INKA STORAGE SYSTEMS

Inka Storage Systems

Edited by TERRY Y. LeVINE

UNIVERSITY OF OKLAHOMA PRESS : NORMAN AND LONDON

This book is published with the generous assistance of the Edith Gaylord Harper Press Endowment.

Library of Congress Cataloging-in-Publication Data

Inka storage systems / edited by Terry Y. LeVine.—1st ed.
    p. cm.
    Includes bibliographical references and index.
    ISBN 0-8061-2440-7 (alk. paper)
    1. Incas—Economic conditions. 2. Incas—Politics and government.
  3. Physical distribution of goods—Andes Region—History.
  4. Warehouses—Andes Region—History. I. LeVine, Terry.
  F3429.3.E2I54 1992
  381—dc20   92-54157
                                                   CIP

The paper in this book meets the guidelines for permanence and durability of the Committee on Production Guidelines for Book Longevity of the Council on Library Resources, Inc. ∞

1 2 3 4 5 6 7 8 9 10 11 12 13 14 15 16 17

Contents

Figures   vii

Foreword, by *Craig Morris*   ix

Part I: Introduction
1. The Study of Storage Systems
   Terry Y. LeVine   3

Part II: The Broad Perspective
2. Staple Finance, Wealth Finance, and Storage in the Inka
   Political Economy
   Terence N. D'Altroy and *Timothy K. Earle*   31
3. Imperial Infrastructure and the Inka State Storage System
   James E. Snead   62
4. Inka State Storage in Three Highland Regions: A
   Comparative Study
   Terry Y. LeVine   107

Part III: Recent Research in Regional Storage: Case Studies
5. Huánuco Pampa and Tunsukancha: Major and Minor
   Nodes in the Inka Storage Network
   Craig Morris   151
6. Inka Storage Facilities in the Upper Mantaro Valley, Peru
   Terence N. D'Altroy and *Timothy K. Earle*   176
7. Inka Storage in Huamachuco
   John R. Topic and *Coreen E. Chiswell*   206

Part IV. Analyses of Storage Structures
8. The Technology of Highland Inka Food Storage
   Craig Morris   237
9. The Architecture and the Contents of Inka State
   Storehouses in the Xauxa Region of Peru
   Terence N. D'Altroy and *Christine A. Hastorf*   259

10. Stores and Homes: A Botanical Comparison of Inka
    Storehouses and Contemporary Ethnic Houses
    Heidi A. Lennstrom and *Christine A. Hastorf*   287

Part V: Comments and Suggestions for Future Research
11. Storage and the Inka Imperial Economy: Archaeological
    Research
    Timothy K. Earle   327

Notes   343

Glossary of Spanish and Quechua Terms   346

Bibliography   348

Contributors   375

Index   377

Figures

1-1. Chronological time scale   7
1-2. Map of the Andean area indicating places mentioned in the text   8
2-1. Schematic representation of the function of storage in the subsistence economy   42
2-2. Schematic representation of the function of storage in the political economy   46
3-1. Map of Tawantinsuyu illustrating distribution of large state centers with storage components   70
3-2. Map of Tawantinsuyu illustrating distribution of centers of production and special function containing storage components   73
3-3. Inka state storage and related sites in the Cochabamba Valley, Bolivia   74
3-4. Inka-period sites in Salta Province, Argentina   75
3-5. Map of Tawantinsuyu illustrating distribution of secondary state facilities with storage components   80
4-1. The research area in the Andean Central Highlands   109
4-2. The Huánuco Pampa Inka administrative center   115–16
4-3. The Pumpu Inka administrative center   120–22
4-4. The main part of the Chacamarca subcenter   124–25
4-5. The Hatun Xauxa Inka administrative center   128
5-1. The Huánuco Pampa center   156
5-2. Closeup of the Huánuco Pampa storage complex   157
5-3. Tunsukancha tampu: the site and its associated storehouses   165
6-1. The distribution of zones of agricultural production in the Upper Mantaro Survey area   185
6-2. Circular storehouses from site J10, above Laguna Paca   188
6-3. Storage facility J20, overlooking the main Mantaro Valley   190
6-4. Inka state storage complex J31 on west ridges bordering the main Mantaro Valley   191
6-5. Storage facilities J15, J16, and J17 on the terraced hillslopes just west of Hatun Xauxa   193
6-6. Regression of state storage volume, by 1-km bands, against (a) log of the distance from Hatun Xauxa   196–97
6-7. Regression of state storage volume, by 1-km bands from Hatun Xauxa, against Wanka population   200–201
6-8. Inka state storage complex J22, on top of a hill on the east side of the main Mantaro Valley   203

7-1. The location of qollqa around Huamachuco and some other important sites 209

7-2. Diagram of the qollqa and a group of larger buildings on Cerro Cacañan 212

7-3. A reconstruction drawing of the plan and facade of the qollqa excavated on Cerro Santa Barbara 214

7-4. A plan and reconstruction drawing of a qollqa excavated on Cerro Cacañan 216

7-5. A plan and reconstruction drawing of the large building excavated on Cerro Cacañan 217

7-6. A plan and reconstruction drawing of a storeroom at Cerro Amaru 228

8-1. Diagram of a circular qollqa at Huánuco Pampa 238

8-2. Diagram of a two-room rectangular qollqa at Huánuco Pampa with paved floors and ventilation ducts 239

8-3. Diagram of a qollqa in Row 10 at Hauánuco Pampa, with rock paved floor and ventilation ducts faced with rock 240

9-1. The distribution of sites in the Upper Mantaro Valley during the Inka occupation 260

9-2. The distribution of storage complexes and Wanka villages above the Inka administrative center of Hatun Xauxa 263

9-3. Inka state storage site J17 above Hatun Xauxa 274

9-4. Storage structure J17=F2: plan view and cross-section 276

9-5. Storage structure J17=F4: plan view and cross-section 277

10-1. Map of Hatun Xauxa area 289

10-2. J16=2 level 2: relative proportions of plant area 298

10-3. J16=2 level 4: relative proportions of plant area 299

10-4. J17=2 level 1: relative proportions of plant area 300

10-5. J17=4 level 3: relative proportions of plant area 301

10-6. J2=1-1 level 4: relative proportions of plant area 303

10-7. J2=2-1 level 3: relative proportions of plant area 304

10-8. J54=2-1 level 2: relative proportions of plant area 305

10-9. J54=2-1 level 3: relative proportions of plant area 306

Foreword

CRAIG MORRIS

FOR many years storage and storable surpluses have played important roles in theoretical thinking about the growth of early complex societies. On the one hand, there have been arguments for the key nature of agricultural surpluses in supporting the nonsubsistence activities of elites and craft specialists (Childe 1951). On the other hand, there have been concepts of redistributive or "storage" economies whereby exchange of goods is accomplished by a central political, or temple, organization through its storehouses rather than through open exchange in markets (Polanyi 1957).

Even though there has been a long period of theoretical interest, until relatively recently, storage has received little systematic archaeological field study. This is surprising because storage forms a material focal point on which many factors of the economic, social, and political organization of a society impinge. The study of storage facilities and their contents can give the archaeologist direct access to data on the size and nature of the stored surplus of a society, and studies of the locations and contexts of storage can illuminate various aspects of economic, social, and political institutions.

Information that the Inka state maintained a vast, elaborate and well run storage system reached Europe soon after the invasion of the Andes in the sixteenth century. The massive wealth accumulated in state storehouses is indeed a major theme in the early sources on the Inka:

> From the fortress [of Sacsaywaman above Cuzco] one can see many houses . . . and many of these are the houses of pleasure and rest of the past rulers and others are of the leaders or chiefs of all the land who now reside in the city: the others are houses or storehouses full of blankets, wool, weapons, metals and clothes—and of everything that is grown and made in this realm. There are houses where the tribute the vassals bring in are stored . . . and there is a house in which are kept more than 100,000

dried birds, for from their feathers articles of clothing are made. . . . There are shields, beams for supporting tents, knives and other tools; sandals and armor for the people of war in such quantity that it is not possible to comprehend how they had been able to tribute so many and different things (Sancho 1917 [1532–33]:194–95).

In the 1920s Louis Baudin (1928), picking up on the exaggerated pro-Inka vision of Garcilaso de la Vega (1963 [1604]), reached the conclusion that the storehouses were part of a scheme to protect the populace against hunger and famine. Baudin saw Inka storehouses as the great common larders of a beneficent socialist state. To be sure, storehouses commonly are built to correct some kind of disjunction between production or supply and consumption. Stored contents are waiting to fill a gap between needs and the goods that can be supplied from current production. The simple interpretation of massive warehousing of food, especially in a preindustrial context, is that it was intended to keep people from going hungry in the face of a bad harvest.

The first valid anthropological consideration of Inka warehousing was John V. Murra's analysis of the early written evidence for storage as part of his landmark study, *The Economic Organization of the Inca State,* completed in 1955 (Murra 1980). One of Murra's main contributions was to move the welfare functions down the socioeconomic scale from the level of the state to the level of local communities where questions of subsistence and survival were primarily addressed. Murra related state stores to state functions and to state institutions. In part they were seen as a substitute for markets in a redistributive economy, giving people access to goods from other regions and from other production specialists.

The first systematic archaeological study of Inka storage had its origin and inspiration in Murra's work. My own field work began with the qollqa at Huánuco Pampa in 1964 (Morris 1967, 1985; Chapters 5 and 8, this volume). One aim was simply to verify on the ground the sixteenth-century reports of quantitatively impressive storage by the Inka state. The more important aim, however, was to look at the contents and locations of warehouses so that we might begin to answer the questions of the role of storage in the overall scheme of state economics. The results of that work readily confirmed the size and importance of Inka warehousing facilities as well as their significance as part and parcel of the state's administrative apparatus.

In my estimation, one of the effects of the warehousing system was to make goods available for state use in regions where they would otherwise have been either inadequate or entirely absent. However, the primary results of the study of the Huánuco Pampa storage system suggested that most of the storage volume was devoted to the warehousing of food. I suspected that this was also true in other parts of the empire, except for the region of Cuzco, the capital, and under certain special circumstances such as warehousing at fortresses where the emphasis may have been on sumptuary materials and on arms (see Sancho quote above). The locations of major Inka storage complexes tied them to strategic infrastructural and administrative nodes along the extensive road system in the provinces. Storage basically supported the administrative and infrastructural system.

Additional study carried out in sections around the central plaza of Huánuco Pampa during the 1970s and early 1980s provided details on activities in the center and insight into the probable uses of stored goods (Morris 1982; Morris and Thompson 1985). Part of the explanation for the size of the storage system and the quantity of stored goods seemed increasingly to be the great and expanding necessity to provide for state hospitality as part of the functioning of Inka reciprocal administration. An equally important requirement was to supply the labor crews that, in various organizational forms, supported the state and its elite, and labored to fill state warehouses.

In the late 1970s Terence D'Altroy (1981) carried out a second major field study of Inka storage, this time concentrating on what is probably the largest of all the preserved Inka warehousing complexes—that in the Upper Mantaro Valley near the Inka administrative center at Hatun Xauxa. D'Altroy's work was in conjunction with the Upper Mantaro Archaeological Research Project (Earle et al. 1980, 1987). D'Altroy also collaborated with Christine Hastorf who brought sophisticated archaeobotanical techniques to the study of storehouses (D'Altroy and Hastorf 1984; Chapter 9, this volume) and with Timothy Earle in important articles on the role of storage in the exchange systems of early state societies (Earle and D'Altroy 1982, 1989; D'Altroy and Earle 1985; see Chapters 2 and 6, this volume).

The late Geraldine Byrne de Caballero and her colleagues at the archaeological museum in Cochabamba, Bolivia, carried out preliminary investigations of the large storage complex at Cotapachi near

Cochabamba. This material has not yet been brought together in systematic publication; however, careful reporting in the local press has provided evidence of perhaps 2,000 storehouses that may have been related to storage of the maize produced by the *mitmaq* placed in the region by Huanya Capac (Wachtel 1982; see also Snead, Chapter 3, this volume). Terry LeVine brought storage into her comparative consideration of the Central Highland areas of Huánuco, Jauja, and Pumpu (LeVine 1985), drawing interesting comparisons of storage in relation to site size, function, and population estimates.

As the chapters in this volume demonstrate, there are minor differences in results and interpretations relating both to details of how the storage system functioned and what it meant for the state economy. Some of these differences probably reflect the regional differences so characteristic of the Inka empire. Others reflect the differing methodologies and theoretical orientations of the investigators. Although there are differences in detail, there is strong concurrence in the central conclusion that the Inka state made major investments in the production and accumulation of key goods and that it used these goods to support itself and to finance its expansion.

The stores were critical in supporting the elites, facilitating state-level production, supplying the military and other logistical operations, and in providing for lavish state hospitality in a variety of settings and contexts. Excavations at Huánuco Pampa have uncovered tons of jars used for the preparation and serving of maize beer (*chicha*) in the zones of formal public architecture (Morris 1982). This and other evidence of feasting, related to rites of legitimation, and to other key political and religious rituals, was part of the royal generosity that played an integral role in Inka governance and expansion (Rostworowski 1988). The storage system supported these elaborate hospitality operations and assured that important state obligations could be met. Storage brought technologically and administratively sophisticated solutions to disjunctions in time and place, adjusting needs to available supplies, as these were defined by the state.

Twenty-five years of storage studies have thus brought substantial advance. There is, however, much more work to be done. The origins and development of formal storage systems in the Andes needs additional investigation. As LeVine discusses in Chapter 1, such a complex system obviously did not spring full grown in Inka times. Several studies (for example, Moseley 1985, and Anders 1975, 1981, 1982, 1986) show that there are antecedents. The developmental trajectory needs to be worked out.

As the present volume reflects, our best data on Inka storage come from the Peruvian Central Highlands where, as it seems clear, storage was unusually important. However, we need more intensive work in other areas in order for a more complete and comparative perspective to emerge. The Cuzco region is one of many that needs additional research. The tentative beginnings (Morris 1967; Chapter 5 this volume; see also Snead, Chapter 3) should be followed up by more complete surveys and excavations. Our knowledge of the region around the Inka capital has increased substantially over the past two decades; storage sites throughout this area could now be approached with a more complete model of the economic and social organization of the region.

We need more careful tracking of stored goods both before and after being placed in storage, first in locating their sources of production and second in showing how the materials were used; archaeobotany could play an important role here. With the continuing growth of quality context archaeology, work on these issues will be addressed as part of concerns with broader economic and political questions.

In spite of the substantial work that still awaits us, the chapters in this volume more than fulfill the early promise of an archaeological focus on storage. They have brought increasing methodological sophistication to the solutions of a series of problems relating to Inka economics and state administration. In particular they have greatly increased our understanding of the economic basis for the expansion of the Americas' largest state. At the state level, storage was a key tactic in the balancing and maximizing of diverse Andean resources to achieve political growth.

Storage studies marked a turning point in the archaeology of the Inka. They demonstrated that an archaeology guided and informed by the written record can successfully address complex anthropological issues. The encouraging results in the Andes will hopefully encourage more intensive efforts to look closely at storage in other early complex societies for a more thorough comparative understanding of the development of complex societies in general and of the role of storage in that development.

PART I

INTRODUCTION

CHAPTER 1 **The Study of Storage Systems**

TERRY Y. LeVINE

THIS is a book about financing an empire. It is the first book that fully explores the importance of the Inka storage system as the basis for financing the expansion and consolidation of its empire. Scholars who study this Andean state recognize that the key to Inka finance was a decentralized storage system. During the 100-year period they dominated the Andes, the Inka built storage structures, known as *qollqa*, in storage centers distributed, north to south, over 4,500 km of rugged highland terrain. They constructed these circular and rectangular qollqa where the natural climatic conditions of high-elevation locations in the Andean mountains aided in protecting and preserving the contents.

The Inka were the last indigenous empire of the Americas to fall under Spanish dominance. Spaniards who first saw the extent of Inka storage were amazed and perplexed at the ability of this New World empire to amass so extensive a supply base. We have come to understand that the qollqa were filled through an elaborate system of taxation based mainly on a system of corvée labor-service that the state imposed. The system was tailored to each region's resources, and to the level of political sophistication of its populations. Storehouses stocked agricultural products, textiles and other manufactured goods, as well as products resulting from the working of state-owned mines.

Our goal for this book has been to make available in one volume information derived from archaeological research at Inka storage sites. Our aim is to facilitate an understanding of the Inka political economy, and to encourage continuing research into the relationship between developing political complexity and economic integration that will be useful in cross-cultural research.

This chapter summarizes storage in early agricultural societies, the role of storage in developing and maintaining complex state societies, and the development of storage management in pre-Inka polities.

Next, it reviews Inka economic policy to illustrate the pivotal place of the storage system in Inka administration. A demonstration of how ethnohistorical documents augment archaeological research follows. The chapter concludes with an overview of the chapters of the book that follow.

In early pre-state agricultural societies, the capability to store food and other commodities was basic to the success of human adaptation to the rhythms of agricultural production cycles. Storage evened out seasonal fluctuations in production and mitigated the threat of crop failure. Crafts, produced during periods of time free from the demands of agriculture, could be stored for future use. Once populations were settled permanently, increases in population density tended to increase the risk of a shortfall. Under the management of centralized leadership, it became possible to reduce the required per capita storage by averaging the risk across more producers. Thus storage management also created the opportunity for increasing centralized control (Johnson and Earle 1987:209).

Anthropologists, economists, and historians have long recognized that storage played a critical role in developing and maintaining complex state societies (Thurnwald 1932; Polanyi 1957, 1968; Vermeule 1964; Service 1975; Godelier 1977; Price 1982; D'Altroy and Earle 1985; Cherry 1986). Their research acknowledges, first, that proper management of accumulated economic surpluses is often the key to the political success of state systems. Second, state taxation programs are most effective when the surpluses they produce are distributed and available at strategic points to supply state consolidation and expansion plans, workers on state agricultural and construction projects, and other state requirements.

With the development of archaic expansionist societies, centrally organized storage became crucial to the successful management of increasingly complex economies. Archaeological data and historical records indicate that expanding archaic societies constructed vast storage facilities to accommodate necessary commodities in support of increasing state military, bureaucratic, and ceremonial activities. The role that storage played was particularly essential to economic management when the production of staples provided the primary financial base of a state system (Polanyi 1968:14, 186–87, 323). Because the storehouses supported staple finance systems, analyses of their remains are crucial to an understanding of the economic organization of staple-supported archaic states.

In the New World as well as in the Old World, centrally controlled storage systems maintained the developing agricultural state societies. Research in the Andes has shown that the organization and strategic deployment of storage provides the critical link between state operations supported by the extraction of an economic surplus and the subsequent use of that surplus (Murra 1980 [1956]; Morris 1967, 1981, 1982, 1986; Earle and D'Altroy 1982, 1989; D'Altroy and Earle 1985).

Andean South America has a strong tradition of efficiently used storage; current data trace the earliest evidence back to 1400 B.C. during a period that saw the development of civic/ceremonial centers in coastal valleys where populations were increasingly dependent on irrigation agriculture. This early Andean development is analogous to the palace economies of the Mycenaean cultures around the Aegean Sea. In the Andes, during the next almost 3,000 years of development before the expansion of the Inka empire, central authorities supported themselves and consolidated their power over various portions of the Andean territory by controlling access to concentrated resources that supplied the fluctuating demands of official state activities.

Unlike the Mediterranean archaic states, only 450 years have elapsed since the Inka empire was at its zenith. In the past two decades, research has moved from focusing on the broad picture of how the Inka empire administered its economy to a study of individual portions of the empire, and from a concentration on coastal sites to a focus on Inka regional installations in the Andean highlands. This research is relevant to an understanding of the Inka economy for several reasons. First, the Inka built their most important administrative centers along the major highland road that linked the far-flung empire to its center at Cuzco. Second, the most extensive Inka administrative sites are above 3800 m and are ill suited to agriculture and urban growth. Thus preservation at highland installations with their associated storage complexes is relatively good.

Recent survey, excavation, and analysis at a series of Inka highland sites has been adding significantly to our understanding of the Inka political economy. It is now possible to contrast differences in storage facilities between one highland center and another, as well as differences in facilities between the highlands and the coast. Recent research shows that the Inka state used regional strategies in developing and deploying its stored resources.

STORAGE MANAGEMENT IN PRE-INKA ANDEAN POLITIES

Investigators of pre-Inka societies have raised questions concerning continuity and change between pre-Inka and Inka-period imperial political economies. These questions are related to an assessment of the extent to which elements of Inka statecraft drew on existing models. However, another consideration is the degree to which storage management (particularly staple storage) played a central role in the economies of pre-Inka polities. This section begins with a review of data for those earlier polities for which investigators believe they have conclusive evidence for storage facilities, during the Initial Period, the Early Intermediate Period, the Middle Horizon, and the Late Intermediate Period (Figure 1-1 shows the divisions used for Andean pre-Contact time and places the polities mentioned throughout this chapter, and those that follow, in time and space). The section then concludes with an assessment of continuity and change between the pre-Inka period and the Inka imperial economy.

INITIAL PERIOD

Recent research traces the earliest evidence for storage to 1400 B.C. (see S. Pozorski and T. Pozorski 1986:381–401; 1989). This was a period when the archaeological record shows the development of polities in coastal valleys where societies were becoming increasingly dependent on irrigation agriculture. In the Casma Valley of the north central Andean coast (Figure 1-2), evidence exists for controlled access storage within one of the site's two major mounds. Studies of the architecture indicate that these mounds were the locus of centralized authority. The analysis of pollen samples taken from storage rooms discloses what appears to be an emphasis on comestibles including sweet potatoes, beans, avocado, and peanuts. Evidence suggests textiles may also have been stored.

EARLY INTERMEDIATE PERIOD MOCHE

The archaeological record for most of the Moche period (Andean north coast) between A.D. 100 and 600 indicates that storage was

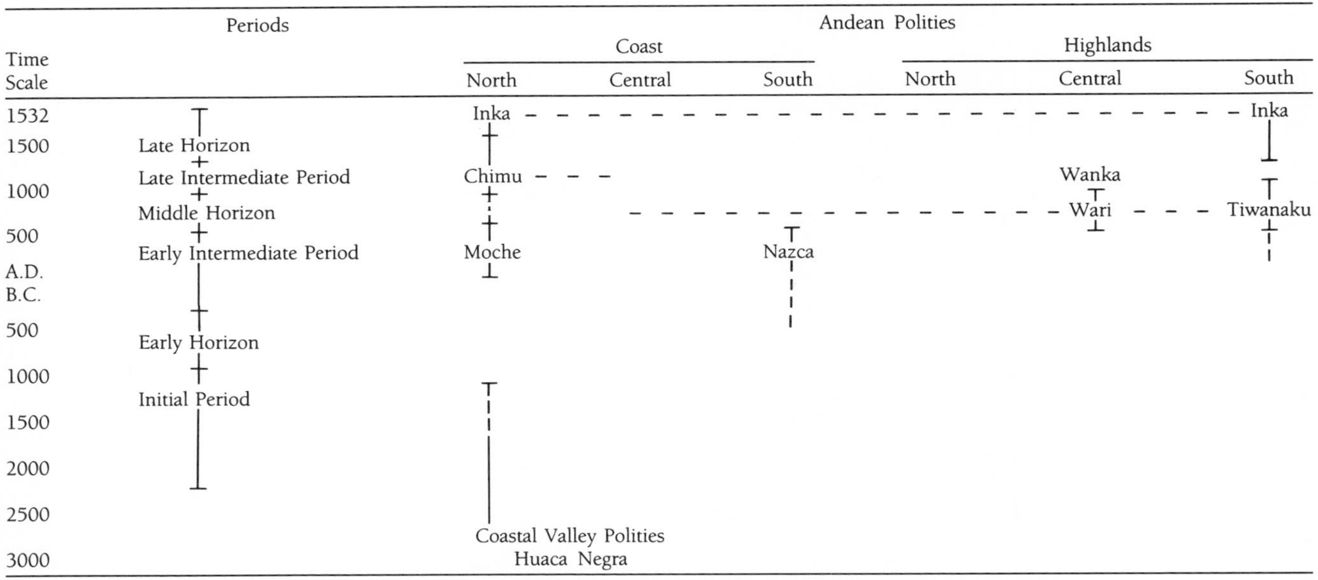

Periods		Time Scale	Andean Polities					
			Coast			Highlands		
			North	Central	South	North	Central	South
Late Horizon		1532	Inka					Inka
		1500						
Late Intermediate Period			Chimu				Wanka	
Middle Horizon		1000					Wari	Tiwanaku
Early Intermediate Period		500	Moche		Nazca			
		A.D.						
		B.C.						
Early Horizon		500						
Initial Period		1000						
		1500						
		2000	Coastal Valley Polities					
		2500	Huaca Negra					
		3000						

Figure 1–1. The relationship between pre-Contact archaeological time periods and calendric time; polities mentioned in the text and calendric time.

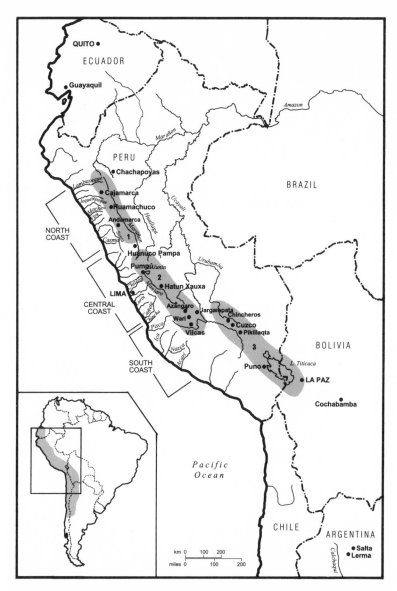

Figure 1–2. Map of the Andean area indicating location of place names mentioned in the text. Inset map shows extent of the Inka empire. River valleys named are those mentioned in the text. Highland zones are indicated by (1) Northern Highlands; (2) Central Highlands, and (3) Southern Highlands. For additional sites mentioned in Chapters 3, 4, 6, 7, 9, and 10 see detail area maps in individual chapters.

associated only with domestic architecture (Topic 1982:274–75, 283). However, the last years of the Moche period (A.D. 600 to 700) brought changes in settlement pattern and in material organization. The capital value that stored materials represented evidently was becoming so critical to Moche political and economic systems that large-scale, standardized storage facilities with controlled access begin to make their appearance at late Moche-period sites (Shimada 1978:588–89; Anders 1981:390–403; Day 1982:341–43). This parallels transitional changes noted in the organizational base of societies in Middle Helladic southwest Greece (*ca.* 1500 to 1400 B.C.), at the site of the walled village of Dorian-Malthi, where storerooms were attached to the "entire inner face of the wall" accessible to all inhabitants. By 1300 B.C., at the nearby palace of Pylos, for the first time, storerooms were being designed with controlled access (Vermeule 1964:77–79, 163–69; see also Polanyi 1968:323).

The final political capital of the late Moche-period intervalley polity is considered to be the ceremonial center of Pampa Grande, located 58 km inland in the Lambayeque Valley. Fieldwork at Pampa Grande has revealed the presence of eight groups of contiguous, rectangular storehouses containing 84 storerooms, identified on the basis of high threshold entrances, a lack of domestic refuse, standardized design, and limited access (Shimada 1978:588; Anders 1981:398). Five of the storage groups with 62 storerooms are located within two large rectangular enclosures surrounding the two largest *huacas* (pyramids) of Pampa Grande; storerooms contain an estimated volume of 2,400 m^3 in rooms ranging from 3 to 4.5 m wide by 3.8 to 7 m long. Sample excavations revealed no objects. Pollen analysis disclosed no direct evidence for the comestibles that were part of subsistence in that time period, only fern spores in one storeroom and monocot in another (Anders 1981:398). A sixth group, located 700 m from the two central compounds had 14 storerooms, 3 m wide and 5 m long, with an estimated volume of 487 m^3, all empty. However, the two remaining groups (total of 8 storerooms with 180 m^3 volume, 2.25 m wide by 7.7 m long and 2 m wide by 2.55 m long) had both been burned, leaving charred contents containing beans and degrained corn (Anders 1981:398).

According to Shimada's (1978:589) assessment, concerning the larger, empty storerooms, there is no a priori reason to believe that these large storerooms (those within walled compounds where there is monumental architecture) contained comestibles. Regarding storerooms in which charred food remains were found, Shimada suggests that "dispersed, small-scale storage facilities provided the daily necessities for much of the population at the site," possibly for a commuting labor force engaged in supervised craft production (1978:589).

Over a 100-year occupation period, construction technology at Pampa Grande shows improvements that attest to the increasing importance of storage to institutionalized hospitality, reciprocity, and redistribution in the restructuring of Moche social, political, and economic relations. Investigators argue that in this final Moche period, spatial separation of closely administered craft production (metalworking, weaving, and figurine manufacture) in an "industrial" sector, possibly destined for state storerooms, mark the beginning of economic specialization (Shimada 1978:588; 1987:136; Anders 1981:404). Production of *spondylous* artifacts, which may be equated with elite status (wealth goods), took place under close supervision in a workshop contiguous to a major *huaca* (Shimada 1982:164).

At the late Moche-period site of Galindo, located inland in the Moche Valley, organized storage represents about one fifth of overall site space. According to Garth Bawden (1982:304–7), storage is separated from other formal architecture and is located on terraced hillsides rising above the site. There is strictly controlled access to uniformly built, small, stone complexes with a single entrance, and with small interconnecting rooms. The small size of these interconnecting rooms, as well as the absence of domestic refuse or cooking facilities, and the lack of fine ceramic vessels, identify these as storerooms. Materials were stored in stone-walled storage bins and in large roughly made storage vessels that apparently stood in rows on wall benches. As storage vessels were invariably empty, there is no evidence as to their original contents (Bawden 1982:304–7).

MIDDLE HORIZON WARI

In the Andean Central Highlands there is no evidence for centralized storage before the development of the Wari polity (*ca.* A.D. 600–1000), and even during this period no clear case can yet be made for the establishment of similarly designed storage facilities at all major Wari sites. In fact, among state-level formal architecture at Wari, the capital, definite storage space has yet to be identified. Rooms with hemispherical cache pits carefully hidden under the plastered floors have been excavated (Isbell 1987:84–89), but these would hardly allow for the bulk volume one would expect for an expansive state system.

Indications for the extension of power and/or influence outside the Wari Central Highland core are present from Cuzco to Cajamarca, as well as on the central and south coasts (Schreiber 1987b:92–95). In fact, the two most extensive Wari sites, Pikillaqta and Azángaro, have similar facilities that are possible storage units. A distinctive feature at Pikillaqta, southeast of Cuzco, is the 285 m × 205 m area containing some 500 rectangular 5.7 m × 4.7 m conjoined rooms with rounded corners and with a single doorway. Rooms are arranged in rows with wooden gates closing off row ends and groups of rooms are divided into walled quadrants. Despite the lack of corroborating excavated data, the standardized design and the restricted access have led some investigators to tentatively interpret that these rooms served as storage facilities (Sanders 1973:399, 404–405; see also Schreiber 1978:160, 1989).

At the Wari site of Azángaro, located in the Ayacucho Valley 15 km northwest of the Wari capital, the central sector of the site, representing more than one third of the total site's 175 m by 447 m enclosure, is composed of 19 rows of equal-sized rooms and a twentieth row of smaller rooms, all with low doorways (80 cm × 60 cm), separated by corridors with controlled access (Anders 1986:201–24). In fact, the supervision of passage through the entire site appears to have been a major consideration. There is no consensus of opinion as to whether or not the previously described rooms were used for storage. Some investigators, because of low doorways and small size, believe these rooms could not have been used for habitation. They tentatively identify them as storerooms (Schreiber 1989); they see similarities between the arrangement of floor supports allowing for air circulation beneath the floors of these Azángaro structures and a system the Inka used to enhance preservation in some storehouses (see Morris Chapter 8, this volume). However, Anders (1986:214) interprets these subfloor passages as part of a water conduit system. On the basis of her excavations, and on features found, Anders rejects a storage function and opts for the possibility that these rooms were used for short-term, rotational residence by people, possibly workers under tight security.

Although the identification of storage facilities at many Wari sites has yet to be clarified, the cost of establishing major architectural facilities, along with the distribution of Wari wealth goods, denotes the class differences and the organization of a long-distance trade network consistent with an organized state system "that must have . . . stored large volumes of material . . . to support the state bureaucracy" (Schreiber 1985, 1987b:94, 1989, 1991). Schreiber argues that centralized storage would have been needed to underwrite state activities, a strategy that we would expect, given the demands of state support under conditions of poor transport technology.

MIDDLE HORIZON TIWANAKU

Tiwanaku (A.D. 500–1200) dominated the Southern Highlands and southern coastal valleys. Recent research characterizes Tiwanaku as a dynamic, expansive state with a three-tier administrative system. This polity was apparently supported by its ability to intensify agricultural production in the vicinity of Lake Titicaca and by its control of all resources on the altiplano of the Southern Highlands (Kolata 1986:748–62). In turn, these resources generated adequate surplus to institute a redistribution system, supplying colonies in the coastal valley and on the Andean eastern slopes with highland products, thus bringing the production of these areas under Tiwanaku control (Mujica 1985:103–40). Tiwanaku also controlled long-distance trade routes using llama caravans to carry elite wealth goods as far as the northern Chile area. Llama caravans brought back exotics (probably including wealth goods) needed, or desired, by the central polity (Mujica 1985:114–16). Recent studies stress agricultural intensification, exchange relationships, and surplus production but have not yet progressed to the point where they can discuss either the presence or absence of Tiwanaku storage.

LATE INTERMEDIATE PERIOD CHIMÚ

Archaeological evidence, consisting of a proliferation of storage units at north coast Chimú sites (A.D. 900 to 1470), is being interpreted as an indication of increasing manipulation and control of craft production and wealth goods to bolster the political power and status of

Chimú leaders (Pozorski 1987:119–20). At Chan Chan, the Chimú capital, storage structures are the most numerous of the adobe structures, most of them associated with royal palace compounds and some incorporated into compounds occupied by the Chimú elite. Storerooms with 1 meter thick walls are 2 m^2 to 4 m^2, arranged in contiguous rows (Day 1982:60). Single entrances, 1 meter high, face the interior of courts that were reachable only along a system of narrow corridors, protected by control point rooms where goods were probably received. According to Kent Day (1982:338), because nothing was found in the excavated storerooms of Ciudadela Rivero, the last Chimú palace to be built at Chan Chan, identification depends upon a lack of evidence for domestic activities and on their similarity to Inka storerooms. Day argues that the isolated location and the difficulty of access to storerooms attests to the value the Chimú placed on stored goods. The *extent* of this regulated access and the location of storerooms within royal palaces and elite compounds suggest that wealth goods may have been among the most important items being stored.

In a recent paper in which storage at Chan Chan was discussed, Ulana Klymyshyn (1987:97–110) argues that there was a reorganization in storage management and changes in the distribution of storage at Chan Chan that resulted from expansion of the Chimú empire and from an increase in the flow of goods from the provinces. She believes that two of the monumental compounds originally identified as palace compounds may not have been used as palaces (they lack burial compounds, have a different internal layout and have increased accessibility) but were converted to storage facilities to house less prestigious materials. Klymyshyn (1987:99–101) acknowledges that the identification of storerooms and stored materials is through indirect evidence because artifacts are rarely found. She argues from archaeological and ethnohistoric evidence that the Chimú economic system was redistributive and would thus have included commodities other than high-status (wealth) goods, including foodstuffs.

Research at two strategically placed secondary Chimú centers along the coast indicate that, unlike those of the Inka period (see Chapters 4, 5, 6, and 7), storage was not a major function at secondary centers and has not been identified at tertiary centers. In the Jequetepeque Valley, north of Chan Chan, at the site of Farfán, Carol Mackey

(1987:121–29) identified 42 square storerooms in the compounds that were excavated; storerooms are either 5 m^2 or 25 m^2 in size. Despite the lack of identifiable remains, the guarded access to these storerooms suggests to Mackey that there may have been an emphasis on elite wealth goods over comestibles. South of Chan Chan, at Manchan, in the Casma Valley, 49 rectangular storerooms were identified, incorporated into five of the nine compounds investigated. All 15 of the medium-range (8 m^2 to 30 m^2) storerooms have guarded access, suggesting again the storage of wealth goods destined for Chan Chan. Unlike storage at Chan Chan, the remaining small-range and large-range storerooms that can be entered directly from an open patio could have been used to store more mundane items (Mackey 1987:127). Overall, the storage function was greatly curtailed at these secondary centers compared to Chan Chan, the primary center.

LATE INTERMEDIATE PERIOD IN THE CENTRAL HIGHLANDS

Despite extensive centralized control of storage present on the Andean north coast in the period before the Inka conquest, evidence for centralized storage in the Central Highlands for the Late Intermediate Period is questionable. From the Upper Huallaga and Marañón drainage areas, south through the Mantaro Valley, storage was concentrated at the level of dispersed household groups, or at the compounds of low-level village leaders or clan chiefs (Morris 1967:20–40; Parsons and Hastings 1988:202–215; D'Altroy 1992, see also Chapter 6).

Browman (1970, 1985), who conducted his doctoral research in the Mantaro Valley, has argued for extensive storage facilities during the Late Intermediate Period. However, more recent Mantaro Valley research found no evidence for massive, discrete, pre-Inka storage facilities (Earle and D'Altroy 1982; Chapter 6, this volume). All of the preserved complexes follow architectural canons common to Inka state storage elsewhere in the empire. At the rare sites that have extensive associated ceramic refuse, both Inka and the local Wanka ceramics were invariably found. An even more persuasive point, however, is that the Late Intermediate Period phase was characterized by intense intravalley warfare (LeVine 1979; D'Altroy 1981). Settlements were protected both by their hilltop locations and by surrounding fortress walls, and it would have been strategically unsound to place the storage basic to political finance and security undefended outside the walls (Earle et al. 1987; D'Altroy 1992) .

CONTINUITY AND CHANGE

Administratively, the most likely source for elements of Inka statecraft would have been the Chimú and the Wari. The Inka may have adopted the concept of a decimal hierarchy from the Chimú (Rowe 1948; although see Netherly 1978). The north coast polities also may have relied heavily on corvée labor as the principal means of mobilizing state economic support, at the same time that economic specialization in sumptuary craft production was directly underwritten by the nobility (see Moseley 1975; Moseley and Day 1982; Topic 1982). Further, networks of new, regional administrative centers were apparently tied together by road systems in the Chimú, Wari, and Tiwanaku states, as in the Inke empire, and, like the Inka, they appear to have undertaken extensive land and water improvement projects (see, for example, Isbell and Schreiber 1978; Kolata 1986; Schreiber 1987a, 1991). Also, the Inka apparently borrowed much imperial architectural design from earlier styles (Gasparini and Margolies 1980).

As D'Altroy (1992) makes clear, the Inka drew from centuries of Andean statecraft in creating their new polity. Nonetheless, Tawantinsuyu was distinct from preceding polities in scale, in degree of integration, and in reorganization of subject societies. No earlier state encompassed a remotely comparable territory, population, diversity of ethnic groups or languages, or range of political and economic configurations. With respect to storage facilities in particular, it is well to bear in mind that although the problems of preservation and the distinctiveness of Inka storage facilities would favor their recognition and investigation, nevertheless, the storage systems described in this volume were unprecedented in scale and spatial extent.

The extent to which staple materials played an important role in pre-Inka storage management has yet to be adequately proved. Actual remains of stored materials have not often been recovered and have yet to be adequately reported, for example, for the Chimú. Assumptions about the contents of pre-Inka storehouses are often based on indirect evidence (see Klymyshyn 1987:97–110). The presence of "mouse bones" (Pozorski and Pozorski 1986:381–401) is seen as an indication of the former presence of foodstuffs. The presence of guarded access is seen as an indication of highly valued materials, possibly wealth goods. The similarity to Inka storehouses is noted. In recent years, the availability of more sophisticated methods of ethnobotanical analysis show promise for making more direct evidence for stored contents in pre-Inka storehouses more accessible in the future (see Chapters 7, 9, and 10 this volume).

It is possible that the extension of Inka economic models back to earlier polities has been over emphasized. For example, there are definite limits to the extent that Inka models can be useful in interpreting Wari-period storage sites. Unlike Inka storage sites, Wari sites are not located in separate, well-aerated areas that lend themselves to the preservation of staple goods. Staple storage may not have been as great a priority for the Wari as it was for the Inka. Similarly, Chimú storage differed markedly from Inka storage in one respect. Although Chimú storage had guarded access and usually was hidden within compounds that had multiple functions, Inka storage is found in separate, specialized storage complexes, placed on highly visible hillsides distributed across the backbone of the Andes, serving almost as a symbol of state power. The bulk of Inka storage was composed of the staple goods that the state invested in capital improvements, and in a major Inka goal, empire expansion.

STORAGE AND INKA ECONOMIC POLICY

After the Inka conquered all preexisting polities and molded them into their expanding empire, the role that storage played in the development and maintenance of the Andean state changed dramatically. For the first time in Andean prehistory, a polity faced the logistics of provisioning a bureaucracy that stretched from Quito in contemporary Ecuador to Santiago in contemporary Chile. This distance can be compared to the expanse of the Roman Empire from Britain in the northwest to Damascus at the east end of the Mediterranean. The expansion of storage was a logical necessity for the Inka domination of the Andes (A.D. 1425–1533). In fact, efficient organization and the control of state surpluses became a hallmark of Inka-period administration. This organization included a complete differentiation between the stockpiling of staples and utilitarian craft goods, which underwrote the cost of basic state services, and the management of prestige and wealth goods used to maintain relations between the state and a hierarchy of subordinate elites (see Chapter 2 for an in-depth discussion of these concepts).

Reorganization of the economy required the Inka first to solidify control over conquered populations and then to implement finance policies carefully adapted to the wide range of existing social, political, and economic realities of conquered polities. The state suppressed market and trade. It maintained symbolic ownership of all natural resources, setting aside strategic portions of conquered territories as production enclaves to supply state needs, and to support the state-approved religion. Where feasible, the state augmented agricultural production by increasing irrigation and by expanding the terracing of hillsides.

The state acquired its major revenues through the mobilization of labor using three methods: first, they imposed a universal labor service tax, the *mit'a,* based on a thorough periodic census; second, over time, they steadily increased the number of permanently attached craft specialists; and third, they forcibly resettled portions of the population, known as *mitmaq,* in order to increase agricultural production in key areas and also to discourage rebellion in areas crucial to the state's economic planning. Strategies for labor organization and production were flexible, depending on population size and density and on the regional resources that the state considered to have priority.

In a current publication, D'Altroy (1992) makes an important point concerning the impact of military logistics and transportation costs on the imperial political economy. A number of chroniclers described the transport of materials by llama caravans of tens of thousands, as well as the remarkable capacities of Andean porters to transport goods in support of the Inka armies (e.g., Atienza 1931:113–14; Zárate 1862:Bk. II:ch. xii:483). Pedro Pizarro (1986:ch. 15:97–98) recounted the story of a man from Cajamarca who told him he twice carried half an hanega of maize (about 21.8 kg) to Cuzco for the Inka, a distance of about 1,200 km. However, La Lone (1985) reminds us that such accounts do not imply that goods could be transported at the will of the empire without respect to the energetic requirements of the porters or the llama.

As D'Altroy (1992) demonstrates, logistical capacities provide necessary constraints on the capacity of states and the military to conduct activities, no matter the level of technological development (see also van Creveld 1977; Engels 1978). D'Altroy makes some interesting calculations showing that the porter interviewed by Pedro Pizarro would have consumed more in the round trip than he would have delivered. Thus the transportation of this maize cannot be seen as part of a regular system supplying subsistence support to the capital.

The Inka fully understood that there are realistic limitations to transportation. The Licenciado Polo (1940:170) recounted the relationship between kinds of goods and the distances that they were transported to Cuzco: "[F]rom the lands that were far away, little was brought . . . except gold and cloth, because it weighed little . . . and food was brought from the other neighboring areas, those that were closer brought more and those farther away less."[1] In fact, the limited ranges of bulk goods implied that virtually all long-distance exchange was conducted in prestige goods in both Mesopotamia and the Aztec empire (Adams 1974; Berdan 1975; Schneider 1977; Hassig 1985), as well as in the Inka polity. It was precisely because regular, long-distance bulk transport of foods was not feasible, with the available technology, that staple storage facilities were built throughout the Inka empire (D'Altroy 1992).

The range of goods the Inka state amassed through control of the vast labor supply it controlled can be divided into three categories. The first two, general staples and utilitarian crafts, were transported and stockpiled at the central capital, at regional state storage centers, and at *tampu*, way stations dispersed along the major Inka roads to service state-approved travelers. In lieu of a monetary system, stockpiled staples financed a variety of local projects for the state and served the empire's military, security, transport, construction, and communication needs. The third category, specialized prestige and wealth goods, was directed mainly to the state capital at Cuzco (Murra 1980, 1982; Morris 1967, 1974, 1985; Wachtel 1982; D'Altroy and Earle 1985; LeVine 1987).

Growing quantities of surplus goods required an unusual investment in state management that included construction of great numbers of strategically placed storage facilities to hold the surpluses derived from the imposition of labor service quotas. Archaeological remains of these Inka storage facilities are readily identifiable based on the following attributes: the construction of modular units within a limited size range and the use of a linear layout rather than the grouping of structures around a patio, an arrangement common to habitation facilities. A third attribute is the Inka penchant for separating rows of storehouses into either rectangular or circular structures and for constructing them on hillsides, in locations separated from other state activities (Morris 1967; D'Altroy 1981; Chapters 5, 6, and 7).

A centrally controlled storage system was vital to the Inka state because its economy was based largely on staple finance. Seasonality of staple production, as opposed to fluctuations in use demand, required effective systems of storage, making storage management a key element in Inka finance. The stockpiling of key agricultural and artisan-made goods permitted the state to support designated services when and where they were needed. Over time, as the empire grew in size and complexity, storage management increased in importance, in an effort to keep up with growth in the number of nonfood producers who had to be supported: the military cadre, administrative and religious elites, and full-time state supported artisans.

Storage became even more critical as the state expanded north and south from Cuzco, extending the empire over 4,500 km of rugged terrain. Because travel was almost exclusively on foot, it became necessary to compensate for the lack of efficiency in transport methods by careful planning of Inka storage distribution. The provisioning of military personnel, considered by sixteenth-century writers to be the primary use for goods stockpiled in state storehouses, became crucial to expansion planning. Major storehouse complexes were concentrated at state installations adjacent to the major road system, a scheme that provided several additional advantages.

First, officials were able to monitor closely the allocation of goods to support state operations. Second, raw materials were available for specialized craft workshops at administrative centers where regional artisans labored as part of their annual labor service commitments. Third, supplies were at hand for the regional civic/ceremonial celebrations that took place at provincial centers. Fourth, proximity of supplies to the road system made them readily available to fulfill the logistical needs of traveling state personnel. Finally, well-stocked storehouses had psychological value at highly visible hillside locations above state centers where they symbolized state power and represented a promised safety net for provincial populations at times of localized disasters.

In recent years, a debate has surfaced regarding the organization of material flow under the Inka system. Whether the Inka economy would be more aptly labeled a "redistributive" or a "mobilization" economy has been addressed by both Morris (1967, 1981, Chapter 5, this volume) and by Earle and D'Altroy (1982) and D'Altroy and Earle, Chapters 2 and 6, this volume). Morris (1985) has convincingly argued that elaborate ceremonial feasting and public hospitality at regional state centers and the reciprocal exchange of ceremonial gifts between local and state elites maintained the consent of conquered populations and legitimized the system of domination initiated by the Inka empire (Morris 1985:481). Although vast quantities of materials flowed into regional storehouses, or were shipped directly to Cuzco, little evidence exists for redistribution, an interregional transfer *between* major storage centers (Morris 1967). In fact, where regional resources to supply major centers were lacking, as they were for Pumpu, a Central Highland Inka center, the state required porters from adjacent regions to transport the necessary supplies, from agricultural production zones in adjacent regions, directly to Pumpu (Helmer 1955–56 [1549]41–42; Ortiz 1967 [1562]:57; Rostworowski 1978 [1549]:223–24).

Redistribution to hinterland populations is also questionable. The exchange of local subsistence products between regions and between ecological zones for use by regional populations appears to have taken place below the level of the state (Ortiz 1967–72 [1562] vol. I:63, 68, 73, 178–79; for a more detailed discussion see Morris 1967:174–79; LeVine 1985:144–45, 1987:29). Recent research views massive storage mainly as a solution to supply problems, a way of stabilizing the economic base and ensuring the provisioning of state activities (Earle and D'Altroy 1989).

INKA STORAGE AS SEEN THROUGH DOCUMENTAL RESEARCH

Long before sustained archaeological research in Peru, the nineteenth-century publication of William Prescott's (1961 [1847]) book based on the writings of sixteenth-century Spanish chroniclers, soldiers, administrators, and men of the church, inspired interest in the Inka empire. Most chroniclers traveled, observed, and wrote first-hand descriptions. They interviewed Inka administrators and wrote detailed descriptions of how the empire worked; they described the economic system and the storage facilities that supported it. Despite their bias, early writers provide an important first-hand look at the Inka administrative system while it was still relatively intact. More recently, late sixteenth-century court cases and administrative documents, long buried in state archives, have added a significant new dimension to standard chronicle sources.

John V. Murra's (1980 [1956]) excellent analysis of Inka economic organization, based on sixteenth-century writings, provides a fresh view of chronicle sources bringing to them an anthropological perspective. Murra's work continues to be an important resource both for the value of his analysis and for locating and reading and evaluating, at first hand, sixteenth-century sources on specific aspects of Inka economic organization. Data on storage facilities are concentrated in Murra's (1980) Chapter VI.

It is interesting to read at first hand the Spaniard's astonishment at the quality and the quantity of the Inka storage network. The chroniclers did not begin to comprehend, however, the extent of individual storage facilities; archaeological survey serves us best for these data. For example, when Pedro Cieza de León ventured to estimate the number of units in any one storage complex, he writes of the "more than 700 storehouses" at Vilcas, located in the central part of the empire (Cieza 1862 [1551]:435). Bernabé Cobo's general description of storehouses is that they were located "in high, cool, windy places close to the royal road . . . many small, square structures separated by two or three steps . . . in orderly rows . . . of twenty, thirty, fifty, and more buildings" (Cobo 1956 [1653]:124). These descriptions hardly suggest the 2,700 some units in the vicinity of Hatun Xauxa in the Central Highlands, the 2,400 units at Cotapachi, in the Cochabamba Valley of Bolivia, or the more than 1,600 units at Campo del Pucara, in the Lerma Valley of northwest Argentina (see D'Altroy and Earle, Chapter 6, and Snead, Chapter 3, this volume).

Cieza recognized that great numbers of storehouses were associated with provincial administrative centers, collection points for the manufactures and staples made and grown by people in the countryside surrounding Inka centers. Cieza enumerated, among other centers, Huánuco Pampa, Pumpu, Hatun Xauxa, and Huamachuco (Cieza 1967 [1553]:65); description and analyses of storage at these sites is addressed in Chapters 4, 5, 6, and 7, this volume).

Recent research is clarifying the function of the great concentrations of storage at sites like Cotapachi. Cotapachi was not an administrative center but was one of a number of vast state farms established in fertile valleys and geared toward intensive agricultural production. The best source of information on the storage facilities at Cotapachi has not been the standard chronicles but administrative documents that Nathan Wachtel discovered in the historical archives at Cochabamba, Bolivia, documents that clarify the status of the thousands of workers transferred to the valley to operate this Inka "production enclave" and to deliver harvested materials into Inka state granaries (Wachtel 1982:199–222; LaLone and LaLone 1987:49–63; D'Altroy: 1992).

Chronicle descriptions of the quantity of materials stored in the storage units they observed are also fascinating. They give us some idea of the awe the Spaniards felt as they became aware of the ability of what seemed to them a "primitive" empire to amass materials in staggering quantities. Francisco Xerez, Pizarro's secretary, described his first view of the contents of Inka storehouses, along the Ecuadoran coast where he saw enough supplies to "maintain the Spaniards for three or four years" and in the Northern Highlands where there was "clothing tied in bundles stacked nearly up to the roofs of the structures . . . the Christians took all that they wanted and still the storehouses remained full" (Xerez 1862 [1533–34]:326, 334). Cobo estimated "more than 500,000 *fanega* [each about 1.5 bushels] stored at Hatun Xauxa" (1956 [1653]:126). The conquerors were particularly awed by the storehouses associated with Cuzco, the capital, "in such quantity that it is not possible to understand that they have been able to give such great amounts of tribute and of such diversity" (Sancho 1917 [1532–33]:195).

Some chronicle descriptions provide interesting data not available through archaeological fieldwork. For example, they relate how the state protected the contents of state storehouses. Cobo describes guards to oversee both the entries and the withdrawals from the state's stores and the maintenance personnel to protect stored materials from damage by fire, rain, or rodents (Cobo 1956 [1653]:124). Several chronicles give detailed explanations of the use of *khipu* to keep careful accounts: "they count by some knots in some string whatever each local chief has brought . . . and they take off some knots when they bring to us loads of wood or *llamas*, or *maize* or *chicha* beer" (Hernando Pizarro 1959 [1533]:88). Cobo also notes that the *khipu* devices were used to record events and to keep track of the periodic census, as well as serving in place of ledgers and account books (Cobo 1956 [1653]:143). Cieza's excellent detail informs us that *khipu* had strings of varied colors, each color representing a different product, and that there were knots to represent quantities of from 1 to 10, from 10 to 100, and from 100 to 1,000. Being dubious about the system, Cieza requested a demonstration when in the Mantaro Valley at Hatun Xauxa some years after the conquest. The local Wanka Lord showed him the *khipu* on which was recorded all of the provisions distributed to and stolen by the Spaniards from the Hatun Xauxa storehouses, covering the years following the Spanish conquest in 1533 (Cieza 1967 [1553]:35). Cieza's report is corroborated by court documents filled with data recorded from these same *khipu*, found in the state archives at Seville (Espinoza Soriano 1971 [1558–61]; LeVine 1979:99–105; Earle et al., 1980; see D'Altroy and Hastorf, Chapter 9, this volume, for a discussion of this document).

Excavation yields only limited data on stored materials because most storehouses were stripped clean of any valuables (see Chapters 7, 8, 9, 10, this volume). Through documents we discover a wider range of materials than is obtainable through any other method. Most chroniclers put great emphasis on the quantities of military supplies stored throughout the empire. Cieza (1862 [1551]:397), impressed with the organization imposed on storehouses that he saw soon after entering the territory that had been under Inka domination, describes "the provisioning of the soldiers. . . . [I]n one of these storehouses there were lances, and in others darts, and in others sandals and in others whatever arms they used." At Sacsquaman on a hill overlooking Cuzco, Pedro Pizarro (1965 [1571]:196–97) saw "rooms full of weapons, spears, arrows, darts, clubs, shields . . . [and] helmets." Pedro Sancho (1917 [1533]:191, 194–95) adds to the list axes, quilted jackets, footgear, metal materials, and he was impressed with storerooms stacked with 100,000 (?) dried birds, highly valued for their multicolored feathers, because it was the custom to weave feathers into garments for military personnel. Sancho also describes the food supplies that probably required the major amount of space in storehouses. These included maize, legumes, root crops, and "herbs" similar to those in Spain. Cobo (1956 [1653]:126) adds highland food staples to this list including the grain, *quinoa, chuño* (dried potatoes), and *chárqui* (dried meat).

The chronicles, when used with care, can be a useful resource. However, Colonial-period administrative documents, census reports, regional questionnaires circulated by *visitadores* (inspectors), and court records provide the important and surprisingly detailed data Andeanists are using with good success to augment archaeological research (Morris 1967; LeVine 1979; Murra 1980; see D'Altroy and Hastorf, Chapter 9, this volume, for a concrete example).

ORGANIZATION OF THE CHAPTERS

The chapters in this volume begin with the broad perspective in Part II, move to descriptions of storage in specific Inka provincial regions in Part III, then examine technological aspects of Inka storage structures and their contents in Part IV. Chapter 2 is a theoretical paper published in *Current Anthropology* in 1985 by Terence D'Altroy and Timothy Earle in which the authors investigate the nature of the political economy in a nonindustrial state. In this chapter, using a vocabulary amenable to cross-cultural research, the authors discuss the relationship between developing political complexity, economic organization, and storage. The authors are primarily concerned, first, with the reorganization of the economic systems of states and their subject polities to meet the requirements of expansion, and second, with the development of new forms of finance, for example, state-run farms, and semiindustrial textile shops, to develop the stored staples and wealth goods to support state projects.

As D'Altroy and Earle point out, it is mainly through the study of storage that staple finance systems can be understood; clearly, storage provides the basic facilities that support staple finance systems. The authors argue that the key factors affecting finance organization are (1) the capacity of subject groups for gross surplus production; (2) a required state investment in political and economic security; (3)

the potential efficiency of the mechanisms of production; and finally (4) the logistics of management and disbursement.

D'Altroy and Earle also enter the debate regarding the extent to which bulk materials moved between storage centers. As they argue, long-distance movement of staples is labor-intensive and cost-ineffective, thus placing more emphasis on regional storage and regional management. Under this plan, materials in storage optimally would be moved to another region only when required (see also Morris 1981:358, 368, and Chapters 4 and 5, this volume; and especially D'Altroy 1992).

In the next chapter, James Snead draws together storage data from a series of archaeological investigations in which the storage aspect was often only a peripheral portion of more extensive research projects. Snead has collected data from the past 40 years of research, and he uses it to evaluate the Inka state storage network as a system. In reviewing this corpus of material, he emphasizes the relationship of storage to furthering economic, military, and political goals. His aim is to assess the overall spatial arrangement of the storage system to gain insight into the interacting forces within Inka imperial economic organization, visible particularly when comparing patterns of difference between concentrations of storage in the highlands and along the coast.

Only recently have adequate data become available to approach a perception of storage and Inka finance policies from a comparative perspective. Terry LeVine's chapter compares Inka state storage sites in the Central Andes, using data from storage sites within the boundaries of three adjacent regions. LeVine compares storage distribution, storage volumes, storehouse design, and stored contents. She then analyzes storage based on regional labor potential and on the variability of localized resources. Her data are archaeological, ethnohistorical, and environmental. She uses her data to examine the logic motivating Inka economic decisions, showing that Inka strategy required a balancing of broader policies for ruling the empire with regional policies for managing labor in the successful extraction of resources.

Part III focuses on the specific details of three case studies where recent research has stressed the storage component of Inka administrative installations. Craig Morris, whose 1967 study of storage in the

Huánuco region laid the foundation for further Central Highland studies, evaluates the position of the Huánuco Pampa Inka center as part of the storage network that supported the integration, administration, and expansion of the Inka empire. In appraising the nature and function of the storage network, Morris poses two main sets of questions. First, how are the various parts of the network linked? Second, how do the goals of the overall storage network relate to the function of an individual network node? He describes and analyzes storage in the Huánuco region in order to assess its position within the Inka storage network by comparing this site to other points in the storage network and then to storage in the region of Cuzco, the empire capital.

Terence D'Altroy and Timothy Earle approach the storage systems of the Mantaro Valley, a strategically located Central Highland basin, from the perspective of the overall organization of the Inka political economy. As the authors argue, an evaluation of storage is critical to understanding state/local relations. Beginning with an analysis of how the economic mechanisms of reciprocity, redistribution, and mobilization apply to the Inka political economy, the authors suggest a fourth model to provide a better understanding of the Inka economy. In addition to detailed descriptive data on Mantaro Valley storage complexes, the authors analyze the reasoning behind the spatial distribution of storehouses around the Hatun Xauxa administrative center and throughout the Mantaro Valley. They also discuss the location of storehouses associated with sites identified as state-controlled agricultural enclaves that took advantage of the agricultural potential of this productive area. The Mantaro Valley is central to a study of the Inka political economy because of its unusually dense population both before and during Inka occupation. The authors evaluate the region's unusual distribution of storage sites as evidence of how the state integrated the strategic Mantaro Valley into the overall economic system of the empire.

The final case study is in contrast to the extensive storage complexes described in Chapters 5 and 6. John Topic and Coreen Chiswell present data on a less elaborate storage complex associated with the Huamachuco Inka administrative installation. Their research team mapped over 200 Inkaic storerooms and associated structures in the vicinity of Huamachuco. Evidence from 10 of the structures they excavated indicates distinct functional types based on architectural as well as macro- and microbotanical evidence. Data on Inka storage are then discussed within the more general context of Inkaic Huamachuco including the relationship of storage to the state road system and to other Inka installations in the vicinity.

Part IV is concerned mainly with specific data on the technology of storehouse construction and storehouse contents. In Chapter 8, Craig Morris focuses on the sophisticated Inka planning that provided specialized conditions critical to the long-term maintenance of stored staples. He presents evidence to show the ability of the Inka to take advantage of the great natural refrigerator of the high-elevation *puna* to facilitate effective storage. The effort that went into providing specialized conditions for the storage of a variety of staples tells us almost as much about the importance of storage to the Inka as does the overall capacity of their storage system. Morris stresses that storage is one of the most important aspects of ancient technology that supported the logistical supply for political integration and for the administration of archaic societies.

Next, Terence D'Altroy and Christine Hastorf use analyses based on three sources: early documents, field survey and mapping, and botanical analysis of excavated materials. The spatial distribution and the architectural standardization of storage facilities are indicative of the central management of storage in the Mantaro Valley. Documents indicate that the Wanka elite played an important role in managing the state storage system. Documents also show that the native Wanka population was wholly self-sufficient, independently producing the full range of goods stored in Mantaro Valley storehouses; the authors' test excavations in six storehouses recovered all major prehistoric highland crop taxa that were grown by Wanka farmers. Both documentary and archaeological evidence suggest that Inka organization of stored commodities was complex and probably varied over time.

In the final chapter of Part IV, Heidi Lennstrom and Christine Hastorf suggest a method to aid future research in differentiating storage structures from residential units by means of botanical analysis. Their chapter presents botanical data from seven storehouses where excavated sample materials were compared to samples excavated from seven Inka period Wanka domestic structures as a way of interpreting the material that has and will continue to be recovered from Inka storage units.

Finally, Timothy Earle assesses the progress and future research directions for clarifying the role that economics played in the success of expanding state systems like the Inka. If the key to political success of the Inka state lay in its economic organization, then our understanding of the Inka finance system lies in continuing research into Inka storage facilities.

We hope that this volume will stimulate more emphasis on the study of storage systems in other early societies, to the extent that negative as well as positive evidence for storage management can aid in interpretations of economic organization in earlier Andean polities. We cannot assume that pre-Inka systems were the same. We need the same kind of systematic study of pre-Inka storage management systems as has been attempted in this volume to reach some conclusions as to how storage was managed by pre-Inka polities. In addition to issues of access, we need data on volume in order to estimate the number of people storage could have served, as well as data on standardized design, distribution of storehouses, and the use of recent advances in ethnobotanical analysis to assess contents. We need to document whether there was continuity, as well as change in storage management practices over time.

ACKNOWLEDGMENTS

I would like to express my appreciation to Timothy K. Earle for his recognition that the time was right to collect in one volume the accumulating data on Inka economics, and more specifically on storage, research that has resulted from recent studies focusing on Inka storage sites. This book benefited from his advice and encouragement throughout the planning and development stages. Special appreciation is extended to Terry D'Altroy, and also thanks to Craig Morris, Christine Hastorf, Coreen Chiswell, Heidi Lennstrom, James Snead, and John Topic whose cooperation made the volume possible. Melissa Hagstrum, Katharina Schreiber, and Timothy Earle read this opening chapter that benefited from their comments.

PART II

THE BROAD PERSPECTIVE

CHAPTER 2 **Staple Finance, Wealth Finance, and Storage in the Inka Political Economy**

TERENCE N. D'ALTROY AND TIMOTHY K. EARLE

THE evolution of complex society is a central issue in recent anthropological thought. Analysts of cultural evolution have adopted various perspectives to understand the relationship between developing political complexity and economic organization. Particularly influential have been the functionalist arguments that seek to explain the development of new institutions, such as centralized leadership and regional political organization, as means to solve problems of production, security, and privileged access to economic resources. Such theories emphasize the way new forms of integration manage problems created by increasing population density and the concomitant intensification of subsistence activities or the way privileged access to necessary resources is maintained in the face of competing claims (see Service 1975). Arguments centered on the requirements of information processing (e.g., Wright and Johnson 1975; Wright 1977) and the social relations of production (e.g., Godelier 1977; Friedman and Rowlands 1977) have also stimulated considerable interest in the recent literature.

An alternative approach focuses on the relationship between the evolution of social complexity and increasing energy capture. This perspective, which underlies the present discussion, is based to a certain extent on principles of cultural evolution worked out by prior researchers. For example, Childe (1951), drawing from nineteenth-century Marxian ideas, argued that the evolution of complex society required technological progress and the production of a food surplus. The surplus was seen as necessary to support social elites, government bureaucrats, craft specialists, and the other non-food producers that characterize complex societies. In a sweeping general formulation, White (1959) proposed that cultural evolution was based on progressive levels of energy capture and related cultural elaborations. As Steward (1960) noted, however, the problem is not simply how much energy is available but how that energy is used. In simple terms, an increase in the amount of energy brought into a cultural system can result in either more biomass (more people) or more complex systems. Analyses of the development of social complexity must therefore be concerned with how energy is channeled to finance the creation and maintenance of new social institutions and the elaboration of old institutions (cf. Adams 1978; Price 1978, 1982; Harris 1979).

Included among these institutions are regionally integrated government, religion, and social elites (Fried 1967; Service 1975). The development of these complex features is predicated on the growth of existing systems of finance to channel needed resources from local production. Of comparable importance is the establishment of new socioeconomic institutions to develop alternative sources of revenue, such as centralized taxation, tribute, and administered exchange. Sources of finance are thus essential to the evolution of the sociopolitical and religious institutions that provide the authority and power components of the state.

In this chapter, we are primarily concerned with (1) the reorganization of the economic systems of the state and its subject polities to meet the requirements of the expanding state and (2) the development of new forms of finance, drawing on both staple and wealth products, to meet state needs. Assuming that the state's economic goal is to expand its labor and natural resources, we argue that the key factors affecting the finance organization are the capacity of the subject groups for gross surplus production, a required state investment in political and economic security, and the potential efficiency of production, logistical, and disbursement mechanisms. We focus our discussion here on Inka state finance, although the arguments are not necessarily restricted to this case.

STAPLE FINANCE AND WEALTH FINANCE

For the purposes of the present discussion, we may dichotomize systems of finance in archaic states into two general types, *staple finance* and *wealth finance,* on the basis of the form in which the material support is mobilized. *Staple finance* (Polanyi 1968:321; Earle and D'Altroy 1982:266) generally involves obligatory payments in kind to the state of subsistence goods such as grains, livestock, and clothing. The staples form accounting units (a bushel of wheat or a head of sheep) that have established values. Staples are collected by the state as a share of commoner produce, as a specified levy, or as produce from land worked with corvée labor. This revenue in staples is then used to pay personnel attached to the state and others working for the state on a part-time basis. The obvious advantages of such a finance system are its simplicity and directness in collecting generally available products needed by the households that are involved in state activities rather than solely in subsistence production. The main disadvantage is the cost of bulk storage and transportation. Such goods are typically heavy in relation to their value, and it is inefficient to move them over long distances. For this reason, staple finance is most appropriate for relatively small agrarian states and for empires with highly dispersed activities that can be supported by regional mobilizations. Staple finance includes systems that have been called redistribution (Polanyi 1957; Dalton 1961; Murra 1980 [1956]), mobilization (Smelser 1959; Earle 1977) and tax in kind.

Wealth finance involves the manufacture and procurement of special products (valuables, primitive money, and currency [cf. Dalton 1977]) that are used as a means of payment. These wealth items often have established values with respect to other goods of a similar nature but vary in their convertibility into staples (Bohannan 1955; Earle 1982). They may be amassed as direct payment from subservient populations, or they may be produced by craft specialists attached to the central authorities. In the latter case, raw materials given as tribute are often used in the manufacture of these goods, and the craftsmen may be provided as part of a labor obligation from local communities. Wealth held by the state is used to pay political officials and other personnel who work for the state. The obvious advantages of such financial units are their storability and transportability, which allow a more centralized control over finance than is possible with bulky staples. Wealth is also appropriate for territorially extensive states, such as the Aztec, in which the goods used in finance are moved over long distances. The main disadvantage of wealth items is that they often have restricted intrinsic use value and so must be converted into subsistence or utilitarian goods used to support the nonagricultural personnel. As Brumfiel (1976, 1980) shows for the Aztec case, conversion on a large scale requires a market system in which the tribute goods used as state payment are sold for subsistence goods.

The division between staple and wealth finance is of course largely heuristic, and the financial base of complex societies typically involves a mixture. For example, in an agrarian society such as the complex Hawaiian chiefdom, staples mobilized from community production are used to support craft specialists who are attached to the chiefs and who manufacture wealth items (Earle 1978:184–85). In this way, staples are converted into wealth directly. Alternatively, special goods may be manufactured for trade with outside groups that manufacture valuables or control valuable resources. On the other side, materials received as tribute may not be "wealth," strictly speaking, but may be a highly desired utilitarian material not locally available. The materials can then be exchanged in markets for subsistence goods from local farmers, as in the Aztec case. As we will describe for Inka state finance, staple finance is often used to support local administrative activities, and wealth finance is used to support more centralized state functions requiring long-distance movement of goods.

THE INKA POLITICAL ECONOMY: THE PROBLEM

The institutional organization of the Inka state economy has been extensively studied, primarily through reference to ethnohistoric sources (e.g., Baudin 1928; Rowe 1946; Moore 1958; Morris 1967, 1974; Métraux 1969; Murra 1975, 1980 [1956]; Godelier 1977; Wachtel 1977). Early researchers' perception of the state economy as a monolithic structure has been discarded since the recognition of significant variation among imperial provinces in economic and political organization. Nonetheless, general organizational features and policies are discernible, and it is these with which we are most concerned here.

The empire of Tawantinsuyu, encompassing approximately 984,000 km^2 was divided into four administrative quarters centered at Cuzco. The empire comprised about 80 provinces, roughly corresponding to the territories of subject populations (Rowe 1946:262; Schaedel 1978:292). Provinces were subdivided into two or three political units called *saya*, each subsuming a variable number of *ayllu*. The nature of the *ayllu* is widely debated, but it is generally considered to be an endogamous kin group with a communal territory; it formed the basic corporate productive group above the household (Rowe

1946:254; cf. Moore 1958:22; Zuidema 1964:26–27; Murra 1980 [1956]:191).

Governance was vertically oriented, as political control was vested hierarchically in offices filled by ethnic and honorary Inkas and elites from subject groups. Horizontal compartmentalization was key to Inka administration because it discouraged interethnic alliances against the state (Schaedel 1978). Both the Inka (and local ethnic) kinship structure and numerical orderings seem to have played a major role in organizing the political hierarchy. The state seems to have made an effort in some instances to make state and local hierarchies congruent with one another, apparently to facilitate use of the local elites as middle-level management (Murra 1958; D'Altroy 1981). In a complementary policy, a substantial proportion of the subject populations was resettled, apparently to reduce threats of insurrection and to meet economic needs in other parts of the empire (Rowe 1946:269–70; Espinoza 1975).

As is shown most clearly in the work of Murra (e.g., 1975, 1980 [1956]), economic support for the state came primarily from use of the productive capacities of the local populations. Much of the state's economic output was produced through a corvée labor tax, assessed to each household on a rotating basis. Craft-specialist enclaves were also established, and some levies were directly laid on goods produced or traded. The state's intent seems to have been to phrase economic relations with the local populace in terms of the relations the local elites had maintained with the commoners prior to the Inka conquests (Wachtel 1977:62; Murra 1980 [1956]:90).

The literature on the Inka political economy has tended to focus on institutional organization, relations of production, land tenure systems, and the social relations of exchange between the state and its subordinate populations (e.g., Espinoza 1978). Conversely, the importance of control of goods and their role in underwriting the state political economy is usually minimized either implicitly or explicitly. It is generally argued, for instance, that state activities were funded almost solely through application of a labor tax (e.g., Rowe 1946:265; Lumbreras 1974:229–30; Godelier 1977:64; Murra 1980 [1956]:92). Tribute in goods is said not to have existed (Murra 1982:288; compare Salomon 1986 for an alternative view) or to have been phrased in such a way that only labor, not goods, was extracted from the local populations (Murra 1975:243–54; cf. Murra 1982). Sumptuary goods are typically assigned the role of (asymmetrical) reciprocal gifts between elites, and it is often argued that they were limited in circulation and therefore played a minor role in the state economy (e.g., Wachtel 1977:70).

Although these analyses have been illuminating, we remain uninformed about key aspects of state finance. In particular, knowing the form of the institutional framework does not inform us directly about choice of policy or allocation of resources within or among institutions. The focus of this chapter is therefore primarily the production, management, and disbursement of goods and only secondarily the state's control of labor.

The central point we wish to make is that the energetic requirements of production and management of goods were at least equal in importance to the social relations of labor and exchange in the organization of the state economy. Analysis of the state's use of a mixture of subsistence and utilitarian goods and valuables and semimonetary goods to fund its activities provides a perspective to explain the development of the state economy alternative to that which currently dominates the literature. Production of staples was primarily for use in local or provincial material sustenance, whereas the developing wealth finance system provided a means of underwriting management and of integrating local elites into the state economy interregionally. The use of a mixture of these goods afforded the Inkas a measure of flexibility in allocating resources among the various local and interprovincial requirements of the political economy. We argue that, in both staple and wealth sectors, the state took costs of production and management into account in its organization and altered both institutions of production and exchange relationships to meet its material needs.

The study of the institutional relations of labor organization and elite-elite exchange is, of course, critical to understanding the Inka economy. Similarly, we agree that the labor tax was the principal source of surplus production for the state. It should be equally apparent, however, that the mobilization and allocation of that labor were to a large degree contingent on the intended use of the labor's products. Additionally, because control of access to both staples and valuable/monetary goods lay at the core of the state's ability to fund its activities, the balance in the use of the two general classes of goods merits careful consideration.

INKA STAPLE FINANCE

For the purposes of the present review, we may characterize Andean economies under the Inkas as comprising two related but distinct organizations: the local subsistence economy and the state political economy. Because the staple finance aspect of the political economy was initially constructed on a base analogous to the local subsistence economies, we will review their central features here briefly (see Murra 1975, 1980 [1956] for a more thorough review).

The *subsistence economies* of Andean highland communities were generalized to incorporate a wide range of economic resources. The vertically compact Andean landscape made a vast array of products accessible to highland communities within short distances of their principal residences. The apparent ideal was to integrate the distinctive economic zones within a single community through autonomous production and reciprocal exchange, an organization that circumvented the need for extensive market exchange. Communities in the Mantaro Valley of the central Peruvian highlands, for instance, had ready access to flat valley bottomlands (3,150–3,400 m) suited to intensive maize agriculture, the adjacent rolling uplands and hillslopes (3,400–3,800 m) conducive to extensive tuber and quinoa cultivation, and the surrounding *puna* grasslands (3,800–4,800 m) suited to camelid herding. Products such as coca, capsicum pepper, and fruit could be procured either directly or through exchange from the nearby *montaña* and *selva* on the eastern side of the Andean *cordillera* (Earle et al. 1980:6–8). Under certain circumstances, control over land was extended by colonization to more distant, economically significant zones to obtain goods such as coca, pepper, and marine products (Murra 1972). This organization did not obviate barter exchange of goods or exchange of use rights to resources among communities or ethnic groups, however (Ortiz de Zúñiga 1967–72 [1562] vol. 1:31, 63, 73, 179, 219, 329; see Burchard 1974).

This mainstream central Andean highland pattern may be contrasted with those of the north and central coasts of Peru and the highlands of Ecuador, where economic specialization in production and exchange was more highly developed. On the north coast of Peru, for instance, entire corporate groups functioned as economic specialists (e.g., in fishing), with the intention of exchanging the products for other goods of specialized production (e.g., sandals, salt, pottery, agricultural products) (Netherly 1978:209; Rostworowski 1977). Trading specialists have also been noted for Ecuador and the Peruvian coast, trafficking in shell beads (*chaquira*), gold, copper, salt, coca, and a variety of other commodities, apparently in systems of administered exchange or incipient market exchange (see Rostworowski 1970, 1981; Salomon 1983, 1986). These sources clearly show that, among the societies conquered by the Inkas, subsistence economies varied considerably in strategy and complexity. This diversity seems to have directly affected the way the Inkas economically integrated conquered regions.

These local economies may be contrasted as a group with the *state political economy,* that is, the system that mobilized and allocated the goods and services that funded state activities. As noted above, it is generally argued that the principal source of state support was a corvée labor tax and that local communities made no material contributions from their own goods or produce. This assertion is supported by statements in major chronicles and in some local inspections (e.g., Polo 1940 [1561]:165, 169; Cobo 1956 [1653], vol. 2:119; Diez de San Miguel 1964 [1567]:80; Ortiz de Zúñiga 1967–72 [1562]); see Murra 1980 [1956]:95).[1] The labor tax was assessed to the local populace on a rotating basis, phrased in terms of reciprocal economic relationships between the households of the *ayllu* and the state (Wachtel 1977:66). As has been noted by numerous authors, the state was thus extending a relationship of obligations that had already obtained between the local elites and their populace. The state established this relationship by arrogating to itself the rights to all productive resources in the empire, including agricultural and grazing land, undomesticated biota, and raw materials for craft production. Local communities therefore held their land only in usufruct, for which right they were obliged to render labor service to the state. In return, the state materially supported people who were performing their tours of duty, provided security through military protection and fall-back storage, and performed religious ceremony (Polo 1916 [1567]:20).

Mit'a (labor service) included collective labor on the lands of the state and of the state religion and personal periodic service for specific activities (Cobo 1956 [1653] vol. 2:121; Wachtel 1977:71; Murra 1982). Most subsistence goods were produced on state lands either alienated from the local communities or created through agricultural intensification such as terracing, irrigation, or expansion of fields (e.g., Chincha [Castro and Ortega Morejón 1936 (1558):244]; see also Murra 1980 [1956]:31, 94). The state also developed and amplified specialized labor institutions. The mitmaqkuna were displaced colonists (either individuals or entire communities) who served as specialized farmers, military police, and artisans (for discussion, see Espinoza 1975). The responsibilities of the aqllakuna (chosen women) included textile manufacturing and chicha (maize beer) production (Morris 1974). The yanakuna (specialist servants) performed such varied tasks as palace and temple service, tilling of the Inka's private lands, herding, and administration (Cieza de León 1967 [1553]:69; see also Wachtel 1977:73–74).

The products of the labor of the communities and the craft specialists were collected and stored by the state in immense warehouse complexes (e.g., Cieza de León 1862 [1551]:397; Vega 1965 [1582]:169). In general, the staples were stored locally to support permanent provincial personnel throughout the year and to fund periodic labor projects (Morris 1967). Many of the craft products (such as ceramics and rough cloth) were probably consumed locally, but many of the finer wealth goods were shipped to Cuzco as tribute, phrased as gifts (e.g., Ortiz de Zúñiga 1967–72 [1562], vol. 1:26).

The recognition that a labor tax on local communities and the establishment of labor specialists were the principal means of state finance should not, however, obscure two key features of the Inka political economy. First, a distinction exists between what the local communities saw themselves as paying to the state and what the state was actually receiving. Although the state ideology may have maintained that the populace was rendering only labor and the local populations may have often reported paying taxes as such, the state was receiving both goods and services (Moore 1958:49). The sources cited above also suggest that the labor input varied to meet the required material output in the production of several classes of goods. For instance, the quantity of land to be cultivated (or the amount of seed to be sown) and the amount of wool to be woven into cloth by the local communities were determined annually (e.g., Diez de San Miguel 1964 [1567]:31, 39, 92). The state was thus apparently estimating its material needs and requiring the local communities to contribute whatever labor was necessary to meet those needs, taking into account their productive capacities as determined from the census counts.

Second, the state's economic relations with the populace were distinct from those with the local elites. Manipulation of these relations led to the incipient development of a partially independent state staple finance sector, on the one hand, and a state-elite sphere of exchange based on wealth goods, on the other. The latter process suggests a shift away from a state finance system based solely on local labor to one incorporating increasingly "monetized" state-local relationships. The state directly obtained wealth and monetary objects from local elites, often phrasing the exactions as reciprocal gifts. Direct mobilizations of manufactured and gathered products from local elites are recorded, for example, for the Quito area (Salomon 1983, 1986), for Chucuito in the Lake Titicaca area (Diez de San Miguel 1964 [1567]:39), and for the Guancayo polity of the Upper Chillón Valley of the central Peruvian coast (Martínez Rengifo [1571] in Espinoza 1963:63). We return to this issue in greater detail below.

Although this review provides us with an understanding of the basic institutional organization of the state economy, we remain uninformed about the relationships among the different sectors. One key to the problem lies in the way we view what are generally termed the redistributional features of the staple finance system. As applied to the Inkas, redistribution is often seen as a means of commodity exchange and of integrating subject populations into the centralized economic system (e.g., Wachtel 1977:62; Murra 1980 [1956]:121–34). We suggest that *mobilization* more accurately describes the system of finance used to obtain goods from both the subsistence producers and the local elites than does the more general term *redistribution* (Smelser 1959; Earle 1977:215; Earle and D'Altroy 1982:266). Redistribution in complex societies combines aspects of centrally administered exchange (Service 1975:75–78) and economic integration (Polanyi 1957:253–54) with extraction of the goods needed to fund centrally controlled activities. As societies become more complex and a larger fraction of the collected goods is allocated to support a managerial sector, what appears structurally to be redistribution takes on the role of centralized finance (i.e., becomes mobilization) while maintaining the trappings of political and ritual integration. The key to this transition lies in the central authority's increasing capacity to enforce an extractive economic relationship with the subordinate populations, while reinvesting a smaller proportion of the goods collected in supporting unattached producers or political relations with the subordinate populations.

In most current analyses of the Inka political economy, the costs and economic constraints of such mass mobilization of goods are often overlooked. Therefore, to exemplify the relationship between the energetic requirements of centrally controlled goods production and management, on the one hand, and the organization of state labor, on the other, we will examine the role of centralized storage in the mobilization of goods to fund intraprovincial activities. To provide the theoretical rationale for this argument, we will also briefly review the developing role of storage in an expanding state economy.

STAPLE FINANCE AND STORAGE IN THE STATE POLITICAL ECONOMY

Storage is a mechanism to average fluctuations in the availability of a material over time. It is employed to synchronize variable production and use of goods, a function that is critical in both subsistence and political economies. A second function is to average annual variation in food production that unpredictably affects total yearly harvest of food. To hedge against crop failures with environmental causes such as random variability in climatic and disease conditions, or social causes such as warfare, crops harvested in good years may be carried over from year to year.

In the subsistence economy of a local community, the most important use of storage is to average out the variable seasonal supply of food to meet the nearly constant daily household demand for it (Figure 2-1a). In agricultural societies, the availability of foods typically varies with the seasonal cycles of cultivation, harvest, and con-

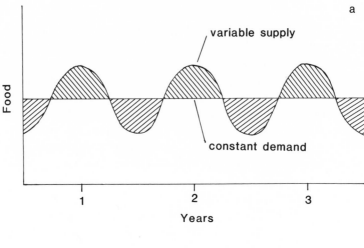

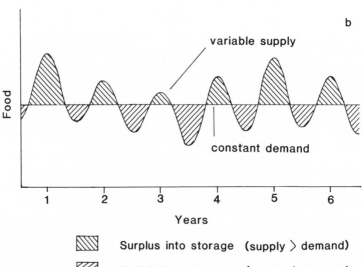

| | Surplus into storage | (supply > demand) |
| | Deficit from storage | (supply < demand) |

Figure 2-1 Schematic representation of the function of storage in the subsistence economy: to bridge the gap between variable supply and constant demand; *a*, annual cycle with no year-to-year variation; harvest in one year provides food until the next harvest; *b*, annual cycle with year-to-year variation; harvest in good year (e.g., *1*) is partly carried over for use in bad year (e.g., *3*).

sumption. Food harvested during a relatively brief period of abundance is stored through the year to feed the family and community. For example, among the Gwembe Tonga of modern Zimbabwe, bulrush millet harvested by a woman in February is held for use by her and her family through one yearly cycle (Scudder 1962:26–27). Such household control of and access to stored foodstuffs provide economic independence and security, with the result that the close association of living and storage areas characterizes many domestic units. The use of household storage appears in numerous prehistoric Andean societies (e.g., Preceramic Huaca Negra [Strong and Evans 1952:19], Early Intermediate Moche [Bawden 1982:310], central Peruvian highland groups from the Early Intermediate Period through the Late Horizon [Browman 1970:262–65; Earle et al. 1980:22; Lavallée and Julien 1973:47–48]; and Chimú [Topic 1982:153]). This tactic continues to be important today in rural households (Werge 1977).

Storage may also serve the local community as a hedge against random fluctuations in domestic food availability (Figure 2-1b). Possible ethnographic examples include storage of dried maize among the Hopi and Zuni (Stevenson 1905:352; Hough 1915:62; Forde 1931:393; Bradfield 1971:21) and of fermented breadfruit among the Marquesans (Handy 1923). Many groups, however, do not normally carry stored goods past one season despite having developed extensive systems of household storage (e.g., the Gwembe Tonga [Scudder 1962], the Trobrianders [Malinowski 1965]). The avoidance of storage from year to year probably reflects the high loss rate from spoilage with most traditional storage technologies. In Ghana, for example, the loss rate for maize is about 30% per year, although it is considered one of the most storable crops (Nyanteny 1972). Only crops that keep well with minimal treatment or that can be treated in bulk with traditional techniques, such as freeze drying of potatoes, are suitable for storage past one season without prohibitive losses. Highland Andean peoples may have had the capacity to store household foods over several years because of the importance of maize and the development of freeze-drying techniques (see Morris 1981).

In the political economy of a complex society, storage often plays a critical role in economic management. The formation of institutions, such as governmental bureaucracies, the military, and religious hierarchies, requires a constant and reliable supply of materials. When these institutions are financed primarily by staple production, storage facilities are usually necessary. Polanyi (1957:254; cf. Thurnwald 1932:108) has noted that the staple finance of the ancient states of Egypt, Sumeria, Babylonia, and the Andes (see also Morris 1967; Anders 1977) relied on massive storage systems. Storage in state finance was also important in the Aegean during the Bronze Age (Renfrew 1972:190–96, 287–88). Centralized storehouses were often built in conjunction with administrative and religious centers to supply permanent and temporary personnel and to meet the demands of ceremonial feasting. The storage facilities serve essentially the same averaging functions as the household granary. Their scale and significance differ radically, however, because they are used to guarantee the independence of the institutions funded through political finance. The effect of concentrating this material is thus to consolidate the power of the central authorities who control access to it.

It should be noted that massive storage is not a necessary element of staple finance but partially an outcome of seasonality in availability. Where seasonality is minimally important, as in tropical forest environments, central storage can be deemphasized. Traditional Hawaiian society, for example, was a series of highly developed chiefdoms (or simple states) in which non-food-producing personnel included an aristocracy, managers, and craft and military specialists (Sahlins 1958:13–22; Goldman 1970:200–42). To support this personnel, large amounts of food, labor, and raw materials were mobilized through a hierarchy based on land tenure and the careful management of production (Earle 1978). What is striking is that this system of finance required little central storage because the dominant staple— irrigated taro—was produced throughout the year and crops could be left in the fields until needed. Where seasonality is an important feature of subsistence production in the political economy, however, the intensification of agriculture associated with the rise of early states exacerbates the risks involved in relying on such crops, because of a reduction in the complexity of the agricultural base (i.e., by increasing dependence on a limited crop mix). This is especially critical for a complex state with a high proportion of non-food producers to food producers, in which a large segment of the population may not be able to rely on fall-back household agricultural storage.

In our description of the role of storage in the subsistence economy, it was assumed that the need for storage reflected variation in supply while demand/use was fairly constant (see Figure 2-1). In the political economy, however, demand/use also fluctuates. First, seasonal part-time labor places peak demands on state stores at specific times, especially during the agricultural off-season, which is the time of greatest food supply (Figure 2-2a). Second, annual fluctuations in demand reflect such changing conditions as the financial needs of warfare and welfare (Figure 2-2b). War places often unexpected and unusually high demands on a region's resources. In archaic and traditional societies, it generally occurs during the agricultural off-season, when the demands of food production are minimal. For example, planned warfare in seventeenth- through nineteenth-century Dahomey was conducted after the harvest (Polanyi 1968), and the Yucatec rebellion (Reed 1964) and the Inka siege of Cuzco (Santillán 1968 [1563–64]:114, 116, 132) failed in part because of the combatants' need to tend their crops. Welfare, as in the state's support of a destitute population undercut by major drought, can be equally demanding. The temporal demands on storage for this purpose are not restricted to the agricultural off-season, however, and may be concentrated during the planting and cultivation season, when household stores are most depleted. Examples of this include the opening of central Aztec storehouses during the famine of the year One Rabbit (Hassig 1981:177) and similar use of Inka stores in time of local shortfall (Garcilaso 1943 [1609]:382; Cieza de León 1967 [1553]:63; see Murra 1980 [1956]:130–34).

When comparing the seasonal and annual fluctuations in Figures 2-1 and 2-2, the main point to observe is that the gap between income and expenditures is at times proportionally much greater for the institutional finance because of the fluctuating demand. For this reason, the development of the new institutional forms of statehood is often dependent on the development of effective systems of storage. In addition, the mechanisms complementary to storage that are used in a subsistence economy (e.g., reliance on kin ties or diversification of food sources) are undesirable or impracticable for a state because they create a dependency on external sources of finance that may not be available quickly enough (if at all) to respond to a major shortfall. Interdistrict movements of goods are possible (see, for example,

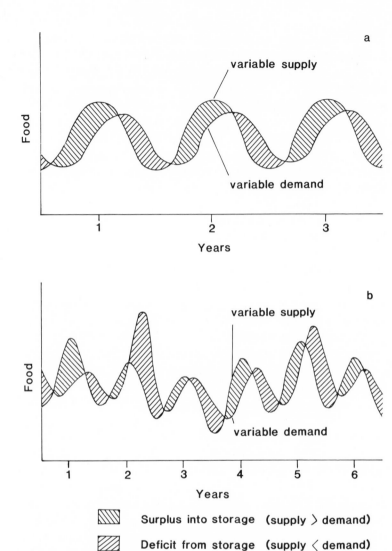

Figure 2-2. Schematic representation of the function of storage in the political economy: to bridge the gap between variable supply and variable demand; *a*, annual cycle with no year-to-year variation (supply from harvests is used to pay for laborers during the off-season); *b*, annual cycle with year-to-year variation (harvests in good years and low use are stored for years with poor harvests and/or high use).

Wachtel 1982:214), of course, and the ecological diversity in an extended empire such as that of the Inkas offers alternative food sources. However, long-distance movement of staples is labor-intensive and cost-ineffective and appears to have been of less importance than storage in regular management of the state economy.

As noted above, the importance of storage in the political economy also reflects the central problem of economic and political control. Control of storage in a staple finance system is equivalent to control of the economy and hence the dependent population. In a household economy, a family uses storage to retain control over its subsistence base and economic survival. In a state, the control of central storage by the government implies control over all people who depend on the stored goods for their livelihood. This includes both part-time workers for the state and households relying on the safety provided by state support. The development of central warehouses in the agrarian state is thus a key element in the centralization of power and direction within the society. The importance of storage in social control was clearly articulated by David Malo, a Hawaiian chief who grew up in the court of the paramount chief Kamehameha (1971 [1898]:195):

> It was the practice of kings [ali'i nui or paramount chiefs] to build houses in which to collect food, fish, tapa, malo, pa-u, and all sorts of goods.
> These store-houses were designed by the kamaimoku [chief counselor to the paramount] as a means of keeping the people contented, so they would not desert the king. . . .
> As the rat will not desert the pantry (kumuhaka) where he thinks food is, so the people will not desert the king while they think there is food in his store-house.

INKA STATE STORAGE IN THE UPPER MANTARO VALLEY

The rapid expansion of the Inka empire created wide-ranging problems of finance for the state administration. As discussed above, to effect control over its subject provinces, the Inkas developed a system of subordinate political units, each relatively independent of the others but owing allegiance to the central authority at Cuzco. Partially as a consequence of this, the staple finance economies of the provinces functioned autonomously to a great extent (see Morris 1967, 1972a). The labor tax was assessed by governors within provinces, and the staples accumulated through the tax were stored in warehouses at the state administrative centers and stations where the goods were to be used.

According to oral tradition, the state storage system originated in the mid-fifteenth century when the emperor Pachacuti ordered facilities built to expedite the construction of Cuzco (Betanzos 1880:75, 77). Additional storehouses (*qollqa*) were built at provincial centers and at roadside way stations over the following century (Garcilaso 1943 [1609]:238–39). Recent archaeological and ethnohistoric research has provided significant insight into some of the organizational and technological features of the state storage system (e.g., Morris 1967, 1972a, 1981; D'Altroy 1981; Earle and D'Altroy 1982). This research has additionally demonstrated the concentration of state activities funded by stored goods at provincial centers, where we would anticipate the concentration of those goods.[2]

As yet, however, the intraprovincial organization of the staple finance system has not been addressed as a function of collection and disbursement of supplies. To examine the intraregional organization of this system in detail, we will discuss the state storage system in the Upper Mantaro Valley of the Peruvian Central Highlands. This valley, conquered by the Inkas about A.D. 1460, was critical both in terms of troop movements and population concentration and in terms of grain production to the central part of the empire. In the period just prior to the Inka conquest, the native Wankas comprised a series of competing political units (LeBlanc 1981). The total population probably approached 200,000 (cf. Cook 1975, 1982), although estimates range from 135,000 (Rowe 1946:184) and 243,000 (Smith 1970). Under the Inkas, communities moved down from their hilltop locations to live in a more dispersed settlement pattern along the valley margins (LeBlanc 1981). At the same time, the Wanka polities were drawn into state government through a policy of centralizing local authority and inducting Wanka elites into the state administrative structure (D'Altroy 1981). In the process, the Wankas were organized into three provincial subdivisions (*saya*). Each of these was headed by a Wanka paramount elite, who held the office of *hunu curaca,* or leader of 10,000 households (roughly speaking), in the imposed Inka decimal hierarchy (Toledo 1940 [1570]).

The main Inka highlands highway from Cuzco to Quito ran

through the valley, with its provincial capital of Hatun Xauxa. Smaller state settlements were built along the road to support transient state personnel, and stations were established to control traffic and to provide message service (D'Altroy 1981; see Morris 1972a).

The basis of the staple finance system in the valley was the labor tax described above for the empire in general. In 1582, the Wankas reported in a Spanish inspection that they had, in effect, been required to produce staples for the state. The Wankas were thus characteristic of many highland groups in that their corvée labor provided the basic intraregional support for the military, the elites, state laborers, and retainers (Vega 1965 [1582]:169).

The Upper Mantaro Valley became the location of the empire's largest storage complex (D'Altroy 1981; Browman 1970; Parsons and Hastings 1977; Earle and D'Altroy 1982; see Chapters 6 and 9 for detailed descriptions of state storehouses in the Mantaro Valley). Archaeological test excavations in six structures in the main storage facilities above Hatun Xauxa, the Inka administrative center, have recovered the remains of all the major highland crops: maize, potatoes, quinoa, and lupine (D'Altroy and Hastorf 1984). From documentary sources, we know that the Inka qollqa housed a vast array of utilitarian and prestige commodities besides food, such as military supplies, rough and fine clothing, sandals, and firewood, although we do not yet know what proportion of the storage space was allocated to the various types of goods (Cieza de León 1862 [1551]:397; Espinoza 1971 [1558–61]).

The administrative center Hatun Xauxa was the focus of the state's regional activity. The first Spanish travelers who passed through the valley in 1533, when it was still under Inka control, reported that the Inka army, estimated at 35,000, was garrisoned across the river from the center and that 100,000 people were assembling daily in its streets (Estete 1917 [1532–33]:96–97). Cieza de León (1862 [1551]:432) later recorded that smiths and aqllakuna had been present and that 8,000 laborers were available for the service of the temple and the elite residences.

Given that the state storage system was centrally controlled and that Hatun Xauxa was the focus of state-funded activity, the distribution of storage might be expected to reflect two interdependent aspects of the provincial state economy. First, storage should be concentrated at the administrative center. Second, the distribution of state-funded activities should be a function of distance from the center, particularly if transport costs of bulk goods were a significant factor in state planning.

Both of these expectations are met. Over half the regional storage capacity (about 64,600 m^3) is concentrated within 1.0 km of Hatun Xauxa. The remaining storage capacity is distributed in systematically decreasing amounts as the distance from the center increases. In fact, we can account for about 79% of the spatial distribution of storage as a function of distance from Hatun Xauxa (see Earle and D'Altroy 1982 and Chapter 6 for a detailed discussion of this point). The implication is that state funding of work was strongly tied to a system of central economic control, with transport costs apparently being important to the disbursement of staple support throughout the valley.

It is intriguing to observe, however, that the distribution of the state storage complexes is not a function of the distribution of the local communities. The largest concentration of Wanka population in the immediate vicinity of Hatun Xauxa—in the Yanamarca Valley to the northwest—is not associated with state storehouses. Although we do not yet understand the reasons for this, it is apparent that the state was not simply organizing its storage capacity to conform to the distribution of the sources of corvée labor (see Chapter 6 for an elaboration of this idea).

To summarize our discussion of the Inka staple finance system and storage, staples were the principal source of funding for the intraprovincial economy. The high cost of transport and the consistent but occasionally unpredictable need for large quantities of staples made concentrated storage the most reasonable solution to the problem of supporting state personnel within each largely autonomous province. The organization of storage within a province can be used to estimate the spatial distribution of state-supported activities. These activities, while centrally focused, are not restricted to the immediate environs of the administrative center. Further, the distribution of storage facilities is not a clear function of the distribution of the local population. Although we understand a great deal more about the organization of staple finance and storage now than we did prior to Morris's (1967) important first work, it is clear that much work remains.

WEALTH FINANCE IN THE INKA POLITICAL ECONOMY

Wealth finance, as noted above, involves the use of valuables, primitive money, or currency as a means of payment of taxes or tribute to a central authority, which then uses these goods and others manufactured by attached specialists to fund governmental activities, particularly political services. We are deliberately extending the term to include goods that have previously been treated solely as prestige objects in the Inka economy because their role appears to have included some monetary features. In Inka and other societies heavily dependent on staple finance to support state activities, wealth finance plays a complementary role. It economically integrates the managerial ranks, consisting primarily or partially of subject elites, into the central state authority structure. Goods move directly to the state and are paid out by the central authorities for political services.

The utility of valuables and of special- and general-purpose money in facilitating economic transactions has been extensively discussed elsewhere (see, for example, Dalton 1967; Schneider 1976; Earle 1982), but several points bear repetition here. The first of these is that a state may increase the efficiency and control of its political finance system by shifting toward wealth finance. The use of goods with monetary characteristics reduces state costs in proportion to the value of the goods being transferred. Transport costs are reduced, wealth goods being lighter and more readily transportable than staples. The costs of management are also diminished because fewer storage facilities and fewer personnel to manage such facilities are needed. A tax or payment for services also reduces the proportion of the finance lost through decay because wealth goods are typically less perishable than staples. An additional key benefit of wealth finance is that it provides the means of interregionally integrating the economies of the state's disparate ethnic groups. A generalized medium of payment facilitates collection and transport of taxes and the payment of government obligations among provinces.

For example, the Aztec state actively promoted the use of craft goods and exotic valuables as currencies in the tax-tribute system and the Central Highlands marketing system. Even in provinces that did not grow cotton, the state often required tribute of *quachtli* (white cotton cloth). These textiles, which appear to have lost their use function over time, were used in state-administered foreign trade and in market transactions for fine clothing and luxury raw materials, the latter available through ports of trade outside of the Aztec heartland (Chapman 1957; Berdan 1975:292). Similarly, some Aztec campaigns may have been directed to the conquest of cacao-producing regions, the beans being a key medium of exchange in highlands markets (Berdan 1975:297). The production and distribution of these goods were promoted by the state elites, who used them in part to obtain subsistence products from specialized agricultural communities in the Valley of Mexico (Brumfiel 1980) and to pay off political and military debts.

In the Andes, the circulation of prestige goods was widespread millennia before the rise of the Inka state. For instance, during the Early Intermediate Period (*ca.* A.D. 100–600) and before, precious metals (e.g., gold and silver) from the Central and Northern highlands, *Spondylus* shell from south coastal Ecuador, feathers from the tropical forest, and semiprecious stones (e.g., chrysacolla, lapis lazuli), some of which came from the Southern Highlands, were circulating in long-distance exchange networks (Earle 1974; Paulsen 1974; Shimada 1982). Given the known circulation of these and similar wealth goods prior to and under the Inkas, it is reasonable to ask to what extent, if any, the Inka state was employing these goods as special-purpose media of tribute and as payment for services. The evidence on this point is limited and often regionally specific, but sufficient information exists to permit some preliminary conclusions concerning the state's use of such goods in the management of the political economy.

Before entering this discussion in detail, however, we should anticipate two possible objections to our argument. First, we do not imply here that the Inka state was actively promoting a market economy comparable to that of the Aztecs (La Lone 1982; cf. Hartmann 1971). Barter did, as we have said, occur beneath the political economy, but widespread market exchange seems to have been primarily a north Andean phenomenon (Salomon 1983, 1986), with some elements of entrepreneurial exchange occurring on the central and north Peruvian coasts (Netherly 1978; Rostworowski 1978, 1981). Second, the imputation of monetary characteristics to goods whose transfer is often couched as gift-giving does not preclude their serving other functions. The combination of social, ideological, and economic features is typical of special-purpose moneys (Dalton 1977), and it would be surprising if Inka wealth did not share this feature. The Aztecs' cacao and *quachtli* are just two examples of such consumable currencies in a complex state economy.

In general, wealth goods were mobilized in the Inka state in two ways. The first of these was through direct prestation of finished products in the form of obligatory gifts from local elites to the state or taxes on economic specialists. These goods included qumpi cloth (Salomon 1986), various gold, silver, and copper objects (Cobo 1956 [1653], vol. 3:291), and unfinished *Spondylus* shell (Murra 1975; 1982:249). The second was through conversion of staples into wealth objects by support of craft specialists attached to the state (see below).

The increased importance of the control of wealth by the Inka state appears to be exemplified by the distribution of metals recovered in our Mantaro Valley excavations. Preliminary analysis of the metals recovered through 1982 suggests a major contrast between the latest phase of the Late Intermediate Period (Wanka II: *ca.* A.D. 1350–1460) and the Late Horizon (Wanka III: A.D. 1460–1532, during Inka domination). These data come from household groups we have been excavating at four sites: two (Tunanmarca and Umpamalca) represent Wanka II, and two (Hatunmarca and Marca) represent Wanka III. The change in distribution of metals is clearest in terms of the materials themselves (Table 2-1). While both copper and lead increase in occurrence, silver becomes less common. Assuming that lead is a by-product of silver production (a point we are currently trying to document), silver production in the Mantaro region appears to increase at the same time that finished silver products become quite rare in Wanka sites. To what can we attribute this change? Most likely, the silver production is becoming directed toward the state, which is removing it from local use. Ethnohistoric sources (e.g., Cieza de León 1862 [1551]:432) speak of silver manufacture at the local Inka administrative center, Hatun Xauxa; however, the silver was apparently not destined for general local consumption.

The combined archaeological and documentary information for the Xauxa region suggests that metal products may have flowed to the state through (1) metal procurement and production systems in which the local elites played a controlling managerial role through their own attached specialists and (2) systems in which the state

Table 2-1. Percentage of Excavated Proveniences (Upper Mantaro Archaeological Research Project 1982 Fieldwork) Yielding Metals in Wanka II (prior to Inka Conquest) and Wanka III (during Inka Domination)

	N Proveniences	% Silver	% Lead	% Copper
Wanka II	473	2.3	0.2	1.5
Wanka III	433	0.2	1.6	5.1

controlled all aspects from mining to final disposition of the finished products. The evidence for increased ore processing at the local communities, particularly in elite areas, suggests an increase in metal manufacturing managed by local elites. It is not clear, however, whether the products of this work were transferred to the state as finished products or as refined metal ready for conversion into finished products by attached specialists (Cieza de León 1862 [1551]:432). We consider it possible that the two systems functioned simultaneously for different metals and for different finished products. Current field research may shed more light on this issue.

Two ethnohistorically documented cases of the use of wealth goods by the Inkas to finance relations with subject elites are also pertinent here. The first case involves the cooption or integration of semimonetary and material tribute systems into the state political economy in relations with societies in which they were already present. The most clearly defined case for this is in the highlands of Ecuador, although state-local relations on the central Peruvian coast may have been similar. The second case involves the massive production and promotion of more generally used wealth objects, especially *qumpi,* or fine cloth.

In an incisive study of highland societies of Ecuador prior to and under the Inkas, Salomon (1983, 1986) has observed marked differences in political and economic organization from societies of the central Andes. Prior to the Inka conquest of the region in the late fifteenth and early sixteenth centuries, the societies were fairly small, independent polities that Salomon calls *chiefdoms.* Rather than drawing their basic support from internal production, as was the ideal in the central and southern Andes, the communities were integrated into complex exchange networks. This included market exchange, particularly in special products such as salt, coca, pepper, and cotton.

Various kinds of monies, such as polished gold buttons (*chaguales*), copper axes, and shell beads also circulated within the region. These were graded in value and were variably convertible into subsistence goods in market exchange by commoners, elites, and trading specialists.

Two features of this economic organization are especially interesting here. First, the local lords received direct payment of tribute in the form of *mantas* (cloth), gold, shell beads, bone beads, copper axes, and coca. These goods moved freely up and down the political hierarchy and were used as means of payment for political services as well as for purchase of goods in the market. These goods thus played a role in underwriting the local elites' relations with other communities and within their own hierarchies. Second, there was a hereditary merchant sector (*mindalaes*) that trafficked in wealth goods (see Salomon 1978 for a comparison with Aztec *pochteca*). They paid no tribute in labor but paid the local *caciques* (elites) in gold, cloth, and beads and perhaps coca and salt. The amount to be paid was calculated as a portion of their trade goods.

When the Inkas conquered the Ecuadorian highlands, they established Quito as the northern capital of the empire and laid an additional level of political organization over the local elites. In addition to establishing state lands for production of staples, the state usurped the elites' rights to dominate the flow of wealth goods and required new prestations of cloth. Salomon (1983) observes that the more distant Pasto groups had a much more widespread *mindalá* sector than did the communities surrounding the Quito and Otavalo areas, which had been integrated more fully into the Inka state as a result of their domination for several decades. In the latter areas, the traders were coopted and regulated by the Inka state perhaps to ensure the continued flow of sumptuary items, such as Spondylus (*mullu*), from areas that the Inkas systematically failed to incorporate, including the Ecuadorian coast.

The key point to be taken from this Ecuadorian example is that the Inka state regulated a monetized tax/tribute system, associated with an indigenous market economy, for its own ends in the northern part of the empire. The Inkas added a new level of control over the existing system and used its own wealth goods to underwrite the elites' political services to the state. The Inkas concentrated the merchant sector under their control not to eliminate its activities within the regional economy but to articulate it with the state's own means of generating funds for the political economy.

Salomon (1983) points out that a comparable situation may have existed in the central Peruvian coastal Chincha Valley, where an ethnohistoric source from 1570–75 records the presence of a class of merchant traders (Rostworowski 1970). These traders were apparently allowed to maintain an independent status under the Inka state. They circulated from Guayaquil, Ecuador, to the Ica Valley of southern Peru and traveled to Cuzco, bringing, among other goods, various raw and finished *Spondylus* products into the central Andean economic sphere. The *Spondylus* was especially important to the Inkas and their subordinate polities because it was extensively used in rituals designed to induce rain and to make springs flow (Paulsen 1974; Murra 1975:257; Marcos 1978). Whether the Chincha merchants were independent entrepreneurs under Inka rule, as Rostworowski (1970) suggests, or whether they served as delegates of administered trade is not clear. The important point is that the Inka state recognized and exploited an established trading institution to provide wealth goods to the central authorities, who could then distribute them to subordinate elites as part of payment for service to the state.

The second general case for the use of wealth finance in elite-state relations lies in the state-subsidized and controlled manufacture and circulation of sumptuary goods. The outstanding example of this occurs in the production and distribution of fine cloth. Murra (1962) has detailed the role of textiles in the Andes under the Inkas, showing its pervasive significance in many social, political, and economic situations. For instance, cloth was given in bridewealth, presented as gifts at weaning, buried in mummy bundles, sacrificed in rituals, and used as a status marker. Of importance here is the systematic presentation of cloth to subordinate elites for political services and economic management. In an inspection of the province of Chucuito west of Lake Titicaca in 1567, it was reported that the predecessors of Martin Cari, the paramount of the *parcialidad* (sociopolitical division) of Anansaya, received 50 to 100 pieces of cloth per year from Inka state warehouses. The cloth, presented in addition to a wide range of other goods and services, was for the consumption of the *kurakas,* their families, and the travelers passing through (Diez de San Miguel 1964 [1567]:25, 34). It is not clear what (possibly variable) proportion of the cloth and other goods was at the personal disposal of the paramount and what proportion was consumed by state travelers, but the fact remains that the cloth was a perquisite of office. Further, the subordinate elites of the *parcialidad* of Urinsaya reported annually giving up to 35 pieces of cloth of their *own* wool (about half *qumpi* and half *awasqa* or rough cloth) to the paramount, Martin Cusi, in addition to the cloth woven from his wool (Diez de San Miguel 1964 [1567]:33). The paramount thus had access to fine cloth through systematic awards from the state, less systematic presentations from subordinate elites, and weaving by the community and his own household.

The state produced fine cloth through two basic mechanisms. The first was as part of corvée labor production, in which craft specialists made cloth from wool provided by the state as their labor tax. The second was through the growing system of displaced colonists and specialist female weavers employed full-time by the state. The colonies of craft producers included weavers, such as the inhabitants of the town of Lamay, near Cuzco, at which a Wanka *qumpi camayoc* (master weaver) reported that his father had held the position of *pichqapachaca kuraka,* or head of 500 households (loosely speaking) (Toledo 1940 [1571]:159). Other attached craft specialists included potters, such as those from the 14 ethnic groups represented at Wayakuntu or the north coastal potters relocated in Cajamarca (Espinoza 1973). Similarly, the Inkas transported the Chimú metalsmiths wholesale to Cuzco to produce for the state after taking control of the north coast (Rowe 1948). Other cloth producers recorded archaeologically include those who occupied a compound at Huánuco Pampa at which a high concentration of spindle whorls was recovered (Morris 1974:103).

The state's production and distribution of cloth is clearly too complex an issue for us to address fully in this chapter. However, without pushing the point too far, it seems reasonable to view some Inka cloth as a special-purpose money, circulating in a restricted sphere of exchange (Bohannan 1955). In this sense, *qumpi* may be analogous to the Aztec *quachtli* but less generalized and less easily convertible to other goods. That is, the cloth served as a standard of payment for service to the state in a limited sphere of exchange relationships.[3] It is important to note that this cloth flowed in *both* directions, from the local elites to the state in the form of obligatory gifts and back from the state as part of payment for work rendered in office.

The state's heavy investment in the production of fine cloth has two significant implications for our argument. First, the state was structuring economic relations with its subordinate elites in terms of a flow of valuables. By investing high value in certain commodities, the state could minimize transport costs for tax relations with subject elites, and interregional integration of disparate subject polities could be controlled through a state-regulated system of wealth manufacture and payment. Second, the state's control over the circulation of these goods allowed it to set their value within the political economy. Whether a system of exchange equivalencies existed is not clear, but within the sphere of exchange of political services and valuables/ special-purpose money, the state controlled access to the wealth associated with power.

In an analogous fashion, the state controlled a large portion of the production and distribution of a specialty crop, coca. The state maintained fields of coca in the *yungas* (coastal piedmont) and in the *montaña,* cultivated by designated laborers, often *mitmaqkuna.* As part of the regular dole to corvée laborers, the state and local elites provided a ration of coca (e.g., Diez de San Miguel 1964 [1567]:22, 82), whose amount is unclear. Basing her account on ethnohistoric sources, Rostworowski (1978) has suggested that coca was one of several (consumable) currencies circulating on the central coast of Peru during Inka hegemony and may have been used as a medium of exchange to obtain metals from neighboring highland people. Salomon's (1986) work has documented that coca served as a currency in highlands Ecuador in the Colonial period. Similarly, we have seen that coca was produced as a specialty crop on the eastern side of the Andes in the early Colonial period, with the intent to exchange it for other subsistence or specialty goods, such as salt (Burchard 1974, Ortiz de Zúñiga 1967–72 [1562]).[4] Alhtough the state's mass production and circulation of coca may be viewed as part of its ceremonial hospitality, it also suggests a state interest in providing a good to its workers that was valued both for its use as a comestible and as an item with recognized exchange value.

From the foregoing, we may argue that the Inka state promoted and employed circulation of wealth goods in its finance system both with groups that were marginally incorporated into the empire politically (Ecuador and coastal Peru) and with groups that were intensively integrated into the state. As mentioned earlier, the Inka state attempted to retain control over regions by compartmentalizing them economically and establishing strong vertical ties between the ruling Inka and the regional elites. Control of valuables was of course instrumental in establishing and maintaining these vertical ties in the Inka state as it was in the Aztec (Brumfiel 1983).

CONCLUSION

We have attempted to lay out some of the conditions affecting an archaic state's political finance policy. We have argued that the requirements of gross production and the constraints of security and of management costs will lead the state to develop a finance system based on production and circulation of both staple and wealth goods. The staple finance system will be largely focused within a region because of the regular and stochastic needs for large-scale funding of personnel throughout the state's territory and the prohibitive cost of transport among regions on a regular basis. Regional concentration of storage is therefore a highly adaptive strategy for a territorially expansionist state. At the same time, it creates a major problem; the stored goods may be used to fund rebellion against the state. For example, in the Mantaro Valley, from the Spanish arrival in 1533 until 1554, supplies from the massive warehouse complexes were given by the local leaders to support the Spanish war against the Inkas (Espinoza 1971 [1558–61]). Decentralized finance may thus result in weakened controls from the administrative center.

We have also argued that the organization and allocation of labor resources is not an independent variable in the state's economic planning; the use of labor depends upon the requirements of goods production and management as much as on the socioeconomic relationships between the various producing and consuming sectors of the economy. To argue that the peasants paid taxes to the Inka state only in labor may be essentially correct, but to assert that this was the sole means of state finance obscures a range of systematic economic interactions based on goods, especially among elites. To integrate the disparate provincial economies into the centralized state political economy, the Inka state adopted a complementary system of circulating wealth goods, often in a form already compatible with those in use in the subject provinces. Controlling the procurement and circulation of wealth goods was a means of interregional economic integration that was cost-effective and subject to central authority. An additional benefit to this approach, of course, was to give local elites who received wealth from the state a vested interest in the maintenance of the system.

The use of a mixture of staple and wealth finance in the state political economy allowed the Inkas flexibility in regional and interregional finance. The establishment of a separate staple finance system within each province guaranteed, as much as was possible under the agricultural conditions, the support of permanent, temporary, itinerant, and security personnel for the state. The risk of production and the variability in labor costs of the staple finance system were borne by the local populace in that cultivation of state lands took precedence over cultivation of community lands (see Mitchell 1980 for a discussion of the logistics of this problem). In return, the state provided a security umbrella in the form of concentrated storage, and, in fact, the support of corvée laborers by the state in the agricultural off-season can be viewed, in part, as a means of providing security for the local populace (see Murra 1980 [1956]).

In sum, archaic states were confronted with simultaneous problems of gross energy capture to support its dispersed activities, a need for security, and a need to integrate its subject regions into a centralized system of control. A mixed strategy of labor taxation, control of staple goods, and production and circulation of wealth goods permitted the Inka state to meet its disparate economic requirements. Although we have chosen the Inkas as a case to demonstrate our argument, we feel that the reasoning presented should also apply to other preindustrial states.

ACKNOWLEDGMENTS

The reader is referred to the *Comments* and *Reply* sections in the original publication of this paper in *Current Anthropology* (Vol. 26, No. 2, 1985:197–204) that are not repeated here to conserve space. We are gratified that our work has been of comparative interest to researchers working elsewhere on archaic political economies (Hunt 1988; Alcock 1989; O'Connor 1990). We would like to thank Morton Fried, Ross Hassig, John Hyslop, William Macdonald, Alison Paulsen, and Barbara Price for reviewing various drafts of this paper. Although we have incorporated a number of their comments into the text, we, of course, remain responsible for the interpretation and any errors of fact.

CHAPTER 3

Imperial Infrastructure and
the Inka State Storage
System
JAMES E. SNEAD

INTRODUCTION

THE remains of storage complexes constructed by the Inka state
provide extensive physical evidence concerning imperial organization. Attempts to use these data to better understand the relationship
between state storage and the political economy of Tawantinsuyu are
hindered by problems of scale. The vast size of the empire, variation
in the political and ecological units of which it was composed, and
the patchiness of archaeological research in much of the Inka empire,
make generalizations tentative. A century and a half of scholarly
inquiry within the Andean region has, however, produced a significant quantity of data regarding Inka state storage sites. This evidence,
when examined within constraints, does allow for a limited degree of
comparative study. Collation and preliminary analysis of the resultant
body of documentation is an important step upon which further
inquiry must be based.

The focus of modern archaeological research on Inka state storage
has been on storage technology (Morris 1981; see Chapter 8, this
volume; D'Altroy and Hastorf 1984; see Chapter 9) and local/regional
organization (Morris 1967 and Chapter 5; D'Altroy 1981; D'Altroy
and Earle, Chapter 6, this volume; Topic and Topic 1984; Topic and
Chiswell, Chapter 7; LeVine 1985, and Chapter 4). This has resulted
in several fine-grained analyses of storage complexes at major Inka
sites in the northern and central Peruvian Andes. Archaeological
evidence for Inka storage from much of the rest of the empire has
been less systematically treated. Efforts to use archaeological data to
study the state storage system on a panregional level have been few,
with the discussions in Morris (1967, 1981) and Hyslop (1984) being
the principal sources.

The present study compares some of the results of the last two decades of detailed research on the infrastructure of the Inka state with a selection of data from a wide array of less available and less detailed sources. This approach allows for the reestimation of the scale of state storage throughout the empire and of some of the organizational principles behind the Inka state storage system as a whole. It will be argued here that the disposition of state storage within Tawantinsuyu reflects economic, military, and political goals of the state. Examination of the spatial arrangement of the system can, in turn, give insight into these interacting forces as they existed within the Inka polity.

ARCHAEOLOGICAL DATA

In this analysis archaeological evidence for Inka sites containing state storage components has been gathered from throughout the regions formerly encompassed by Tawantinsuyu. All of the sites have been identified as facilities under Inka state control on the basis of architecture or context, although in some areas the persistence of local architectural styles or a lack of recognizable state facilities in the vicinity make the relationship between local Late Horizon (Inka-period) storage and state installations difficult to determine. Instances where patterns of control are poorly defined will be discussed in a later section.

Evidence for state storage in the vicinity of Cuzco has been consciously omitted from this study. It is predictable that the role of commodities stored in the capital and surrounding precincts might vary substantially from that found elsewhere. Maintenance of larger populations, a greater concentration of the elite elements of Inka society, and the presence of imperial "estates" would have placed different requirements on state stores. This is probably reflected in an organizational pattern at variance with the more peripheral areas of the empire. Archaeological evidence (see Morris 1967; Niles 1980; Kendall 1985) indicates that the situation is complex. The intrusion of state planning and control at the local level is evident (Morris, chapter 5). The work of Bingham (1922) and Fejos (1944) on Machu Picchu and nearby sites revealed few features that resemble state storage structures as known from other Inka sites. Given such evidence and its implications, state storage in the imperial core proper would require separate analysis and is thus not discussed here.

The sample of storage sites cannot be considered definitive. Although attempts have been made to review thoroughly the existing literature, as well as unpublished material, omissions are unavoidable. Vagaries of preservation, "coverage" of areas by field researchers, and publication of results weigh against the sample being considered representative. The sites examined, however, have been taken from most of the geographical regions encompassed by the empire along with many of the cultural and political subunits that it incorporated. Under these circumstances the sample is as broad as the data allow.

The identification of state storage in archaeological contexts is problematic. Ethnohistoric information associates storage with architectural forms known as *qollqa,* typically one-room structures built of unshaped fieldstones, or *pirca.* In form *qollqa* are variable; Morris (1967:181) identifies seven structural forms of *pirca*-walled *qollqa* in the Central Highlands and the Cuzco area alone. They are initially distinguished from other buildings of similar dimensions on the basis of context. Their orderly arrangement in rows make them distinct in the Inka architectural canon (Gasparini and Margolies 1980). Excavations at Huánuco Pampa and in the Mantaro Valley support the association of storage activity with these structures.

Pirca-walled qollqa are not found throughout the empire, and other techniques must be used in the identification of state storage outside of the Central Highlands. The following criteria were used by Anders (1981:392) to segregate state storage at the Moche V (*ca.* eighth-century A.D.) site of Pampa Grande, in the Lambayeque Valley on the north coast of Peru: the presence of regular and repeated architectural features such as "equally sized, contiguous rooms arranged in a linear pattern," together with a low level of domestic debris and high thresholds. In regions where storage architecture evidently deviates from the Central Highland pattern, structures meeting this definition may be tentatively identified as having a storage function.

It cannot be assumed that architectural data will identify all forms of storage originally present in state complexes. There is evidence that storage structures identified in the Lerma Valley of Argentina (Figure 3-4), for example, had superstructures of adobe that might not have been preserved under less favorable circumstances (Gonzalez 1983:347). Hyslop's (1984:291) comment on the likelihood that corrals for camelid herds would have been "storage" of state property is relevant. Byrne de Caballero (1975) describes several forms of storage found in the Cochabamba Valley of Bolivia (Figure 3-3), not all immediately recognizable. This variation can be partially attributed to the storage conditions required for different types of commodities. Sample error also must be considered. Imperial requirements for certain staple crops, however, make it likely that small, regularly arranged structures or multiple rooms within larger units formed a primary mode of state storage and one that can be detected within the archaeological record.

GENERAL CHARACTERISTICS OF THE STATE STORAGE SYSTEM

Using the criteria discussed above, 44 sites with a recognizable state storage component have been identified. They are descried in Appendix I; Appendix II contains information from 3 sites in Argentina received after the analysis was completed. Although the inconsistent quality of the data cited in the appendices affects direct comparison between the different storage complexes, evidence for their organization on internal and regional levels can be examined. Not all variables can be used effectively. Individual structure type, for example, is a measurable component of state storage complexes, but its significance is poorly understood. Research in this direction is thus reliant on excavation (Morris 1967; see Chapters 5 and 8, this volume; D'Altroy 1981; D'Altroy and Hastorf 1984 and Chapter 9, this volume; Chiswell 1984; Topic and Chiswell, Chapter 7). Two categories of variables are described in sufficient detail and lend themselves to a study of regional organization: (1) complex size and (2) associated facilities (the type and proximity of other state facilities).

COMPLEX SIZE

A minimum number of storage units present in the individual sites reviewed is identifiable in all but six cases (Table 3-4). This data can be used as a rough indicator of the size of the complex and the potential commodity storage that would have been available. Although comparisons of the surface area or volume of storage structures would be desirable, the measurements needed to make such calculations are missing for 18 of the 44 sites sampled. Some variation in the size and form of storage structures must be assumed but in most cases should not be of such magnitude as to invalidate rough comparison. Table 3-1 illustrates the range of structure/room counts for the sites in Appendix I. The extent of a storage complex can be considered an indicator of the significance of storage at that location.

ASSOCIATED FACILITIES

All of the storage units listed in Appendix I existed in some degree of association with other physical aspects of state operations. These nonstorage elements of the sites provide the context in which the storage component existed. Again, given little archaeological data on the specific function of different structures, in each case it is necessary to rely on general scale and cultural affiliation. Storage units are found in both large and small state complexes; facilities at Huánuco Pampa (2) occupy approximately two square kilometers (Morris and Thompson 1985:56), whereas small *tampu* (inns serving travelers) such as Tambo Blanco in Ecuador (34) have only a few associated structures (Uhle 1969). Given a general absence of quantitative measurement of site size, a simple four-level hierarchy of units is applied here (see Tables 3-2, 3-3, and 3-4). Terms such as "small *tampu*" and "large *tampu*" are admittedly impressionistic but convey a generally reliable sense of the scale of the site being considered.

As an essential element of the imperial infrastructure, state roads must be considered "facilities" as well. All of the sites reviewed have some association with roads. The extent and importance of those roads is, however, variable. The principal coastal and highland arteries north into Ecuador and south through Chile and Argentina would have been more strategically significant on a broad level (Hyslop 1984:257) than roads connecting sites or regions to them. The location of a storage complex within this system is a significant indicator of its function. For the purpose of this analysis, three distinctions of road type are made; primary roads (the two main north-south highland and coastal roads), secondary roads (highland-coastal laterals, while often of significant strategic importance, are included in this category), and junctions (access to more than one route). For roads in northwest Argentina and Chile, reference has been made to Raffino (1981); in all other areas Hyslop (1984) is used as a source.

An examination of the interrelationships of these elements as present in the sites reviewed here reveals a certain amount of co-variance. Typological treatments of Inka state storage are prominent in the

Table 3-1. Storage Units Sampled, with Associated Variables

Sites	Storage Units	Associated Facilities	Roads
Agua Hedionda	103	*tampu*	S
Camata	43	*tampu*	S
Campo del Pucara	1,717	domestic?	S
Capis-Cerrillos	200	nd	P/J
Cerro de las Rueditas	68	nd	S
Chichipampa	x	nd	nd
Culluma Baja	46	none	S
La Cima	17	*tampu*	P
Chacamarca	118	large *tampu*	P/J
Cochabamba (Chachapoyas)	23	large *tampu*	S
Corral Blanco	19	*tampu*	P
Cotapachi	2,400	domestic	S
Graneros	x	*tampu*	P
Hatunqolla	x	extensive	P
Hatun Xauxa	1,069	extensive	P/J
Hualfin	23	*tampu*	S
Huamachuco	144	extensive?	P
Huanuco Pampa	496	extensive	P/J
Ingapirca	x	large *tampu*	P
Inkallajta	20	extensive	S
Inkawasi	202	extensive	S
Inka Tampu	25	*tampu*	S
Kharalaus Pampa	80	*tampu*	S
Kullku Tampu	4	*tampu*	S
Mantaro Valley	1,657	variable	P/J
Millpu	16	none	S
Nevados de Aconquija	x	extensive	P
Paredones (Azuay)	38	*tampu*	P
Pocona	21	*tampu*	S
Potrero de Payogasta	x	extensive	P
Pumpu	325	extensive	P/J
Quebrada de la Vaca	27	large *tampu*	P
Quitaloma	5	large *tampu*	nd
Raqchi	120	extensive	P
Tambo Blanco	12	*tampu*	nd
Tambo Colorado	5	large *tampu*	S
Tambo Viejo	40	extensive	S
Taparaku	20	*tampu*	P
Tarmatambo	38	large *tampu*	P
Telarnioj	15	*tampu*	P
Tumuyo	63	domestic?	S
Tunsukancha	24	*tampu*	P
Turi	x	extensive	P
Yacoraite	4	*tampu*	P
Storage unit total	9,167		

x = insufficient data for unit count.
Roads: S = secondary, P = primary, J = junction.

Table 3-2. Storage at Large State Centers, in Descending Order of Size

Sites	Storage Units	Associated Facilities	Roads
1. Hatun Xauxa	1,069	extensive	P/J
2. Huanuco Pampa	496	extensive	P/J
3. Pumpu	325	extensive	P/J
4. Huamachuco	144	extensive?	P
5. Raqchi	40	extensive	P
6. Hatunqolla	x	extensive	P
Storage unit total	2,074		
Percentage of total sample	.23		

x = insufficient data for unit count.
Roads: S = secondary, P = primary, J = junction.

Table 3-3. Storage at Centers of Production and Special Function, Shown in Descending Order of Size

Sites	Storage Units	Associated Facilities	Roads
7. Cotapachi	2,400	domestic	S
8. Campo del Pucara	1,717	domestic?	S
9. Inkawasi	202	extensive	S
10. Capis-Cerrillos	200	nd	P/J
11. Chacamarca	118	large *tampu*	P/J
12. Agua Hedionda	103	*tampu*	S
13. Kharalaus Pampa	80	*tampu*	S
14. Cerro de las Rueditas	68	nd	S
15. Tumuyo	63	domestic?	S
16. Culluma Baja	46	none	S
Storage unit total	4,997		
Percentage of total sample	.54		

Roads: S = secondary, P = primary, J = junction.

ethnohistoric literature; both Garcilaso de la Vega (1943 [1609]) and Cobo (1956 [1653]) describe a system which was hierarchically organized on local, regional, and state levels. The archaeological evidence suggests a more complex picture. Using the variables described above, certain general characteristics of storage in different types of state installations can be defined.

1. *Storage at Large State Centers* (Sites 1–6: Table 3-2, Figure 3-1). Storage units are found in association with extensive state facilities and in close association with primary state roads in six of the sampled

Table 3-4. Storage at Secondary State Facilities, Shown in Descending Order of Size

Sites	Storage Units	Associated Facilities	Roads
17. Mantaro Valley[a]	*	variable	P/J
North Valley	923		
South Valley	734		
18. Camata	43	*tampu*	S
19. Tambo Viejo	40	extensive	S
20. Paredones (Azuay)	38	*tampu*	P
21. Tarmatambo	38	large *tampu*	P
22. Quebrada de la Vaca	27	large *tampu*	P
23. Inka Tampu	25	*tampu*	S
24. Tunsukancha	24	*tampu*	P
25. Cochabamba (Chachapoyas)	23	large *tampu*	nd
26. Hualfín	23	*tampu*	S
27. Pocona	21	*tampu*	S
28. Inkallajta	20	extensive	S
29. Taparaku	20	*tampu*	P
30. Corral Blanco	19	*tampu*	P
31. Millpu	17	*tampu*	P
32. AY5-66	16	none	S
33. Telarnioj	15	*tampu*	P
34. Tambo Blanco	12	*tampu*	nd
35. Tambo Colorado	5	large *tampu*	S
36. Quitaloma	5	large *tampu*	nd
37. Kullku Tampu	4	*tampu*	S
38. Yacoraite	4	*tampu*	P
39. Turi	x	extensive	P
40. Portrero del Payogasta	x	extensive	P
41. Nevado del Aconquija	x	extensive	P
42. Graneros	x	*tampu*	P
43. Ingapirca	x	large *tampu*	P
44. Chichipampa	x	nd	nd
Storage unit total	2,096		
Percentage of total sample	.23		

[a]48 separate storage sites have been documented for the Mantaro Valley (D'Altroy 1981, 1989, 1992; Browman 1970, 1985), which are grouped together under these two headings.

x = insufficient data for unit count.

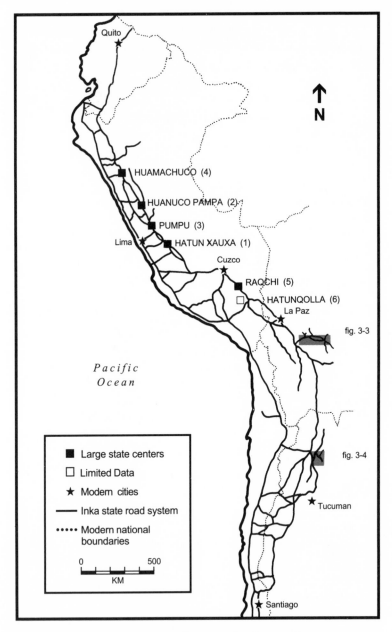

Figure 3–1. Map of Tawantinsuyu, illustrating distribution of large state centers with storage components along the state road system. Numbers refer to sites listed in Table 3-2. Road network based on Hyslop 1984; Raffino 1981.

cases. These sites are typically identified as regional administrative centers for the state (LeVine 1985:5). Four of them, Hatun Xauxa (1), Pumpu (3), Huanuco Pampa (2), and Hatunqolla (6) are on the list of Inka provincial capitals provided by Cieza de Leon (1967 [1553]:65). Archaeological and ethnohistoric evidence for Huamachuco (4) (Topic and Topic 1984; Topic and Chiswell, Chapter 7; Netherly 1978) and Raqchi (5) (La Lone and La Lone 1987) indicates that they were also centers of extensive imperial activity. All of these sites are located on primary highland roads, and with the exception of Raqchi lie close to junctions with lateral roads leading either to the coast or to the Selva (Figure 3-1). Although archaeological reconnaissance at Hatunqolla remains preliminary, the work of Julien (1983) suggests that the complex contained a storage component of uncertain extent.

Size is also a significant factor. Although comprising only 14% of the number of sites examined, the 6 together contain 22.6% of the total number of storage units in the sample. Four of the sites (1–4) are within the top 10 sites in terms of storage capacity. The comparatively high percentage of state storage located in these administrative sites would undoubtedly increase if similar complexes believed to have had significant storage components were included. Cieza's (1862 [1551]:435) count of 700 storage structures at the administrative site of Vilcas is credible in comparison with these other figures but has yet to be archaeologically verified.

The close association of storage complexes with other imperial facilities underlines their functional interrelationship. The role of the administration centers in the context of an expanding empire seems to have been to provide a support base for a variety of economic and political activities in the surrounding region. Management of labor service and ritual activity were centralized in these locations (D'Altroy 1981; Morris 1982; Morris and Thompson 1985; LeVine 1985, 1987) and required logistical support. Although arguments that large quantities of staple goods may have been stored and transported elsewhere have been advanced (Topic 1985), the high volume of storage in these complexes is clearly related to the size of the entire installation and the extent of the economic and political activity focused on it (see also LeVine, Chapter 4 this volume for a discussion of the correlation between storage volume and regional population size).

The importance of storage in administrative centers can be seen from an empirewide perspective as well. The variable nature of political and economic circumstances throughout the territory of Tawantinsuyu meant that demands upon imperial resources were not constant in space or in time. Security and the mobilization of a surplus, in particular, were problems faced by expansive states (D'Altroy and Earle, Chapter 2; see also D'Altroy 1992). Provisions for the army are believed to have come directly from state stores (Bram 1941:53). The positioning of administrative centers and their associated storage along primary routes of communication and at the junctions of key lateral roads suggests that they were designed so that commodities stored at these sites could be used to support state activities in more distant regions when needed.

In terms of organization, at most of these sites the storage complexes are within or adjacent to the administrative centers themselves. The more dispersed organization of storage facilities in Huamachuco varies from this pattern only in detail. The map of qollqa distribution provided by Chiswell (1984; Topic and Chiswell, Chapter 7) for the Huamachuco area depicts all three groups as within a 3-kilometer radius of Huamachuco itself; they are essentially satellites of the center.

State storage at Raqchi may have been organized along different lines. The site itself is walled and occupies 80 hectares (La Lone and La Lone 1987:54). Although the remains of only 40 circular qollqalike structures are currently visible (Gasparini and Margolies 1980:238), 120 were counted in the last century (Squier 1973 [1877]:411). The principal feature of the site is a major temple of Wiracocha, and Raqchi is generally considered to have been a religious center. Ethnohistoric evidence suggests that storage for the support of the state cult may have been considered separately from that intended for other state functions (Morris 1967:119). Storage at Raqchi may thus have been used to further a different set of goals than those of administrative centers. Its extent and strategic location, however, indicate that commodities stored there provided support for a broad variety of functions. Further consideration of storage at religious centers will require a better understanding of the role of the sun cult within the broader state structure.

2. *Storage at Centers of Production and Special Function* (Sites 7–16; Table 3-3, Figures 3-2, 3-3, 3-4). Of the 44 sites in the sample, 10 share the characteristics of having limited associated facilities in

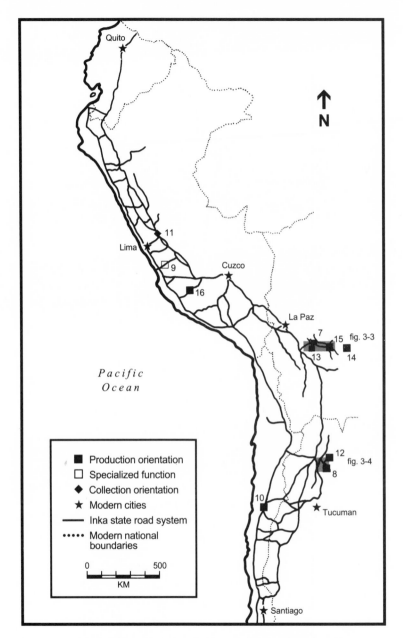

Figure 3-2. Map of Tawantinsuyu, illustrating the distribution of centers of production and special function containing storage components along the state road system. Numbers refer to sites listed in Table 3-3. Road network based on Hyslop 1984 and Raffino 1981.

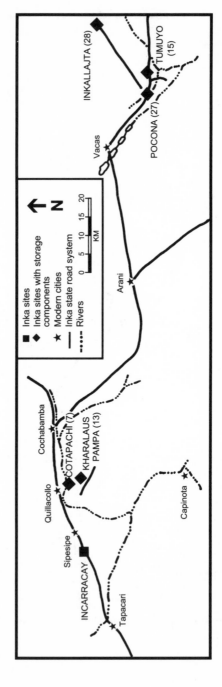

Figure 3-3. Map of Inka state storage and related sites in the Cochabamba Valley, Bolivia. Map based on Pereira 1982a; Cespedes Paz 1982.

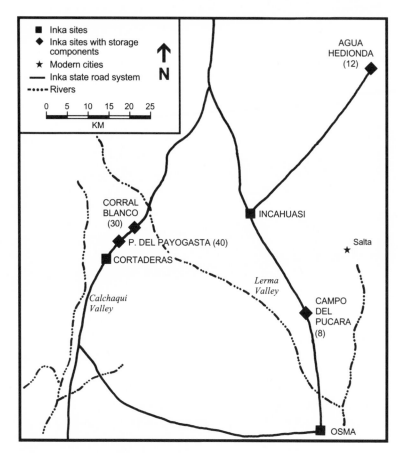

Figure 3-4. Map of Inka-period sites in Salta Province, Argentina.

combination with a large number of storage units. In most cases they are located along secondary roads away from the main highland and coastal routes. Approximately 54% of the storage units in the sample fall into this category. Although linked by common features, variation between these sites indicates that they were used to support diverse functions related to the goals of the state.

The two largest sites in the category, Cotapachi in Bolivia (7) and Campo del Pucara in Argentina (8), together contain 44% of the total number of storage units in the survey. There are no significant state complexes within 10 kilometers of either site, and both lie upon lateral routes to the east of the main highland road. At Cotapachi an unspecified number of domestic structures are related to the complex, but the nearest state facility of any size is at Incarracay, 15 kilometers distant (Byrne de Caballero 1978) (see Figure 3-3). Cotopachi is not entirely unique; large state storage complexes have been noted at Capinota and other locations in the region but have yet to be thoroughly described (Pereira 1982a).

Although Cotapachi is a single large complex, Campo del Pucara is composed of three storage facilities separated by 2.5 km. Fock (1961:72) identified domestic structures with Inkaic associations near the site, and a badly disturbed compound east of Groups B and C is mentioned in Boman (1908:288). Extensive Inkaic architecture is found at the site of Incahuasi (in the vicinity of Salta), 30 km to the northwest (Raffino 1981:146) that was probably connected to Campo del Pucara by road (see Figure 3-4). In design, the storage complexes are similar to Cotapachi, in that they are organized in evenly spaced grid patterns with a north-south orientation.

A third site of similar configuration is Capis-Cerrillos (10), near the Chilean city of Copiapo, for which little additional information is available (Latcham 1927). Although Capis-Cerrillos is located near a significant junction between the coastal road and a transcordilleran lateral, the available reports describe no directly associated installations. Copiapo lies at the end of the long Atacama stretch of the coastal state road, and it was significant to the Inka both because of its strategic location and for the presence of local resources (Rivera 1987).

In most of these cases, identifiable imperial political activity in the immediate vicinity, as measured by investment in associated facilities, cannot account for the volume of storage present. The labor involved in the construction of extensive qollqa complexes at these locations far outweighs that devoted to installations of an administrative nature. The concentration of state storage sites away from administrative facilities suggests that their location can be attributed to factors other than the support of local state operations. The logical inference is that local state facilities were intended to support the prime function of the storage complexes rather than the reverse.

A close relationship with resource production seems indicated in nine of the sites listed in Table 3-3. In the case of the Cochabamba

Valley (Figure 3-3), state storage in the region is clearly a material correlate of the well-documented maize-production enclave established in the region by the Inka ruler Wayna Qhapaq. The large size of the operation as described in sixteenth-century litigation records (Wachtel 1982) is corroborated by the vast number of storage structures present.

The ethnohistoric documentation for northwestern Argentina is limited (González 1982:318). The similarity of design and context between Campo del Pucara and Cotapachi, however, argue for a similarity of function. Direct evidence for extensive Inka-period cultivation in the Lerma Valley is not evident, but, allowing for sufficient water, the surrounding terrain is productive (Dougherty 1972). Some of the evidence discussed by Fock (1961:79) suggests that an Aymara-speaking *mitmaq* colony was associated with the Lerma Valley, and Gonzalez (1983:356) attributes the presence of Inca-Pacajes pottery and certain architectural details at Incahuasi to ties with the Lake Titicaca area. The possible association with *mitmaq-kuna* (resettled colonists) is similar to the Cochabamba circumstances and supports the identification of the Campo del Pucara site as storage for a production-oriented state installation. Gonzalez (1983:356) suggests that Incahuasi and sites along the primary highland road were the most significant Inka centers in the region. All are within 100 km of Campo del Pucara, and some percentage of the staples collected there can reasonably be assumed to have been devoted to their support.

Although somewhat more extensive, nonstorage facilities at Agua Hedionda (12) indicate that the site may have been a *tampu* or similar facility, the amount of storage present clearly outstrips the demand exercised for goods at a site of that nature. It is close enough to Campo del Pucara and Incahuasi to have been a part of the same supply system. A similar situation is evident in the Cochabamba Valley, where sites devoted to storage but of smaller size such as Kharalaus Pampa (13) are found in proximity to the massive complex at Cotapachi. The presence of smaller satellite complexes may have been a feature of the organization of storage at state production enclaves.

Several of the smaller sites that seem to have been devoted primarily to storage are found in closer proximity to state sites with a broader range of functions. Cerro de las Rueditas (14) (Byrne de Caballero 1981), Tumuyo (15) (Pereira 1982a), and Colluma Baja (16) (Schreiber 1987a) all have similar characteristics. The first may have originally consisted of 80 *qollqa* and lies in close proximity to a Inka-period site known as the Fuerte de Samaipata. Byrne de Caballero (1981) considers the two to have been functionally related. Tumuyo (15) is a storage site within the Cochabamba region that is also located near larger state installations. The site of Culluma Baja (16), in the Carhuarazo Valley of the Peruvian sierra, is located in a context of other Inka and local Late Horizon sites (Schreiber 1987a) and may be similar. Centers of indigenous population in the area may, however, suggest an organizational pattern more along the lines of that evident for the Mantaro Valley (see below).

Sites of this nature are all located away from primary roads and close to other state sites but lack features which would identify them as *tampu*. Although significantly smaller, their similarity in design to large production-oriented sites may suggest a related function at a smaller scale. One hypothesis is that they were elements of a regional distribution system. Locally produced commodities were stored at these sites and used to support state outposts within a fairly limited area.

The two remaining sites that have similar characteristics seem to be products of unique geographical and political circumstances. The ratio of storage to complex size at the Central Highland site of Chacamarca (11) (LeVine 1985:226; see also chapter 4) argues for the primacy of the storage function there, although it occupies an estimated 10.9 hectares and includes several structural complexes. Tarmatambo (11) to the south is nearly three times the size of Chacamarca but has less than a third of its storage capacity. Chacamarca is also only 40 km from the administrative center at Pumpu. LeVine (1985:292) suggests that its location may have made it favorable as a collection point for regional resources as well as a center of production. This would explain the presence of a greater administrative presence while still supporting the primary role of storage in the function of the site.

Inkawasi (9) (in the Cañete Valley of Peru) is organized along quite different lines. Large but only briefly occupied, the site is believed to have been constructed as a base of operations for military campaigns in the region and subsequently abandoned in favor of the coastal site of Cerro Azul (Marcus et al. 1983–85). Inkawasi seems to have largely served as a supply center; possibly as many as one third of the rooms at the site filled a storage function (Hyslop 1985:75). Administrative activity apparently played a minor role, as the unsuitability of the site for that purpose is suggested by its eventual relocation. Current information would suggest that its primary function was as a strategic stockpile supporting regional military activity.

The data indicate that a variety of special function sites related to production and distribution of resources were a fundamental element of the Inka state storage system. These sites share a common spatial organization, and all seem to have had storage as their primary function. That they comprise such a large percentage of the known number of storage units is informative. Identification of the uses to which the stored commodities were placed, however, is reliant on other categories of information.

3. *Storage at Secondary State Facilities* (Sites 17–44, Table 3-4, Figure 3-5). Storage at the remaining 28 sites in the sample can be classed as serving largely local functions. Although these complexes are found with the full range of possible associated facilities and are located on all types of roads, storage capacity is lower. With the exception of four of the Mantaro Valley sites (17), the number of storage structures in each of these sites does not exceed 50 (see Chapter 6 for a detailed description and analysis of Mantaro Valley sites). Such a small scale implies that storage units present in these sites would have been intended to support state activities in the immediate vicinity. As in other cases, the role of state storage in this context is thus dependent on the type of installation in which it is found.

Evidence for storage in sites of a specifically military nature is rare. Storage units have been identified in the fortress sites of Quitaloma in Ecuador (36) (Oberem 1968:199) and at Inkallajta (28) in Bolivia; they may also be a feature at other sites along the frontier between the Cochabamba Valley and the Chaco region to the east (Byrne de Caballero 1981). The number of *qollqa* found in these sites is low, as would be expected in a situation where storage therein was intended to primarily support the operations of the site itself. Inkallajta is within 20 kilometers of the storage site of Tumuyo discussed in the

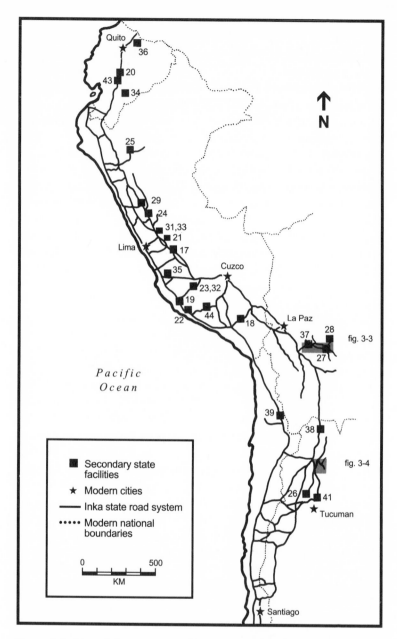

Figure 3-5. Map of Tawantinsuyu, illustrating the distribution of secondary state facilities with storage components along the state road system. Numbers refer to sites listed in Table 3-4. Road network based on Hyslop 1984 and Raffino 1981.

previous section and probably used Tumuyo as a source of supply. The lack of centralization in these military sites clearly differs from the pattern at Inkawasi (Cañete Valley) that is organized on a scale more indicative of focused regional activity.

Tampu sites included in the sample range in size from single hectare sites such as Kullku Tampu (37) and La Cima (31) to more extensive facilities such as those at Pocona (27). The smallest state installations surveyed by Hyslop (1984) along various road segments do not seem to include permanent, special storage structures. Although considered to have been designed to provide support for road traffic, there is evidence that *tampu* performed a variety of other functions, of an administrative and ceremonial nature (Hyslop 1984:279). The amount of associated state storage seems to fluctuate regionally. Heavy use of the major north-south highland road, for instance, may partially explain the relatively large storage capacity of the *tampu* in the Central Highlands. The level of state storage at *tampu,* however, is low when compared to that of larger sites, which indicates that even sites designated large *tampu* in Table 3-1 had only limited involvement in the production of goods or in the use of those goods to support multiple activities.

Eleven of these sites contain small numbers of storage units within a context of a greater number of associated facilities; these are considered "large *tampu*" and "extensive" in Table 3-4. Tambo Colorado (35) is architecturally one of the more significant of coastal Inka sites (Gasparini and Margolies 1980:124), but only a few structures with probable storage function have been identified to date. Evidence for state storage at Ingapirca in Ecuador (Franch 1978), Tarmatambo in the central highlands (LeVine 1985), and at the Chachapoyas site of Cochabamba (25) (Schjellerup 1984) also fit this pattern of small numbers of storage units within a context of a greater number of associated facilities. State storage at Tambo Viejo (19) in the Acari Valley on the Peruvian south coast (Menzel and Riddell 1986) is more extensive; facilities of similar design have been identified at other south coast Inka sites. Although the size and organization of Tambo Viejo would suggest that it was functionally similar to highland administrative sites, its storage capacity is low in comparison. As it currently stands, the evidence indicates that state storage at Tambo

Viejo and similar sites would have been on a scale compatible with the support of the center and purely local activities.

Identification of storage features and the level of state control at some of the sites from the southern regions of Tawantinsuyu is problematic. A small number of possible storage features in association with Inka architecture are visible on plans of the sites of Turi (39) in the Atacama Desert of Chile and Potrero de Payogasta (40) and Nevados de Aconquija (4) in highland Argentina (Raffino 1981:118). Their organization is different from that evident elsewhere. Rectangular structures with multiple rooms at the Argentine *tampu* of Corral Blanco (30) are suggested to have had a storage function (Hyslop 1984:178). A similar divergence from the Central Highland norm is evident in Ecuador (Hyslop 1984:290). Raffino (1981:110) suggests that large sites such as Potrero de Payogasta were important outposts of the Inka state; although further examination of these sites may identify more extensive storage facilities, it seems nevertheless evident that they have a significantly lower storage capacity than administrative sites further to the north.

A discussion of state storage in the Mantaro Valley can be found elsewhere in this volume (Chapters 4, 6, 9, and 10). Although in the aggregate, Mantaro Valley storage (17) dwarfs others in this category, 17 of the 25 sites described by D'Altroy (1992; see Chapter 6) have less than 40 units. It is the hypothesis of D'Altroy and Earle (Chapter 2) that the function of these scattered complexes was the support of state activities being carried out by or in local communities. Their decentralization does not follow the pattern of storage at production centers, which seem to be concentrated rather than dispersed. The repeated pattern of association with particular villages, sometimes within a few kilometers of each other, indicates that the distribution of storage facilities reflects a particular set of state-local relationships.

REGIONAL PATTERNS IN STATE STORAGE

HIGHLAND-COAST DICHOTOMY

Beyond the basic distribution of different types of storage sites throughout Tawantinsuyu, larger patterns exist. Although variations in population and resources were clearly important, it is evident that other factors were critical and were considered by imperial planners as the state storage system evolved. The data on state storage suggest that the sociopolitical organization of subject groups was an important factor in the organization of the imperial infrastructure (LeVine, Chapter 4).

The distribution of storage in state complexes throughout the empire forms a significant highland-coast dichotomy. The highlands are the locus of the bulk of state storage; with the exception of the Inkawasi, storage capacity reported for coastal sites is limited. The total of 274 storage units identified for the coast, from the sites of Quebrada de la Vaca (22), Tambo Colorado, Tambo Viejo, and Inkawasi, comprise only 3% of the total sample. The inclusion of unquantified data from Inka-period sites such as La Centinela (Chincha Valley) and Pachacamac (Lurín Valley) on the central coast of Peru seems unlikely to elevate this count to as high as 10%. This figure is surprisingly low given the potentially major role of coastal production in the state tribute system as well as the likelihood that the bulk of regional population in the prehistoric period was found on the coast (Shea 1976).

Physical evidence for state storage on the coast is ephemeral in spite of a century of archaeological investigation. In some areas, it is entirely absent; no single Inka site with more than domestic storage capacity has been identified on the north coast. Excavations on an Inkaic site in the Chicama Valley failed to uncover any significant storage facilities (Conrad 1977). Archaeological evidence for state storage at other state installations such as Tambo Colorado or at many Inka-period urban centers is quite sparse. Incomplete reconnaissance is an inadequate explanation for this pattern. Willey (1953) found no Inka storage complexes in his survey of the Virú Valley on the north coast, and only one small potential storage facility is evident from Wallace's (1971) surveys in the Chincha and Pisco regions further south. Agurto Calvo (1986:165) suggests that one of the small *tampu* sites in the vicinity of Lima has a storage component; as visible on an associated site map the area is small and of ambiguous association. The range of current evidence indicates that storage at coastal state Inka sites was at a significantly lower frequency than in the highlands.

Storage site design also differs significantly between the two regions. Sites in the highlands are thematically consistent; in most of the Peruvian sierra circular and rectangular qollqa in linear arrangements is the norm. Where storage with clear state associations is found on the coast it varies in form both when compared with the highlands and with other coastal areas. Extensive gridlike subterranean bins at Pachacamac (Lurín Valley) (Uhle 1903) have been identified as storage units (Morris 1967:153). The role of the state in their maintenance is uncertain. The storage units at Inkawasi are similar in design to those at Pachacamac and probably reflect coastal architectural traditions within a state-controlled context. Storage units described for Inkaic sites in the vicinity of the Acari Valley are linear multiroomed structures with courtyards, a form unreported for the Central Highlands. A similar architectural pattern is evident at the site of Camata [18] in the Osmore drainage (Mathews 1987). The qollqalike foundations at Tambo Colorado are the only coastal storage units in a form analogous to the highland qollqa.

Two general explanations can be proposed to explain the low level of state storage on the coast and its variable form: adoption by the Inka of local construction and storage technology that has gone unrecognized, or a relationship between the state and the stored surplus fundamentally different than that found in the highlands. The former is difficult to assess without excavation. The resemblance between storage unit design at state-controlled Inkawasi and the probable indigenous pattern at Pachacamac indicates that architectural borrowing occurred. The general absence of intrusive state facilities of any type for much of the coast, however, indicates that the pattern is rooted in state-local relationships.

Variability in the Inka patterns of integration of subject populations has been well established: "[T]he Tawantinsuyu is more a complicated and extensive network of relationships than it is the apparently monolithic and showy apparatus of power that the chroniclers described in the sixteenth century" (Pease 1982:190). Direct rule in much of the highlands can be inferred by the extensive and intrusive state facilities concentrated in that region. The predictable patterning of storage at state sites in the highlands is a result of this overt state control. The archaeological manifestations of indirect rule in coastal and valley areas have been described by Dillehay (1977), who notes that Inka involvement in different zones of the Chillón Valley seems to have been conditioned by local sociopolitical complexity and the distribution of valuable resources. Indirect rule is inferred, for instance, for the middle valley areas surrounding the local Late Horizon site of Huancayo Alto in the Chillón Valley of the central coast. The continuity of local traditions of storage there may be interpreted as implying local control of tribute that was then sent to centers such as Pumpu in the highlands to the east. Ethnohistoric evidence indicates, for instance, that agricultural production from the lower elevations of the Canta Valley was taken by local people to the highland centers of Huánuco Pampa, Pumpu, Hatun Xauxa, and Cuzco (Rostworowski 1978; LeVine 1985:287).

The distribution of state storage on the coast reflects the patterns of indirect rule. In the Chincha Valley, a region with some autonomy in the Inka period, there is little evidence for the presence of state-controlled storage. A similar condition seems to have prevailed on the north coast. Although the Inka dismantled the Chimú state (Rowe 1948), there is little evidence for subsequent direct rule (Netherly 1978). State surpluses seem to have gone directly to highland sites such as Cajamarca and Huamachuco (Cieza de León 1967 [1553]:195; see Chapter 7). The lack of evidence for storage on the north coast substantiates this. The probable continuation of local storage techniques at sites such as Pachacamac underscores the variable quality of imperial authority even at significant sites (Patterson 1983). The largest group of coastal storage sites is located on the south coast where pre-Inka integration was low (Menzel 1959:140).

The logistics of moving materials from the coast to the highlands is complicated by the fact that the transport distances involved may have made the movement of staple goods from the coast to the highlands highly inefficient (D'Altroy 1988). The small amount of coastal storage indicates, however, that any commodities collected were not being amassed locally. The explanation may be that labor service requirements were of a different nature in the absorbed coastal polities than elsewhere. Regardless, it seems evident that the highland-coast dichotomy in state storage capacity is a product of the political geography of the day rather than of poor site preservation.

The strategic imperative behind this approach is clear. One direct result is a decentralization of storage in politically volatile regions. In a system based on the mobilization of staple goods, there is a close relationship between storage and political power (D'Altroy and Earle, Chapter 2). The urbanized coast contained the most integrated societies faced by the Inka; although providing economic opportunity, they were also potential rivals. The absence of state storage complexes in those areas may underlie a political intent to bypass former centers of power and to undercut their ability to revolt.

Evidence of this pattern exists in other regions. A general negative correlation exists between the location of state storage and centers of local population. In the Mantaro region, although some storage is spread throughout local villages, it is virtually absent from the adjacent Yanamarca Valley, a center of local Wanka population (D'Altroy 1981:256; see also Chapter 6). In no case is a storage complex of greater than 50 units in size located in proximity to a center of local population. The furtherance of state economic goals in the construction of storage complexes may have been contingent on the strategic realities of local political relationships.

OTHER PATTERNS

Other distribution patterns of state storage across Tawantinsuyu as a whole are evident. Figure 3-2 clearly demonstrates the marginal locations of production facilities and associated storage in relation to the state road system. In all, this supports the assertion that those locations were selected for reasons other than their potential for rapid mobilization of resources.

Tampu and similar small facilities are spread generally throughout imperial territory; the distribution of storage at smaller state sites as seen in Figure 3-5, however, demonstrates a general absence of state storage in areas where state interests were more influenced by security requirements than by economics. Low levels of storage at Inka sites in the Atacama Desert of northern Chile, such as Catarpe, are an example of this. Rivera (1987) indicates that state installations in the region were focused upon the protection of the communication routes between the imperial core and the far south. In sum, variability in the material record seems to mirror the flexibility of the Inka state in its management of subject territory.

CONCLUSION

Analysis of Inka state storage as visible in the archaeological record reveals an intricate physical manifestation of the economic and political machinery of the empire. The major storage facilities associated with the state administrative centers of the Peruvian Central Highlands formed the core of the system: Of large size and strategic location, these complexes were intended to support a wide range of state goals on a regional level. Such facilities were typical only in what might be termed the "peripheral core" of the Inka state, the highland region outside of Cuzco most thoroughly integrated into the state structure. In other regions of the empire, extensive installations with significant storage components were rare, even when intrusive state facilities were present. State storage throughout this area was more typically of modest scale, designed to support the communication and administrative infrastructure on a purely local level. This system functioned to concentrate labor service tribute in regions under direct rule while still allowing for the maintenance of symbolic state presence in all areas under the control of Cuzco. Potential rivals, particularly the developed coastal cultures, were thus deprived of a source of supply while remaining vulnerable to highland intervention.

In addition to this two-level structure, a series of sites were created to respond to specific conditions requiring storage. Specialized production facilities in peripheral regions of the empire required centralized storage for commodities destined for points of high demand. In some cases stockpiles were built at strategic road junctions. Use-related storage facilities formed temporary support installations, in some cases supplying ongoing military operations. While accounting for a large percentage of the total volume of state storage, installations devoted to storage alone were relatively few in number. Ethnohistoric evidence suggests that at least some were late developments, perhaps a result of an evolutionary trend toward state ownership (Schaedel 1978).

The degree to which these patterns of state storage have been skewed by poor preservation remains to be seen. Ultimately it is clear that state storage functioned in concert with the entire array of imperial operations. As archaeologically verifiable data, its organizational principles form a sensitive indicator of the political, military, and social conditions that composed the imperial infrastructure of Tawantinsuyu.

ACKNOWLEDGMENTS

This research was originally conducted as part of the requirements for a master's degree in Anthropology at the University of California, Los Angeles, under the direction of

Christopher Donnan, Timothy Earle, and Merrick Posnansky. The principal stimulus for the project was Timothy Earle, who along with Terence N. D'Altroy, Terry LeVine, and other members of the Upper Mantaro Archaeological Research Project have been of great assistance. Data and discussion provided by Katharina J. Schreiber were particularly helpful; other archaeologists contributing unpublished information included A. Rex Gonzales, Thomas Lynch, Jim Mathews, Fritz Riddell, and Mario A. Rivera. Among my fellow graduate students I would like to thank Coreen Chiswell and Monica Smith for their useful comments.

Inka State Storage Sites

THIS appendix provides a distillation of spatial information on the 44 state storage sites discussed in the text. Distinction is on the basis of architecture, associated facilities, and the results of other archaeological investigation. Multiple sites within a single area (i.e., Huamachuco, Campo del Pucara) are treated as subunits under a single number. The state storage sites in the Mantaro Valley are grouped under a single entry due to space constraints and previous extensive publication (e.g., D'Altroy 1981). Sites are listed by type as defined in chapter 3, and within' that type in order of decreasing size.

STORAGE AT LARGE STATE CENTERS

1. *Hatun Xauxa*

Location	Vicinity of Jauja, Department of Junin, Peru.
Environment	3,410–3,530 m; slopes of watered highland valley.
Structure Type	Circular and rectangular *pirca*-walled qollqa; circular exterior diam. 5.5–6.0 m; wall thickness 0.5–0.6 m; max. estimated H 3.5 m : rectangular, exterior 6.0–8.0 × 4.0–5.0 m.
Organization	Five separate sites (J15-18, J62). Organized into single and multiple linear rows following contours. J18 and J62 contain only rectangular structures, while the others have varying percentages of each type.
Size	1,069 units; 562 circular, 507 rectangular. Size range of discrete sites ranges from 20–479
Associations	Within 1 km of the administrative center of Hatun Xauxa. Various nonstorage structures incorporated into storage complex, assigned administrative function.

Roads   On primary highland route, junction of secondary route to Pachacamac and the coast.

Citation   D'Altroy 1981; Earle and D'Altroy 1982; LeVine 1985.

2. Huánuco Pampa

Location   Department of Huánuco, Peru.

Environment   3,800 m.

Structure Type   Circular and rectangular *pirca*-walled qollqa. 3 types: circular (Q-HC), average interior diam. 3.5 m: rectangular singleroom (Q-HR1), mean width 3.1 m, mean length 9.5 m; rectangular multiroom (Q-HR2,12,14).

Organization   Multiple linear rows following hill contours.

Size   496 units.

Associations   On hillside adjacent to administrative center of Huánuco Pampa. Various nonstorage structures incorporated into storage complex, assigned administrative function.

Roads   On primary highland route

Citation   Morris 1967.

3. Pumpu

Location   Department of Junin, Peru.

Environment   4,100 m; Puna, northwest shore of Lake Chinchaycocha.

Structure Type   Circular and rectangular *pirca*-walled qollqa.

Organization   Four groups; (1) hillside storage in linear rows (93 rectangular, 57 circular); (2) S-4, single nonlinear row arrangement (97 circular, mean diam. 5.7 m); (3) S-6, linear arrangement with double row section (approx. 50);(4) S-7, single linear row (20+, mean diam. 5.28 m). 2–4 on flat pampa. 70% of qollqa at Pumpu are circular.

Size   325 units.

Associations   Physically separated from core of administrative site of Pumpu.

Roads	At junction of primary highland route and secondary road to the coast.
Citation	LeVine 1985.

4. *Huamachuco*

Location	Vicinity of Huamachuco, Department of La Libertad, Peru.
Environment	3,300–3,400 m; hillside.
Structure Type	Rectangular *pirca*-walled qollqa with raised floors; 5–7 m length, 2.5–4 m width.
Organization	Three distinct sites on adjacent hillsides. Cerro Santa Barbara: 4 preserved linear rows on terraces following contour lines containing 62 qollqa (of an estimated 125). Cerro Mamorco: 3 linear rows containing a total of 60 qollqa along same contour line over approx. 1 km. Cerro Cacanan: single linear row of 23–26 qollqa following contour.
Size	144 units (of an estimated 215).
Associations	1–3 km from Huamachuco.
Roads	Above secondary road from Cajamarca to the coast.
Other	Possible administrative structures at Cerro Cacanan.
Citation	Topic and Topic 1984; Chiswell 1984.

5. *Raqchi*

Location	San Pedro de Cacha, Department of Cuzco, Peru; 118 km Southeast of Cuzco.
Environment	3,460 m; highland valley.
Structure Type	Circular structures, some with diam. of 8 m.
Organization	Several linear rows within rectangular compound
Size	40 units (currently visible; Squier counted 120 in 1877).
Associations	Adjacent to *kancha* group at the temple of Wiraqocha at Raqchi.
Citation	Squier 1973 [1877]: 411; Gasparini and Margolies 1980: 235, 238; Pardo 1937; La Lone and La Lone 1987.

6. *Hatunqolla/Qollqa Chupa*

Location	On hill north of Hatunqolla, Department of Puno, Peru.
Environment	Altiplano.
Structure Type	Foundations of long, rectangular structures.
Organizatiom	No data.
Size	No data.
Associations	Inka ceramics; adjacent to Inka center of Hatunqolla.
Roads	Adjacent to road along southwest side of Lake Titicaca.
Citation	Julien 1983.

STORAGE AT CENTERS OF PRODUCTION AND SPECIAL FUNCTION

7. *Cotapachi*

Location	Cochabamba, Bolivia: 3 km south of Quillacollo.
Environment	Highland valley, on hill overlooking zone of maize cultivation.
Structure Type	Circular qollqa, *pirca* foundations with probable adobe or turf superstructure; average 3 m in diameter.
Organization	Two adjacent complexes in rectangular grid plan, north/south orientation.
Size	2,400 units, 1,200 in each complex; 9.5 m between rows, 5.15 m between columns.
Associations	Domestic structures attested: approx. 15 km E/NE of small administrative site of Incaraccay.
Roads	On secondary road network between Paria and the Chaco frontier.
Other	Other storage sites attested in the Cochabamba region.
Citation	Byrne de Caballero 1974, 1975; Gasparini and Margolies 1980.

8. *Campo del Pucara*

Location	Valle de Lerma, Province of Salta, Northwest Argentina

Environment   *Ca.* 1,200 m; semiarid valley.

Structure Type   Circular qollqa, *pirca* foundations with probable adobe or turf superstructure; 2.5–3 m diameter.

Organization   Three separate complexes, each of rectangular ground plan in a north/south orientation spread over 2.5 sq km area.

Size   Total, 1,717. Group A: 1047. B: 158. C: 512.

Associations   Domestic structures w/Inkaic artifacts, fragmentary structural remains of unclear cultural association.

Roads   Secondary road.

Other   Within 100 km of Inka sites on primary highland route.

Citation   Boman 1908; Fock 1961; Dougherty 1972; Gonzalez 1983.

9. *Inkawasi*

Location   Lunahuana Valley, Cañete, Department of Lima, Peru.

Environment   Coastal valley.

Structure Type   Aggregate multiroom construction; large stones mortared with mud-clay mixture, rooms 3.5–4 m square.

Organization   Site sector A: courtyard surrounded on three sides by multiple rows of doorless rectangular storage rooms.

Size   202 (of an estimated 250 units).

Associations   Integral structural unit of Inkawasi site. Also limited access, little domestic or ceramic debris.

Roads   On secondary route from the highlands to the coastal road at Huarco.

Other   Two other sectors of the site may have had additional storage function.

Citation   Hyslop 1985, 1984:85.

10. *Capis-Cerrillos*

Location   Near Copiapo, Chile; Plain south of Cerro Capi.

Environment   Coastal desert.

Structure Type	Circular qollqa, *pirca* foundations with probable adobe or turf superstructure; average diameter 2.5 m.
Organization	Arranged in rectangular grid plan, with 10 rows of 20 units each in north/south alignment.
Size	200 units.
Associations	No artifactual data reported; other Inka sites in Copiapo region.
Roads	Near junction of primary coastal road coming S through the Atacama and lateral route to Tucuman region in NW Argentina.
Citation	Latcham 1927; Dougherty 1972; Raffino 1981.

11. *Chacamarca*

Location	Department of Junín, Peru.
Environment	4,100 m; puna.
Structure Type	Circular *pirca*-walled qollqa; mean exterior diameter. 5.8–6.8 m.
Organization	Three linear rows.
Size	118 units.
Associations	West of large *tampu* of Chacamarca.
Roads	Junction primary highland road and secondary route.
Other	Associated rectangular structures assigned administrative function.
Citation	LeVine 1985:229.

12. *Agua Hedionda*

Location	Rio Las Sauces, Dept. of San Antonio, Province of Juyuy, Northwest Argentina.
Environment	1400 m; semiarid.
Structure Type	Circular qollqa, *pirca* foundations with probable adobe or turf superstructure; 2.90–3.70 in diameter.
Organization	Within walled enclosure; irregular N/S alignment.
Size	103 units.
Associations	Small structural complex w/walls.
Roads	Possibly on secondary road.

Other	Approx. 55 km N of site of Campo del Pucara.
Citation	Dougherty 1972; Gonzalez 1983.

13. Kharalaus Pampa

Location	Cochabamba, Bolivia: 5 km south of Quillacollo.
Environment	2,750 m: on hill overlooking zone of maize cultivation.
Structure Type	Circular qollqa, pirca foundations with probable adobe or turf superstructure ext. diameter 2.70–2.85 m; wall thickness 0.30–0.4 m.
Organization	Four linear rows, oriented east-west; units 2.0–2.5 m apart.
Size	80 units.
Associations	Adjacent rectangular structure.
Roads	On secondary road network between Paria and the Chaco frontier.
Other	Near site of Cotapachi.
Citation	Pereira 1982b; D'Altroy, field notes, 1989.

14. Cerro de las Rueditas

Location	Santa Cruz, Bolivia.
Environment	Highlands.
Structure Type	Circular qollqa, pirca foundations with probable adobe or turf superstructure; average internal diameter 2.66 m.
Organization	Two parallel rows 9 m apart, north/south orientation; units 3.5 m apart, 34 units per row.
Size	68 units (of an estimated 80).
Associations	None recorded; near site of Fuerte de Samaipata.
Roads	No data.
Citation	Byrne de Caballero 1981; Trimborn 1967.

15. Tumuyo

Location	Department of Cochabamba, Bolivia; approx. 17 km east of modern town of Pocona.
Environment	Ca. 2,500 m; hilltop overlooking highland valley.
Structure Type	Circular qollqa, pirca foundations with probable adobe or turf superstructure; average diameter 2.9 m.

Organization	Rectangular grid plan, 9 columns by 7 rows; aligned NE-SW.
Size	63 units.
Associations	No adjacent structures described.
Roads	On secondary road between Paria and the Chaco frontier.
Citation	Pereira 1982a; Cespedes Paz 1982.

16. *Culluma Baja (AY5-75)*

Location	Carhuarazo Valley, Department of Ayacucho, Peru.
Environment	3,330 m; highland valley.
Structure Type	Circular *pirca*-walled qollqa, interior diameter 2.2–2.6 m.
Organization	Two linear rows following contour.
Size	46 units; 5 in upper row, 39 in lower row.
Associations	No adjacent contemporary architecture recorded.
Roads	Near secondary highland-coast route.
Other	Within 2 km of Late Horizon site of Queca.
Citation	Schreiber 1987a, 1987b.

STORAGE AT SECONDARY STATE FACILITIES

17. *Mantaro Valley Region*

Location	Department of Junin, Peru.
Environment	Slopes of watered highland valley.
Structure Type	Circular and rectangular *pirca*-walled qollqa; circular; exterior diameter 5.5–6.0 m, maximum estimated height 3.5 m. rectangular; 6.0–8.0 × 4.0–5.0 m.
Organization	48 separate sites (see D'Altroy, Chapter 6) along east and west sides of the Mantaro Valley and north/northwest of the site of Hatun Xauxa.
Size	1,657 units, with sites containing from 4–99 units each. D'Altroy (Chapter 6) identified a total of 923 in his survey area; Browman counts 734 storage units in the southern portion of the valley.
Associations	Sites discussed by D'Altroy are within 17 km of Hatun Xauxa, and 16 of the sites are within 200 m of local (nonstate Inka) Late Horizon sites.

Roads	Primary highland road in addition to secondary lateral routes to the coast.
Citation	Browman 1970; D'Altroy 1981, and Chapter 6; Earle and D'Altroy 1982.

18. Camata

Location	Department of Moquegua, Peru.
Environment	2,800 m; coastal desert.
Structure Type	Multi-roomed structure.
Organization	Three long rectangular structures subdivided into 10–12 rooms each, grouped around a plaza: some additional structures.
Size	43 units.
Associations	Both Late Horizon and Late Intermediate Period components.
Roads	Secondary.
Citation	Mathews 1987.

19. Tambo Viejo

Location	Acari Valley, Department of Arequipa, Peru.
Environment	Coastal valley.
Structure Type	Rectangular *pirca*-walled structures, possibly semi-subterranean; average 2×3 m.
Organization	Four adjacent walled compounds containing double rows of 4–5 units each.
Size	40 units.
Associations	Group 1E of Tambo Viejo, at northern end of site.
Roads	On primary coastal road.
Other	Similar to complex at the Inka site of Ingenio in Nazca.
Citation	Rowe 1946; Menzel and Riddell 1986.

20. Paredones (Azuay)

Location	Canar Province, Ecuador.
Environment	4,000 m; Paramo.
Structure Type	Narrow, multiple-roomed rectangular structures with stone foundations.
Organization	Four structures divided by narrow passageways.
Size	38 units.

Associations	*Tampu* of Paredones.
Roads	On primary highland road south of Quito.
Other	Similar to Tambo Blanco site [34].
Citation	Hyslop 1984:31.

21. *Tarmatambo*

Location	Department of Junin, Peru.
Environment	3,500–3,800 m; highland valley/puna
Structure Type	Circular and rectangular *pirca*-walled qollqa. Circular: average exterior diameter 5 m. Rectangular: average 6×3.2 m.
Organization	Two groups, one a linear single row with 14 units both circular and rectangular, the other 2 linear rows containing 14–22 circular units.
Size	38 units.
Associations	On hillside directly south of Tarmatambo site.
Roads	On primary highland route.
Citation	LeVine 1985:346.

22. *Quebrada de la Vaca*

Location	Quebrada de la Vaca near Chala, Department of Arequipa, Peru.
Environment	Coastal valley.
Structure Type	Pirca-walled multiroomed structures.
Organization	Two adjacent structures each containing single rows of parallel rooms with individual doors; one structure has enclosing courtyard.
Size	27 units.
Associations	Local Late Horizon and state Inka components.
Roads	On primary coastal route through southern Peru.
Other	Similar structure noted for nearby *tampu* of La Caleta.
Citation	Rowe 1946; Trimborn 1985; Menzel and Riddell 1986.

23. *Inka Tampu* (AY5-39)

Location	Carhuarazo Valley, Department of Ayacucho, Peru.
Environment	3,300 m; highland valley.

Structure Type   Circular *pirca*-walled qollqa, average interior diameter 3.1 m.
Organization   Linear row following hill contour.
Size   Approximately 25 units.
Associations   Four rectangular structures, two in qollqa row, two parallel
Roads   On secondary highland-coastal route.
Other   1–2 km from local Late Horizon site of Apucara.
Citation   Schreiber 1987a, 1987b.

24. *Tunsukancha*

Location   Department of Huánuco, Peru.
Environment   ca. 4,000 m; puna.
Structure Type   Circular *pirca*-walled qollqa; average interior diameter 3.5 m.
Organization   Single linear row.
Size   24 units.
Associations   Part of Tunsukancha *tampu* complex.
Roads   On primary highland route.
Other   36 km south of Huánuco Pampa.
Citation   Morris 1967; Hyslop 1984.

25. *Cochabamba (Chachapoyas)*

Location   Department of Cajamarca, Peru.
Environment   Ceja de la Montana.
Structure Type   Rectangular, *Pirca*-walled qollqa.
Organization   Two linear rows along hillside.
Size   23 units.
Associations   State administrative complex of Cochabamba.
Roads   Secondary.
Citation   Schjellerup 1979–80; 1984.

26. *Hualfin*

Location   Catamarca Province, NW Argentina.
Evidence   Series of circular structures in various linear and circular groupings, associated with rectangular-plan Inka architecture; minimum number of units is 23. Probable *tampu* complex.
Citation   Bruch 1904: Gonzalez 1983:345; Hyslop 1984:289.

27. Pocona

Location	Department of Cochabamba, Bolivia; west of modern town of Pocona.
Environment	ca. 2,500 m; highland valley flank.
Structure Type	Circular qollqa, *pirca* foundations with probable adobe or turf superstructure.
Organization	Single row with less organized section.
Size	21 units.
Associations	Within site of Pocona *Tampu* (Inkarracaycito).
Roads	On secondary route between Paria and the Chaco frontier.
Other	Other state storage units attested for nearby sites.
Citation	Pereira 1982a: Cespedes Paz 1982.

28. Inkallajta

Location	Department of Cochabamba, Bolivia.
Environment	Highlands.
Structure Type	Circular qollqa, *pirca* foundations with probable adobe or turf superstructure; probable diameter 3.6 m.
Organization	Two complexes, rough linear arrangement.
Size	18–20 units in total; 12 in one group and an unspecified number in another.
Associations	Within the site of Inkallajta.
Roads	Probable secondary road connection from Pocona.
Citation	Nordenskiold 1915; Gonzalez and Cravotto 1977; Gasparini and Margolies 1980:119.

29. Taparaku

Location	Department of Huánuco, Peru.
Environment	Puna.
Structure Type	Circular *pirca*-walled qollqa.
Organization	Single linear row.
Size	20–25 units.
Associations	Taparaku *tampu*.
Roads	On primary highland route.

Other   23 km n of Huánuco Pampa; described from aerial
                   photographs.
Citation   Thompson and Murra 1966; Morris 1967.

30. *Corral Blanco*
Location   Province of Salta, northwest Argentina.
Evidence   Two parallel rectangular structures with multiple
                   rooms aligned with road; total 19 units.
Other   15 km from Portrero del Payogasta.
Citation   Hyslop 1984: 178–79.

31. *La Cima*
Location   Department of Junin, Peru.
Environment   4,150 m.
Structure Type   Circular *pirca*-walled qollqa; diameter 6–6.5 m.
Organization   Linear single row.
Size   17 units.
Associations   120–130 m from *tampu* of La Cima; complex is 13
                   km south of Chacamarca.
Roads   Primary highland route.
Citation   LeVine 1985:236.

32. *Millpu (AY5-66)*
Location   Carhuarazo Valley, Department of Ayacucho, Peru.
Environment   3,150 m.
Structure Type   Circular *pirca*-walled qollqa, average interior diame-
                   ter 3.3 m.
Organization   Linear row following hill contour; built into terrace.
Size   16 units.
Associations   Adjacent to local Late Horizon site.
Roads   Near secondary highland-coast route.
Citation   Schreiber 1987a, 1987b.

33. *Telarnioj*
Location   Department of Junín, Peru.
Environment   Highlands.
Structure Type   Square-to-rectangular *pirca*-walled qollqa; 6×5 m.
Organization   Single linear row.

Size	15 units.
Associations	Hillside above Telarnioj *tampu* complex.
Roads	On primary highland route.
Other	Three associated small rectangular structures.
Citation	LeVine 1985: 243.

34. *Tambo Blanco*

Location	Loja province, Ecuador.
Evidence	Two narrow, parallel rectangular structures, each containing 6 rooms, separated by a narrow passage; total 12 units.
Citation	Uhle 1969:98.

35. *Tambo Colorado*

Location	Department of Ica, Peru.
Evidence	Foundations of 4–8 circular, qollqalike structures within the site.
Citation	Urteaga 1939: Morris 1967:153; Hyslop 1984:109.

36. *Quitaloma*

Location	North of Quito, Ecuador.
Evidence	Five circular structures, 2.6–3.5 m diameter, within walls of Inka-occupied fortress.
Citation	Oberem 1968:99.

37. *Kullku Tampu*

Location	Approximately 40 km northeast of Oruro, Bolivia.
Environment	4,100 m; puna.
Structure Type	Rectangular structures with rounded interior corners.
Organization	Single row.
Size	Four units.
Associations	Possible *tampu*.
Roads	On secondary road from Paria-Cochabamba region.
Other	Heavy modification of structures for modern corral construction.
Citation	Hyslop 1984:145.

38. *Yacoraite*

Location	Quebrada de Humahuaca, Department of Juyuy, northwest Argentina.
Evidence	Four doorless rectangular rooms along one side of a small plaza. Gonzalez (1983) suggests 15 structures in complex have similar characteristics.
Citation	Krapovickas 1968: Gonzalez 1983:345.

39. *Turi*

Location	Río Loa, Antofagasta Province, Chile.
Evidence	Unspecified number of circular structures identified as storage units on the basis of architecture.
Citation	Mostny 1948: Raffino 1981:110.

40. *Potrero de Payogasta*

Location	Calchaqui Valley, Province of Salta, northwest Argentina.
Evidence	Unspecified number of circular structures identified as storage units on the basis of architecture.
Citation	Raffino 1981: Hyslop 1984:177.

41. *Nevados de Aconquija*

Location	Tucuman, Argentina.
Evidence	Unspecified number of circular structures identified as storage structures on the basis of architecture.
Citation	Paulotti 1967.

42. *Graneros*

Location	Calchaqui Valley, Salta Province, northwest Argentina.
Evidence	Circular and rectangular adobe-walled structures located beneath a rock overhang.
Citation	Gonzalez 1983:345.

43. *Ingapirca*

Location	Canar Province, Ecuador.
Evidence	Unspecified number of circular structures in of possible storage function; other storage areas suggested.
Citation	Franch 1978:142; Hyslop 1984:290.

44. *Chichipampa*

Location   Vicinity of Colta, Department of Arequipa, Peru.
Evidence   Long, rectangular structure with regular small, windowlike openings.
Citation   Bingham 1922:65, illustrated facing page 66; Morris 1967:199.

Addendum

EXAMINATION of some of the Inka sites in Argentina and Bolivia conducted by Terence D'Altroy in 1989 provided additional information on state storage at three locations. Although there was insufficient time to include this material in the body of the analysis, it is appended here for purposes of reference.

1. *Anocariri*

Location	8 km west-northwest of Paria, Bolivia.
Environment	3,900 m; in shelter of hill on altiplano.
Structure Type	Circular qollqa; rock foundations with probable adobe superstructures; exterior diameter about 3.0 m.
Organization	Two parallel rows.
Size	8 units.
Associations	In central part of large *tampu* of Anocariri, adjacent to open plaza and probable residential sectors.
Roads	On primary north-south highland road.
Other	Anocariri has been associated with the Inka center of Paria, which Cieza (1967 [1553]:65) identifies as a provincial capital.
Citations	Hyslop 1984: 143–45; Vaca de Castro 1908 [1543]: 435; Cieza 1967 [1553], 1984:ch. cvi:286; D'Altroy, field notes 1989.

2. *Shincal*

Location	Vicinity of Belen, Provincia de Catamarca, Argentina.
Environment	Approximately 300 m; low hill crest adjacent to open valley lands.
Structure Type	Circular qollqa, stone foundations, probable adobe

superstructures; exterior diameter 2.5–2.8 m; wall thickness 0.35 m; maximum estimated height 0.5 m.

Organization	2–3 rows curving along the hill crest; structures 2.0–3.0 m apart. One rectangular structure at west end, 8.0 × 8.0.
Size	60 units.
Associations	Immediately adjacent to the administrative center of Shincal.
Roads	On trunk route east of Watungasta.
Citations	D'Altroy, field notes, 1989.

3. *Punta de Balasto*

Location	Santa Maria Valley, Provincia de Salta, Argentina.
Environment	2,050 m; on flat river terrace adjacent to main valley watercourse 100–150 m to the west.
Structure Type	Circular qollqa; river cobble foundations, probable adobe superstructures; exterior diameter 3.0 m; wall thickness 0.4 m.
Organization	Two parallel rows, structures 2.0–2.5 m apart.
Size	Eight units.
Associations	Within large *tampu* of Punta de Balasto, adjacent to large central plaza containing *usnu* and to apparent residential structures.
Roads	Adjacent to Inka road through the Santa Maria Valley.
Citations	Raffino 1981; D'Altroy, field notes 1989.

All three of these sites fall within the range of variation evident from the larger sample. Both Anocariri (possibly the Paria of the chroniclers) and Shincal have been suggested as regional administrative centers. Further archaeological reconnaissance would clarify the storage capacity situation in either, although the relatively small number of storage units reported is in keeping with the general trend in the southern regions of the empire.

CHAPTER 4

Inka State Storage in Three
Highland Regions
A Comparative Study
TERRY Y. LEVINE

ALTHOUGH research focusing on regional Inka state storage systems
has been increasing (Morris 1967, 1981, 1986; D'Altroy 1981; D'Altroy and Hastorf 1984), the possibility of delineating the logic of
Inka finance policy archaeologically by comparing similarities and
differences in Inka storage facilities has yet to be adequately explored.
It seems reasonable that a comparison of the capacities, the distribution, and the contents of Inka storage complexes, data available
through archaeological research, could illuminate the rationale behind the implementation of Inka state finance policies specific to
individual regions, data that also could be useful to those studying
the role of storage organization and management in archaic state
economies in other parts of the world.

In the century before the Spanish conquest, the Inka consistently
demonstrated a capacity to set up a functioning administration to
undertake state business. They developed an overall strategy to incorporate and manage a wide variety of conquered polities with different
languages and cultures and occupying diverse geographical settings.
Given variability in the distribution of human and natural resources
within their imperial borders, the rise of the Inka empire was predicated on the Inka talent for organization and on their ability to
develop flexible strategies that balanced general imperial policies with
regionally specific methods to accommodate the diverse problems of
integrating individual conquered polities into the overall state system
(Rowe 1946; Schaedel 1978; Earle and D'Altroy 1989).

Thus reorganization of the economy required first the solidifica-
tion of control over conquered polities and then the implementation
of policies adapted to the economic realities of each of the
conquered ethnic groups. The state acquired symbolic ownership
of all natural resources and then proceeded to alienate portions of
conquered territories for state use, particularly in microzones

producing resources that the state considered to have high priority. In order to maintain full control, the state suppressed most market and trade. It used a periodic census to aid imposition of a universal labor service tax. Using this tax system, it mobilized labor to produce and store the economic surplus that provided its major revenues (Murra 1980 [1956]; Morris 1986; D'Altroy and Earle, Chapter 2, this volume).

The purpose of this chapter is to examine the reasoning motivating the policies that organized state-stored surpluses. Data on Inka storage presented here are a portion of the results of a research project that had as its goal the comparison of Inka administrative strategies in three adjacent but diverse central highland regions (LeVine 1985). Understanding the organization of revenue raising and storage management became a major focus in the course of the investigation. Although some have argued for the repetitiveness of Andean environments (MacNeish et al. 1975), the basic thesis being argued here is that regional variability in the demographic and political realities of conquered populations, as well as differences in the focus of regional economies, necessitated flexibility in Inka administrative planning (Menzel 1959). The implicit argument is that an important source of insight into the Inka political economy is an understanding of the degree to which flexibility was present in Inka planning of the organization and control of storage.

Archaeological and documentary data derived from regions administered from three great Inka administrative centers known as Huánuco Pampa, Pumpu, and Hatun Xauxa, all located in the central Andean highlands, will be used to address the following questions: Did the provisioning of state projects affect the location of administrative centers and intraregional storage distribution? Is there a correlation between population size and storage volume on a regional basis? To what extent were resources moved between regions? How did differences in regional resources affect storage organization?

RESEARCH AREA

In the Andean Central Highlands, the major volume of state storage was centered at Huánuco Pampa, Pumpu, and Hatun Xauxa (Figure 4-1) (Morris 1967, 1981, 1982, 1985, 1986, Chapters 5 and 8 this volume; D'Altroy 1981, 1987, 1992, Chapter 6, this volume; Earle

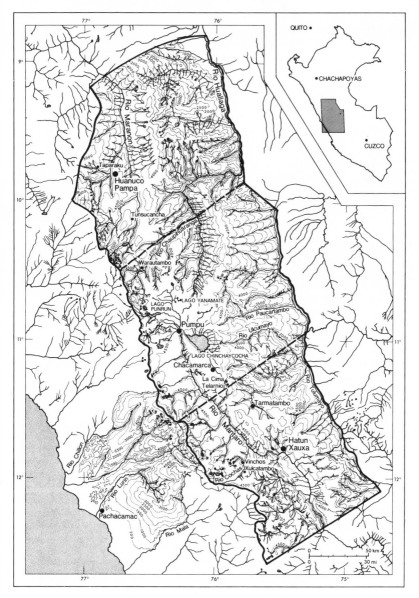

Figure 4-1. The research area in the Andean Central Highlands: the Huánuco, Pumpu, and Xauxa regions established for purposes of comparison (after LeVine 1985).

and D'Altroy 1982, 1989; LeVine 1985). These three Inka installations were secondary-level administrative nodes below Cuzco, the primary-level capital; for purposes of analysis, they were a logical focal point for delineating three regions in order to draw comparisons.

Thus, for purposes of comparison, Huánuco, Pumpu, and Xauxa are the terms used in this chapter to designate three central highland regions. The assumption I am making is that the storage complexes of the three centers would have been the focal point for the bulk of surplus materials that the labor services of the 12 or more central highland ethnic groups, distributed within the research area, generated. It is likely that the 12 conquered ethnic polities also would have had access to specialized services at the administrative installation closest to them. There they could participate in the periodic civic/religious ceremonial rites that involved conquered groups, making them feel a part of the greater state system and, at the same time, wrapping state authority within an aura of religious ideology.

The regional boundaries used in this analysis are, in part, artificially defined. The extent to which the Inka state thought in terms of regional boundaries, or administrative regions, is not clear. It *is* clear that the state had a strong interest in retaining ethnic relationships for administrative convenience; the state maintained and reinforced the role of cooperative ethnic elites, fitting them into the hierarchy of the state bureaucracy. Although the pattern of approximately 130 to 140 km between the three centers suggests that the Inka based this spacing on the logistics of military, communication, travel, and administrative needs, available documents indicate that administered populations transported the bulk of the products generated from their labor service to the storehouses of the center that was closest to them (Helmer 1955–56 [1549]; Vega 1965 [1582]:169; Ortiz 1967–1972 [1562] vol. 1:25, 51–52). The data used in this chapter are organized around the distribution of storage associated with the major centers, Huánuco Pampa, Pumpu, and Hatun Xauxa, and with other less elaborate Inka installations within the boundaries of regions established for purposes of analysis.

To review: based on the above reasoning and on topographic features, I placed northern and southern regional boundaries at a point halfway between major centers. Similarity in regional size (Table 4-1) is primarily a function of the relatively equal distances of approximately 130 to 140 km between centers (equal to a 3- to 5-day walk, see Hyslop 1985:297–300 for a discussion of distances walked during the Inka period and the relation of walking distances to the spacing of Inka installations). The continental divide represents the west boundaries, and east boundaries approximate the border of the tropical forest.

For purposes of comparison, all Inka installations within these established regional boundaries below the size level of Huánuco Pampa, Pumpu, and Hatun Xauxa are considered to have been subsidiary installations within each center's administrative jurisdiction, possibly subordinate to the major centers. Differences in size between a major center and subsidiary Inka installations were considerable. For example, at Pumpu, the smallest center, the nonstorage portion of the site covers approximately 64 ha (hectares). Chacamarca (40 km south of Pumpu) and Tarmatambo[1] (40 km north of Hatun Xauxa) are designated subcenters in this analysis; their sizes are estimated at 10.9 ha and 20 ha respectively (Parsons and Hastings field notes). The quantity of public architecture at major centers compared to subcenters varies in hierarchical order in keeping with the differences in site size. Considerably reduced in size, *tampu* were wayside stations established in a pattern of about a 1-day walk apart, fulfilling the food and lodging needs of travelers on official state business. *Tampu,* ranging between 1 and 4 ha, commonly have limited storage space adequate to supply short-term needs (see Snead, Chapter 3, for a discussion of storage at *tampu*). *Tampu* must be considered adjunct state installations fulfilling a need unique to the geographical extent of the empire and to the mode of transportation. However, in estimating regional storage volume, any known storage associated with subcenters, as well as *tampu,* are included with the major center in a figure representing regional storage volume.[2]

The three regions being compared, Huánuco, Pumpu, and Xauxa, lie within the central Andean highlands. The northwest-southeast trending Andean cordillera dominates the Central Highlands. Within these mountains lie an extensive potential in mineral wealth (Peterson 1965:417). High elevation *puna* (plateaulike surfaces above 4,000 m) serve as pasturage for grazing herd animals, whereas intermontane valleys between 3,000 and 3,400 m provide agricultural zones. Meandering rivers and streams, headwaters of some of the westmost tribu-

Table 4-1. Comparison of Population and Regional Size

Region	Regional Size	Total Estimated Population	Population per Km^2
Huánuco Pampa	16,390 km^2	55,000	3.4
Pumpu	16,829 km^2	60,000	3.6
Hatun Xauxa	15,100 km^2	217,000	14.4

NOTE: In order to estimate and compare regional size and population density, the above data were created by using Instituo Geografico Militar maps and a planimeter. Boundaries for regions are those established for this research project. Population figures used are the total maximum estimated for each region (LeVine 1985:450, Table 7-1).

taries of the Amazon River, drain these high plateaus and valleys. When rivers reach the steep gradients of the eastern Andean slopes, water flow is increased considerably as it descends through narrow valleys toward the low elevation zones bordering the tropical forest (Drewes and Drewes 1957). Here heat and humidity provide a setting for growing the tropical products adapted to low elevations.

Although similar physical features and, in a general sense, similar resource possibilities are present in all three regions, local land masses combine into mountains, plateaus, and valleys that emphasize the differences between regions. Contrasts between Huánuco, Pumpu, and Xauxa occur in the extent to which each of the above physical features and associated resource potentials dominate. Because climate and resource focus in the central Andes correlate so directly with altitude, a comparison of differences in percentages of land at various altitudes makes contrasts evident (Table 4-2).

The varied ethnic groups occupying the three regions prior to their incorporation into the Inka empire provide another important area of contrast. Comparisons show differences in settlement size, overall population size and population density, as well as differences in the levels of sociopolitical complexity at which ethnic groups were organized prior to incorporation into the Inka empire. The distribution of the population in relation to the locations the Inka chose for the three major administrative centers also varied.

REGIONAL DATA

HUÁNUCO

Land masses of the Huánuco region (Figure 4-1) combine to form narrow twisting valleys in the 71% of the region above 3,000 m. This

Table 4-2. Comparison of Regional Land Distribution

| Region | Size | Tropical Products Zone | | Root Crop Zone | Herding Zone |
		1,000–1,999m	2,000–2,999m	3,000–3,999m	Over 4,000m
Huánuco					
Pampa	16,390 km^2	13%	16%	36%	35%
Pumpu	16,829 km^2	8%	6%	24%	62%
Hatun Xauxa	15,100 km^2	4%	6%	38%	52%

NOTE: All above data were created in order to estimate the percentage of land at various elevations. Instituto Geografico Militar maps and a planimeter were used. Boundaries for regions are those established for this research project (LeVine 1985:450, Table 7-2).

encompasses the zones of root crop agriculture and high-elevation *puna* herding (Table 4-2). However, the potential for herding is of limited extent except on the west side of the region. Also, although maize will grow above 3,000 m, yields are less satisfactory, and land between 3,000 and 3,400 m in this region tends to be steep. The remaining 29% of the region, below 3,000 m, occurs mainly in the relatively open, productive, and frost-free Huallaga River valley that descends to the warm, humid, tropical forest toward what was the Inka empire's eastern border (Drewes and Drewes 1957; Troll 1958).

Prior to Inka domination, the Huánuco region was home to a series of small, independent, ethnic groups living in villages and hamlets distributed throughout the Marañón and Huallaga valleys. They appear to have been at the sociopolitical level of leadership by nonhereditary village *ayllu* (lineage) chiefs (Ortiz 1967–72 [1562] vol. I:22, 45, 91). At least half the estimated population of 55,000 people[3] was settled in and around the Huallaga Valley from 50 to 70 km distant from the main highland road where the Inka built the Huánuco Pampa center. Documents describe how the Inka reorganized these ethnic groups by appointing village chiefs to low-level leadership positions and creating higher level leaders for the upper end of the local elite hierarchy (Ortiz 1967–72 [1562] vol. I:81).

Before being incorporated into the Inka empire, the varied ethnic groups of the region had access to a full range of resources either in their own territory or through exchange with neighbors (Mayer 1985:48; LeVine 1987:29). The likely focus of Inka management policy in the east part of the region was the organization of labor to produce maize, *coca,* and *ají* (hot peppers) in the fertile fields of the Lower Huallaga Valley, and to oversee the collection of wood, honey, and the feathers of tropical birds from along the border of the tropical forest. The west side of the region was developed to emphasize herding and mining resources.

Storage of the materials produced in the Huánuco region were concentrated at Huánuco Pampa, the Inka center, at 3,800 m (Figure 4-2a). In the Huánuco area, the Inka road and the administrative center were located close to the western, high-elevation part of the region (Figure 4-1). The level of public architecture at this major site and the amount of labor organized for its construction attest to the position of Huánuco Pampa as a highly important secondary-level node of the Inka state (Morris 1967; see Chapter 5; Morris and Thompson 1985). The remains of storehouse structures stretch in 11 rows that follow the contour of the hill rising to the southwest of the main part of the site (Figure 4-2b see Morris, Chapter 5 for a detailed description of this storage complex). The greatest diversity in storehouse design occurs at the base of the hill in the first two rows. Upper rows contain either all rectangular or all circular storehouses. Morris estimates that 62% of the volume at Huánuco Pampa was in rectangular structures, and 38% was in circular structures.

The main Inka road connected Huánuco Pampa to Tunsukancha, a small *tampu* to the south and Taparaku, a small *tampu* to the northwest (Figure 4-1). These *tampu* appear to have had a minimum of public architecture and relatively small amounts of storage space. Morris suggests supplies were brought from the stores collected at Huánuco Pampa. A survey of some of the larger villages located on the east side of the region disclosed no evidence for state storage facilities. Estimates of storage volume are 37,123 m³ for long-term storage at Huánuco Pampa, Rows 2 through 11, plus 825 m³ for Row 1 (Morris 1967:137). Adding 400 m³ for Tunsukancha plus 400 m³ projected for Taparaku storage (for which no figures are available), the regional total is 38,748 m³, with 98% at the center (Table 4-3).

PUMPU

Land distribution in the Pumpu region (Figure 4-1) suggests a concentration on herding activities on the broad expanses of the Junín

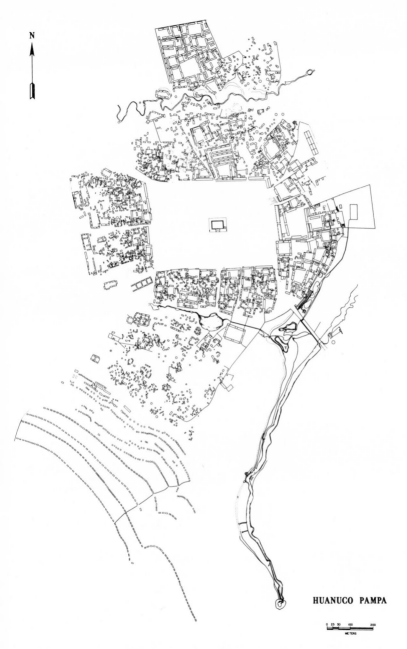

N

HUANUCO PAMPA

0 25 50 100 200
METERS

Figure 4-2A. The Huánuco Pampa Inka administrative center showing the central plaza and the relation of the storage complex to the site (after Morris Chapter 5).

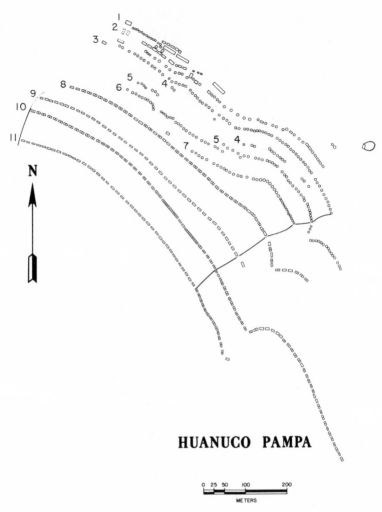

Figure 4-2B. Enlarged view of the storage complex southwest of the center (after Morris 1981).

Table 4-3. Comparison of Regional Storage Volumes

Installations by Region	Volume of Storage	Storage Volume, Rectangular	Storage Volume, Circular	Volume by Region	Regional in Rectangular	Regional in Circular
Huánuco Pampa	37,948m³	.62	.38	38,748m³	.62	.38
Tunsukancha	400m³		1.00			
Taparaku	400m³	(projected)				
Pumpu, hillside	9,806m³	.66	.34			
Pampu	14,697m³	.05	.95			
Chacamarca	8,680m³	.09	.91	36,245m³	.26	.74
La Cima	1,607m³		1.00			
Telarnioj	1,455m³	1.00				
Hatun Xauxa—0–1 km	64,618m³	.51	.49			
1–3 km	16,187m³	.84	.16			
East side 3–17 km	29,310m³	.83	.17	171,192m³	.57	.43
West side 3–17 km	13,601m³	.19	.81			
Mantaro Valley south	44,329m³	.50	.50			
Tarmatambo	3,147m³	.31	.69			

NOTE: The above data compare storage volume in rectangular and circular storehouses, first by installation and then by region (adapted from LeVine 1985:463, Table 7-4).

puna; 62% of the region is above 4,000 m (Table 4-2). Extensive salt sources and some of the richest central highland deposits of lead and copper, occur in the mountains rising above and surrounding the open *puna*. Today, pastureland for herd animals and resources from the mines of Cerro de Pasco and Huaron Mining Companies give the area the same economic focus as in the Inka period.

Agriculture apparently was more important on the *puna* in prehistoric times than it is today (Matos 1975:62). Root crops, especially *macca*, were commonly grown using a protective, ridged-field system, remains of which are still visible on the *puna*. Agricultural land between 3,000 and 4,000 m is limited and accounts for only 24% of the region. This occurs within the steep and narrow valleys descending from the *puna* to the north and east. The tropical products zone represents 14% of the region, on the east edge, where access from the Inka road was limited and difficult to reach (LeVine 1985:282–84).

The estimated population of 60,000 tribal level herdsmen[3] and simple village agriculturalists, organized around *ayllu* leaders, were dispersed in small settlements surrounding Lago Chinchaycocha (today called Lago Junín), on the *puna* northwest and south of the lake, and in the lower elevations of the Paucartambo, Ulcumayo, and Upper Huallaga valleys. These ethnic groups probably required administrative strategies of a different nature than those for Huánuco ethnic groups. It seems likely that integrating egalitarian tribal *ayllu* leaders into the hierarchical organization of the Inka state demanded strategies specific to the area. It may have been difficult for independent lineage leaders to accept intermediaries between themselves and representatives of the state.

In addition to local labor, the state increased manpower to work the mines and to husband enlarged state-owned herds by requiring *mit'a* labor service as part of the labor quota from the ethnic groups of Pumpu as well as importing labor from adjacent regions (Helmer 1955–56 [1549]:3–50; Rostworowski 1978 [1549]:179).

Fieldwork at Inka installations in the Pumpu region (LeVine 1985:171–250) included mapping, measuring, and estimating the volume of storehouse complexes at four Inka installations, all adjacent to the Inka highland road that crossed the Junín puna (Figure 4-1). Storage volume estimates were based on formulae developed by Craig

Morris (1967) for Huánuco, and by Terence D'Altroy (1981) for the Xauxa region.

Although the Pumpu administrative center (elevation 4,100 m, see Figure 4-3a) is less impressive in size and in formal public architecture than Huánuco Pampa, the presence of extensive Inka state style structures around an expansive central plaza, identify Pumpu as an important Inka administrative center. The unique distribution of storage structures sets the site apart from other Inka installations. As is common in Inka planning, there is a storehouse complex on the hillside, separated from the main part of the site by the Mantaro River; here there are rows of rectangular and rows of circular storehouses. However, *unlike* most Inka sites, there are three extensive areas of circular storehouses on the pampa to the south and across a shallow river from the main part of the Pumpu site. The volume of storage on the hillside above the Pumpu center is estimated at 9,806 m^3: 66% in rectangular and 34% in circular structures (Table 4-3). The estimated storage volume in storehouses on the pampa (95% in circular structures) is 14,697 m^3, with a total of 24,503 m^3 for the center.

Although hypotheses for the location of storehouses on the Pumpu plain across the river from the main center can be tested only by excavation, some interesting possibilities may be suggested. First, the elevation of the plain, at 4,100 m, was high enough and cool enough to protect stored contents. Second, the proximity of these circular storehouses to the major part of the site brought stored contents conveniently closer to the activities of the center; or their contents may have been a greater security risk than ordinary staples, requiring closer supervision. Third, given the regional resource potential, contents could have been cloth and metals, either the raw materials, or craft goods in process; if pampa storehouse contents included fine *qumpi* cloth, or precious metals such as gold and/or silver, then temporary location in a well-supervised area would be understandable.

In the Pumpu region, the Inka road crossed the high Junín Puna. In addition to the major center, three additional Inka installations, all associated with the state road, were located in the Junín survey (Parsons and Hastings 1976, 1977:47–48; Field Notes; Matos and Parsons 1979). Because of its large size (approximately 10.9 ha) when

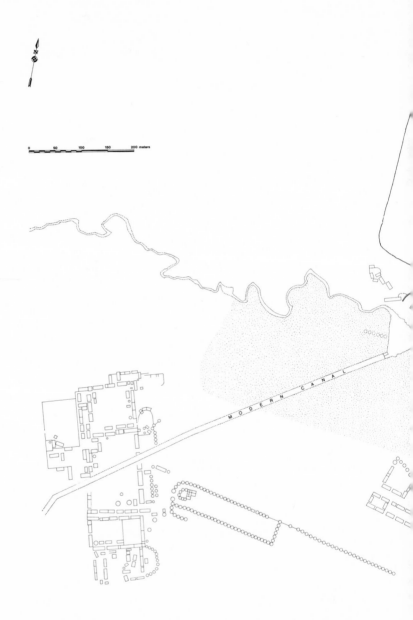

Figure 4-3A. The Pumpu Inka administrative center showing the position of the varied storage sectors on the pampa and across the Mantaro from the center.

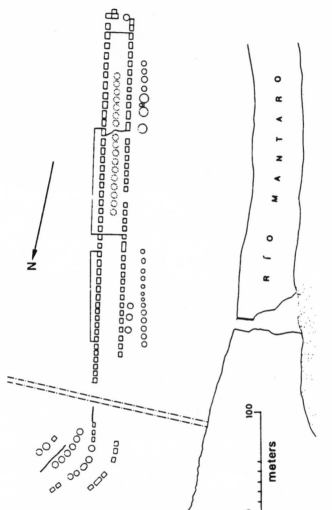

Figure 4-3B. Enlarged view of the main storage section on the hillside across the river from the center; dotted circular storehouses were visible only on aerial photos taken before foundation stones were removed by ranchers for wall construction (after LeVine 1985).

compared to *tampu* waystations, as well as the presence of Inka design public architecture and an extensive storage complex, Chacamarca (Figures 4-1 and 4-4) is classed here as a subcenter. Storehouses at Chacamarca, also on the hillside above the site, were almost entirely circular and had a surprisingly high volume—estimated at 8,680 m³, 91% in circular structures (Table 4-3).

Telarnioj and La Cima (Figure 4-1) are the names assigned to two small Inka *tampu* where public architecture is minimum. However, storage facilities were considerably more extensive than for *tampu* in the Huánuco region, with 1,455 m³ at Telarnioj (rectangular structures) and 1,607 m³ at La Cima (circular structures). From the regional perspective, a total storage volume of 36,245 m³ was distributed between the major center (68%), the subcenter (24%), and the two *tampu* (7%).

It seems obvious that the Inka economic focus in this region was mining, cloth production, and the raising of *llama* for burden bearing, for wool and meat. It is likely that these activities produced less bulk storage than the heavily agricultural focus of Huánuco and Xauxa. Metals and cloth, in particular gold, silver, and *qumpi* cloth, wealth items with a high value for the state, are known to have been regularly transferred to Cuzco (Helmer 1955–56 [1549]:40; Ortiz 1967–72 [1562] vol. I:26). This raises the question of the extent to which storage of materials other than staples in the Pumpu region was long-term. In fact, when describing the Inka period, early statements also suggest the limitations of certain staples at Pumpu, reporting that the state ordered carriers to bring staples and tropical resources from adjacent regions on a regular basis to augment the region's lack of adequate agricultural production (Ortiz 1967–72 [1562] vol. I:47; Vásquez 1969 [1617]:331–32; Rostworowski 1978 [1549]:223–24).

XAUXA

The broad and open Yanamarca and Mantaro valleys, located north and south of the Hatun Xauxa Inka center, were the setting for warring chiefdoms who were consolidating their power in the century before their incorporation into the Inka empire (LeBlanc 1981:297–373). A rich agricultural base, augmented by mining and herding resources, had supported the growth of more dense populations and relatively more complex sociopolitical groups than in the Huánuco

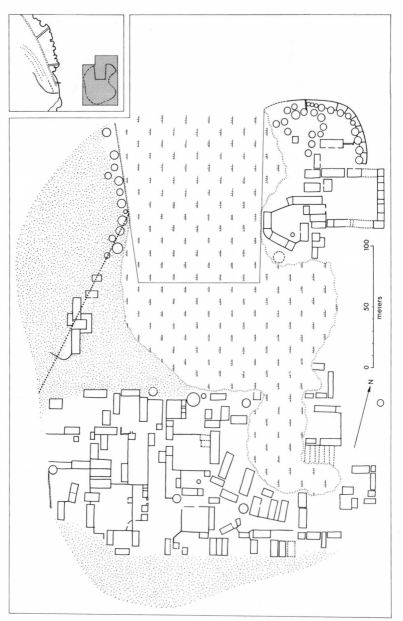

Figure 4-4A. The main part of the Chacamarca subcenter. The stippled area represents areas of poorly preserved structures. The central part of the site including the plaza was under water and was visible only

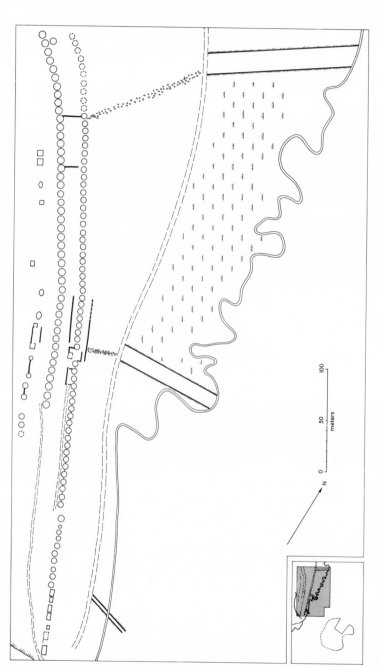

Figure 4-4B. The hillside storage area showing the three causeways crossing the marshlands and connecting the storage section to the central part of the site (after LeVine 1985).

and Pumpu regions described above. *Puna* pasture areas were mainly on high ridges and plateaus above the major valleys, with a more extensive *puna* zone between the Yanamarca Valley and the Tarma valleys in the northeast part of the region.

Although the agricultural zone is represented by only 48% of the region (Table 4-2), this is concentrated in the extensive fertile fields of the Yanamarca, the Mantaro, and smaller, intermontane valleys ranging between 3,000 and 3,400 m. Unlike Huánuco, the frost-free tropical zone is limited in extent and separated by a mountain barrier on the east side of the Yanamarca and Mantaro valleys. Archaeological data from middens in these valleys reveal few tropical products either before or during the Inka period (Earle et al. 1987:83–84). However, the documents indicate that some tropical products were supplied to the state from the Tarma Valley groups, north and east of Tarmatambo where access to tropical zones was relatively convenient (see Vega 1965 [1582]:171, 173; Espinoza Soriano 1971 [1558–1561]). It seems reasonable that in the Xauxa region the Inka probably were emphasizing staples grown between 3,000 and 4,000 m.

Despite similarity in regional size, the unusually high population of the Xauxa region, 217,000 people[3], is approximately four times that of the other two regions. This estimate includes the dense populations of the Yanamarca and Mantaro valleys (189,000), and an estimate of 28,000 people for the small ethnic groups of the Tarma valleys. Population density is the highest of the three regions being compared (Table 4-1). The Wanka represented the largest and most politically complex population aggregation. Before their incorporation into the Inka empire, they had been organized into hierarchical chiefdoms where leadership positions were partially hereditary (LeVine 1979:37–46; LeBlanc 1981:238–75). Unlike the Huánuco and Pumpu regions, while under Inka state control, larger Wanka settlements in the Yanamarca Valley show the presence of public architecture in the Inka style, located in elite, or civic/ceremonial, sectors (D'Altroy 1981:127, 135), suggesting the possibility of third-level nodes below the level of the Hatun Xauxa. Although Wanka population density was greater than that of the other two regions being compared, the Inka apparently were able to integrate the Wanka into the state political hierarchy. Given the high labor potential and the sociopolitical level of development in the central part of the Xauxa region, it seems reasonable to assume that administrative problems and solutions differed markedly from those of Huánuco and Pumpu.

The major Inka highland road from Cuzco, to the south, passed directly through the central part of the Xauxa region, through the Mantaro Valley to reach Hatun Xauxa (Figures 4-1 and 4-5). It continued north through the Yanamarca Valley and across the Huari-colca *puna* to Tarmatambo and then veered northwest toward Chaca-marca. The state chose a location for Hatun Xauxa that lay at the juncture between the two main valleys within which the major popu-lation had been concentrated in large villages and towns.

Using the Parsons/Matos survey, D'Altroy located and mapped Inka state storehouse complexes associated Hatun Xauxa (Figure 4-5; see also Chapters 6 and 9 for a detailed description of Hatun Xauxa storage facilities and for an analysis of storage organization). D'Altroy evaluated the storage volume at sites within 17 km of the center that included the north part of the Mantaro Valley. He found that about 52% (64,618 m^3) of this volume of storage was located in storage units within 1 kilometer of the center, indicating that storage capacity was centralized near the center (51% in rectangular structures and 49% in circular structures, see Table 4-3). An additional volume of 59,098 m^3 of state storage was distributed within the next 16 km, along the east and west sides of the Mantaro Valley, south of the Hatun Xauxa center, in small storage units systematically separated from local Wanka villages. Browman (1985:198) reports 44,329 m^3 for the south half of the Mantaro Valley, the volume being equally distributed between rectangular and circular structures.

Tarmatambo, a site located at 3,800 m (Figure 4-1), has definite Inka design public architecture and Inka ceramics, and is designated a subcenter in this chapter. This Inka installation apparently served to administer the needs of several small-scale, independent ethnic groups settled within a series of narrow, steep valleys in the northwest part of the Xauxa region, north of the Huaricolca *puna* (Rowe 1946:187). Moist winds from the Amazon Basin warm the air of the Tarma valleys providing zones suited to the growing of maize and tropical products. Pasturage for herd animals is available on the Huaricolca *puna*.

Although the estimated population of 28,000 in this region is proportionately low compared to the estimate of 189,000 for the

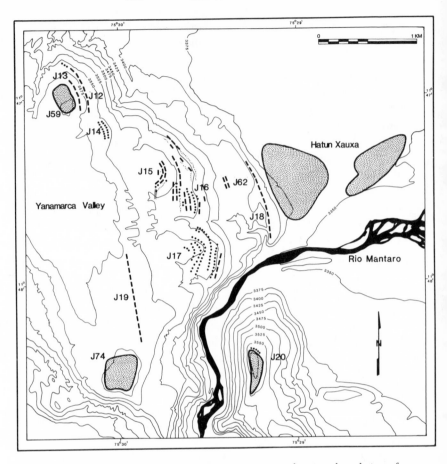

Figure 4-5. The Hatun Xauxa Inka administrative center showing the relation of storage complexes to the center. Areas of rectangular and circular storehouses are represented schematically by dashes and dots (D'Altroy 1981, 1992).

complex chiefdoms of the Yanamarca/Mantaro valley systems, 28,000 people represents half of the population estimated for the entire Huánuco region. This may well explain the need for an administrative presence at this site.

Tarmatambo storage, considerably lower than the 8,680 m³ volume estimated for the Chacamarca subcenter, was yet far above the simple *tampu* storage seen in the Huánuco region. Possibly Tarmatambo served as a reshipment point for products to supply the needs of the Hatun Xauxa center (LeVine 1985:235–36, 350). For purposes of regional comparisons, the minimum storage volume of 3,147 m^3 (LeVine 1985) estimated for Tarmatambo storehouses is included in the Xauxa regional volume. At Tarmatambo, 31% of the volume was in rectangular structures and 69% in circular structures.

To review, environmental and demographic data presented in this section delineate definitive differences: (1) in the percentage of land distributed between the three major land use zones of the Andean highlands; (2) in the resource focus that resulted; (3) in population size and density; (4) in settlement size and population distribution; and (5) in sociopolitical level. It seems reasonable to assume that all of these variables, individually or in combination, affected regional differences in Inka administrative policy and, concomitantly, differences in storage volume, storage distribution, and storage contents.

DISCUSSION OF COMPARATIVE DATA

Two models are useful as a basis for discussing the data presented in this paper: a geographical model and a model of increasing energy capture.

GEOGRAPHICAL MODEL

Although the Inka state represents a complex centralized system, the Inka suppression of most market and trade (Murra 1980 [1956]; La Lone 1982) precludes the use of a locational model based on central-place settlements affected by a market-oriented economy. Many of the organizational features present in the Inka state political economy indicate a better fit with aspects of the locational model that Vincas Steponaitis (1978:417–53; 1981:320–63) developed for hierarchical societies with nonmarket economies. Steponaitis (1981:321) focuses on three dimensions for evaluating these societies: "(1) the number of levels in the political hierarchy, (2) the degree of centralization at the uppermost level, and (3) the relative amount of surplus . . . mobilized to support the political establishment."

The geographical extent of the Inka conquest and the succeeding hegemony developed over conquered polities place this expansive empire within the category of a politically centralized state system with a multitiered political hierarchy. To review: the greatest level of decision-making power, the monopoly on force, as well as the control of access to labor service and to stored state surplus goods, lay in the central node at Cuzco; decisions, and the power to implement them, were distributed in hierarchical order to provincial administrative centers (in the position of secondary-level nodes), and through them to lower-level ethnic leaders. Within the administrative hierarchy, positions of authority carried with them state-appointed fixed duties (as well as state-authorized prerogatives) sanctified by religious ideology and reinforced in civic/ceremonial rituals. These rituals have been discerned archaeologically at Huánuco Pampa (Morris 1985:88–91), and they are suggested in a description of Hatun Xauxa recorded in a sixteenth century document (Xerez 1862 [1533–34]:349–58).

Although the location of central places in a market-based economy is dictated by the fact that centers operate as suppliers for their hinterlands, in the Inka empire, secondary-level nodes as central places served state political and economic needs and were imposed from above. One of the important activities at Inka centers was administrative control, much of which involved organizing production and labor-service delegation resulting in the accumulation of the materials that filled the great storage complexes and were used to supply government activities (LeVine 1987:14–46).

The Inka political economy was a mobilization economy rather than a redistributive economy (see D'Altroy and Earle, Chapter 6). Whatever redistributive aspects of the economy remained were more symbolic than substantial and most households were expected to be self-sufficient within their own communities. Craft specialization was connected with the political establishment and was supported from materials in state warehouses. Thus, if the degree of political power is relative to the amount of surplus extracted, the volume of storage in the Central Highlands leaves no doubt as to the power of the Inka state.

In the Steponaitis model (1978:427), there are two important differences between state administrative districts and market hinterlands. The first relates to how hinterlands are formed. Market hinterlands are formed through decisions made by the people. Inka administrative districts were based in part on pre-Inka corporate land-use rights vested in the kin-based *ayllu*. Although conquered polities sometimes challenged boundaries, decisions concerning political boundaries were imposed, and reinforced, from above by the central government (see Cieza 1967 [1553]:217; LeVine 1979:26–28). The second difference is connected to the nature of the relations between centers of equivalent order. Market centers may be in competition with each other, and thus spacing and distribution mitigate competition. Although there are relatively equal distances between the three Inka centers described in this chapter, it is my contention that this spacing reflects the requirements of transportation and supply in the Inka state, where labor-service assignments included walking porters and only *llama* assisted with carrying supplies.

A final and conclusive point in the nonmarket locational model is that the ideal location for a secondary-level node is not necessarily in the geographic center of the producing population. In consideration of the importance of minimizing the movement of materials, secondary-level installations are located for easier access to primary-level capitals to which surpluses flow (Steponaitis 1978:436; see D'Altroy and Earle, Chapter 2). In the Central Highlands, the location of secondary-level nodes is always on the major highland road, but locations vary in their relation to populated zones.

Distribution of Inka Installations and Storehouses

The location and relative spacing of Inka installations in the Central Highlands appears to have been based on political concerns that overrode regional concerns. In this section, I will discuss the data presented in an earlier section of this chapter that demonstrate interesting variations between regions: differences in the size of secondary nodes; differences in the number of state intraregional installations; and differences in the volume and distribution of storage associated with state sites.

The strategic needs of the empire-state rather than the convenience of administering regional populations also dictated the positioning of the state road system. It follows that the organization of supply was oriented toward state supply needs. My argument is that the location of major centers was an interregional pattern imposed from above, according to central decisions from Cuzco, rather than a pattern that developed from natural conditions within regions. On the other hand, intraregionally, the configuration of conquered populations as well as variable resource potential had an effect on the size and number of Inka installations as well as the size and distribution of storage. These variations might be explained by a series of factors.

1. *State control.* Because all state storage complexes in the Central Highlands were associated with major routes of the state road, the most basic consideration in the location and distribution of storage was apparently the requirement that the state be able to maintain, control, and protect stored materials.

2. *Movement patterns.* The Inka transportation system was a critical element in the success of the state. Thus a consideration of movement patterns is crucial to understanding strategies for locating major centers and for planning storage distribution.

According to John Hyslop (1984:262–63) evidence points to the importance of the highland routes of the state road in preference to travel along the arid coastal desert. Starting from the south, the road connecting Cuzco to the empire's northern borders passed through Hatun Xauxa carrying the heaviest traffic of the Central Highlands. This made Hatun Xauxa an important provisioning point for those traveling on state business. A major lateral road from Hatun Xauxa connected the highlands with the central coast and with Pachacamac, the most important coastal religious center. This siphoned off, toward the coast, a portion of the traffic moving north from Cuzco and increased, with coast traffic, traffic from the north as it passed through Hatun Xauxa on its way south. Hatun Xauxa's strategic position explains both its location and also the concentration of storage at this state center.

The Inka road continued north from Hatun Xauxa passing through Tarmatambo. From the perspective of movement patterns, it is interesting to consider why the Inka road took the route through Tarmatambo and why an Inka installation of more than 20 ha, with considerable public architecture, was built here. The Inka road is still visible archaeologically. H. Pizarro approached Hatun Xauxa along this route in 1533 (LeVine 1985:433–36). I believe there are several explanations: The preferred high elevations were suitable; this was a strategic location for access to and protection of the empire's eastern border; Tarmatambo is located strategically at the interface between the resources grown in the tropical valleys descending to the Amazon Basin, and the resources derived from pasturing flocks on the Huaricolca *puna.* The position of Tarmatambo in the state political hierarchy will be discussed under population distribution.

The Inka road continued northwest to Chacamarca and Pumpu. The variety of routes taken by the Inka roads through the Pumpu region were diverse enough to have affected regional storage organization and distribution. The major road bifurcated at Pumpu: One route moved northwest to connect with lateral routes reaching Inka installations further north on the coast; another branch route, a portion of which is described by John Hyslop (1984:71–77), continued north from Pumpu through Huánuco Pampa. The routes reconnected south of Huamachuco (Cieza 1862 [1551]:430; LeVine 1985:419–33; see also Chapter 7). Xerez, Pizarro's secretary, describes each of these routes, first approaching Pumpu on Wednesday March 11th, from the northwest route, and again, on March 25th, on the return trip, leaving Pumpu to go northeast through Huánuco Pampa (Xerez 1862 [1533–34]:340–42). A lateral route departed Pumpu to the southwest reaching the coast through the Chillón Valley (Rostworowski 1978 [1549]:224; LeVine 1985:425–28).

The 1976 field season of the Junín Archaeological Survey (Parsons and Hastings, 1977; Field Notes) discovered the remains of two Inka roads in the vicinity of Chacamarca. In addition to the route between Chacamarca and Pumpu on the west side of Lago Chinchaycocha, part of the north-moving traffic flow could have taken a subsidiary branch of the main road on the east side of the lake, bypassing Pumpu and connecting directly with Huánuco Pampa to the north. The route along the east side of the lake became the preferred route during the Colonial period, but as per the Parsons survey, it also appears to have been a viable Inka-period route.

Although Pumpu's total estimated storage volume of 24,500 m^3 was lower than storage volumes at Huánuco Pampa and Hatun Xauxa, the quantity of storage at the region's three additional state installations, Chacamarca, La Cima, and Telarnioj, alerts us to differences in the Pumpu region's storage distribution (see Table 4-3). The bifurcation of a more direct sub-route at Chacamarca through to Huánuco Pampa would in part explain the surprisingly large quantity of storage at Chacamarca. The position of Chacamarca in the Inka political hierarchy is problematic. Given the fact that the site's storage volume amounts to about one third of the volume at Pumpu, the second-level node, it seems unlikely that it could be defined as a third-level node and a transshipment point for the major center, 40 km northwest. It was more likely to have been an Inka installation serving specialized needs related either with the organization of supply for the transportation system, or the collection of specialized resources in the area. Only excavation will provide an answer to this problem.

There are also indications of more than one section of the Inka road in the vicinity of the Huánuco Pampa center. In addition to the main route through Huánuco north to Huamachuco described above, a route to Chachapoyas in the northeast part of the empire was recounted in early documents (Vaca de Castro 1908 [1543]:447; Espinosa Campos 1965 [1592]:85, 87)). This route along the Marañón River is part of the road system described by Strube Erdman (1963:23–26, 99–101). Although its importance may have increased in the Colonial period, it seems likely this was also a viable route during the Inka period (see also Hyslop 1984:83; LeVine 1985:411–13). The location of Huánuco Pampa at the juncture point of two Inka-period routes would reinforce its strategic importance and the concentration of almost 38,000 m^3 of storage at this major center.

3. *Provisioning state projects.* An important factor is the extent to which the distribution of storage correlates with the location of storehouses at junctures in the road system known to have been strategic to the provisioning of state projects. There is little doubt that administrative centers and subsidiary installations varied to some degree in their logistic importance to empire operation. The state's requirements for financing empirewide supply lines in the service of military and security forces, communication operations, construction projects, as well as for state conquest and expansion schemes, represented a highly important allocation for storage. Storage concentration at Huánuco Pampa, Pumpu, Hatun Xauxa, and Chacamarca, demonstrates the importance of the Central Highlands in fulfilling this requirement.

4. *Population distribution.* Population density is a factor in understanding the distribution of Inka installations and especially their associated storehouses. As argued above, the positioning of the state road system and the regional centers was much more concerned with the strategic needs of the empire-state than with the convenience of

administering regional populations. The emphasis on state storage in its association with state business is particularly clear in Huánuco where half or more of the region's population was settled in the productive Huallaga Valley on the east side of the region, whereas Huánuco Pampa with about 98% of the region's storage was on the west side of the region. Ethnic groups of the Huallaga Valley complained of the long distances they walked to carry bulk staples to Huánuco Pampa, and also to Pumpu (Ortiz 1967–72 [1562] vol. I:25, 51–52; LeVine 1985:111–15). At approximately 89 ha, the size of Huánuco Pampa may have been related to the number of hinterland people carrying staples and manufactured goods to the center or staying on to participate in craft production at the center.

Pumpu's population appears to have been dispersed throughout the region in agricultural villages in the steep narrow valleys descending to the northeast and east, in settlements around Lago Chinchaycocha, and on the surrounding high-elevation *puna* (LeVine 1985:255–71). The state road and Inka installations in the Pumpu region were also at a distance from much of the administered populations. Pumpu, the major center is smaller, and Chacamarca, the subcenter has a storage volume out of proportion to its overall size. Although difference in size often is equated with difference in function, until Chacamarca is excavated, we can only use reasoned guessing to assign either production and/or administrative functions to the site, in addition to its function provisioning state approved travelers.

The above patterns contrast with the ease of transport in Xauxa where the road passed directly through the well-populated Yanamarca and Mantaro valleys, facilitating transport to the storage units associated with Hatun Xauxa. A balance between state objectives and population distribution created the pattern for Inka administration and storage in the Xauxa region. Only in the Xauxa region is there archaeological evidence for large-size towns with central civic/ceremonial sectors suggesting third-level nodes below the Hatun Xauxa secondary-level node. State storage is also dispersed. Only about 52% of the storage volume was within 1 km of the state center, whereas 48% was distributed in storage complexes along the east and west sides of the Mantaro Valley through which the major state road passed. D'Altroy (1981:236) suggests that the contents of storehouses associated with villages may have been used to support labor services for the state performed by local villagers, thus reducing congestion at storage complexes and at the center's workshops where specialized production was carried out. This seems a reasonable solution, first based on the high population density in the Mantaro Valley, and second, considering that villages were close enough to the Inka road and the Inka center to permit relatively good supervision of materials in storage.

The density of population in the northeast part of the Xauxa region may be part of the explanation for the location of Tarmatambo. The size of the population settled in the Tarma subsidiary valleys (estimated at 28,000) appears to have been a factor in the location of this Inka site. Because of the small volume of storage at Tarmatambo, as well as the site's small size compared to the three major centers, Tarmatambo may represent a third-level node below Hatun Xauxa, as in the Steponaitis model discussed above. The 20 ha estimated represents the central portion of the site surrounding the central plazas. This was reduced from an approximately 30 ha estimate based on the distribution of Inka ceramics (Parsons and Hastings 1977). Site size appears to correlate with the amount of productive arable land in the vicinity. Much of the site is overlain with contemporary village homes and gardens. Comparing the high population density in the vicinity of contemporary Tarmatambo and the low population density around contemporary Chacamarca, with population estimates for the same areas during the Inka period (Parsons and Hastings 1977), suggests that population distribution is relative for both periods. This argues for the need of an administrative function at Tarmatambo during the Inka period. As discussed above, the low storage volume suggests that Tarmatambo was a reshipment point supporting Hatun Xauxa, a major Inka regional center, again suggesting this site might fit the description of a third-level node in the Inka political hierarchy.

INCREASING ENERGY CAPTURE MODEL

Inka empire expansion fits the materialistic model of increasing energy capture. The ability of the Inka state to extend power by establishing hegemony over a series of diverse and less organized polities was enhanced further by their proficiency at reorganizing and expanding regional economies with a resulting increase in the amount of energy controlled. Expansion increased not only the number of people under Inka empire jurisdiction but also the amount of energy harnessed per capita (White 1959). This met the state's increasing labor requirements for production intensification in both subsistence and nonsubsistence goods to maintain itself and to underwrite further expansion (Steward 1960; Price 1978; D'Altroy and Earle Chapter 2; Earle and D'Altroy 1989).

The manner in which the state managed the new surplus, specifically its skill at organizing and centrally directing its storage system, were key elements in the control of increasing amounts of energy. Control of power is costly, and for this reason the location and distribution of political nodes on the empire landscape, represented by state administrative installations, required access to energy. This energy is represented by the storage sector that was an important part of every Inka administrative installation.

Research in the Central Highlands has demonstrated that Inka state storage facilities show sufficient similarity to indicate centralized state planning. They were most often located on terraces built along hillsides to achieve the cool temperatures of higher elevations. They were sturdily built, utilizing local materials, and they were either rectangular or circular in design. Structure size ranged between 3 m and 8 m diameter for circular structures; rectangular structures were more variable, depending on whether they were single or multiple room structures (Morris 1967:184–93; D'Altroy 1981:205–10; see also Chapters 5, 6, 8, and 9). State storage facilities were regularly associated with the main state road or with important branch roads. Finally, major regional storage volumes most commonly were associated with the great Inka centers.

Aside from the above similarities, data also demonstrate the following: (1) strong differentiation in storage volume per installation and per region; (2) patterning in the design of storage units; and (3) probable variations in stored contents (Morris 1971:139; D'Altroy and Hastorf Chapter 9, this volume; LeVine 1985:188–98). The extent to which these variations were the result of state policies to maintain a balance between meeting local needs and broader imperial needs will be discussed.

Storage Volume

If we can assume that productivity was efficiently used and that storage management minimized waste, then population size can be used as an index of energy capture (Price 1978:729) and variations in population size per region can be a factor limiting or increasing potential regional productivity. This could help to explain differences in regional storage volumes. Table 4-4, comparing total regional estimated storage volume to total estimated regional population, demonstrates a correlation of volume with population size for two of the regions. The ratio of storage per 1,000 people for the Huánuco region at 705 m^3 and for Xauxa at 780 m^3 is relatively similar, despite great differences in each region's total estimated population size.

Correlation between storage volume and population size for the above two regions is less surprising when viewed from three perspectives. First, given that labor service expectations per capita for production were likely to have been relatively equal in Central Highland regions, similar population size should be expected to generate similar quantities of stored materials. This would be especially valid if similar proportions of materials produced were stored locally. Warehousing locally and delaying shipment until need was demonstrated would minimize labor expenditure and maximize labor efficiency (see D'Altroy and Earle Chapter 2, this volume).

Second, similar per capita storage for Huánuco and Xauxa may be explainable by the fact that both regions had mainly an agricultural orientation. Bulk staples generated per capita should require a similar volume of storage space. From a third perspective, it is logical that Xauxa's storage volume should be four times greater than that of Huánuco. A portion of the volume of stored staples was allocated for reinvestment in provisioning local *mit'a* (annual labor quotas) in the form of specialized state agricultural work, mining, public construction projects, and craft production. To judge only from the fact that the Inka-provisioned subject populations engaged in service for the state (Murra 1980:98), it seems reasonable to propose that Hatun Xauxa storehouses required greater storage volume for reinvestment in the region's significantly higher potential labor force.

Regional resource focus might also affect storage volume. For example, regions producing bulk staples might require a greater

Table 4-4. Correlation of Population Size to Regional Storage Volume

Region	Estimated Total Regional Population	Regional Storage Volume	Storage Volume per 1,000 Population
Huánuco Pampa	55,000	38,748m³	705m³
Pumpu	60,000	36,286m³	605m³
Hatun Xauxa	217,000	169,249m³	780m³

NOTE: Table 4-4 represents compiled regional data showing estimated maximum population per region and estimated total storage volume per region. By dividing the estimated storage volume by the estimated population size, it is possible to compare the storage volume per 1,000 people (Adapted from LeVine 1985:457, Table 7-3).

storage volume than regions with a focus on craft production. The consensus is that luxury materials were more likely to be moved to the empire capital at Cuzco. This would reduce the volume of long-term storage in regions with high productivity in luxury materials such as gold, silver, and fine cloth.

Note that the ratio of storage per 1,000 people for Pumpu in Table 4-4 (605 m³) is less than for Huánuco (705 m³) even though population estimates are similar. Assuming that labor service expectations were equal for all populations, this might be explained by one or both of the following reasons: (1) the major Pumpu region resources, mined metals, meat, and wool, as well as llama bred for caravaning, logically would have required less storage space than bulk staples; (2) these resources resulted in the production of wealth items like silver, gold, and *qumpi* (finely woven cloth) that, according to sixteenth-century interviews, were not placed in long-term local storage but were sent to Cuzco (Helmer 1955–56 [1549]:40; Ortiz 1967–72 [1562] vol. I:26).

Storehouse Design

Storehouse design, specifically the shape of storage units, shows systematic patterning. Storehouse structures in Inka storage facilities are either rectangular or circular and most often are grouped by shape. Morris (1967) has suggested that structure shape may have been an accounting device related to organizing storage by specific crops. One question that has intrigued investigators is to what extent differences in the shape of storage structures, rectangular or circular, reflect differences in the kinds of goods stored (Morris 1971:139; D'Altroy and Hastorf 1984:346–47). Although data from test excavations are not conclusive and no agreement regarding correlation of shape with specific contents has been reached, investigators are in agreement with the basic idea that the Inka probably organized storehouse contents systematically.

Approached from another perspective, a hypothesis could be proposed that, if locally generated surpluses were stored locally, differences in resource focus between one region and another might well be reflected in differences in the predominant storehouse design from one region to another or from one storage group to another. For example, regions with high productivity in bulk staples might require different storage accommodations compared to regions with high productivity in craft goods. Table 4-3 presents a comparison of Central Highland storage complexes showing the volume of storage in each of the two storehouse designs common to Inka storage sites. At the main center of the Huánuco region, where storage is located on the hillside rising above the center to the southwest, 62% of storage volume is in rectangular structures.

In the Pumpu region because storage distribution is divided between the Pumpu center, the Chacamarca subcenter, and the two *tampu,* the proportional differences between rectangular and circular storehouse volumes is more complex. At the Pumpu center, there are two separate areas of storehouses (Figure 4-3). The hillside zone across the Mantaro River has 150 storage units where the estimated volume of storage in 93 rectangular structures represents 66% of the volume compared to 34% of the volume in 57 circular structures. On the *pampa,* across a small stream to the south, there are approximately 177 units where the proportion changes dramatically with 95% of the volume in 167 circular storehouses. At Chacamarca, circular structures also predominate, holding 91% of the estimated storage volume. Telarnioj and La Cima had 100% rectangular and circular structures respectively.

In no way do I wish to imply that circular structures were used exclusively to store craft goods; however, it is interesting to note the predominance of circular structures in the Pumpu region. I have suggested the possibility that regional economic focus may have affected storage complex design—if so, then the circular storehouses prevalent in the Pumpu region could have been due to the region's dominant focus on products associated with large-scale mining and weaving. From a different perspective, the low number of rectangular structures in this region may be related to the minimum amount of agricultural staples storage (see, however, Chapter 6 for another interpretation for the prevalence of circular structures).

In Xauxa, the division between the two storehouse types is more complex and more interesting. Among the storehouses within 1 kilometer of the main center (those considered by D'Altroy to be closely associated with activities at the center; see Table 6-1 in Chapter 6), the proportion of volume is 51% in 507 rectangular units and 49% in 562 circular units (Table 4-3). Outside this core group, storage sites within 1 to 3 kilometers of the center are associated with villages D'Altroy (1992) has defined as state-run farming communities (Chapter 6). Within this group the proportion of storage volume changes radically with 185 rectangular units holding 84% of the volume compared to only 16% in 41 circular units.[4]

Distinctions are even more apparent among the dispersed facilities between 3 and 17 kilometers from Hatun Xauxa.[4] These storehouses are distributed east and west of the Mantaro River in the north part of the Mantaro Valley where data are more detailed than data available for the south part of the valley (Earle et al. 1980:34; D'Altroy 1981:472–73; Earle and D'Altroy 1982; D'Altroy 1992). Analysis indicates that on the east side of the valley, 303 of the 417 units are rectangular and represent 83% of the storage volume; the 114 circular units represent 17% of storage volume (Table 4-3). Factors of population distribution and ceramic identification have influenced the interpretation that the east side of the valley was an additional area where the state established state-supervised farms. The fact that the east side of the valley has a superior agricultural potential due to more fertile soil, reduced threat of frost, and greater rainfall (Franco et al. 1979; D'Altroy 1992), reinforces this interpretation and also suggests that rectangular units correlate with the storage of bulk agricultural products.

The west side of the Mantaro Valley has 280 storage units, and the proportionate volume is reversed with only 19% in 40 rectangular units and 81% in 240 circular units suggesting the possibility that craft production may have been more important on the valley's west side. For the south half of the Mantaro Valley it is estimated that storage was equally divided between rectangular and circular units (Browman 1985:198). The small storage volume at Tarmatambo, the subcenter, about 40 km north of Hatun Xauxa, has been included in the regional totals because the site appears to stand in a similar relationship to Hatun Xauxa as the subcenter of Chacamarca to Pumpu.

In sum, when evaluated from the perspective of the total amount of storage within 17 km of the Hatun Xauxa center, overall volume stored in 1,035 rectangular units is 59% and 41% in 957 circular units. This is surprisingly close to the proportion of storage volume in rectangular to circular structures for Huánuco Pampa and could well have been a function of the fact that both of these regions had a high productivity in agricultural staples. On the other hand, the predominance of circular structures in the Pumpu region could be interpreted as the result of the regional focus on herding and mining.

Thus, although correlation of storehouse shape with specific contents is difficult to establish (see Lennstrom and Hastorf, Chapter 10), the data gathered for this comparative study suggest a correlation between regional focus on production in agricultural staples and a predominance of rectangular structures in storage sites.

Storage Contents

The limited amount of excavation accomplished to date restricts our ability to compare storage contents. Nevertheless, an understanding of the major resources within regions, plus clues from relevant documents, adds to our knowledge of materials warehoused in Inka storage complexes. Data available for each of the three regions will be discussed.

Huánuco: The Documents. Ethnic groups from the high-elevation west part of the region responded to questions from Colonial officials in 1549 about the materials they produced for the Inka. The herding focus of the region is evident in their answer that their major contribution was meat from herds of llama, as well as from hunted deer (Espinoza Soriano 1974b:59–60). Answers to questions recorded in another Colonial-period document indicate that the state expected these same ethnic groups to travel to the eastern slopes of the Andes to trade for commodities like feathers, cotton, and coca to be taken to state storehouses at Huánuco as part of the labor service requirements (Espinoza Campos 1965 [1592]:84).

Much more detailed documents containing interviews with Huallaga Valley ethnic groups from the east side of the Huánuco region suggest a more varied and a more agriculturally oriented production. Just a few years after the Spaniards conquered the valley, answers to questions described labor services that produced gold, silver, feathers, honey, cloth, maize, peppers, salt, coca, sandals, wood products, and pottery (Helmer 1955–56 [1549]:41–42). In interviews conducted a few years later (Ortiz 1967–72 [1562] vol. I:25–27) informants listed the same products, with the addition of products that resulted from local fishing and hunting activities, plus the manufacture of war implements (see LeVine 1987 for a detailed discussion of this document).

Huánuco: Excavation. Morris conducted sample excavations in Huánuco Pampa storehouses. Of the 95 storehouses excavated, he found pottery only in circular structures (Morris 1967:Appendix III). Botanical evidence for Andean staples in sample excavations was limited: Six structures had maize and three tubers. Morris noted an association between circular structures, pottery, and maize, suggesting that maize was stored in jars in circular structures. He associated root crop storage with rectangular structures in which he found no pottery, suggesting the use of other methods of storage (Morris 1971:139; 1981:333,339; see Chapter 8).

Pumpu: Documents. Evidence for the Pumpu region is tenuous. There are few direct documents for the area, and there has been no excavation of storehouses. However, answers to questions asked by inspectors of occupants of Huallaga valley to the north and Chillón to the west show that Inka *mit'a* labor service required that the people of these regions transport maize, coca, peppers and potatoes to Pumpu storehouses (Ortiz 1967–72 [1562] vol. I:47; Rostworowski 1978 [1549]:223–24). Early sixteenth and seventeenth century travelers emphasized, first, that the majority of ethnic groups administered from Pumpu had concentrated on herding, hunting, and salt mining; and second, that they had always supplemented their personal diet with agricultural products that they could exchange for the salt, wool, and meat they produced.

Thus, one might infer that long-term storage in the Pumpu region did not include agricultural products. Early documents indicate that fine cloth woven from the region's concentrated vicuña population, (Vásquez 1969 [1617]:331–32; Duviols 1974–76 [1614]:276) and precious metals from local mines, were major end results of Pumpu regional production. However, a reasonable proportion of these may have been taken directly to Cuzco (see D'Altroy and Earle, Chapter 2). This leaves ordinary cloth, less-precious metal goods, and staples on an as-needed basis, as major products stored in the Pumpu storehouses.

Hatun Xauxa: Documents. Two documents suggest the contents of Hatun Xauxa storehouses. One, Andres de Vega (1965 [1582]), a *visitador* (inspector), questioned the local Wanka leaders who reported that the Inka demanded "staples and clothing, the most they were able to produce;" Vega also notes that the Xauxa area was "a land of mines of lead, silver, and copper" (169–71).

A much more detailed list of products derives from litigation instituted by Mantaro Valley Wanka ethnic lords against the Spanish Colonial government. These documents will be discussed in more detail in Chapter 9 (Espinoza Soriano 1971 [1558–61]:9–407). The list includes metals (gold, silver, copper), artisanal goods (fine cloth, blankets, ceramics, sandals), staples (maize, quinoa, potatoes), dried birds (for feathers?), and fish, fruit, maize beer, charcoal and firewood, straw and grasses.

Hatun Xauxa: Excavation. The results of test excavations in storehouses at Hatun Xauxa will also be described more fully in Chapter 9 (see also D'Altroy and Hastorf 1984). Ceramic fragments were almost entirely Inka and were mostly from large storage jars. They occurred mainly in the circular structures tested. Flotation procedures yielded maize, highland products (quinoa, potatoes, and legumes) as well as wood and grasses, all materials reported in the litigation discussed above, and all consistent with agricultural products grown within the environs of the Mantaro Valley today (Hastorf 1983).

D'Altroy and Hastorf's data (1984; Chapter 9) leave the question of a consistent correlation between architectural design and specific stored contents still open to discussion. Data are neither sufficient nor conclusive. Based on her work with botanical remains, Hastorf (personal communication) believes that it may be too simplistic to try to correlate storehouse shape with the specific type of products stored. She feels that, to be successful, the Inka would want to be flexible in what they stored in their warehouses. Long-term, versus short-term, storage may have had a greater effect on storehouse design than the specific contents they contained.

SUMMARY AND CONCLUSIONS

This chapter has stressed that proper storage management and well-planned storage deployment were crucial to the economic success of early archaic empires like the Inka, especially those supported primarily by staple finance. The underlying purpose has been to search out the motivations influencing Inka state administration and especially the state's economic planning. The thesis being argued is that a successful Inka policy was flexible enough to balance the requirements of empire management with the inherent variability of the microecologies and the preexisting political structures found within Andean central highland regions. I have attempted to demonstrate, through a comparison of three administrative regions, the extent to which this policy effected the location of state administrative centers and storage distribution, why flexibility in administrative policy was necessary, and how the increased energy capture, represented by incorporation of new sources of labor and a newly expanded resource base, required careful planning.

The location of Huánuco regional storage at a great distance both from the region's most productive agricultural fields, as well as from population centers, reinforces what many have already concluded: The location of Inka centers and the distribution of storage was not necessarily convenient for local populations. The energy represented by a stored surplus was organized to accommodate the unique needs of the state. The labor of ethnic groups from the Huallaga Valley were required to move materials to where they would be used, whether it was to Huánuco Pampa, to Pumpu, where adequate agricultural staples and tropical products were lacking, to supply regional *tampu*, or to the state capital at Cuzco. This contrasts with the location of Hatun Xauxa centered between the densely populated Yanamarca and Mantaro valleys.

Storage distribution in the Xauxa region where almost half of regional storage was associated with production sites is of particular interest. Given the high density of population in the Mantaro Valley, it seems clear that dispersed storage methods served the state's specific needs for production. It had several advantages. First, storing staples close to the fields where they were grown decreased unnecessary movement of the great quantity of agricultural materials grown in the Mantaro Valley. If some workshops could be dispersed to Wanka villages, it would also eliminate congestion at the Hatun Xauxa center. The close proximity of Wanka villages to the administrative center and the location of the major Inka road passing through the Mantaro Valley enabled the state to continue to maintain control over both the production and the materials in storehouses.

The data presented in this chapter make clear that in the regions being compared there were important contrasts with respect to both the microenvironments and the varied polities occupying them. Data show a strong differentiation in storage volume that correlates with population size. My contention is that this reinforces arguments, previously made, for regional storage of resources and a minimum amount of transshipment interregionally. A correlate to this argument is that a substantial percentage of storage volume was maintained within each region for reinvestment in future productivity. This is supported by the fact that almost half of Xauxa's storage volume was distributed in small complexes associated with Mantaro Valley production sites, many of which may have been connected to state-run agricultural production areas.

Pumpu's lower per capita storage volume when compared to the other two regions is consistent with the major resource base of the Pumpu region. This suggests that regional resource focus affected storage organization with the strong probability that a high ratio of production in wealth goods required less long-term storage space. Documentary evidence supports the minimum agricultural production in the Pumpu region with testimony from adjacent regions showing that agricultural products were regularly taken to Pumpu state storehouses to supplement local agricultural production, while precious metals and fine cloth commonly went directly to the Inka capital. It is likely that agricultural products were not brought in bulk for long-term storage at Pumpu but were carried in on an as-needed basis. It seems reasonable that this arrangement would have affected storage planning.

Several conclusions can be drawn from these patterns. Both volume and distribution in the three regions are consistent with requirements to supply the traffic moving along state roads through the Central Highlands on state business. Traffic patterns, bifurcations on the major road into branch routes serving the northwest and northeast sections of the empire, as well as lateral roads serving traffic to and from the coast, dictated the placement and volume of storage needed to supply those traveling on military, communication, economic, or bureaucratic missions. This is particularly evident in the Pumpu region, where the variety of routes through the region appear to have affected storage distribution.

Even though there is no agreement regarding the correlation of storehouse design to storehouse contents, comparison of storehouse design in the three regions has been useful. In comparing the prevalence of rectangular to circular structures, note that in the two regions that were high in agricultural production, more than half the structures were rectangular. This relationship is further emphasized in the Mantaro Valley where rectangular structures predominated in areas where it is believed the Inka established state-operated farms. However, in the Pumpu region, where agricultural production was low, circular storehouses predominate. This suggests a connection that Morris (1967) originally made between rectangular structures and the long-term storage of agricultural production (Morris 1967). It is also consistent with the close correlation in per capita storage volume between Huánuco and Xauxa, the two heavily agricultural regions.

Research combining archaeology with the use of documents related to specific regions is beginning to point out variations in how the Inka organized revenue raising even within seemingly similar areas. In order to understand the variability in Inka policy between one region and another, it is advantageous to look closely at the role that storage played in the Inka economy. I believe that comparisons made between regions in this chapter will point out that Inka administrative policy was flexible and was adapted to regionally specific problems.

ACKNOWLEDGMENTS

I wish especially to thank Timothy Earle and Terence D'Altroy who read versions of this paper at several stages of its development and offered important suggestions for improvement. Bruce Owen's comments were also helpful. I appreciate the help of Ramiro Matos Mendieta, Craig Morris, John Hyslop, Jeffrey Parsons and Charles Hastings who shared data and offered helpful advice in the early stages of research planning. Anna Mujica B., of Lima, and Mel LeVine, my field assistants, provided invaluable help, as did Elizabeth

Rivera Damián of Tarma, Peru. I also thank my colleagues of the Upper Mantaro Archaeology Research Project, Christine Hastorf, Cathy Scott, Glenn Russell, Elsie Sandefur, and especially Melissa Hagtrum for their ongoing discussions and support. I am grateful to the Fulbright-Hays Commission for a Doctoral Dissertation Grant, and to the Friends of Archaeology at UCLA, for the support that made the fieldwork for this study possible.

PART III

**RECENT RESEARCH IN REGIONAL STORAGE,
CASE STUDIES**

CHAPTER 5 **Huánuco Pampa and Tunsukancha**

Major and Minor Nodes in the Inka Storage Network

CRAIG MORRIS

A key problem in the maintenance of a large state society is the coordination of its numerous subunits and its multiple geographic zones. People, information, and goods must be moved about and frequently "stored" in such a way that they will be available when and where they are needed. Indeed the technologies of preindustrial complex societies can perhaps be more meaningfully distinguished from those of simpler societies by the emergence and elaboration of these infrastructural and logistical components than by innovations in production.

One of the most important aspects of infrastructural and logistical technology is storage. Although storage systems in early societies have attracted considerable theoretical interest (Polanyi 1957) and have stimulated research based on ethnohistorical documents (Murra 1980:chapter 6), they have relatively recently begun to receive direct archaeological study in the field (Morris 1967; D'Altroy 1981:Chapter 8; LeVine 1985:especially 188–98). This is surprising, because storage forms a material focal point on which many factors of economic, social, and political organization impinge. The study of storage facilities and their contents can give the archaeologist direct access to data on the ability of a society to produce and collect a usable "surplus" of goods, and studies of the locations and contexts of storage can illuminate various aspects of economic and sociopolitical institutions.

In 1964 and 1965 I began an investigation of a small portion of the Inka storage system as part of the *Study of Inka Provincial Life,* a research project directed by John V. Murra. That study examined storage during the Late Horizon (Inka period) in three different contexts: the local community, the provincial logistics network of the state, and the center of state control at Cuzco. I was interested mainly in the kinds and quantities of goods stored in these different contexts as they reflected concentrations of resources in various sectors of the economy and were relevant to the systems by which certain classes of goods were exchanged.

I have outlined elsewhere several aspects of the coordination and planning of logistics and administration through a network of roads and state administrative centers that was such a notable feature of the Inka empire (Morris 1972a, 1982). Storage was naturally a key part of that strategy. In fact, without an organized system of storage and an extremely successful storage technology, it is doubtful that either the administrative and logistic network or Tawantinsuyu (the Inka empire) itself, would have been possible.

I will discuss (Chapter 8, this volume) how the builders and keepers of the storehouses designed their facilities and procedures to take maximum advantage of an extraordinary storage climate. But like the settlements in which they were built, the warehousing facilities comprised a network, and the organizational features of the storage network were fully as essential to success as were the methods and procedures of storage technology.

The Inka storage network included storehouses in administrative centers and at *tampu* (roadside way stations), along thousands of kilometers of roads in the highlands and to a lesser extent on the coast. There were also some state storehouses in places away from the principal roads. Some were in the vicinity of state-controlled agricultural areas (see Wachtel 1982, and Chapter 6); others were connected to state-supported religious establishments, although except for Pachacamac in the Lurín Valley (Jimenez Borja, personal communication) and Rowe's suggestion based on the survey at Huanacauri near Cuzco (Rowe 1944:41), few have been documented. It is also difficult to ascertain the extent to which storage for the state or the state religion may have been linked to storage systems controlled by local communities and at other organizational levels below the state. Some of the questions of storage outside the network of state controlled centers have been treated in an earlier article (Morris 1972b).

In appraising the nature and function of the storage network we need to pose two main sets of questions. First, how are the various parts of the system linked? Are they coordinated in such a way that goods are regularly moved back and forth one to the other? Do the various storage centers place emphases on different kinds of food products? If so, are these differences influenced more heavily by the kinds of goods produced in the surrounding region or by a center's suitability, because of its altitude for example, for the storage of certain goods?

The second set of questions relates to the nature of storage and to the functions of the centers. Are there correlations between the amount of residence space in a center and the size of its storage facility? How does storage relate to the political importance of a settlement? Documents frequently stress the military importance of storage. Does storage of food and other militarily important items occur in places that make them easily available in critical military situations? Finally, perhaps the most famous of all functions attributed to the storage network is its role in the public welfare. Were the storehouses indeed the repositories of a benevolent state with their goods distributed to the general populace in times either of famine affecting large numbers of people, or of personal misfortune involving individual households? Or was the storage network instead an instrument of the ruling elite in the maintenance of its power and domination?

In order to deal adequately with these many questions we need massive information based upon fieldwork on various geographic and sociopolitical segments of the far-flung system. Recent research confirms the existence of elaborate storage facilities in various parts of the Inka empire and gives some comparative information (see Chapter 3 for a review of Inka state storage sites). Only recently have data become available to indicate what was stored in such facilities. Especially important is our material from Huánuco Pampa, where site preservation and the availability of unusually detailed information recorded in early sixteenth-century documents provide data lacking for many other storage sites we surveyed. At some sites it is difficult even to distinguish Inka-period storehouses from those built earlier. It is thus not yet possible to answer many of the questions just raised, because their solutions depend as much on the contents of the *qollqa* as they do on the mere existence and size of warehousing facilities.

The individual storage houses, according to early documents, are called *qollqa* (Guaman Poma 1936 [1613]:335, 339, 369). We know these Inka qollqa best from the Peruvian Central Highlands where Delfín Zuñiga, my assistant, and I counted more than 2,000, made detailed measurements of about 800, and excavated 112. However, unless otherwise specified, the data reported here come mainly from the sites of Huánuco Pampa and Tunsukancha. The most productive excavations were in the site of Huánuco Pampa and the major data on storehouse use for this chapter come from that large, well-preserved center. Our knowledge of the use and significance of the storage facility at Huánuco Pampa is far better than that for any other center.

Excavation revealed important information on the kinds and quantities of goods stored there, and, equally important, we have relatively good control over the context in which the storage occurred. This is the result of excavations carried out in the settlement proper (outside the storage zone) and also of the excellent written data contained in the *visita* (inspection report) of Iñigo Ortiz (1967 [1562], 1972 [1562]) about part of the region that supplied the Huánuco Pampa storehouses.

Our surveys also identified, counted, and in some cases measured storehouses at (1) the *tampu* of Tunsukancha about 36 km south of Huánuco Pampa; (2) Pumpu, Tarmatambo, and Hatun Xauxa (for data on Pumpu, Tarmatambo, and Hatun Xauxa see Chapters 4, 6, and 9); (3) in the immediate vicinity of Cuzco; and (4) such coastal sites as Inkawasi in the Cañete Valley (later studied by Hyslop 1985 in more detail) and Tambo Colorado in the Pisco Valley. Excavations were undertaken only at Huánuco Pampa and Tunsukancha.

Before proceeding to some general comments on the nature of the storage network, it is necessary to summarize the pertinent evidence from those segments that my own research investigated. I am essentially omitting here the small amount of coastal evidence at hand. In addition to its meagerness, it would lead to a whole series of new questions that are best treated elsewhere.

HUANUCO PAMPA

The Inka administrative center is located on a small flat *pampa*, a high triangular-shaped plain about 140 km from modern Huánuco, the Peruvian departmental capital. The major subsistence base of Huánuco Pampa lay some distance away, as the 3,800 m elevation of the Inka center is too high for most crops. The ceramics found in several parts of the site suggest the varied groups supplying the center and indicate contact with various neighboring regions. However, the state's major provisionment in this region was dependent on the coordination of a variety of lands and resources in a broad hinterland.

The sustaining hinterland included at least the rich valleys of the Huallaga and the Marañón to the east and probably the Callejón de Huaylas (upper valley of the Santa River) to the west. References to the regular transport of food and other products to Huánuco Pampa, as well as to other state centers, are frequent in Iñigo Ortiz's interviews with the Chupaychu and the Yacha, two ethnic groups of the Huallaga Valley. Such groups at lower, more auspicious, altitudes for agriculture sustained the Inka center (Iñigo Ortiz 1967 [1562], 1972 [1562]).

During a series of 10 trips to Huánuco Pampa in 1964 and 1965, we spent a total of more than 5 months in survey, excavation, and mapping the site. The main section covers more than a square kilometer, and in addition the storehouses (Figure 5-1) much more sparsely cover about half that much area. The *usnu,* a large platform of well fitted cut stones, is set in an expansive open plaza about 550 m long. Extensive architectural remains are grouped along the four sides of this main plaza. East of the main plaza, many long rectangular structures surround unusually large open patios connected by gates of fine cut stone. Excavation in this area indicates that the eastern area of the site was probably the main administrative and ceremonial section, and also likely the residence of the administrative elite (Morris 1982; Morris and Thompson 1985).

An attempt was made to locate storage in the site proper, outside of the main depository zone. We investigated two groups of circular structures that were similar to storehouses in general shape. Sample excavations in these areas convinced us that the large scale and deliberate accumulation of goods was concentrated in the major depository zone on the hillside rising above the site to the south (Figure 5-2). Our major initial goal was to investigate the storage sector and to understand its functioning in relation to the site as a whole and especially to the broader state storage network.

1. *Architecture.* Our survey counted 497 probable storehouses in the main depository zone and 25 nonstorage structures. The 278 circular structures were numerically the predominant storehouse form at Huánuco Pampa and proved to be the only form for the storehouses at Tunsukancha. The form varied from an almost perfect

N

HUANUCO PAMPA

0 25 50 100 200
METERS

Figure 5-1. The Huánuco Pampa center.

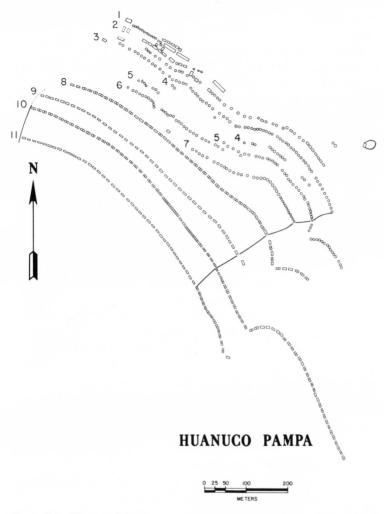

Figure 5-2. Closeup of the Huánuco Pampa storage complex.

circle to a roughly elliptical shape that was dependent on topographic peculiarities such as unusually steep slope or outcrops of rock. The interior diameter ranged from 2 to 6.3 m with four modes clustering around 2.7, 3.3, 4.3, and 5.0 m. Evidence for height is limited because only a small percentage of the structures have walls preserved to their original heights. The range in interior heights for those circular measured was from 3.2 to 3.45 m; the mean, 3.3 m.

The *pirka* masonry of the qollqa is of stones fractured on a vertical plane, and the stones reflect the use of locally available materials. The small doors and windows of these structures always open uphill to the southwest. The openings vary between 45 and 60 cm in width with a mean of 51 cm. Height varies between 55 and 70 cm with a mean of 63 cm. The slope of the hill affects door height; it varies between 70 and 135 cm above the storehouse floors.

The rectangular structures in the depository zone at Huánuco Pampa include 111 single-room, *less* well-preserved structures, and 132 multiroom structures containing a total of 186 rooms, where construction, and *therefore* preservation is better. Most multiroom structures have two almost equal rooms (one long structure has 14 rooms, another 12 rooms). The masonry of rectangular structures is similar to that for the circular structures described above. Interior widths of single-room structures vary from 2.5 to 3.4 m with a mean 3.1 m. Their lengths vary from about 7 to 10 m and cluster around 9.5 m. Major divergence from the 9.5 m mode can largely be explained by topographic features that affected structure size. The two windows preserved in single-room qollqa face downhill to the northeast. It seems likely on the basis of the preserved windows that these structures had four openings, two uphill and two downhill.

The width of multiroom structures varies from 3.5 to 4.9 m, and clusters around 4.5 m. However, the two long structures are only 2.5 and 2.8 m wide. Rooms within multiroom structures vary in length from 2.9 to 5.1 m and cluster around 4.6 m. Several of the better preserved structures have windows in both their north and south walls, and we assume that less well preserved walls had similar windows. The openings range in width from 47 to 57 cm with an average of 51 cm. Height ranges from 74 to 79 cm with an average of about 76 cm.

The small sample of completely preserved qollqa walls range in height from an average of 3.1 m, as mentioned above, for circular structures to 2.9 m for rectangular ones. Although no roofs are preserved, we presume they were made of straw as was the general Inka custom. The roofs of circular storehouses may well have been conical or hemispherical (see Guaman Poma 1936 [1613]:335) but, if so, excavations suggest they were without center supports. Rectangular qollqa probably had flat roofs that sloped slightly, being lower on the downhill side. We saw no examples of gabled roof storehouses in the Peruvian Central Highlands, though they do occur in the Cuzco region.

Floors of qollqa vary. Many have unmodified floors, with no evidence of alteration. In others, floors have been modified by the addition of earth to level the floor when the structure is built on a steep slope (see Figure 8-2, Chapter 8). Stone fill, usually a mixture of stone and earth, is also used for leveling. Some structures have had an additional level of small stones set in hard claylike earth added after the basic leveling was accomplished.

The more complex floors were found mainly in Row 10 (see Figure 8-3, Chapter 8), but no two of these floors were exactly alike. An association between more complex floor types and multiroom structures was noted. Such floors utilize a loose stone fill of irregular stones with no earth binding. The result is an "open" floor through which air or liquid can pass easily. This openness is enhanced further by the construction of from one to four canals (drains or vents) within the floor. Canals may exit either on the uphill or downhill side, and provision was made for closing these exits with stones. The openings in the foundation are usually coupled with small covered ditches. The open construction of the floor would support the stored goods, yet allow air, or possibly water, to circulate through the floor. Thus, as an alternative to ventilation, there is the possibility that water was added to increase humidity, or perhaps lower the temperature, without wetting the stored goods (see Chapter 8 for a more detailed discussion of floor drains and humidity control).

From the interior measurements and height approximation, it is possible to calculate maximum volume capacities. Maximum volume capacity of the zone of circular qollqa at Huánuco Pampa was calculated at approximately 14,300 m^3; for the zone of rectangular qollqa, 22,800 m^3. Of course these maximum volume capacities are in excess of the quantities of any goods actually stored, because containerization and provision for air circulation consumed substantial space. The figures, nevertheless, assist comparisons of various parts of the Inka system, and of Inka storage, with warehousing arrangements in other time periods and in other parts of the world.

2. *Organization.* The grouping of the rectangular structures into four rows was clear cut, but as the plan shows, the divisions of the circular structures was less orderly. Due to time limitations, 50 qollqa, a 10% sample, were chosen for excavation; later experience expanded this number to 95. However, the additional storehouses were chosen based on visible surface features and the promise of a greater amount of data being obtained, rather than by random sample. Circular structures yielded pottery, and the additional group chosen concentrated on the circular structures.

The organization of the storehouses suggests that patterns of use varied in terms of the location of the storehouses, or groups of storehouses, within the facility. Because architectural variation is also related to storehouse position, a pattern of differing uses of the major architectural forms also emerges. The depository zone may be divided into three main parts as suggested by these architectural groupings within which the major variation seems to occur on an essentially vertical axis. Rows 1 and 2, at the bottom of the hill, did not show a rigid pattern in either architectural arrangement (both rectangular and circular structures are present) or in the patterning of contents. It is not immediately apparent why this area is different. Possibly goods in lower, more convenient, rows were stored on a short-term basis for more immediate needs; or these stores ($800m^3$) may have been set aside for religious purposes. It is also possible that both of these kinds of storage could have been carried out in this area.

The remaining rows seem more rigidly planned both in terms of their architecture and their apparent use. Rows 3 through 7 contain all circular structures and Rows 8 through 11 contain all rectangular structures. Charred remains of tubers were found only in rectangular storehouses; maize (with one exception) was found in circular structures. These excavated findings suggest that the groupings have functional as well as spatial and architectural meaning as will be discussed.

We were not able to determine the function of all of the warehousing, but its overwhelming concern with food products seems indisputable. The only nonfood product we found was charcoal, and of course this might have been employed in cooking. There was, nevertheless, a series of circular qollqa with floor types that were never found in association with maize. The architectural characteristics of these qollqa are quite generalized and are not suggestive of special storage conditions or functions. Based on the association between foods found and the architecture with which they were related, it is likely that between 40 and 65% of the 37,900 cubic meters of space in the warehousing facility was devoted to the highland tubers. Between 5 and 7% was probably devoted to maize. The minimum percentages are based on parts of the facility for which functional determination is relatively secure. The larger percentages include storehouses whose function is only indirectly suggested by the data.

The function of at least 28% of the space in the qollqa is undetermined. Cieza (1862 [1551]; 1967 [1553]) and other sixteenth-century writers mention large quantities of cloth, military equipment and other nonsubsistence goods as part of the contents of Inka storehouses. There is no reason to doubt the accuracy of these accounts because such goods were produced in various sectors of the Inka economy and would have been needed in the state cities along the road system. It is possible that craft goods were stored in those types of storehouses for which we were not able to determine a function. Another possibility is that durable goods were stored in the city proper. They would not necessarily have benefitted by the slightly cooler temperatures on the hill. However, our research has so far not revealed any nonfood stores in the city, and my impression remains that the overwhelming emphasis in storage at Huánuco Pampa was on comestibles.

The grouping of storehouses of similar architectural types has been referred to above. Examination of the plan of the storage zone (Figure 5-2) shows that the major organizational feature is the distinction between the rows of circular qollqa low on the hill and four rows of rectangular ones higher up. This parallels the functional separation between tubers and maize elaborated above. But there are three other aspects of the arrangement of the zone that provide some indication of the organization and administration of storage. First it is noted that Row 2 contains rectangular structures as well as circular ones. Some of our best preserved stored tubers were found in Qollqa 2-38, confirming that at least some of the rectangular buildings in that row were used for tuber storage. I have suggested (Morris 1967) that this varied row at the foot of the hill comprised a somewhat separate and more accessible part of the facility maintained for temporary storage. This evidence is admittedly indirect, but it would seem more efficient to set aside a sector of the zone for short-term storage of goods scheduled for prompt disbursement.

A second notable feature of the arrangement of the facility is the occurrence on the western side of Rows 1 and 2 of an almost separate unit of qollqa where a row of rectangular storehouses is placed above a row of circular ones. This small subdivision is almost a microcosm of the zone as a whole. We encountered no evidence of what had been stored in these buildings, and it is not possible to specify the significance of the subdivision. This, too, could have served as short-term storage. It is also possible that it housed goods destined for purposes different from the other stores. Chroniclers frequently refer to storage for the Sun, apparently kept apart from that of the state—administratively if not physically. If there were stores set aside for the state-sponsored religion, they were very small in comparison with the remainder of the facility.

There is a small amount of storage with clearly defined purposes. Two smaller than usual circular qollqa in Row 2 are located on either side of a rectangular building (2-24). The rectangular building contained a ceramic complex, consisting mainly of plates and low bowls, typical of religious structures used for religious purposes and distinct from the ceramic forms associated with storage. One of the qollqa (2-25) was the only example in which several kinds of food were stored together. These structures demonstrate a relationship between storage and religion, but they are likely a purely local manifestation related to the city or simply to the qollqa hill. The stores were not large enough to be part of the support for a large, statewide Inka religion.

A third important aspect of the layout of the facility is the group of nonstorage structures at the northern edge of the storage zone. It is not possible to determine the exact function of the structures in most cases, but as a group they almost certainly served the administration of the zone, and some may have been related to prestorage processing, packing and unpacking. Structures A-24 through A-29 (see Figure 5-2) appear to have been residential. For example, the ceramics compare interestingly with ceramics recovered from obvious residential contexts in the main part of the site. There was storage-type ceramics within these nonstorage structures, and the overall quality of the ceramics tended to be higher than in residential structures excavated elsewhere in the site (Morris 1967:129–31). These structures may have housed storage administrators.

To the west of Structure A-17 are groups of low steps and a slightly sloping ramp. These appear to have formed a formal entrance to the complex. The long Building A-17 contained 10,963 sherds of pottery, almost all of it from the type of jars associated with maize storage. Such a large quantity of jars suggests that they may have been used for packing maize (and perhaps some other goods) in the state's vessels. Buildings A-21 and A-22 contained fewer sherds, representing a less homogeneous group of pots and jars. Although there seems little doubt that these last two structures had some relation to storage administration, it is not possible to suggest the exact nature of the activities within them.

The importance of food storage at Huánuco Pampa is demonstrated both by its quantity and the substantial effort that went into operations of the facility. Storage was one of the major activities within the site. More than 12% of the approximately 4,000 structures of which the city originally consisted are qollqa. The percentage of covered floor space devoted to storage is only slightly less. Our tentative estimates of the housing capacity of the center indicate that as many as 12,000 to 15,000 people might have been housed there, although the actual population at any given time probably fluctuated considerably (Morris and Thompson 1970, 1985; Morris 1972a). Using this estimate, the ratio of storage space to housing capacity is approximately 2.0 to 2.5 cubic meters per person—allowing for 25% unused space in the storehouses due to room taken by containers, packing materials, and the like. This does not sound particularly high until we realize that 1.6 cubic meters is adequate to store a metric ton of potatoes (Burton 1966:287).

The scope and methods of food storage at Huánuco Pampa are thus relatively clear. So, too, is the source of the food. Because there is no firm evidence of intensive food production adjacent to the center, most of the food must have been brought from other areas, and the *visita* of Iñigo Ortiz (1967 [1562], 1972 [1562]) is filled with statements of how goods were carried several days from Yacha and Chupaychu villages.

The deployment of thousands of tons of stored food is far less clear. There is little evidence, either archaeological or written, of a movement of goods from the storehouses out into the hinterland. The only substantial archaeological evidence of a close tie to Huánuco Pampa was found in the Chupaychu capital of Ichu where Cuzco-style Inka sherds of Huánuco Pampa varieties were numerous. But of course foodstuffs would not necessarily have been accompanied by state pottery. And in any case Inka disbursements might have been funneled through the local capital. In his numerous references to goods being carried to the Huánuco Pampa storehouses, Iñigo Ortiz does not mention goods being carried from the storehouses back into the countryside. This may in large part be the result of the nature of the questionnaire on which the *visita* is based, but it seems likely that the receipt of goods by the local towns would be noted if it had been of real economic importance.

The size of Huánuco Pampa, its functions in terms of servicing travelers and state personnel and its isolation from rich food-producing regions all suggest a pressing need for stored food. In many respects, the storage capacities seem large in relation to the probable number of people usually in the center, but some of the stores were probably used as a guarantee of long-term security, beyond merely keeping the center supplied from harvest to harvest. Although some of the food may well have been transferred to other centers, particularly other centers along the road system, I am convinced that the great bulk of it was used to maintain state operations and that most of it was intended for use in Huánuco Pampa itself.

TUNSUKANCHA

The site of Tunsukancha is located about 36 km south of Huánuco, on a high *puna* at almost 4,000 m elevation. Figure 5-3 shows the 24 small, circular qollqa and their relation to the remainder of the site. The storehouses are located on a small rise on the eastern edge of the site at an elevation slightly higher than the main body of the site. The average diameter of the storehouse structures is 3.5 meters, and their total volume capacity is slightly less than 400 m^3. The volume is calculated using the height of similar storehouses at Huánuco Pampa because none of the Tunsukancha qollqa are preserved to their original heights. Remaining walls are also too low to determine door or window position.

The evidence from Tunsukancha gives only a partial picture of

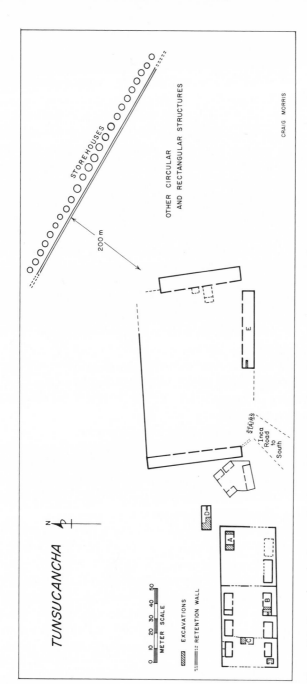

Figure 5-3. Tunsukancha *tampu*: the site and its associated storehouses.

storage in a Central Highland *tampu*. We excavated 12 of the storehouses, but post-Conquest disturbance in several of them made associations questionable, and we found but a single kernel of corn as direct evidence of what might have been stored. The architecture of the storehouses and the relatively small amount of pottery recovered, however, are sufficient to suggest a contrast with Huánuco Pampa. In addition to the very obvious difference in the sizes of the two storage facilities, the storehouses are homogeneous in terms of architecture, and the ceramics they contained do not suggest the functional specialization that is such an important aspect of storage at Huánuco Pampa. The floor was a quite simple one and was not associated with openings in the base of the wall. However, the sherds found were from the same form of jars used for maize storage at the administrative center, although they were smaller in size. This suggests a similar specialization of storage ceramics.

The basically uniform nature of both the architecture and the artifact contents of the Tunsukancha qollqa implies an absence of the complicated internal differentiation present in the Huánuco Pampa warehousing zone. I suspect that specific qollqa were not reserved for specific goods and that all storage was essentially short-term. There is neither the space nor the administrative facilities to cope with long-term storage.

Two items of information suggest that storage administration at Tunsukancha may have been directly subordinate to Huánuco Pampa. First, the pottery in the two centers is of the same materials and techniques and came from the same sources. Because the ceramics were made either by or for the state, this identity of material suggests a direct administrative relationship. Other large centers such as Pumpu and Hatun Xauxa used local versions, in imitation of Cuzco ceramics. Perhaps even more important is the lack of reference in the *visita* of Iñigo Ortiz to the carrying of food to Tunsukancha. Goods were carried to Huánuco Pampa, Pumpu, and even Cuzco, but the small *tampu* located along the Inka road are not mentioned. Of course the much smaller depository at Tunsukancha might have been supplied from sources closer at hand and outside the area covered by Iñigo Ortiz. But there is also the possibility that its supplies were channeled through Huánuco Pampa.

Our general information on the nature of Tunsukancha as a whole is based on a very brief study (Morris 1966). For example, a complete building count is not available. The site includes a fairly extensive zone of small circular and rectangular residential structures as well as long buildings probably for housing travelers, and a compound that may have been a combination of elite housing and temporary quarters for the traveling nobility. The total number of structures must have been somewhere between 200 and 400, not including the storehouses.

Whatever the precise ratio between residence space and storage space may have been, it is readily apparent that storage capacity at Tunsukancha was minuscule in comparison to Huánuco Pampa. The slightly less than 400 cubic meters at Tunsukancha is barely 1% of the capacity at the larger center. The housing capacity of the *tampu*, in contrast, must have been at least 5 to 10% of that at the administrative center. In terms of servicing travelers moving about the empire, however, the burden on the small *tampu* would have been almost as great as that on the larger centers that occasionally replaced them on the road. The differences in the sizes of stored resources in the two centers is then due to something other than their necessity to supply the needs of transients along the road. Two sets of factors seem largely to explain the differences. First the larger centers had to support many more people and a much greater range of activities. Second, only the larger establishments were set up as long-term storage centers.

CUZCO

Having seen the efforts to which the Inka went to provide extensive storage facilities in their centers of provincial administration, we would naturally expect the capital and homeland of the ruling elite to be endowed with even greater and more richly-filled depositories. The amazement of the Spanish when they first entered Cuzco demonstrates that the stores were indeed lavish. Pedro Pizarro (1965 [1571]:191) observes that the storehouses in the valley were a wonder, and to all it seemed impossible to gather so much together. Sancho (1917 [1532–33]:194–95) continues:

> All of the fortress of Sacsayhuaman was a warehouse of arms, clubs, lances, bows, arrows, axes, shields, strong jackets padded with cotton and other arms of diverse types, and clothing for soldiers assembled here

from all parts of the land subject to the Lords of Cuzco. . . . [F]rom this fortress many houses can be seen around the city . . . and many of them are for the pleasure and relaxation of the former lords, and others for the *caciques* from all the land who are continually residents of the city: The others are houses or storehouses full of textiles, wool, arms, metal and clothes, and of all things grown and made in their land. There are storehouses where the tributes brought by the vassals to the lords are kept, and there is a house in which are kept more than one hundred thousand dried birds, because clothing is made from their feathers that are of many colors, and there are many houses for that. There are bucklers and shields, beams for roofing, knives, and other tools. [There are] sandals and breastplates to provision the soldiers, in such quantity that reason is inadequate to understand how they could give such great tribute of so many and such diverse things. [author's translation][1]

Unlike the provincial centers just discussed, where many of the storehouses have remained for more than 400 years for us to see and measure, the city of Cuzco has left little material evidence of its once-rich stores. There are shreds of evidence that suggest where some of the qollqa were, but they cannot tell us of their number, size, nature of constructions, or contents.

In 1966, during a brief survey of some of the hills around Cuzco, we found outcrops of the foundations of buildings with Inka pottery on the surface. There was evidence also that the floors of some of the buildings had been made with a filling of loose stones, in a manner somewhat reminiscent of Huánuco Pampa. Most of the sherds were from the very large *aryballoid* vessels we associate with storage. This evidence was especially common to the north-northwest of the city, low down on hills then covered with eucalyptus trees. Somewhat more positive evidence is noted by Rowe (1967:66) at Qhata-q'asa on a hill south of Belen, where he measured square and rectangular storehouses of about 6 × 6 meters and 6 × 7.5 meters, respectively. We also measured a storage site, pointed out to us by John H. Rowe, above the modern town of San Sebastian about 5 kilometers from the center of Cuzco. The storehouses there were located on a slope similar to storehouse positions in the Central Highlands, but they are quite different in architectural type with multiple doors on the downhill side reaching almost to the floor. The maximum capacity of these buildings is slightly less than 2,500 cubic meters. Oscar Núñez del Prado (1950) describes storehouses similar to these from the site of

Raqchi near Chincheros northwest of Cuzco. Many of the sherds found by Núñez del Prado at Raqchi were of the Killke series. This suggests that storehouses of this type may be earlier than the smaller circular and rectangular structures described above. It also suggests that the Inka either altered their storehouse architecture in general as the empire expanded or that significant regional variation was introduced.

The storehouses near San Sebastian are situated directly across a small quebrada from a residential site. This might lead us to conclude that the storehouses were under the control of the residents of that site. Such an interpretation, however, would not necessarily be valid. The distinction between the state centers along the royal highways and the local villages pertaining to non-Inka ethnic groups is much less marked here. The control of the state probably extended down to a much lower political level in the area near the capital. Garcilaso (1960 [1604]:t. ii, p. 80) refers to a "distrito de la corte" around Cuzco, and Rowe's (1967) analysis of the written and archaeological sources suggests a dispersed but organizationally linked set of settlements surrounding a puma-shaped center. Thus storage dispersed at many different points throughout the region may have been coordinated for the provision of the capital zone as a whole.

Our only other archaeological evidence of storage in the general Cuzco region comes from the site of Ollantaytampu. There, several long multidoored storage structures cling to the very steep hills opposite the major body of the ruins. We measured only one of the difficult-to-reach buildings, and from that estimated very roughly their total storage capacity at 2,000 to 3,000 cubic meters.

Except for Ollantaytampu in the Urubamba Valley 40 km northwest of Cuzco and the site above San Sebastian we do not have even rough estimates of storage capacity to compare with other Inka centers. Thus the question of the quantitative importance of Cuzco in the overall storage network cannot be answered. But I think we might be incorrect in assuming that simply because Cuzco was the capital and most important center in the realm that it would automatically have the largest food stores. If food stores were directly related to a center's importance, we would expect Cuzco to possess at least a few thousand qollqa. Has the destruction of the city and the erosion of surrounding hills really destroyed such a massive number of storage chambers, which, because of their location, frequently survive even when other architecture is wiped out?

Of course it can be only an hypothesis, but I doubt that food storage in Cuzco was as great in comparison to its importance and population as in many provincial centers. I would certainly expect it to have been substantial, but several factors may have reduced the need for massive food storage to provide security for the capital. The most important of these is Cuzco's location near the Urubamba Valley where warm *kechwa* slopes had been transformed by terracing and irrigation into what must have been one of the most productive regions of Tawantinsuyu. The terraces at Pisaq and Yucay, where many of the royal fields were supposedly located, demonstrate a different technological approach to secure a subsistence base. With production increased and made less subject to seasonal variations, storage, particularly long-term protection against crop failure, would have become less vital. There is also the factor of political stability. The state was dependent on the loyalty of the work force that cultivated its fields and delivered the goods to centers of state operations. Political problems that would have interfered with smooth production and delivery were probably relatively rare around the capital itself, whereas in newly conquered and still lightly held areas it was likely a different matter. Finally, there is the relationship between storage and the expansion of the state. One would expect storage to be more important near the frontiers of expansion than in the stabilized heart of the kingdom. On the one hand, the demands upon the state to supply armies and to support construction projects and other activities of political and economic expansion would have been great. On the other hand, local mechanisms of production and delivery would not have been fully set up.

The emphasis by the Spanish observers on nonsubsistence goods in their descriptions of the Cuzco warehouses may be the result of being already jaded by the sight of thousands of food storehouses as they traveled down the Inka state road known as *capac ñan* on their way to the capital, and of course Sancho, as quoted above, does say that there were warehouses "de todas las cosas que se crian y fabrican en esta tierra." But if their observations are an accurate reflection of what the stores of Cuzco largely comprised, then we may have both a partial confirmation of a deemphasis on food storage in Cuzco as well as the suggestion of another important characteristic of the state storage network. As I have indicated earlier in more detail (Morris 1967), the storage of certain classes of luxury goods may have been concentrated in Cuzco. Not only was food less necessary, but goods such as cloth, feathers, and other items that figure importantly in state gifts and in supporting the elite were stored in abundance. The emphasis of the Cuzco warehouses may have rested on items of special significance in the system of political reciprocity. These were already items of great value, but their value was further increased if they came from the Inka and his storehouses at Cuzco. Thus, besides supplying the royal court with luxury goods, such items were brought to Cuzco so that they could flow out from the capital in a classic pattern of redistribution to those people and parts of the realm that were essential to the state's goals of expansion and control. This suggestion would explain the remarks of the eyewitness observers of Cuzco and is also supported by written evidence from the provinces. Iñigo Ortiz in his visita of Huánuco (1967 [1562], 1972 [1562]) mentions only maize as a subsistence good taken to Cuzco, and that only rarely. Cloth, however, is frequently taken to the capital. The pattern is clear: Subsistence goods by and large go to provincial administrative centers a few days distant; luxury goods frequently go all the way to Cuzco. Subsistence and certain nonsubsistence goods seem to have constituted distinct classes of products that flowed through the storage network in somewhat different ways. The pattern is much like what Manning Nash (1966) has described as distinct "circuits of exchange."

SUMMARY

Perhaps the most important features of the Inka storage network were its sheer size and its geographic extent. We shall never know precisely its total capacity, but my 1967 (p. 155) estimate of between 1 and 2 million cubic meters is probably conservative. Connected by well-maintained roads, the various segments of the storage system constituted a remarkable achievement in the deployment of goods where they were needed, when they were needed. Many of the questions posed at the outset of this section about the storage network cannot be answered satisfactorily. A few observations on the locations and sizes of the nodes and the movements of goods within the network as a whole are nevertheless worth summarizing.

My original analysis of highland Inka storage indicated that two major variables determined the location and size of food storage facilities. One of these was need in the locale in question—defined largely in terms of the state's requirements for supporting communication, military operations and perhaps most of all, the hospitality demands of reciprocal obligations. The other was the ability of the region to supply and resupply itself reliably. We have very little data on state storage on the coast. The minimal information available suggests that strictly Inka (state) storage on the coast was also related to the interaction between local state needs and the reliability, whether for ecological or political reasons, of local supplies. The site where Inka storage is most in evidence near the coast is Inkawasi (Hyslop 1985:14–15, 31) a site with probable military functions in an area of insecure supply. Tambo Colorado, an Inka site in the Pisco Valley has storage facilities. To my knowledge they have not been studied, but they seem more like those of highland *tampu,* designed for short-term supply in conditions where resupply was not problematic. Another site with an important Inka presence is La Centinela in the Chincha Valley. It has almost no evidence of Inka storage in the site proper (Morris and Santillana n.d.), although there are a few possible Inka storehouses several kilometers upvalley. Food production in the Chincha Valley was bountiful, and political relations with the local polity were apparently direct and secure.

A second set of variables potentially related to the size and distribution of storehouses are associated with production rather than consumption. Areas of heavy agricultural production are likely to require large storage facilities, particularly if that production is intended for use far away and if the transportation system that moves it is scheduled irregularly. One of the largest preserved Inka warehousing facilities probably owes its size and location to an association with state-managed agricultural production. Although not systematically studied, the site of Cotapachi, near Cochabamba, Bolivia, is said to have the foundations of more than 2,000 storehouses (Byrne de Caballero 1974; Hyslop 1984:289). There the Inka had moved in workers from other regions to cultivate maize at least in part for transhipment to Cuzco (Wachtel 1982:214).

On the matter of movement of goods from one segment of the storage network to another, there is the feeling that at least certain *tampu* centers were supplied through larger administrative centers rather than having goods come to them directly. There is no real evidence, however, that goods were regularly moved back and forth between one major center and another. The archaeological evidence is not such that it would easily shed light on the question, but certainly we do not find large quantities of Hatun Xauxa or Pumpu sherds in Huánuco Pampa. Such movements would likely have been necessary in case of severe, localized famine. Garcilaso (1960 [1604]:t. ii, p. 80) at least implies that state stores were tapped in times of crisis, although he says the storehouses intended to give help in case of scarcity were located in the villages themselves, and if our analysis is correct, these "village" storehouses would probably not have been under direct state control in most of Tawantinsuyu. We know that goods occasionally went to Cuzco from the Huánuco region via Huánuco Pampa or Pumpu (Ortiz 1972 [1562]:38), but this may have been largely for record-keeping purposes and the control of traffic on the royal road. My impression is that, in general, each major storage center was set up to supply itself and to a limited extent its own hinterland and that transport of goods from one major center to another was more the exception than the rule (Cotapachi, just referred to, was probably such an exception). If this was the case, the network would not have been heavily involved in evening out ecological differences between regions. Each administrative center, however, probably had access to certain regions that provided various kinds of food so that regular movements between major centers would have been necessary only if it were considered important to have the proportions of various goods roughly the same throughout the realm. Although some amounts of such goods as maize were probably needed everywhere, we have seen no information that suggests that any absolute evenness of distribution of food or other items was sought.

Related to the issue of the movement of goods from center to center is the question of variations in the proportions of certain goods among different segments of the network. If the functional associations of rectangular and circular storehouses at Huánuco Pampa should apply at such centers as Pumpu, Tarmatambo, and Hatun Xauxa, there is indeed an indication that the kinds of goods stored varied from center to center and that the variation may have been related, in part, to the altitude of the storehouses and suitability of the surrounding areas to different crops (see Chapter 4). Given the storage and production requirements of the tubers and of maize, such variations in stored quantities would be reasonable. However, this does not necessarily mean that the goods were regularly shifted from one center to another to achieve a balance.

THE FUNCTION OF FOOD STORAGE

The obvious function of food storage is that it evens out a society's food supplies so that they are more uniformly or appropriately distributed through time and space. It is the low point in the cycle of availability of food that sets limits on the population of a group (and perhaps also on other aspects of its potential development) not the high point or season of maximum productivity. Storage can bridge the disjunction between these points in time, whether they be from one harvest to the next or through lean years on a longer time scale. In the case of large-scale societies, the bridging of spatial disjunctions is almost as important as the bridging of temporal ones. Communication and administration must be maintained across large areas, regardless of the kinds and quantities of products naturally available in them. Storage is almost always a vital part of the establishment and maintenance of the administrative system and its communication links.

The Inka food storage system was probably a significant factor in the maintenance of a high and stable population. Even if there was no general distribution to the populace from the state's stores in times of hardship, more subtle mechanisms of moving people temporarily into state centers or otherwise assigning them to state chores that would entitle them to eat from the Inka's larder could have effectively and productively taken up the slack. Certainly there is no doubting the role of storage in sustaining the elite and the network of administration and communication.

The implications of storage do not end with their purely practical effects. There is not space here to give the topic the thorough examination it deserves, but a storage system like that of the Inka represents an enormous accumulation of wealth that cannot help but have ramifications beyond the sheer number of people it can supply. If wealth enhances power, then the Inka had only to worry about their ability to continue in control of the masses they had accumulated. But the issues are more subtle; in what the wealth consists and how and where it is deployed are more important than its simple quantity. Many of these critical subtleties will never be known for the Inka system, but it appears that just as food was supplied where food was needed, certain politically meaningful goods were frequently redistributed from Cuzco itself, with their effectiveness thereby enhanced.

A warehousing system such as that documented in this chapter does not emerge full-blown as the result of the command of some powerful and brilliant ruler. The sophistication of its environmental understandings are too great and its organizational scope too vast. It can only be the product of long development processes and can only be understood in terms of the larger patterns of technology and organization from which various aspects of the storage system were drawn.

Some of the principles that underlay both the state centers and the storage network were outgrowths of traditional approaches to the management of the highland Andean ecology: People and goods were moved from one zone to another, as a matter of course; a great variety of ecological floors was understood by each group—a much wider understanding than would be likely in a system based on trading among specialized groups rather than direct management of multiple zones; there was a spatial and territorial perspective that viewed the ecological, political, and economic worlds as widely extended entities not bounded by the physical lines of a single settlement or region. The food storage system was not only made possible by these principles, it is a good point from which to observe them in operation.

ACKNOWLEDGMENTS

Much of the material in this chapter was written in 1976 and published in 1981 as part of "Tecnología y Organización Inca del Almacenamiento de Víveres en La Sierra," in *Runakunap Kawsayninkupaq Rurasqankunaqa: La Tecnología en el Mundo Andino*, edited by Heather Lechtman and Ana María Soldi. Most of the information was originally collected for my 1964 Ph.D. dissertation, "Storage in Tawantinsuyu." I am grateful to the National Science Foundation, the Wenner-Gren Foundation, and the National Geographic Society for support of various aspects of the research and to Delfín Zúñiga D. who was my assistant and collaborator in much of the research.

CHAPTER 6

Inka Storage Facilities in the
Upper Mantaro Valley, Peru

TERENCE N. D'ALTROY AND TIMOTHY K. EARLE

UPON entering the broad Upper Mantaro Valley in the Central Highlands of Peru, the visitor is struck by the sight of numerous storehouses standing prominently on the naked hills. Storage structures
cover the knolls just above the Inka administrative center of Hatun
Xauxa, and many more dot the hill slopes and crests extending south
along the valley. Nothing demonstrates the Inka domination of the
Central Highlands as clearly as these Mantaro storage sites.

The Inka conquests created a need for an economic support system
that could sustain imperial personnel and underwrite political relations between the state and its subordinates. This need was met
through two interlocking components of the imperial political economy: a staple finance economy and an associated system that produced prestige or wealth support (see Chapter 2). Both entailed
production, exchange, and storage of the resources used to finance
the state institutions. This chapter describes and analyzes the organization and distribution of Inka storage sites within the Mantaro Valley
to delimit the economic integration of this strategic central valley into
the Inka empire.

STORAGE AND THE ORGANIZATION OF THE INKA
POLITICAL ECONOMY

The sierra societies upon which the state depended for its early model
tended to be generalized in subsistence production. The *ayllu* formed
the basic resource-holding unit in the central Andes. Ranging up to
several thousand members, the *ayllu* held lands communally, allocating them through usufruct. The basic principle underlying access
to resources was that one held rights to agricultural land, pastoral
grasslands, water, and other critical resources through membership
in the kin group. The community's elite (*kuraka*) had rights to have
their lands worked, herds tended, and some craft products manufac-

tured. In return for this, the elites were responsible for adjudicating disputes, for providing military and ceremonial leadership, and for providing ceremonial hospitality. The ideology propounded throughout the Andes was that this was a relationship of reciprocal obligations (Wachtel 1977).

The ideal *ayllu* territory recorded in the early documents encompassed diverse ecological zones. As sketched out by Murra (1972), sierra community members resided in settlements distributed through their territory, pooling and exchanging resources internally. The principal village would normally be located near the ecotone between the maize and tuber lands, whereas satellite settlements would be located from the high *puna* down to the upper edge of the jungle. Murra has suggested that communities could also establish small settlements at points of specialized productivity, such as in zones favorable to coca cultivation or salt collection. Although solid evidence exists for the establishment of such vertical archipelagos under Inka rule, especially along the eastern slopes, widespread hostilities throughout the Andes immediately preceding the imperial expansion would have made such an arrangement of multiethnic resource sharing highly unlikely in the pre-Inka period.

Upon conquering a region, the state appropriated rights to all resources within the subject territory. In exchange for corvée labor (*mit'a*), the state allocated access to productive agricultural and pastoral lands back to the communities but retained a state monopoly over many wild and mineral resources notably metals. In practice, communities retained a high proportion of their original resources, but yielded prime land.

Members of the local communities were required to perform myriad duties for the state. In 1549 and 1562, for instance, members of the Chupachu ethnic group of the Huánuco region reported having fulfilled 31 separate duties for the Inkas. Among these were generalized agricultural production; construction near the home communities, at provincial centers, or at Cuzco; mining gold and silver; performing guard duty in locations ranging from Quito to Cuzco; growing coca and peppers; collecting feathers and honey from the lowlands; tending state herds; and manufacturing sandals, pottery, and wooden objects (Helmer 1955–56; Ortiz de Zúñiga 1967, 1972; see Julien 1982, 1988; LeVine 1987). Each assignment was allocated according to the population size and particular resources of a region. In return for their efforts, the laborers were entitled to be supported with food and *chicha* while they were carrying out state directives. Other rights included the annual distribution of sandals and a new set of clothing to soldiers.

Most recent authors who have addressed the nature of the Inka political economy have followed either a substantive or a marxist economic perspective. The former, derived initially from the writing of Karl Polanyi (especially 1957) and elaborated through the influential work of John Murra (e.g., 1975, 1980), subscribes to the premise that economic relations were embedded in the sociopolitical matrix. This perspective assumes that the nature and development of economic relations are specific to the society within which they occur. Many studies of the Inka economy thus concern how economic processes, such as production and exchange, were undertaken in contexts peculiar to a given historical circumstance. The values, motives, and policies of Andean societies are taken to have determined economically rational behavior. From this view, the processes that contributed to economic developments are comparable across societies only to the extent that the social and political contexts, the motivations, and values were comparable.

Two substantivist economic notions receiving great attention in the Andean literature derive from Polanyi's (1957:128) classifications of exchange into reciprocity, redistribution, and (market) exchange. In Andean studies, *reciprocity* is generally taken to imply an obligatory relationship of exchange defined by social or political relationships. It has been applied to varied contexts, among them simple dyadic exchanges between members of social groups occupying zones that produced specialized cultivated or gathered subsistence crops. Examples of this kind of reciprocity are found in the exchange of salt and maize among the Chinchaycocha and Wanka societies (e.g., Vega 1965:171) and coca and *ch'arki* (dried meat) between *montaña* and *puna* societies. *Asymmetrical reciprocity* is taken to be the fundamental form of political exchange that characterized relationships between native elites and commoner populations throughout the Andes in late prehistory (e.g., Wachtel 1977:62–75). This relationship, often described in structural terms, consisted of mutual obligations between the elite stratum of society and the subject groups that supported them. In this relationship, the elites received labor and material support, in return for which they provided political, economic, and religious leadership, and, more materially, food, *chicha* (maize beer), and various material goods. Although these exchanges were consistently couched in terms of mutual responsibilities, it does not take a very jaundiced eye to see this relationship as exploitative.

Redistribution in the literature on the Inka and subject economies is seen as constructed on principles of *asymmetrical reciprocity*. As originally proposed by Polanyi (1957:128), redistribution referred simply to "appropriational movements towards a center and out of it again." Murra (1980) initially posited that the Inka state economy functioned as a redistributive agency, taking in the goods produced through the labor of subject populations and reallocating them to the people who performed the labor, after a cut was taken out to support the state apparatus. Although he disavowed Garcilaso's (1960) notion of Tawantinsuyu as a welfare state, Murra viewed the production, storage, and distribution cycle of the political economy as a substitute for a market system. In later writings, especially following the research of Morris (1967), Murra reconsidered this position, but the notion of redistribution as the organizing feature of the Inka and other political economies remains a dominant element in the Andean literature.

Evaluations of redistribution subsequent to the original postulations have shown that the term encompasses several kinds of economic relations. Mobilization, the type of redistribution most characteristic of chiefdoms and states, is essentially a form of political finance, whereby labor and goods are extracted from a subject populace to support the elite sector of society and its associated personnel, such as craft specialists and functionaries (Earle 1977, 1978; Earle and D'Altroy 1982; D'Altroy and Earle 1985). Relatively few of the goods that reach the center ever find their way back down the line, and those that do are exchanged in political and ceremonial contexts. Mobilization thus does not serve as a means of providing the basic subsistence needs of the general populace analogous to reciprocity or market exchange; rather redistributional mobilization provides the support base for political institutions.

Marxist analyses of the Inka economy focus on such issues as inequalities of class, social relations of production, and central control of productive resources. The state is said to derive from class conflict over access to the means of production (Godelier 1977; Lumbreras 1978). It is difficult to understand this perspective, given that Inka society was probably not class-differentiated until military conquests established the need for more complex administrative structures. A more useful element of the marxist approach has been the focus on control of peasant labor by the elite stratum (e.g., Espinoza 1975). A number of analysts (Earle 1987) have drawn attention to the central change in the social relations of production in the Inka economy— from the state's dependence on the corvée labor of the peasantry to the development of independent institutions of attached specialization. This transition was detailed first by Murra (1980), in his seminal dissertation on the Inka economy, but the marxist view offers an alternative perspective. By emphasizing the exploitative aspects of the relationship, rather than the integrative aspects of traditional institutions, the marxists draw attention to the increasing class differentiation that the elites were fostering within the empire.

Although these perspectives provide significant insight into the Inka political economy, they must be extended by evaluating the criteria underlying the shifts in institutional relations developed under state auspices, particularly in latter decades of Inka rule. Given that the state economy developed new institutions of production that differed substantially from existing forms, it is reasonable to ask if the new economic processes or relations were essentially extensions of existing forms or if they represented significant transformations. Wachtel (1977) and Murra (1980) have argued that the Inka political economy can be seen as a local or regional economy expanded to encompass the empire. Conversely, it is clear that the Inkas were transforming relations of production from dependence on corvée labor to development of specialized labor classes. Such variables as the energetics of different forms of production, transportation costs, and the relative security of differing strategies are particularly significant here (D'Altroy 1992). If it can be shown that the new forms of economic activity and institutions created by the state or transformed from prior models were significantly more efficient than those that preceded them, it may reasonably be postulated that the development of the state economy resulted from a calculated interplay between sociopolitical and energetic considerations.

Building on these perspectives, we may conceive of the Inka economy as a nonmarket, central-place, dendritic system (D'Altroy 1992). This structure was characterized by strong vertical ties and few, if any, horizontal exchanges (see Schaedel 1978). Regions were integrated with one another primarily through mutual ties with higher levels in the hierarchy. It is appropriate to a system in which economic interactions were largely structured around political relationships and in which the political economy functioned to extract resources from a region whose economy it did not control directly, as was often the case in archaic empires.

Because markets did not exist in most Inka territories and because, as Smith suggests (1976:323), commercial integration would have eroded the elites' power base, the lack of market development under Inka rule is not surprising (Earle 1985). The Inkas themselves neither were market-oriented nor had the power to control or effectively tap into an economy organized along those lines among subject populations. It is noteworthy that the Inkas took little advantage of the exchange economies of the north and central coasts of Peru (Netherly 1978; Ramírez Horton 1981) and may have suppressed market systems to some degree in the highlands of Ecuador, by pooling control of regional exchange under sanctioned elites (Salomon 1986). Even with a broad interregional peace established by the Inka, exchange did not increase following conquest of the Central Highlands (Earle 1985).

The state economy was designed to channel natural resources and their products upward, mobilizing support for the sociopolitical institutions. It did not provide a means of circulating goods among specialized subsystems of the general populace, nor did it serve as a surrogate market. Because the economy was designed as an extractive system, the flow of goods was heavily weighted in the upward direction. Food and craft goods produced for the state were bulked at central places, where they were consumed by state personnel or redirected to support state activities elsewhere. Storage facilities were the visible side of this mobilization.

State storage played a pivotal role in the management of the Inka political economy. Polanyi (1957) first drew attention to the systematic relationship between mass mobilization and storage in staple finance systems. In his argument, nonmarket state economies extract goods from the general populace through labor obligations or through production of specific goods by commoners attached to the state. Murra (1980) adapted this argument to interpret Inka storage, arguing that goods were mobilized from the local populace through corvée labor to finance state activities at Cuzco and in the provinces. Goods kept in storage were used principally to support administrative and religious personnel, the military, specialists attached to the state, and corvée laborers.

The chroniclers considered military support to be the primary use for the goods stockpiled in state storehouses (see Murra 1980:42, 128). Although the conquistadors' views were often colored by their profession, they were on the mark here. The Inkas also reckoned the magazines to be an important military target, as they attempted to destroy all stores as they retreated before the Spanish advance (e.g., Sancho 1917:141).

Under circumstances of uneven supply, poor transportation, and partially stochastic demand, the most effective solution to ensure support for state need was to develop resources throughout the empire for local storage in state-controlled facilities (see Chapter 2). According to one oral tradition, the Inka state storage system originated in the mid-fifteenth century, when Pachacutec ordered facilities built to expedite constructing Cuzco (Betanzos 1880:75, 77). Additional storehouses were built at provincial centers and at roadside waystations with the expansion and consolidation of the empire over the following century. The resulting multilevel system elicited admiring comments from the Spaniards, who enthusiastically appropriated the stored goods during the early years of their conquest.

The systematic association of storage complexes with provincial centers was recounted by several chroniclers (e.g., Cobo 1956:bk. II:114), some of whom mentioned Hatun Xauxa specifically (e.g., Sancho 1917:141; Castro y Ortega Morejón 1936:244). Cieza (1967:xii:37) and Polo (1917:77) who visited the Mantaro about 15 years after the first Spanish arrival, expressed admiration for the storage system, which was still functioning, despite the demise of Inka power in the valley. Of the documentary sources, the Wanka petitions of 1558–1561 based on *khipu* records (Espinoza 1971) have been especially useful for evaluating state storage because of their detailed lists of stockpiled goods appropriated by the Spaniards (see also LeVine 1979:99–105; Earle et al. 1980:36–37; D'Altroy 1981:466–71).

With the preceding discussion setting the broader context for the regional focus of this chapter, we may now turn to the Upper Mantaro region to examine storage, one aspect of the state's political economy.

THE MANTARO VALLEY IN LATE PREHISTORY

The Mantaro Valley is a high intermontane valley in the Central Highlands of Peru. Our research area in the Mantaro has concentrated on the region surrounding the modern town of Jauja (Earle et al. 1980; Earle et al. 1987). This region includes the broad, main Mantaro Valley, several tributary and isolated valleys, and the surrounding uplands. Three dominant economic zones characterize the Jauja region: (a) the alluvial bottomlands of the main and side valleys (3,300–3,400 m), which were farmed intensively for cereal crops including maize and *quinoa*; (b) the rolling upland soils (3,400–3,800 m), ringing the lower valleys, which were farmed extensively especially for potatoes; and (c) the high grasslands of the surrounding ridges and plateaus (3,800–4,400 m), which were used extensively for grazing of camelids. These environmental zones with their distinctive production strategies are closely juxtaposed, and most prehistoric communities would have had access to lands in all three zones. As mentioned earlier, however, an additional lower agricultural zone important for several crops (e.g. coca, *aji, lucuma*) was more distant, 50 km over the Cordillera Oriental and down the eastern mountain flank toward the rainforest.

UMARP (Upper Mantaro Archaeological Research Project) has concentrated its investigations on the Late Intermediate Period (A.D. 1000–1460) and the Late Horizon (A.D. 1460–1533)—periods in which major social and political changes took place within the region (Earle et al. 1980). During the Late Intermediate Period, population grew rapidly, and settlements shifted from scattered small sites on the valley floor and low ridges to a few large sites (up to 95 ha) and smaller, apparently dependent sites. During the latter part of the Late Intermediate Period, internal warfare was prevalent; sites were fortified and located on defensible hilltops (LeBlanc 1981). Then, during the Late Horizon, the Mantaro Valley was conquered by the rapidly expanding Inka empire and was incorporated into the state administrative system. The Inkas constructed a major administrative center at Hatun Xauxa (near the modern town of Jauja), several smaller state sites, the valley's extensive storage complexes, and the main road running through the valley from Cuzco to Ecuador (D'Altroy 1981). Most defensive local settlements were abandoned at this time, and new, smaller, and unfortified settlements were located in more dispersed locations.

Storage during the Late Intermediate Period and Late Horizon shows strongly contrasting patterns. During the Late Intermediate Period, storage was decentralized and has been found thus far only in household contexts (cf. Browman 1970). Although it seems likely that some larger storage areas may have been connected with the households of community leaders (cf. Morris 1967:20), no separate, recognizable village or regional storage complexes existed. During the Late Horizon, more than 3,000 storehouses were constructed in many special complexes through the valley. These storage sites—strung out along the hills flanking the valley—provide the primary data on the redistributional economy of the provincial Inca in the Mantaro Valley (see Figure 6-1).

The description of these Late Horizon storage complexes in the Jauja region was made by UMARP teams, working from an intensive survey conducted by Jeffrey Parsons (Parsons and Matos 1978; Matos and Parsons 1979). The data were collected primarily under the direction of Terence D'Altroy, in whose dissertation the data were presented (D'Altroy 1981). The descriptive analysis of the Mantaro Valley that follows is drawn from this and later sources (D'Altroy 1992; Earle and D'Altroy 1982, 1989).

Within the survey region studied by UMARP, a total of 1,992 storehouses, with a total estimated capacity of 123,716 m³, have been recorded in 30 sites (Table 6-1). As was characteristic of many Inka facilities, there is extensive evidence of prior planning and supervised execution in construction. It is important to emphasize that the construction of this extensive storage system appears to have been *entirely a state venture* (cf. Browman 1970). Spatial distribution, masonry, and internal layout all bear the stamp of state planning.

Bearing in mind that some variations occurred both within and among sites, a description may be drawn of two typical Mantaro region storehouse plans, circular and rectangular, each containing a single room. The circular structures were low, undivided silos, constructed of mortared stone. They were nearly round, and the walls

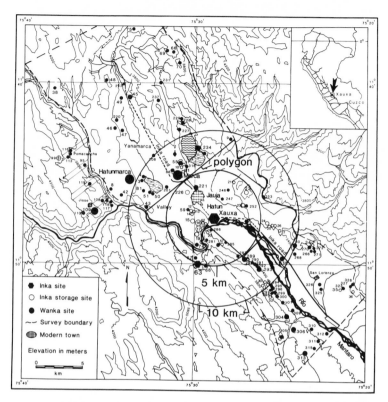

Figure 6-1. The distribution of zones of agricultural production in the Upper Mantaro Survey area: 5-km radius, 10-km radius, polygon (valley surrounding Hatun Xauxa).

canted noticeably inward (Figure 6-2) to a height of 3.5 m or more. The exterior diameter of circular structures varied little, from 5.5–6.0 m, with wall thickness of 0.5–0.6 m; estimated storage volume has been calculated at approximately 52 m³ per structure. The rarely preserved tops of the walls were smoothly mortared, flat, and level. No evidence for wall attachment or roofing techniques was obtained during the field research reported here, but early documents and fieldwork elsewhere suggest that circular structures would have been topped by a conical or semiconical thatched roof, held up by a framework of poles (Guaman Poma 1936 [1613]:336 [338];

Table 6-1. Distribution of State Storage Facilities in Upper Mantaro Valley

Distance from Hatun Xauxa	Sites	Numbers of Structures	Volume (m³)[a]	Cumulative Total of Structures (no/%)	Cumulative Total of Volume (m³/%)
0–1 km	J15	93	5,251		
	J16	359	23,398		
	J17	479	27,075		
	J18	118	7,164		
	J62	20	1,730		
		1,069	64,618	1,069/53.7	64,618/52.2
1–2 km	J14	32	2,112		
	J19	99	7,269		
	J20	18	684		
		149	10,065	1,218/61.1	74,683/60.4
2–3 km	J12	60	4,048		
	J13	35	2,758		
		95	6,806	1,313/65.9	81,489/65.9
3–4 km	J23	66	5,610		
	J57	37	1,838		
	J226	37	1,861		
		140	9,309	1,453/72.9	90,798/73.4
4–5 km	J21	39	3,272		
	J22	75	6,278		
		114	9,550	1,567/78.7	100,348/81.1

Distance	Code	Count	Volume		
5–6 km	J10	29	1,760		
	J11	24	1,286		
	J28	21	901		
	J91	4	183		
		78	4,130	1,645/82.6	104,478/84.4
6–7 km	J24	63	5,079	1,708/85.7	109,557/88.6
7–8 km	J25	23	1,286		
	J26	15	838		
	J27	42	3,515		
		80	5,639	1,788/89.8	115,196/93.1
8–9 km	J29	15	490		
	J30	8	313		
	J31	41	2,207		
		64	3,010	1,852/93.0	118,206/95.5
9–10 km	J32	46	2,078	1,898/95.3	120,284/97.2
10–11 km	J34	17	689	1,915/96.1	120,973/97.8
16–17 km	J35	39	1,517		
	J36	38	1,226		
		77	2,743	1,992/100.0	123,716/100.0

[a]The volume is structure volume to the roofline, based on an estimated height of 3.5 m; it does not take into account accommodations for packaging.

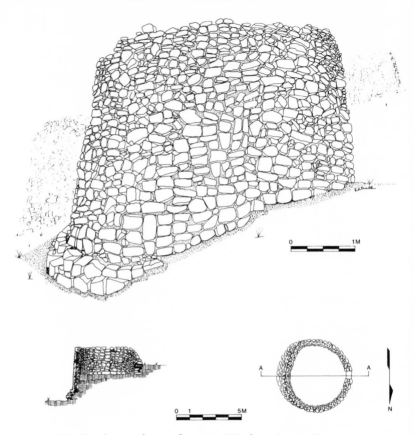

Figure 6-2. Circular storehouses from site J10, above Laguna Paca.

1980:308). Entrances are preserved in only three storage sites with circular form; in all cases structures only had single entrances (cf. Morris 1967), facing uniformly either uphill of downhill. At J10, north of Hatun Xauxa, all preserved entrances lie on the uphill, about 1 m above ground level. Similar entrances are preserved on the upslope of J31 and on the downslope of J29. Overall, the entrances have a mean width of 0.45 m and a height of about 0.75 m. Unmortared stone was neatly laid in each entrance, closing them. Single-stone tenons were preserved on the side walls of three circular structures at J31 and on the upslope walls of two at J20. Several functions have been suggested for such tenons (Kendall 1976b:44), with the most reasonable in this case being to facilitate access to the roof. It seems reasonable that the entrances may have been closed during use to permit filling the entire structure from the roof, and the structure could than be kept sealed until needed.

The masonry was standard *pirka*. Amorphous, angular limestone (or more rarely metamorphic or igneous cobbles depending on local availability) were set in a limestone mortar with small rock (or pebble) inclusions. Typically stones were not well-worked and were apparently quarried or gathered locally; they were placed so as to form a rough facing without coursing for both wall sides. Larger stones (maximum dimension 25–50 cm) were used for the facing, with smaller pieces used as fill in the mortared core. Reddish plaster is preserved on the interior face of one circular storehouse at J31. Worked stone was used primarily to frame the entrances, especially for the lintels. Overall the construction of the circular structures is typical of local residential construction that is also circular in layout (Earle et al. 1987). The main differences are the smaller, raised entrance doorways, larger dimensions (typical exterior diameter of Wanka III houses, 4.0–5.0 m), and perhaps greater care in construction; most distinctive are the site layouts described below.

The rectangular structures were generally similar to the circular storehouses, except for the obvious contrast in layout and the use of more upright walls. The units were not subdivided, and the long axes paralleled the slope contours. Exterior dimensions were 6.0–8.0 m in length and 4.0–5.0 m in width. Wall thicknesses and heights were comparable to those of the circular structures. The estimated mean volume for a rectangular structure is thus approximately 71 m^3. The roofs of rectangular structures were most likely built of the same materials as circular structures but were gabled (*dos aguas*) (Morris 1967; Browman 1970:263; Gasparini and Margolies 1980:303). At site J32, entrances are preserved in only four structures, where they were positioned systematically in the downslope wall. These entrances are similar to those described for the circular structures. No rectangular structures retained exterior tenons. Masonry was essentially similar to the circular structures, except for the larger, shaped blocks used to form the corners. Generally, the rectangular structures were not unlike the rectangular habitation structures built in elite

Figure 6-3. Storage facility J20, overlooking the main Mantaro Valley; facing east.

patio groups during Wanka III; however, their doorways and especially their site layout were distinctive.

To judge from the distribution of rectangular and circular structures, it seems highly probable that the Inkas organized the contents of their storehouses systematically. Morris (1967) has made the reasonable suggestion that the use of two shapes of structures was in part an accounting device and has further suggested that maize was stored in the circular storehouses and tuber crops in the rectangular buildings. Exploratory excavations by UMARP in six structures at two facilities (J16, J17) above Hatun Xauxa, however, did not support the latter suggestion (D'Altroy and Hastorf, Chapter 9 as discussed below).

State storage facilities were internally highly organized. They typically consisted of single or multiple rows of circular or rectangular buildings, following the contours of the hills on which they were built. Two of the more simple facilities, J27 and J31 (Figure 6-4), may be described as examples of sites along the east and west slopes of the valley. J27 (3,600 m) lies on the ridge separating the Masma and Mantaro valleys, about 7.8 km east of Hatun Xauxa. The site

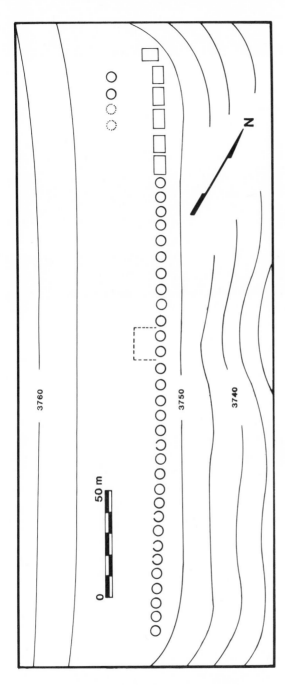

Figure 6-4. Inka state storage complex J31, on west ridges bordering the main Mantaro Valley.

consists of a single line of 41 rectangular structures (3,485 m³) with a circular structure (30 m³) appended at the south end. The building foundations are preserved completely, and the highest standing wall is 2.2 m high; the uphill walls are in worse condition than those downhill, because of agricultural clearing in the fields above. The masonry consists of unworked metamorphic fieldstone and igneous river cobbles set in a mortar of mud and pebbles. A stone-buttressed terrace wall lines the entire length of the line of qollqa. No ceramics were observed in the structures themselves; the deposit along the row ranged from scant to absent.

The single circular structure is analogous to the one at J28, on the opposite side of the valley, where a single rectangular structure was built at the north end of a line of circular buildings. The significance of this organization is not apparent at present, although the anomalous buildings could potentially have been used to house a resident guard or to store unusual materials. The closest storage site to J27 is J26, about 250 m north along the same ridgeline. A Late Intermediate period ceramic scatter running between J27 and J26, containing no architectural remains, is the only evidence for a Wanka habitation site in the immediate vicinity.

Site J31 (3,775 m) lies very high on the hillslopes bordering the west side of the Mantaro Valley, about 8.9 km from Hatun Xauxa. The site contains 35 circular (1,5l6 m³) and 6 rectangular (691 m³) qollqa, primarily in a single row. The buildings were constructed of uncoursed limestone rocks set in a mortar of mud, small rocks, and pebbles. The architecture is well-preserved, as six elevated entrances remain intact (mean height = 0.70 m; mean width = 0.45 m); three stone tenons project from the exterior of circular buildings. The best indication of the fine preservation is reddish plaster on the interior of one building wall. Numerous structures are preserved to a height exceeding 2.0 m, with the highest building standing about 2.8 m high. Unmortared rock walls were constructed between all pairs of adjoining buildings, to form a solid terrace support. A low (0.5 m high), flat, rectangular earth platform (15 m NS × 10 m EW) is situated on the uphill side of the long line of buildings at J31. It is lined in places with a single row of stones, and the corners are squared. It does not resemble any other feature in the study region,

Figure 6-5. Storage facilities J15 (upper left), J16 (upper right), and J17 (center) on the terraced hillslopes just west of Hatun Xauxa; facing north.

with the exception of the earth and stone features of J22, the elliptical storage facility on the opposite side of the valley (see below).

Ceramics were scant along the entire site, as an intensive surface collection of the ground within 10 m of the storehouses yielded only 11 sherds, 3 from Inka jars and 2 from Wanka-style pots. All the vessels were fairly small, however, and would have been more appropriate for domestic use than for large-scale storage. The lack of surface ceramics is not atypical for storage sites and is probably a consequence of limited use of pottery vessels to store goods and the removal of pots upon abandonment of the structures. The closest storage site to J31 is J30, about 350 m to the northeast (downhill). No habitation site is adjacent to J31, as the closest village was a strip settlement 1.0 km downhill. No imperial facilities, other than storage, lie nearby.

In the larger storage complexes, such as J16 and J17, above Hatun Xauxa, a few structures were offset from the principal rows of storage buildings (Figure 6-5). As an example, we may describe site J17 (see

Table 6-2. Chi-square Test for Distribution of Circular and Rectangular Storehouses at State Storage Sites J15-J16 (combined) and J17, above, Hatun Xauxa (J5)

	Circular	Rectangular	Total
J15-J16	147	305	452
	(272.9)	(179.1)	
J17	415	64	479
	(289.1)	(189.9)	
Total	562	369	931

$\chi^2 = \Sigma \frac{f_o^2}{f_e} - N.$

$\chi^2 = 284.8828.$

df = 1.

p < .001.

$\Phi = -0.55.$

Chapter 9, Figure 9-3, for site J17), the largest storage complex in the valley. It contained an estimated 479 buildings with a capacity of about 27,075 m^3. In contrast to other sites, many of the structures at J17 have been reduced almost to rubble, and we were able to count only 335 buildings; however, characteristic lines of rubble correspond to areas where structures probably stood before being destroyed by modern agriculture. Of these buildings, an estimated 415 were circular, and 64 were rectangular. Structures were laid out in 10 parallel rows, usually composed of structures of one shape or the other, or, if mixed, of series of each shape. About 15–20 of the buildings at J17 were isolated from the main rows and may have been used for nonstorage functions, such as the residence of maintenance personnel, accounting, security, administration, or religious ceremony (cf. Morris 1967). The ceramic deposition at J17, which was somewhat heavier than that of most other storage complexes, consisted of Inka and high-quality local Late Horizon pottery. The forms recovered included storage vessels and domestic pottery, suggesting that some residential population was present at the site.

In contrast to J17, the neighboring storage complexes of J15 and J16, although generally similar in layout, were strongly dominated by rectangular structures. Of a total 452 structures with identifiable form, 305 were rectangular. A Chi-square test shows that the distribution of circular and rectangular buildings at J17 and J15/J16 is statistically significant at $p<.05$ ($p<.001$; = $\phi-0.55$; Table 6-2). This patterning of storage facilities both within and between sites indicates to us the probable accounting function of the individual units, a point to which we will return.

Turning to the regional distribution, the storage complexes were found in three major spatial groupings: (1) above Hatun Xauxa in the hills separating the Yanamarca Valley from the main Mantaro Valley, (2) north and south of Hatun Xauxa on the west side of the main valley, and (3) along the slopes and ridges on the east. Viewed from a slightly different perspective, the storage facilities fell into two principal contexts: *adjacent* to the Inka administrative center and *dispersed* throughout the valley.

A little more than half of the storehouses in the survey region were concentrated within 1 km of Hatun Xauxa. Of the 1,992 structures located, 1,069 (53.7%) were found in five complexes on the hills west of the center (see Figure 4-5, Chapter 4); this represented about 52.2% (64,618 m^3) of the total structure volume in the region. The remaining storage fell off systematically as a function of distance from the administrative center. A regression of structure volume—by 1-km concentric bands around Hatun Xauxa—against log-distance yields an R^2 of .6717 (SE$_{\hat{y}}$ = 10,443; Figure 6-6a and b). Even if the facilities within 1 kilometer of the center are removed from consideration to eliminate the effects of the massive storage there, volume still decreases as a function of distance from the center (R^2 = 0.6938; SE$_{\hat{y}}$ = 1,881).

This pattern implies that storage capacity was strongly centralized around the provincial center. Two related explanations for this configuration may be suggested (cf. Earle and D'Altroy 1982; D'Altroy and Earle 1985). First, by concentrating storage around the provincial capital, the expected location of primary consumption, the Inkas would have reduced the costs of transporting goods at the time at which they were required. Second, because agricultural goods were said to have been stored in buildings adjacent to the lands on which they were grown, the concentration of storehouses at the center would conform to a pattern in which state farms encircled the provincial capital (D'Altroy 1992).

The relationship between state production and land use may be examined through an analysis of the distribution of native population and the capacity of state storage facilities, with respect to distance

Storage Volume
around Hatun Xauxa

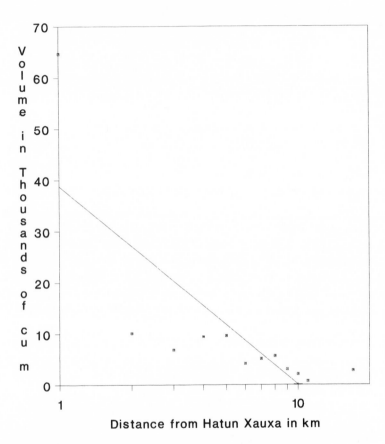

by 1-km band

A

Figure 6-6. Regression of state storage volume, by 1-km bands, against (A) log of the distance from Hatun Xauxa, including all bands, and (B) log of the distance from Hatun Xauxa, outside 1 km surrounding the center.

Storage Volume 1+ km around Hatun Xauxa

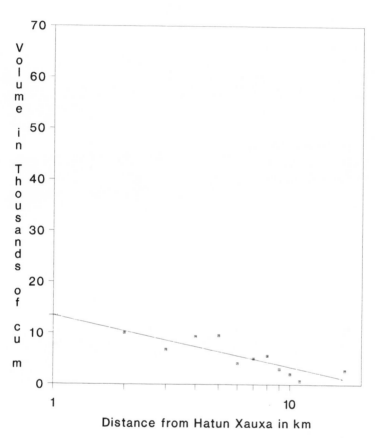

by 1-km band

B

from the administrative center. For this analysis, only the surveyed lands within 11 km of the center have been considered. This includes 96.1% of the storage structures and 97.8% of the storage capacity within the entire survey region. Only two small storage facilities (J35, J36) near Apata lay beyond this radius, about 17 km away.

The data have been treated in three slightly differing regressions. For each analysis, the volume of storage structures was estimated for each of the 1 km-wide bands surrounding Hatun Xauxa (see Table 6-1). This volume was regressed against (1) total estimated population in each band and (2) the population of the Wanka settlements in each band. In the third analysis, only the storage capacity and population of Wanka settlements outside the first kilometer were considered. The last analysis was conducted to compensate for the considerable impact on regional patterning of the immense facilities immediately at the center. The intent of all analyses was to determine if, as appeared to be the case on inspection, there was an inverse relationship in space between the state's concentration of stored goods and the location of the population that labored to produce them.

The first two regressions that we ran show the effect of the large concentration of storage above Hatun Xauxa. In each plot, the point representing the massive facilities above the capital stands out as an outlier, skewing the regional pattern. In neither case does the regression line account for more than 23% of the total variance, and neither regression has an F-ratio significant at $p=.05$ (one-tailed).

When the centralized concentration is eliminated, however, the patterning elsewhere in the valley becomes clear (Figure 6-7). For this analysis, the two villages (J59 and J74) directly associated with the main storage facilities were eliminated from the Wanka III population. The rationale for this analytical reduction was that the artifactual assemblages indicated that these were specialized farming villages run by the state (see Costin et al. 1989). These village had unusually high densities of hoes and virtually no evidence for other productive activities (spinning and ceramic manufacture) normal to households. The total variance accounted for by the regression line is $R^2 = .5057$; ($SE_{\hat{y}} = 2440.7$), and the F-ratio is significant at $p=.05$ ($p=.0211$). Examination of the residuals of this last regression showed them not to be spatially autocorrelated. However, the case accounting for the greatest residual variance was the 1–2 km band, indicating that the regional effects of the concentration of storage above Hatun Xauxa extended beyond the first kilometer around the center.

The results of these sets of regressions indicate two clear trends in the distribution of state storage. First, the state's facilities were highly concentrated around the administrative center and decreased systematically as a function of distance from the center. Second, the local population was settled in locations that suggest that the state personnel were deliberately keeping them away from the lands that were used to produce state foods. In combination with other data reported earlier, this evidence points to the development of state farms around the capital (D'Altroy 1992).

The distinction between the distributions of circular and rectangular storehouses is further suggestive of patterned differences in the productivity of the microzones of the main valley (Earle and D'Altroy 1982:286). The east side complexes were heavily weighted in favor of structures with a rectangular floor plan (303 rectangular, 114 circular), whereas those on the west were predominantly circular (126 rectangular, 281 circular) (see Table 6-3). The estimated structure volume for the east side is about 30% higher than that of the west. Franco et al. (1979:35–39) state that the east side of the valley has more fertile soil, reduced threat of frost, and greater rainfall above the valley floor than does the west and therefore could be expected to have been agriculturally more desirable.

The concentration of Inka storehouses along the eastern ridgeline, coupled with the lack of Wanka population in the immediate area, again suggests strongly that the Inkas reserved this land for state production. Despite the evidence that the eastern side was agriculturally most favored, the 1986 resurvey of the Mantaro Valley settlements failed to identify any major Wanka III settlements in a broad section immediately south and east of the administrative center. Rather, there is a near-continuous line of storage composed mostly of rectangular units (J21, J22, J23, J24, J25, J26, and J27). The extraordinary standardization of the state structures in these special complexes may be exemplified by examining the variations in the complexes extending about 7 km along the east side of the valley. The mean volumes for rectangular structures at J21 and J22 were estimated at 84 m^3; for J23 and J27, 85 m^3; and for J24, 81 m^3. Coefficients of variation for length and width measurements of structures within sites typically

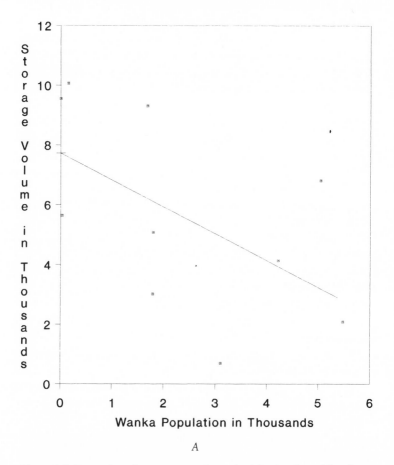

Storage/Population
›1 km from Hatun Xauxa

A

Figure 6-7. Regression of state storage volume, by 1-km bands, > 1 km from Hatun Xauxa, against (A) Wanka III population, and (B) Wanka III population excluding the specialized farming villages Huancas de la Cruz (J59) and Chucchus (J74).

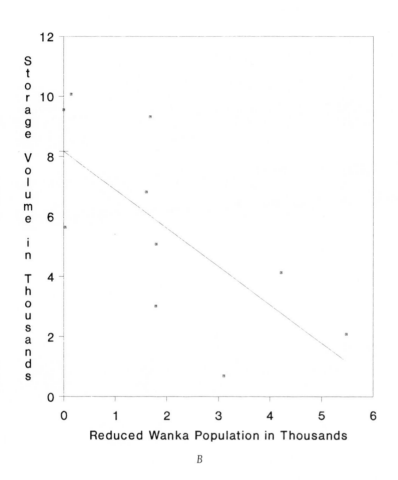

Storage/Population
›1 km, – J59, J74

Storage Volume in Thousands

Reduced Wanka Population in Thousands

B

varied between 5% and 10%, remarkably low for fieldstone buildings adjacent to croplands (D'Altroy 1981:Table I–2). Clearly, the state planners conceived of these storage facilities as *standardized units* and had them built accordingly.

Several characteristics of the storage site J22 (Figure 6-8) illustrate the special nature of these storage facilities on the eastern side. Located

Table 6-3. Distribution of Inka State Storehouses, by Shape, on East and West Sides of the Main Mantaro Valley, Excluding the Core Storehouses above Hatun Xauxa.

Sites on West	Sites on East	Circular Frequency	Circular Volume m³	Rectangular Frequency	Rectangular Volume m³	Total Frequency	Total Volume m³[a]
10		29	1,760	0	0	29	1,760
11		24	1,286	0	0	24	1,286
12		9	542	51	3,506	60	4,048
13		0	0	35	2,758	35	2,758
14		32	2,112	0	0	32	2,112
19		0	0	99	7,269	99	7,269
20		18	684	0	0	18	684
	21	0	0	39	3,272	39	3,272
	22	0	0	75	6,278	75	6,278
	23	0	0	66	5,610	66	5,610
	24	0	0	63	5,079	63	5,079
	25	23	1,286	0	0	23	1,286
	26	15	838	0	0	15	838
	27	1	30	41	3,485	42	3,515
28		21	901	0	0	21	901
29		15	490	0	0	15	490
30		8	313	0	0	8	313
31		35	1,516	6	691	41	2,207
32		33	1,526	13	552	46	2,078
	34	17	689	0	0	17	689
	35	39	1,517	0	0	39	1,517
	36	19	681	19	545	38	1,226
57		21	591	16	1,247	37	1,838
91		0	0	4	183	4	183
221		36	1,824	1	37	37	1,861
Total, west		281	13,545	225	16,243	506	29,788
Total, east		114	5,041	303	24,269	417	29,310
Grand total		395	18,586	528	40,512	923	59,098

[a]Refers to structure volume to roof line, not adjusted for packaging; see text.

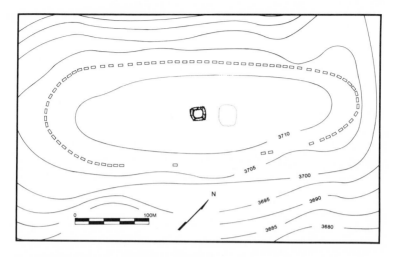

Figure 6-8. Inka state storage complex J22, on top of a hill on the east side of the main Mantaro Valley; the two central features are a rubble and earth mound (*left*) and a ring of rocks (*right*). Elevation is in meters.

on a hilltop 300 m above the plain, a single line of 75 rectangular structures surrounded the hilltop just below its crest. Most of the units were regularly spaced in the primary line, but a 200 m gap existed in the line on the northeast face; three structures were located here. On the hilltop, surrounded by the storage line, a rubble and earth mound and a rock ring enclosure was constructed. The exact use of these special features is unknown, but they certainly emphasize the unusual character of the site.

On the western, less fertile side of the valley, the line of storage sites stands immediately above a strip Wanka III settlement located along the lower slopes adjacent to the valley's agricultural land. These complexes are dominated by circular structures. Even here, however, the storehouses were systematically separated from the local villages. The storage facilities were set apart from the habitation areas by 100–200 meters and often stood by themselves adjacent to small series of terraces.

What is to be made of the east-west contrast in storage observed in the Mantaro Valley? As a working hypothesis we would like to suggest that the contrast represents two different strategies for mobilizing staples for state finance.

1. On the eastern side, storage facilities with rectangular units isolated from local population may be associated with specialized state farms in which production could be controlled directly by the state (Earle and D'Altroy 1989).
2. On the western side, storage facilities mainly with circular storage units associated with local communities may be indicative of the *mit'a* labor system controlled indirectly through the community's organization.

This division into two forms of storage associated with different architectural forms makes sense in terms of symbolic reference. The rectangular structures refer to state architectural style that is seen in the buildings at the administrative centers; rectangular architecture was almost nonexistent prior to the Inka conquest of the region. The circular structures may refer to the local residential architecture that existed in the region prior to conquest. This division into architectural styles in storage may thus recognize the division into direct and indirect mechanisms for mobilization. If this is true, the division of storage facilities into distinctive form groups both on the hills above the administrative center and on the eastern versus western slopes may provide a key for understanding the very nature of Inka imperial finance in the Mantaro Valley.

CONCLUSION

The storage facilities in the Mantaro Valley of Peru provide unambiguous evidence for the specific nature of the Inka political economy. They afford concrete evidence for the ways in which state "redistribution" functioned as a system of staple finance. The concentration of storage in the Mantaro Valley makes good sense. This valley is agriculturally rich and positioned strategically along the central road network of the empire. As discussed by LeVine (Chapter 4), the amount of storage was based at least in part on the natural richness of the region and local population available for corvée labor. On a regional scale, the specific pattern of storage distribution with regard to the local population offers tantalizing details on how production, distribution, and storage of staples were controlled. We have suggested that specific strategies of mobilization should have been associated with distinctive patterns of storage. It is the variation in how storage was handled that may provide the critical key for understanding the economic base of the Inka, the only empire apparently to have existed without a developed market system.

ACKNOWLEDGMENTS

We wish to thank James Hill, Jonathan Ericson, and Terry LeVine for commenting on this chapter and Victor A. Buchli for drafting Figures 6-8 and 9-2 in Chapter 9. We also thank our colleagues on the Upper Mantaro Archaeological Research Project—Co-principal Investigator Christine Hastorf, Cathy Costin, and Glenn Russell—who provided data on ecofactual and artifactual remains. This chapter is an extensive revision of material contained in Earle and D'Altroy (1982). Finally, we gratefully acknowledge support for this research from Friends of Archaeology and the Academic Senate of UCLA, the Columbia Council on the Social Sciences, and the National Science Foundation (BNS 8203723).

CHAPTER 7 **Inka Storage in Huamachuco**

JOHN R. TOPIC AND COREEN E. CHISWELL

INTRODUCTION

HUAMACHUCO is located in the North Highlands of Peru, approximately 115 km from Trujillo and 90 km from Cajamarca, in the southern end of the Condebamba-Cajamarca drainage basin. The area is one of relatively broken topography, where small valleys, drained by northward-flowing rivers, are separated by hills and mountains. The town itself is at 3,160 m, but variations in altitude give local people access to a variety of resource zones. Much of the land in the immediate vicinity is suited to rainfall agriculture, and there is a limited amount of highland pastureland.

Despite references in the sixteenth-century Spanish chronicles to an Inka center located at Huamachuco, remarkably little evidence of the Inka presence survives to modern times. The town of Huamachuco is believed to overlie the original Inka installation, and it has obliterated almost all architectural evidence of the prehispanic settlement. Outside modern Huamachuco, *qollqa* were first recognized in 1981 (Topic and Topic 1982). An analysis of these storage facilities provides one way to better understand the Inka presence in Huamachuco.

Storage was an important aspect of the Inka economy, and sixteenth-century chronicle sources abound in references to Inka storage structures. The chroniclers make clear that there were many types of storage facilities, that a wide range of food and nonfood products were stored, and that facilities were specifically dedicated to a variety of state institutions. For example, the chroniclers tell us that there were storage facilities for each town, and sometimes for individual fields; that the state religion and important shrines had separate storage facilities; and that travelling dignitaries, soldiers, *akllaquna* (chosen women), and people fulfilling state labor obligations were supplied from stores set aside for them.

Although specific details of the chronicles cannot always be taken at face value, they provide a wealth of general information about storage that would be unavailable from archaeological excavation alone. At the end of this chapter, we will consider the degree to which our present understanding of the Huamachuco qollqa concurs with these general descriptions of Inka storage. However, most of the chapter will be devoted to describing what remains of the storage complex, the excavations we conducted, the identification of distinct types of storerooms and their possible functions, the analysis of botanical remains, and the regional and historical context of the Huamachuco complex.[1]

The time frame that encompasses the construction and abandonment of the Huamachuco qollqa is defined with relative precision by historic references. Rowe's (1946:209–10) general chronology of the Inka expansion as it pertains to Huamachuco is supported by local documentation. Although some Inka military activity may have taken place earlier, Huamachuco was effectively incorporated into the Inka realm by Thupa Yupanki probably between 1463 and 1471. Local documentation for this event is sparse, but Thupa Yupanki is mentioned in some documents.[2] There are suggestions that Wayna Qhapaq, who reigned from about 1493–1527, may have played a major role in incorporating Huamachuco into the empire: Espinoza (1974a:22,35) feels that he may have reorganized the local population by creating a *waranqa* (unit of 1,000 tributaries); the Primeros Agustinos (1918) mention him in regard to several local *huacas* (holy places); and Guaman Poma (1980:1094–1103) notes that Wayna Qhapaq had houses in Huamachuco. It was under these two rulers that the Inka town was built, the road system was reconstructed, *mitmaqkuna* (state-sponsored colonists) installed, and the storage facilities discussed in this chapter created (Topic and Topic n.d.).

After Wayna Qhapaq's death, the civil war between Waskar and Atawalpa raged through Huamachuco. During the war, Atawalpa spent several months in Huamachuco, destroying the famous oracle of Catequil in Porcón (Primeros Agustinos 1918:22–24; Betanzos 1987:segunda parte, cap. xvi). Atawalpa's troops executed Waskar in

Andamarca, in the southern part of the province of Huamachuco (Sarmiento 1965:274; Betanzos 1987:segunda parte, cap. xxiv). Undoubtedly, throughout this period both armies were provisioned on occasion from state storehouses in Huamachuco. The Spanish conquerors probably were still drawing on these stores in 1533 as they passed through Huamachuco (Estete 1917:77; Pedro Pizarro 1965:187–88). A rather strange reference by the Augustinians (Primeros Agustinos 1918:36) to finding two mummies hidden in piles of maize may indicate that the storerooms were still functioning to some extent in 1560.

It is unlikely that any system of centralized storage was still functioning in 1567. In that year, Gregorio Gonzales de Cuenca (Ordenanza, folio 343^3) ordered that each *tampu* (state waystation) in the province be stocked with food from surrounding towns. Moreover, the food was to be sold to travelers and the money deposited in the community treasury; he notes that this is a change from what had been customary during and immediately following Inka control.

GENERAL DESCRIPTION

The remains of five groups of qollqa are located on three hills that overlook the modern town of Huamachuco from the south and west (Figure 7-1). In addition, near one of the groups there is a complex of larger rooms that may be related to the storerooms. Rarely are any of these structures very well preserved so that surface observations do not allow even a complete count.

CERRO SANTA BARBARA

The least preserved storerooms are on the northeast facing slope of Cerro Santa Barbara,[4] a rounded knoll located on the southern outskirts of Huamachuco. Four factors contribute to poor preservation: The buildings may have suffered damage when the hill served as a Peruvian position during the Battle of Huamachuco (1883) in the War of the Pacific; the hilltop is under cultivation today, and the slopes also appear to have been cultivated in the past; the slopes are quite steep and subject to slippage; and, as we will discuss below, the construction techniques of these buildings facilitated their collapse.

The qollqa are arranged on four or five terraces, which tend to follow the hill contours. The uppermost row is at the brow of the hill

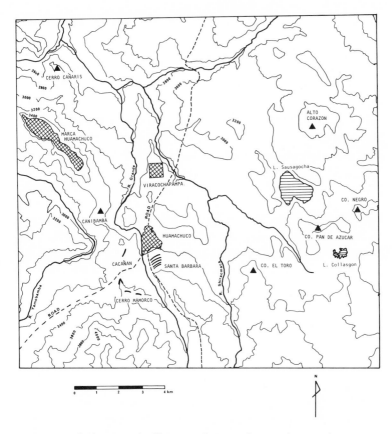

Figure 7-1. The location of qollqa around Huamachuco and some other important sites. Triangles denote Late Horizon sites.

(3,350 m) and is the best preserved. Starting at the extreme southwest, there are either 5 or 6 storerooms, then a shallow ravine, and another 21 rooms. On the next lower terrace there are about 18 qollqa. The third terrace has at least 12 qollqa, but these are much more poorly preserved. On the fourth terrace, we could only define parts of 6 qollqa, but their spacing suggests that there were other qollqa that are now completely destroyed. Finally, a fragmentary terrace wall may indicate the former presence of a fifth row of buildings.

Although we can only count about 62 qollqa on Cerro Santa

Barbara, we think that there may have been as many as 125. The structures measure about 5 × 4 m, with the longer axis always oriented along the contour; they are usually spaced about 3 m apart along the terrace.

CERRO MAMORCO

Preservation at this site is generally much better with some walls standing as high as 2 meters. There are three distinct groups of qollqa, all at about 3,400 m elevation. The first group is located on a northeast facing spur and consists of 19 buildings in a single row. These are situated on the brow of the spur, at the top of a steep slope. There is only one preserved window (or small door?) in the center of a downslope-facing wall. This opening measures 50 cm on a side and is located at least 1 meter above the outside base of the wall.

The second group, about 200 m northwest of the first, probably had about 15 qollqa but is now almost entirely destroyed due to the clearing and cultivation needed for agriculture. This group was located on the northeast facing slope of the hill, rather than on a spur or knoll.

The third group of qollqa is on the northernmost spur of the hill, about 300 m from the second group. Here there are two rows of qollqa arranged in a V-shape that converge on the north end. There were probably 25 to 30 buildings in this group, evenly divided between the two arms of the V. Two small trapezoidal-shape doorways are preserved in qollqa in the eastern row. Doorways face downslope and are located 32 and 35 cm above the modern exterior ground surface. One doorway measures 38 cm (lintel) × 50 cm (sill) × 60 cm (height); the other measures 38 × 52 × 65 cm.

The qollqa on Cerro Mamorco are generally larger (external measurements about 8.0 × 3.5 m) than those on Cerro Santa Barbara, but some smaller examples (about 6.0 × 3.5 m) are interspersed. Here also the long axis is oriented along the contour, and buildings are spaced 2 to 3 m apart. Wall thickness averages 50 cm. The masonry is double-faced with a rubble core, and there is little chinking. The mortar sometimes has gravel and straw inclusions; color variation, red or gray in the first group and orange in the V-shaped group, probably indicates local sources. The stone is a mixture of quarried and fieldstone, but quarried stone seems to predominate in the V-shaped group. External corners are square, but internal corners are often rounded, especially in the first group.

CERRO CACAÑAN

The final group of qollqa is located on Cerro Cacañan at an elevation of 3,350 m (Figure 7-2). These are set in a single row on a terrace just below the brow of the hill and face east and southeast. There are 23 partially preserved qollqa and sufficient room at the southwest end of the terrace to have accommodated about 3 more. The qollqa vary somewhat in size but average about 5.0 × 3.5 m, separated by a space of 4 to 5 m. Largely due to failure of the soft sandstone fieldstones and poor quality mud mortar used, the walls are generally poorly preserved. The walls are about 50–55 cm thick, double-faced, with a rubble core.

About 300 m west of these qollqa there is a group of larger buildings. They vary in size but are about 18.0 × 6.5 m. Six of the buildings are arranged in a row on a terrace and are separated by 2.6 to 2.9 m. The other two are on a higher terrace with their long axes oriented perpendicular to the buildings below. Internal corners are often rounded, and there is one possible example of an external rounded corner. Of the four best preserved buildings on the lower terrace, two have single doors, and two probably have symmetrically placed double doors; doors occur in the downhill-facing wall and are 100 to 104 cm wide. The *pirca* walls are generally poorly preserved, constructed of angular fieldstone, and 50 to 70 cm thick.

In summary, we have surface indications of 144 qollqa but estimate that there may have been as many as 215. In many respects the structures conform to standard Inka storerooms: They are arranged in rows on hillslopes overlooking the main Inkaic center and have small trapezoidal doorways located high in the wall. On the other hand, the lack of circular and multiroomed rectangular qollqa and the very small size range is somewhat surprising because variation in shape and size are sometimes indicative of different storage functions (Morris 1981).

EXCAVATIONS

CERRO SANTA BARBARA

In July 1982 we tested four *qollqa*. They appeared to be rectangular-shaped single-room structures, and we were frankly surprised to find

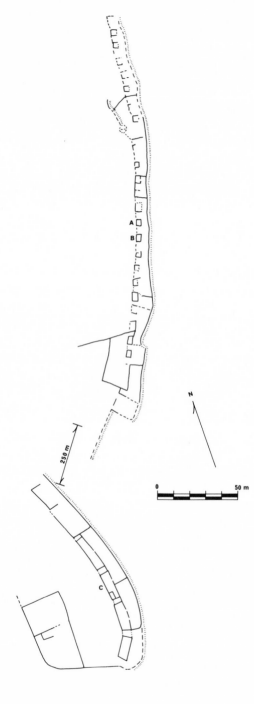

Figure 7-2. Diagram of the qollqa and a group of larger buildings on Cerro Cacañan.

that they were not rooms at all. The first cut made was along what we thought was the inside face of a rectangular room. In attempting to locate the southeast corner, we found that the wall ended and the end was faced. Cut 2 was similar: We began excavating inside what we thought was the northwest corner of a second building but soon determined that this wall also terminated in a finished end.

Interestingly, both walls had three faces, built by first constructing a double faced wall and then adding a third face to bring the total wall thickness to 75–85 cm. The construction of the extra face was notably poorer in quality, having more mortar, less rock, and a more uneven facing. In Cut 1 the extra face was on the *inside* of the wall; in Cut 2, it seemed to be *outside*, but this was unclear because of poor preservation.

At this point we were perplexed by the form of the qollqa and, indeed had doubts if they were qollqa at all. We decided to backfill the first two cuts and completely excavate two more examples. Instead of the rectangular rooms we expected, in both Cuts 3 and 4 we found three parallel walls or piers. In Cut 3 two walls were thinner and less elaborate than the third, which was thickened at each end. The third wall was shaped like an elongated block letter "C" that opened into the inside of the building. In Cut 4, the two outer walls were thicker than the central wall. They were also C-shaped, but the open part of the "C" was filled with poorer quality masonry forming a third face.

The qollqa in Figure 7-3 is based largely on Cut 4, but all four cuts provide evidence for similar reconstructions. The structure was built on three stone piers that were at least 65 cm high and may have been higher. There was some variation in the form of these piers, but generally the outer two were thicker and often had an extra face on the inside of the building. This third face probably formed a ledge to support the floor joists that were also supported by the central pier. In our excavations, only the piers were still preserved, but the quantity of stone between and above them indicates that the qollqa walls were also built of masonry.

All cuts showed some evidence of burning, but only Qollqa 4 was heavily burned. Cut 4 produced a large amount of charcoal, some from poles up to 10 cm in diameter. Cut 1 yielded a small amount of charcoal from what appeared to be a plank. These samples produced uncalibrated radiocarbon dates of A.D. 1475 ± 65 (Cut 4) and A.D.

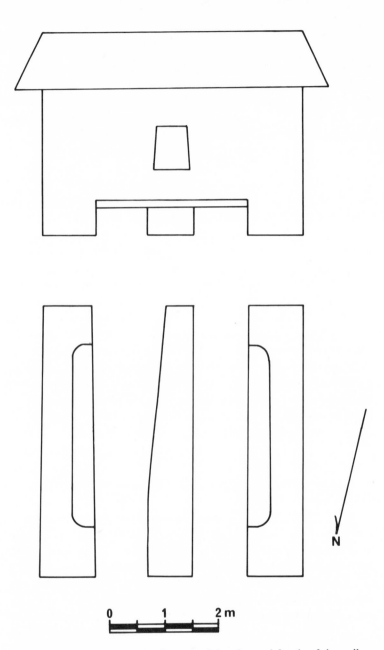

Figure 7-3. A reconstruction drawing of the plan and facade of the qollqa excavated on Cerro Santa Barbara. Although each of the four excavated qollqa varies somewhat from this reconstruction, all had floors elevated above the ground surface on three masonry piers.

1555 ± 75 (Cut 1). Cuts 3 and 4 produced carbonized maize, and in Qollqa 4 we found pieces of burned mud plaster with straw impressions on one face. We recovered 232 sherds, most of which seem to date to an early (900–200 B.C.) occupation in the area. Sherds typical of the Late Intermediate (pre-Inka) period were also present.[5] There were no diagnostic Inka sherds.

CERRO CACAÑAN

In August 1983 we completely excavated two qollqa (A and B on Figure 7-2) on Cerro Cacañan and partially excavated one of the larger buildings (C).

Qollqa A had exterior measurements of 5.25 × 3.90 m; its walls were 50 to 55 cm thick and were built on bedrock. The interior was filled in with relatively loose rock that apparently served as floor and subfloor (there was no recognizable prepared floor surface).

Three canals, about 40 cm wide and averaging 40 cm deep, were built into the fill. Each ran across the width of the building, parallel with the slope (Figure 7-4). The sides of the canals were lined with stones, but the bottom was unlined. The lining reached bedrock at the downslope end but not at the upslope end, giving the canal a greater inclination than the hill itself. The canals seem to have been open to the exterior on both ends. In two cases there were lintel stones that partially defined openings through the upslope wall, and the canal linings partially defined openings through the downslope wall. Because no suitable sized roofing stones were found in the excavation, the canals were probably roofed with poles and floored with rocks and earth.

Qollqa B was similar to Qollqa A. Its external measurements were 4.95 × 3.60 m; the walls were less well-preserved, but construction was the same. Qollqa B had three canals with an average width of 35 cm. The walls lining the canals were less straight and less parallel then those in Qollqa A. One canal had well-preserved openings through both external walls. The openings of the other two canals were destroyed.

We partially excavated one of the larger buildings near the qollqa (Figure 7-5). The building was selected because it had fewer eucalyptus trees planted in it and there appeared to be a small interior room in one corner. Although only a single doorway is preserved, there

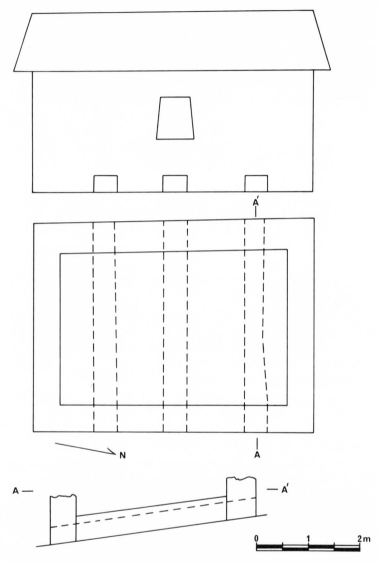

Figure 7-4. A plan and reconstruction drawing of a qollqa excavated on Cerro Cacañan. The subfloor canals could be used to raise humidity within the structure as well as drain away excess water.

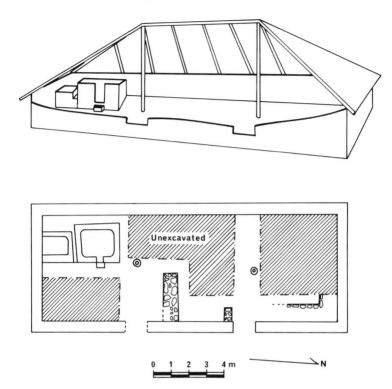

Figure 7-5. A plan and reconstruction drawing of the large building excavated on Cerro Cacañan. The building was probably administrative in nature.

were probably two, placed symmetrically in the downslope wall. The preserved doorway was 1.02 m wide, its sill was about 75 cm above the exterior ground level, and there were no steps leading to it.

Thinking that Building C might be a larger qollqa variant, we started with a trench intended to find evidence of any ventilation or drainage system; neither was present. In the northeast corner, we found part of a bench, which was 18 cm high, faced with stone, and filled with rubble. It was partially destroyed along the east wall but may have originally joined the wall stub located at the south jamb of the door. Because the bench was destroyed inside the door, it is difficult to relate the doorsill to interior floor levels. However, it is likely that the doorsill was at bench level rather than floor level. Where the bench was not preserved, we excavated to bedrock. The floor matrix was 18 cm of compacted reddish clay and earth; below this was about 16 cm of sterile loose gray soil that was probably artificial fill. The walls rested on bedrock.

We then excavated in the vicinity of the room in the southwest corner. Its floor was raised about 30 cm above the floor of the building and was composed of the same material. The ballast below the floor consisted of small rocks and earth. The walls of the room rested on the compact layer corresponding to the building floor. Alongside the room was a raised bin with a floor 67 cm above that of the building. There was also a short section of very low wall that may have been the foundation for a stub wall. Finally, there was a circular pit dug into the floor along the central axis of the building. The pit was 20 cm in diameter, lined with angular stones, and filled with 79 river-rolled cobbles.

Suspecting that this stone-lined and cobble-filled pit might be the base for a post, we excavated a trench across the northern half of the building looking for a similar feature. We found a second stone-lined pit with three river-rolled cobbles. The significance of the cobbles is probably that they allowed drainage away from the post and inhibited water movement from the ground into the bottom of the post. We continued the trench to the west wall that rested on bedrock at a higher level than the east wall. In fact, the base of the west wall was 14 cm higher than the surface of the bench along the east wall; the floor sloped to accommodate the change in bedrock level.

Because of the two postholes, it seems obvious that this building had a single large, pyramidal roof; the room and bin in the southwest corner were probably not separately roofed. The function of the building is unclear. There were no obvious domestic features such as hearths and grinding stones. One hundred eighteen sherds were found, but nearly half of these can be attributed to only two vessels: a shallow bowl and a large jar, both in the local Late Intermediate Period style.[5] A typical Inka rope nubbin found in the building may have been attached to the large jar.

CERRO MAMORCO

In August 1983, we partially excavated three adjacent qollqa in the east-facing arm of the V-shaped group on Cerro Mamorco. They were selected because they were well preserved and appeared to have been burned, thus increasing the probability of recovering charred macrobotanical remains.

Qollqa A and B were similar. Qollqa A had internal measurements of about 7.2 × 2.8 m and Qollqa B was 7.2 × 2.7 m; we excavated approximately half of each structure. Both qollqa had subfloor canals with the sides lined by stone slabs and the bottom formed by bedrock. The sides were not perfectly parallel so that the width varied. The widest canal, in Qollqa A, was 62 cm at its upper end and 72 cm at its lower end; all the other canals were about 50 cm. The canal bottoms were about 30 cm below the floor at the upslope end and about 50 cm below the floor at the downslope end. The slope of the canal followed the natural slope of the bedrock. All the canals appeared to have opened through the walls at both ends, although only one of these openings was completely preserved.

If the canals were laid out symmetrically, each qollqa would have had four canals rather than the three found in the Cerro Cacañan qollqa. The extra canal probably does not indicate functional differences. Rather, it seems to correlate with the larger building size at Cerro Mamorco because the spacing of canals is about the same in both cases.

Qollqa C was smaller than the others, with internal measurements of 5.0 × 2.5 m; we excavated about a third of it. Although we found only minor evidence of burning in Qollqa A and B, Qollqa C was well burned. There were many fragments of burned plaster, some still clinging to the interior faces of the walls. Surprisingly, there were pieces of cane-marked plaster, which we would normally consider as evidence of a finished ceiling. Also surprising was the absence of any subfloor canal. Although the excavation in Qollqa C was smaller than those in Qollqa A and B, we would have found at least one canal if similar canal spacing was used.

No artifacts were recovered from Qollqa A and B, and the only possible artifact from Qollqa C was a piece of lime (cal). Our workmen say that, in addition to its use in coca chewing, lime is commonly used in agriculture and storage. It is sprayed on potato plants to prevent some diseases (plague) and is sometimes sprinkled among stored potatoes to protect them from insects and fungal infections.

STORAGE REQUIREMENTS AND THE HUAMACHUCO QOLLQA

Morris (1981; see Chapter 8) has examined the specific storage requirements of crops in order to correlate probable contents with the design of particular qollqa. His research shows that grain and tubers differ in their requirements for successful storage, and each requires a different type of facility. As Morris points out, major factors inhibiting grain storage include fungus, pests, and sprouting. The risk from these factors is limited by specific environmental conditions: constant low temperature, low humidity, and the use of closed containers. The storage requirements of tubers, however, are different. In the absence of modern chemical treatments, manipulation of the storage environment to lengthen the period of dormancy is the most effective precaution against premature sprouting. This is best achieved by constant low temperatures and high humidity.

By examining Huamachuco qollqa in light of the differing requirements of grains and tubers, we can suggest the likely contents of the Cerro Santa Barbara qollqa on the one hand, and those on Cerro Mamorco and Cerro Cacañan on the other. Of the two type of structures, the ones with elevated floors would probably have most effectively minimized humidity. Air circulating between the ground and floor would have been effective in preventing ground moisture from increasing the humidity within the structure. In contrast, qollqa with subfloor canals would probably have been naturally more humid inside because of direct contact with the soil below. In addition, humidity could have been raised further by using the canals to introduce water into the fill under the structures. Based on data indicating differences in the storage requirements of grain and tubers, it seems likely that maize and other dry goods were stored at Cerro Santa Barbara and tubers were stored in the qollqa at Cerro Cacañan and Cerro Mamorco with subfloor canals.

Qollqa C on Cerro Mamorco, which apparently had neither subfloor canals nor an elevated floor, is anomalous. Possibly it was used to store goods for which humidity control was not crucial. Alternatively, it might have been used for temporary storage of all types of goods before they were transferred to more suitable facilities. The burned cane-marked plaster may indicate a ceiling or internal divisions such as the *pirwa* discussed below.

There is little indication that Building C on Cerro Cacañan was solely devoted to storage. Certainly the bin in the southwest corner suggests a limited amount of storage space, and the small room may also have served for storage.

Storage in bins and cubicles is mentioned by both Cieza (1986:segunda parte, cap. xxvii) and Garcilaso (1963:Libro Tercero, cap. xxiv) in the context of the Qorikancha in Cuzco. Elsewhere, Garcilaso (1963:Libro Quinto, cap. viii) gives a more detailed description of these bins, which he calls *pirua* (*pirwa*), emphasizing that they facilitated keeping account of the materials stored. The Spanish term he uses in describing these bins (*orón* or *horón*) refers to a type of basket, which may have had the connotation of a specific measure. Later, he uses the term qollqa to discuss the storage of materials in buildings.

Guaman Poma (1980) also separates his discussion of *pirwa* and qollqa. Although there is the suggestion that *pirwa* may have the connotation of a unit of measure, the contexts in which Guaman Poma uses *pirwa* (as well as *culluna* and *caway,* two other types of storage) suggests that these are terms for a more rustic, community storage facility, whereas he reserves the term qollqa for state storage facilities (see also, Gonzalez Holguin 1952:54,287,338,686).

Although none of this is very clear cut, it does suggest that there were several, perhaps overlapping, categories of storage facilities: *pirwa* were bins that might have served as a unit of measurement, but the category *pirwa* appears to overlap with *culluna* and *caway,* which, in turn, overlap with the category qollqa.

Returning to the function of Building C at Cerro Cacañan, we can summarize the evidence as follows: There is a lack of domestic features; there is one sherd, the rope nubbin, which dates to the Late Horizon; there are one or two features that may be described as *pirwa*; otherwise Building C provides a large roofed space with few internal divisions or functionally diagnostic attributes. We thus tentatively identify these larger buildings as administrative facilities where goods were received, sorted, perhaps measured, and packaged before being stored in the qollqa. Of course, we have no way of knowing whether these buildings served all the qollqa around Huamachuco or only those on Cerro Cacañan. Intuitively, though, eight administrative structures seems excessive for only the 23–26 storerooms on Cerro Cacañan.

ANALYSIS OF BOTANICAL REMAINS

We tested our hypotheses about the contents of the different qollqa types in Huamachuco by examining micro- and macrobotanical remains (Chiswell 1984, 1986). In addition to the remains of food products themselves, other types of botanical remains may indicate the storage of particular crops. In some qollqa at Huánuco Pampa, Morris (1967:92) found evidence that tubers were stored in layers of *ichu* grass, which he refers to as *pirwa*. These bundles of grass and tubers were probably similar to the modern *chipa* (bundles of poles or bark and leaves) used to transport fruits to market (cf. Gonzalez Holguin 1952:111). We reasoned that if *pirwa* storage were used in Huamachuco, the presence of higher than expected quantities of *ichu* or other grass and leaves in a qollqa might indicate tuber storage. A second possible indicator of stored crops in qollqa is phytoliths.

Archaeologists have only recently begun making extensive use of the analysis of biogenic silica. Numerous problems have been addressed with phytoliths, ranging from environmental reconstruction to analysis of diet (Pearsall 1982; Rovner 1983; Piperno 1987). A significant contribution has been the identification of specific cultivated crops such as maize (e.g., Pearsall 1979:135–50). The potential for identifying particular plants was one of the primary reasons for selecting phytolith analysis for the Huamachuco study.

Phytoliths are microscopic silica bodies that form in the cells of a plant. Upon decomposition of the plant, they are deposited in the soil, where they are resistant to alteration. Phytoliths are less susceptible than pollen to wind transportation, and studies indicate that they move relatively little within undisturbed soils (e.g., Beavers and Stephens 1958). Thus, one would expect to find concentrations of the phytoliths of stored crops in qollqa soils.

Because of specific storage requirements, most Inka crops were probably stored separately, and a limited variety of plants should be represented in a single qollqa. The amount of plant material present should also be greater than in nonstorage contexts. Polo de Ondegardo (in Murra 1980:133) states that annual additions were made to qollqa even though some materials deteriorated before use. The recovery of macrobotanical remains in other qollqa (e.g., D'Altroy and Hastorf 1984:345–46, and Chapter 9) also suggests that some plants remained in storage long enough to contribute their phytoliths to the soil.

The first step of the analysis was to examine a variety of plants to assess their silica content. The quantity and type of phytoliths vary from one part of a plant to another, so it was necessary to evaluate the storable portion(s) of the plants studied. We identified a total of 35 plants or parts of plants as storage possibilities, including the edible portion of several crops, as well as nonfood plants that may also have been present in qollqa (e.g., *ichu* grasses and unidentified plants used in modern *chipas* in the Huamachuco market).

The first observation was simply to note the presence or absence of silica. Four samples—peanut, peanut shell, pumpkin seed, and potato flesh—had no significant silica whatsoever. Most of the remaining samples had nondiagnostic types of silica, but few short cells, the type of phytolith that research has found to be most usefully studied. However, seven samples—four varieties of maize cob, *ichu* grass, *caña brava,* and an unidentified species of grass—had short cells in abundance. In these samples, the number of each short cell form was counted.

Next, we extracted the phytoliths from 22 soil samples collected at Cerro Mamorco and Cerro Cacañan. These samples included two "controls" taken near each group of qollqa and 20 archaeological samples from six structures. Each sample was analyzed in the same way as the plant samples—the short cell phytoliths in each sample were counted.

The resulting data were submitted to two kinds of comparisons. First, we compared all the soil samples from a qollqa with the corresponding control sample. This comparison identified two structures at Cerro Cacañan (Qollqa B and Building C) in which none of the soil samples could be distinguished from the control sample. Either the soil samples from these two structures were contaminated, or there was simply insufficient plant decomposition and phytolith accumulation in these structures to be detected.

We next compared the remaining soil samples with the plant samples to look for evidence of specific plants. The sample from the Qollqa A on Cerro Cacañan did not resemble any of the tested plant samples, but samples from all three of the Cerro Mamorco qollqa resembled the *ichu* grass sample.

The phytolith analysis thus suggests there was an unexpectedly large amount of *ichu* grass in the qollqa of Cerro Mamorco. Based on Morris's association of tubers with large amounts of *ichu* grass in Huanuco Pampa, we can suggest that tubers were being stored at Cerro Mamorco. It will be recalled that two of the Cerro Mamorco qollqa have subfloor channels that we suggested above were used to create the high humidity conditions necessary for tuber storage.

Macrobotanical remains recovered by flotation augment these observations. After we collected the small samples needed for phytolith extraction, the rest of each soil sample was floated in detergent and water, agitated by hand, and the organic material separated in filters. We then examined this material, both visually and under low-power magnification.

The samples from Cerro Cacañan produced very small amounts of fragmentary wood charcoal. The Cerro Mamorco samples yielded slightly more material, including carbonized fragments of two unidentified (presumably nonfood) seeds from Qollqa A, a few burned maize fragments from Qollqa C, and small amounts of fragmentary wood charcoal from all three qollqa. The best recovery of botanical material was from the Cerro Santa Barbara samples. A sample from Qollqa 3 produced large quantities of carbonized maize and wood charcoal. Although the very small flotation sample from Qollqa 4 failed to produce maize, the field notes indicate that carbonized maize was even more abundant there than in Qollqa 3. This supports the predicted association of maize storage with the raised floor qollqa of the Cerro Santa Barbara structure designed for low humidity storage, as suggested above.

Our predicted distribution of stored items in the Huamachuco qollqa seems to hold. The facilities on Cerro Santa Barbara that were thought to be devoted to dry storage produced evidence of maize. The facilities on Cerro Mamorco (Qollqa A and B) that were predicted to be intended for tuber storage produced evidence of *ichu* grass that may have been used to pack the tubers; Qollqa C had macrobotanical evidence for maize storage as well as *ichu* grass phytoliths and may have served to store both grains and tubers. Unfortunately, there was less conclusive botanical evidence of the contents of the Cerro Cacañan qollqa, but the subfloor channels in these qollqa implies they, too, were used for tuber storage.

REGIONAL AND HISTORICAL CONTEXT

The qollqa discussed above can be better understood if they are placed in a wider regional and historical context. Huamachuco is located at a junction of two parts of the Inka road: the main north/south route in the highlands, and a secondary east/west route leading to the coast. Therefore, it is likely that the Huamachuco qollqa were not the only storage facilities in the province.

During the latter half of the eighteenth century, Fray Juan de Santa Gertrudis (1970:225) traveled through the area and mentions that he saw qollqa between Cajabamba and Huamachuco. A modern *caserío* (hamlet) located 13.5 km north of Huamachuco alongside the Inka road is called Colcabamba. Although there are no preserved qollqa known from the immediate area, the toponym is suggestive. Hyslop (1984:61,65) reports no *tampu* between Huamachuco and Cajabamba, so qollqa in this vicinity may have been part of a production-storage complex. At an elevation of 3,050 m, the region is well suited to both maize and tuber agriculture.

There is documentary evidence[6] of another set of qollqa at Chuquibamba in the Condebamba Valley, approximately 25 km northwest of Huamachuco. The document is primarily concerned with a lawsuit concerning the succession in a *curacazgo* (polity controlled by a local level lord) of a *waranqa* of *mitmaqkuna* in the province. In the course of the testimony, it is mentioned that the *mitmaqkuna* were moved to Chuquibamba to serve at some *depósitos* (storehouses) that the Inka had for his soldiers. Chuquibamba survives as the name of an hacienda on the left bank of the Condebamba River about 22 km northwest of Huamachuco. On the opposite bank of the river, 3 to 4 km from Chuquibamba are located the Hacienda Colcas and a *caserío* called Colcas. Again, the toponyms are suggestive. These modern settlements are located between 2,200 and 2,400 m elevation; the Inka may have produced and temporarily stored ají and tropical fruits grown at these lower elevations.

Finally, about 55 km west of Huamachuco there is a site, Llagaday Saddle, which Janet and Mark Mackenzie surveyed in 1979 (Mackenzie 1980:304–10). Llagaday Saddle is located in the general area of a *tampu* called Cucho on the route from Huamachuco to the coast (Topic and Topic n.d.). The site itself is only 20 m from a walled footpath and includes the foundations of two rows of conjoined rooms that curve along the contours of a gentle slope. There are at least 21 rooms in the upper row and 9 in the lower row; average room measurements are about 3 × 5 m. Below the two rows of rooms are several poorly preserved, or perhaps unfinished, terraces, each about 1.5 m wide. There were sherds of large storage jars in the local Late Intermediate (pre-Inka) Period style. Llagaday Saddle does not appear to be located directly on the Inka road and thus is unlikely to be a *tampu*. It was probably a storage facility associated with agricultural production. At an elevation of 3,750 m, the emphasis was probably on tubers, which continue to be important in the area today.

Although information about these three sites is still limited, it does suggest that there were a number of other storage complexes located throughout the province of Huamachuco. These storage facilities occur in zones at widely varying altitudes, suggesting provision was made to store a variety of crops in the zones in which they were produced.

Returning to Huamachuco, we should emphasize that although the excavated qollqa are generally similar to examples elsewhere in the Empire, they are different in detail. Specifically, only rectangular storerooms occur, although these include at least two distinctive types: One type, with an elevated floor, has not been reported in Inka contexts south of Huamachuco; the type with subfloor canals resembles examples from Huánuco Pampa (Morris 1981) but may have functioned quite differently. Ceramics are exceedingly scarce in the Huamachuco storerooms, and those that do occur are predominantly in the local style. In contrast, at both Huánuco Pampa (Morris Chapters 5 and 8) and Hatun Xauxa (D'Altroy and Hastorf 1984 and Chapter 9) diagnostic Inka sherds were commonly associated with grain storage. These differences certainly reflect distinctive variations in storage technology.

Because storage was so important to Andean society, it is useful to trace, to the extent possible, the history of the development of this distinctive technology. Although we as yet only have hypotheses about the history of qollqa with subfloor canals, we have more concrete evidence of the history of qollqa with elevated floors. This type of structure was first identified at Cerro Amaru, located a few kilometers from Huamachuco (Topic and Topic 1984:45–51). Two storerooms dating to the Early Intermediate Period or early Middle Horizon were excavated (Figure 7-6). These structures are round with floors raised above ground level on a masonry support. The support is a stone-faced bench or ledge around the inside of the circular wall; this is similar in concept to the third face inside the C-shaped walls found in some of the Cerro Santa Barbara qollqa. In the Cerro Amaru structures, a low central wall bisects the building and supports the middle of the floor joists, much as the central pier does at Cerro Santa Barbara.

One of us (Topic in press; Topic and Topic 1984) has suggested that the Cerro Amaru storerooms are similar to possible storerooms at Jargampata and Azángaro. These are slightly later in time, dating to Middle Horizon 2, and are associated with the Wari culture of the Central Highlands. At Jargampata (Isbell 1977:37), there are two conjoined rooms with a row of corbels for a second-story floor located only about a meter above a packed clay first-story floor; very narrow doors (65 × 66 cm) open into the first story. Isbell (1977:38,49) interprets these buildings as possible storage structures. We concur and suggest that, as at Cerro Amaru, the actual storage space was on the "second" story, the "doors" are ventilators rather than entrances, and the "first" story functioned only to raise the storage area off the ground. Although Anders (1986:213–14) considers the 340 rooms arranged in 40 rows in the central sector of Azángaro to be temporary residences related to calendric rituals, they are quite similar to the two rooms at Jargampata. The rooms within a row are conjoined, there are stone corbels located only 1 meter above the ground, and very small "doors" (60 × 60 cm) opening into the space below the corbels (Anders 1986:213 and Figure 10.8).

Thus, Inka qollqa on Cerro Santa Barbara are conceptually similar to Early Intermediate Period or Middle Horizon storerooms at Cerro Amaru, which in turn are similar to Wari storerooms in the Central Highlands. However, the historical connections between these storerooms from different time periods are still difficult to unravel. As yet, we know of no Late Intermediate Period examples from Huamachuco that could serve as an historical link between the Cerro Amaru and Cerro Santa Barbara structures. There are also no reported examples from the Central Highlands either earlier or later than the Wari ones. On the other hand, Wari and Wari-influenced ceramics occur at

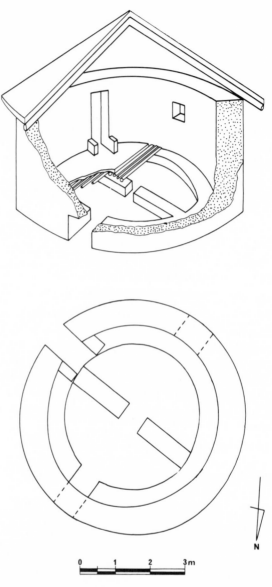

0   1   2   3 m

N

Figure 7-6. A plan and reconstruction drawing of a storeroom at Cerro Amaru. The storeroom was constructed during the later part of the Early Intermediate Period or the beginning of the Middle Horizon.

Cerro Amaru, together with other exotic ceramic styles and trade goods. This evidence of wide-ranging contact provides a mechanism for the diffusion, in either direction, of this type of qollqa during the Middle Horizon.

We should mention one other possible case of qollqa with elevated floors. Schjellerup (1984:172–76) provides very clear descriptions and drawings of Inka qollqa in Chachapoyas province (see Figure 1-1). These occur in two rows of 8 and 15 buildings at quite different elevations. Qollqa in the upper row have a 20 × 25 cm rectangular opening in the front wall at ground level, a door 1 meter above the ground, and six 10 × 10 cm square openings in both the front and back walls just below the level of the door. If the 10 cm square openings are interpreted as beam sockets, these qollqa would have elevated floors similar to the Wari examples discussed above. However, Schjellerup (1984:172–76; personal communication 1990) disagrees with this reconstruction and interprets these openings as ventilators. We admit that in the illustrated example the corresponding openings on the front and back walls are not as well aligned as one would expect of beam sockets. The lower row of qollqa was less well preserved, so that any features located in the upper parts of the walls are probably lost. There were 40 × 14 cm rectangular openings at ground level in each of four walls and a partially preserved masonry bench along the back wall. The bench and ground level ventilators she describes suggest a building similar to those at Cerro Santa Barbara and Cerro Amaru.

In the excavated examples of qollqa with elevated floors, sherds of storage jars are scarce or absent. This statement applies not only to the Cerro Santa Barbara qollqa, where it is clear that maize was stored but also to the structures at Cerro Amaru, Jargampata, Azángaro, and Chachapoyas (see Figure 1-1). The lack of storage jars in all these complexes contrasts with the storage practices documented at Huánuco Pampa and Hatun Xauxa (Morris Chapter 8; D'Altroy and Hastorf Chapter 9) where grain was commonly stored in jars. Perhaps in qollqa with elevated floors, grains were stored in bags. Another possibility, suggested by the Augustinian reference to finding bodies in a pile of maize (Primeros Agustinos 1918:36), is that grains were stored loose and in bulk. A third possibility is that there were internal bins as Garcilaso describes; the straw-impressed plaster at Cerro Santa

Barbara and the cane-marked plaster from Cerro Mamorco (from a qollqa with evidence of maize but no elevated floor) may be evidence of these bins.

Only the excavations at Cerro Santa Barbara and in Building C at Cerro Cacañan produced significant quantities of sherds. As we pointed out earlier, most of the sherds from Cerro Santa Barbara are from an Early Horizon occupation, but sherds in the local Late Intermediate Period style, called Huamachuco-on-White, were also present. The diagnostic sherds from Building C were also in the Huamachuco-on-White style. From both sites the sample of Huamachuco-on-White sherds is very small: The sherds from Cerro Santa Barbara may represent only one jar, whereas those from Building C represent at least one jar and one bowl. Other excavations show that Huamachuco-on-White continues into the Late Horizon and that jars in this style sometimes have rope nubbins, which are an indication of Inka influence. In fact, the one diagnostic Inka sherd from the entire Huamachuco storage complex is a rope nubbin that may be from the Huamachuco-on-White jar found in Building C.

Although the sample of sherds is small, it is surprising that the Huamachuco-on-White style occurs, whereas the Provincial Inka style is lacking. Provincial Inka ceramics, and even a wooden *kero* (drinking cup), have been found in Huamachuco itself (Topic and Topic n.d.; McCown 1945:310), but we know of no Huamachuco-on-White pottery from around the modern town. Because of the small number of vessels from both Huamachuco and the qollqa excavations, we cannot say more about the lack of Inka pottery in the qollqa except that it contrasts with the situation in Huánuco Pampa and Hatun Xauxa.

CONCLUSION

On the hills surrounding Huamachuco there are about 144 preserved qollqa, but we estimate that there may once have been about 215. We excavated or partially excavated nine examples, slightly more than 6% of the preserved qollqa and 4% of the estimated number. In addition, there are eight larger buildings that were probably administrative in nature, of which we partially excavated one example. Ethnohistoric information suggests that the storage complex was constructed after 1463 and fell into disuse by 1567; the radiocarbon dates and associated ceramics are consistent with these dates.

The qollqa are arranged in five groups on three hills. Although the groupings probably reflect significant ethnic categories, it is difficult to determine what those categories may have been. Although it ultimately may be impossible to understand the significance of qollqa groupings, it is interesting to speculate about their meaning.

The largest group of qollqa is located on Cerro Santa Barbara. The excavated examples all have elevated floors and were used for storing maize and probably other goods requiring dry conditions. These qollqa are located adjacent to agricultural terraces that we think are Inka and were probably used for growing maize; crops produced on the terraces were probably stored in the qollqa, and seed for planting the terraces probably came from the *qollqa*. This rather small area of terraces was probably not the sole source of goods stored at Cerro Santa Barbara, but because of the close association of terracing and storerooms, we consider them parts of a single production-storage complex. We further expect that the complex was not under the control of the indigenous community, but most likely was part of a state installation, or belonged to the state religion, or even, as suggested by Poma's reference to houses of Wayna Qhapaq, may have been part of a royal residence.

The presence of administrative structures on Cerro Cacañan suggests that the qollqa there may be the tuber storage equivalent of the maize storage facilities on Cerro Santa Barbara. However, as noted above, it is uncertain whether these structures administered all the qollqa or only those on Cerro Cacañan.

The Cerro Mamorco qollqa are divided into much smaller groups. Although two excavated qollqa had subfloor canals and were probably used for tuber storage, the third had a simple clay floor and was probably used for a variety of goods. From the excavated sample, we cannot be sure whether this heterogeneity is characteristic of each group of Cerro Mamorco qollqa or of only the group tested. Heterogeneity within a group of qollqa would be expected if the storerooms corresponded to a social unit; in other words, if a group of people stored all their goods in one set of storerooms, they would need storerooms suitable for tubers, grains, and various other goods. A similar argument could apply to state institutions, such as administrators, soldiers, or artisans. Although ultimately dependent on state lands, an institution might be assigned its own set of storerooms. The same logic applies to major shrines; the chronicles suggest these had their own lands, and by extension, their own produce to be stored in their own facilities. Perhaps, then, the division of storerooms on Cerro Mamorco into groups corresponded to specific groups of people or institutions, or to shrines.

Although this discussion of the significance of qollqa groupings is speculative, it provides some perspective for evaluating the scale of storage in Huamachuco. Unlike Huánuco Pampa, Huamachuco was not an artificial town; there were indigenous people and numerous *mitmaquna* in the immediate area, as well as the state apparatus. Yet the storage complex is modest in scale. The scale of the complex suggests that it was intended only to provide for local consumption. Possibly any excess production was shipped elsewhere.

As a facility oriented toward local consumption, it is interesting to look at the mix of the two main types of storerooms. Overall, slightly more than half of the storerooms have elevated floors, and, estimating that ⅓ of the qollqa on Cerro Mamorco lack subfloor canals, qollqa specifically designed for tuber storage form about 40% of the total. However, if our speculation about the significance of the qollqa groupings is accurate, this proportion changes dramatically. What we think to be state storage is represented by as many as 125 elevated qollqa (83%) and only about 25 qollqa for tuber storage (17%). Tuber storage predominates in what we think is nonstate storage. However, because the Huamachuco storage complex is only one of several in the province, both its scale and the inferences about consumption patterns may be misleading.

On more solid ground, we have documented the existence of two distinctive types of storage facilities. The distinctive feature of both types is the emphasis on humidity control. Thus far, the type with subfloor canals is known only from the Late Horizon in Huamachuco. The type with an elevated floor has a wider temporal and spatial distribution but at present seems to occur earliest in Huamachuco and only in Huamachuco does it occur during two different time periods. Thus, both types of facilities may represent storage technologies developed in Huamachuco or in neighboring provinces.

Finally, we have demonstrated that phytolith analysis can be useful in storage situations. Although our study has shown on the one hand that the edible portions of many plants lack identifiable silica, we have also shown that phytoliths from nonedible plants used to pack stored tubers can be identified in predictable storage contexts.

ACKNOWLEDGMENTS

This research was funded by the Social Sciences and Humanities Research Council of Canada and authorized by the Instituto Nacional de Cultura. Alfredo Melly, Kaja Narveson, Andrew Nelson, Theresa Topic, Lisa Valkenier, and Sue Wurtzburg all assisted in the mapping, excavation, and analysis of collections. We dedicate this chapter to the memory of Alina Portella who directed the majority of the excavations and, more importantly, was a kind a gentle friend.

PART IV

ANALYSES OF HIGHLAND INKA
FOOD STORAGE

CHAPTER 8 **The Technology of Highland Inka Food Storage**

CRAIG MORRIS

ARCHAEOLOGICAL studies of ancient technology have focused most frequently on the various aspects of production. The concern has understandably been with how the productive base of a society was maintained and increased through changing techniques and strategies of food procurement and production and through improving techniques in the making of tools and other objects of material wealth. Although these factors of production obviously remain important in the case of complex societies such as the Inka, another set of technologies come into play and merit special consideration. These new technologies form the base that supports the integration and administration of the society, and they include such systems as transportation, communication, and storage.

As a result of an emphasis on economic and organizational matters in our study of the Inka storage system, many of the specifically technological aspects of storage were assigned a relatively low priority. However, the evidence is sufficient to show us an extremely sophisticated ability to understand and take advantage of natural climatic conditions for the purpose of effective storage and to give us quantitative information that underscores the enormous importance of storage, particularly to the state.

Central Highland Inka storage units are relatively small buildings arranged in rows, usually on a hillside. They ordinarily overlook the occupation site with which they are associated. Roman y Zamora (1897 [1575]:201) tells us the Inka built their storehouses on hills, and the hillside position of these depositories is one of the main clues to their storage function. The structures, known as *qollqa*, took two basic forms; circular and rectangular (Figures 8-1 and 8-2). The interior diameter of circular qollqa we measured ranged from 2 to 6.3 m, with the most common variety nearly 5 m in diameter. The rectangular qollqa were from 2.5 to 3.4 m wide and 3 to 10 m long,

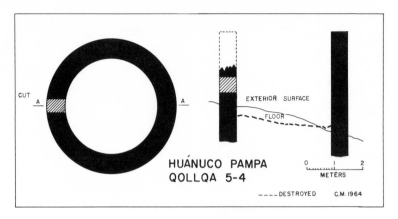

Figure 8-1. Diagram of a circular qollqa at Huánuco Pampa.

occurring in one- and two-room varieties, with very rare examples having more than two rooms. The interior length of the single-room type is usually about 9.4 m, whereas the vast majority of the rooms in multiroom structures are about 4.5 m long (see Chapter 5 for more detailed descriptions of Huánuco Pampa qollqa).

Besides their hillside location the most critical characteristic for distinguishing storehouses from residences or other structures is their doors. The threshold is well above the ground, and the size of the door is small in comparison with the doors of structures that served other functions. Indeed with a mean height of 72 cm. and width of 45 cm, they were more like windows than doors. Circular qollqa had only one door, almost always on the uphill side. Rectangular qollqa usually had two doors, one facing uphill, the other down. Excavation revealed a further distinguishing characteristic of some, but not all, storehouses. Their floors frequently contained elaborate pavements and ventilation and/or drainage ducts. We have found the former very rarely in nonstorage buildings, the latter never (see Figures 8-2 and 8-3 and discussion below).

So far we have found qollqa in groups, never singly. The groups have ranged in number from 4 units to 497. They are arranged in orderly rows (Figure 5-2, Chapter 5) that usually follow the contours of the hills on which they are located. Only rarely do both rectangular and circular storehouses occur in the same row, and in large storage

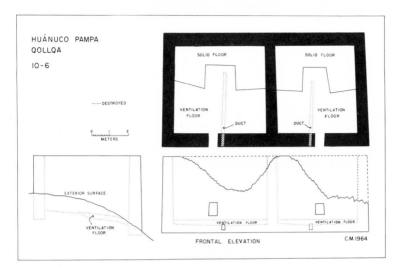

Figure 8-2. Diagram of a two-room rectangular qollqa, 10-6, at Huánuco Pampa, with paved floor and ventilation ducts.

complexes the rows themselves are grouped so that several rows of circular storehouses form one part of the facility and rows of rectangular storehouses form another part (Figure 5-2, Chapter 5).

At Huánuco Pampa the form and arrangement of storehouses is apparently related to their function. We discovered examples of two important commodities, preserved because they were burned. These commodities were probably the most important food products for Andean populations: maize and root crops (mainly potatoes). Identifying their storage conditions allows us to gauge the quantitative importance of each product, gives us some insight into how they were stored, and allows us to understand better the entire question of storage in Inka administrative centers.

The storage of maize and root crops at Huánuco Pampa is intimately related to the difference in shape between the two types of storehouses, that is, between the circular and rectangular storehouses mentioned above. Although it must be stressed that the sample is small, maize was always found in circular storehouses, whereas root crops were always stored in rectangular ones. This differentiation in storehouse design also shows that at least in the major storage facilities

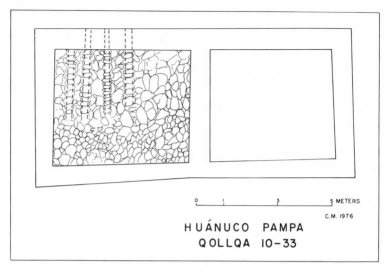

Figure 8-3. Diagram of qollqa in Row 10 at Huánuco Pampa, with rock-paved floor and ventilation ducts faced with rock.

of administrative centers, a conscious effort was made to design storage units in terms of the differing requirements of various goods.

THE STORAGE OF MAIZE AT HUÁNUCO PAMPA

We found charred maize in six storehouses at Huánuco Pampa. The artifacts and architecture associated with the maize were always nearly identical. The structure was approximately circular; the floor was paved with stone; and the building always contained the sherds of several large narrow-necked jars, essentially like Rowe's (1944:48) form "a," often referred to as aryballoid. The maize itself was always shelled; no cobs were found. In three cases the grains were still in the smashed jars, leaving little doubt about the standard storage practice for maize at Huánuco Pampa. The possibility that maize was sometimes stored in other ways cannot be ruled out. Nor can it be said for certain that all circular, paved-floor storehouses were used for maize storage. But our sample found no exceptions to this practice, suggesting that it was at least a very common one.

Our limited investigation of storage customs of the contemporary rural population of the Peruvian Central Highlands suggests that long-term storage of shelled maize in jars is very rare today. Maize is not stored in quantity at altitudes similar to that of Huánuco Pampa except as part of modern commercial operations. At lower altitudes, in or near the areas where it is produced, maize is stored on the cob, hung by parts of its shuck from the rafters or from poles in well-ventilated rooms or porches. Sometimes it is stored shelled in a binlike *troje* woven from straw, but in this case, too, the storage method provides for ample ventilation in contrasts to the closed jars.

Obviously, experimental studies and detailed, year-long climate observations would be invaluable in helping us to understand the many variables involved in high-altitude maize storage, and in evaluating the effectiveness of the Inka practices. Lacking these, we must put together such information as we have in an attempt to explain why the Inka stored corn as they did. Some of the advantages of storing shelled corn are relatively obvious. It takes far less space, and this is doubly important when a product has to be transported great distances from point of production to point of storage and use. The modern practice of on-the-cob storage is largely in a household context where the corn takes up space that would probably not otherwise be occupied and where transportation efficiency is not a factor. Suspending cobs of corn from rafters or poles is also a way of achieving optimum ventilation, and this method is therefore especially suitable for storing recently harvested maize that may not be thoroughly dry.

Modern studies of grain storage (Anderson and Alcock 1954; Genel 1966; Christensen and Kaufman 1969) have shown that the main factors that lead to the deterioration of stored foods are fungi, insects, rodents, and certain characteristics inherent in the grains themselves, such as the tendency to sprout. The extent to which stored grains are susceptible to these problems depends on their condition at the time they are put into storage, the nature of the storage environment, and the length of time the goods are left in storage. The success of a warehousing system thus depends on the ability (1) to create a proper storage environment, (2) to assure adequate prestorage preparation, and (3) to plan for the use of the goods before they have passed the limits set by (1) and (2) and thus become spoiled. The storage environment is perhaps of greatest interest in a consideration of the technology of storage; in any case, that is the aspect most accessible through archaeological remains. However, some facilities thought to have served for prestorage processing have been found adjacent to storage sites. Early documents (Guaman Poma 1936 [1613]:335) inform us that the knotted string records known as *khipu* were used to keep a careful record of the stores.

There are three principal aspects of the storage environment that can be manipulated to control the various factors of deterioration mentioned above and to increase the storage life of grains and other foods. These are temperature, humidity, and the degree to which goods are physically sealed off from invading organisms. In most storage situations these factors are never entirely independent of each other. For example, changing the temperature frequently affects the humidity and vice versa. Moreover, when storage facilities are tightly closed to keep out insects and rodents, there may be adverse effects on temperature or humidity or both. Attempts to achieve optimum storage conditions must take into account the conditions of products when they are placed in storage (temperature, moisture content, contamination, etc.), and storage itself is thus closely interrelated with the kinds of prestorage processing available.

Given all of these complexities, it is easy to see the difficulties in reconstructing how Inka warehouse keepers perceived and attempted to solve storage problems. We cannot always determine exactly why one procedure was chosen instead of another. However, from what we know of the products stored and the general climate of the area of Huánuco Pampa, it seems clear that the major factor being manipulated was temperature. Essentially, foodstuffs were being brought to a natural environment that was highly favorable to their storage. As we shall see, some sophisticated attempts were made to go beyond what the natural climate provided in building the warehouses for tubers that are more difficult to store. But for maize, a simple structure with a good thatch roof to insulate the grain from the extreme of the day/night temperature oscillations of the high elevation *puna* was sufficient.

Looking at maize storage at Huánuco Pampa in terms of potential factors of deterioration we can make the following comments.

1. *Fungi.* Most of the losses of stored grain in the world today are the result of fungi. These microflora can invade grain of relatively low moisture content and can lower the nutritional value and produce

harmful toxins even though the visual damage does not appear to be serious (see Christensen and Kaufman 1969, for detailed discussion). The growth of fungi is mainly a function of temperature and of the moisture content of the grain. There must of course be initial contamination, but the storage fungi (mainly *aspergilllus* and *penicillium*) are so pervasive that grain is almost never entirely free of them when it is put into storage. At very high moisture contents bacteria can also be destructive, but in most cases they are rather easily controlled by drying the grain and keeping it dry.

The storage fungi common to maize and other grains grow most rapidly at temperatures of 30°–32°C, and their growth rate decreases as temperature decreases. At 5°–10°C they grow very slowly. Several studies have been made of the effectiveness of low temperature in controlling fungi. The results are unequivocal: Low temperature is a very effective means of preventing damage by fungi and, if properly used, even allows the storage of grains at relatively high moisture contents. If the grain is carefully dried and is not heavily invaded by fungi before storage, it can be kept at low temperatures for 4 years and longer without significant deterioration (Papavizas and Christensen 1958; Qasem and Christensen 1960).

With the data presently available we cannot ascertain the temperature inside the Inka maize storehouses at Huánuco Pampa. According to Tosi (1960) the mean monthly temperature in zones similar to Huánuco Pampa varies from 3° to 6°C depending on time of year. From the studies of maize storage just mentioned, it can be seen that the temperature is very nearly an optimum one for preventing damage by fungi. The only problems to be overcome in attaining really exceptional storage conditions are (1) to be certain the maize is not or does not become too humid and (2), to control the day-night variations so as to keep the temperature as constant and close to the mean as possible. Although the puna in this area can hardly be described as dry, particularly in the December to March rainy season, the air usually dries out rather quickly after rains. It has been our own experience with short-term storage in the field that if goods are kept away from the earth and not allowed to come into contact with water, humidity is not a serious problem. The stone-covered floors of maize storehouses would have served to protect the goods from the moist ground. There is a common feeling that grain stored in jars is more likely to become humid because of lack of ventilation; however, if it is thoroughly dried before storage, the jars may actually protect it from moist air. In addition, the use of jars serves to break up the grain into small batches preventing moisture of fungi from being transferred from humid or infected grain to portions of the stores free of these difficulties.

The warm daytime temperatures are potentially much more serious. The temperature frequently climbs to almost 20°C during part of the year, although it remains that high for only a few hours before dropping to near or below 0°C. The key here is to protect stored goods from the sun and provide them with adequate insulation. The maize was insulated by the jars in which it was stored, pirka walls about 65 cm thick and a thatch roof. Of course we do not know the exact nature of the storehouse roofs, but we do know that straw is an extremely effective insulator (Phillips 1957). Anyone who has been in a contemporary thatch-roof house on the *puna* during a warm day can attest to its coolness. We do not know for sure whether cloth or some other covering was used on the small doors of the qollqa, but closing them during the day would further contribute to the maintenance of a uniformly low temperature.

The extent to which storage fungi were a problem for the Inka, or were perceived as such, is not known. In modern situations at least it is almost impossible to eliminate entirely damage from all types of fungi, because some can even survive freezing. But assuming the maize kernels were relatively low in moisture when stored, the storehouses and storage methods at Huánuco Pampa would have provided excellent conditions for long term storage with little deterioration due to the familiar fungi.

2. *Insects*. The use of insecticides and fumigation has drastically reduced the loss of grain to insects in modern times. However, in 1947 it was estimated that 16 million tons of stored grain (enough to feed 75 million people for a year) were lost due to insect infestation (Christensen and Kaufman 1969:123). The danger of insect invasion of stored goods is readily perceived by Andean village farmers today and quite possibly was the main threat to maize storage in pre-Columbian times.

Damage from insects can be reduced or even eliminated by establishing a storage environment unfavorable to insect development.

Even in modern times, controlling the conditions that lead to the reproduction and growth of insects is preferable to fumigation with poisonous chemicals.

Again the primary variables are moisture and, especially, temperature. As in the case of fungi, the best storage environment is one that is dry and low in temperature. According to Christensen and Kaufman (1969:131):

> Since most of the [insects that attack stored grains] are of tropical or subtropical origin, they are adapted to a fairly high temperature, 30°–32°C. Their growth and reproduction are greatly reduced at temperatures below about 20°C and many of them cease to develop at temperatures below about 10°C. If the grain is maintained below this, they die. That is, maintenance of a low temperature in grain stocks, will greatly reduce or eliminate most insect problems.

Although high moisture levels slightly lower the temperature range at which insects develop, and some kinds of mites can remain active at temperatures as low as 5°C (Christensen and Kaufman 1969:336) the maintenance of a temperature close to the mean for *puna* areas should essentially eliminate insect damage and greatly reduce any damage that might result from mites.

The protection of stored maize in capped jars would also be a positive factor in insect control, in the event that low temperature alone were insufficient to the task. Christensen and Kaufman (1969:131) recommend "tight bins or warehouses to which insects do not have access."

3. *Rodents.* Low temperature is of course not as effective in controlling rodents as it is in controlling insects and fungi. Mice are relatively common in the *puna,* and when shelter and an abundant supply of food is available they multiply rapidly. The use of ceramic containers would certainly make maize inaccessible to rodents and is perhaps the main reason they were employed.

4. *Sprouting.* It was long thought that a natural tendency to sprout during a certain season was a significant factor in the heating and spoilage of stored grains. However, studies of grain, including maize, have repeatedly shown "no urge to heat and germinate in the spring" (Christensen and Kaufman 1969:106). It is of course the ability of grains to lie dormant almost indefinitely that makes them such a storable and therefore valuable food. Only warm temperatures and

obvious and easily avoidable extremes of moisture initiate sprouting. It is invasion by other organisms, not factors inherent in the grains, that is responsible for most destruction of stored maize.

STORAGE OF TUBERS AT HUÁNUCO PAMPA

Carbonized tubers were found in only three storehouses. The sample again is small but extremely homogeneous: Root crops were always found stored in essentially the same way, and the procedures used contrast markedly with those used for maize. As previously noted, root crops were found in rectangular buildings. The one exception to this was a small circular building obviously associated with a religious structure and apparently used as a small warehouse apart from the main facility and maintained for a special purpose. That building contained maize in jars as well as potatoes and other root crops stored between layers of straw. This clearly special case of goods stored together is also the only one in which root crops were found in a storehouse that contained pottery.

The normal pattern for root crop storage was to place the tubers between layers of straw and then to bind the layered combination with rope into what were essentially "packets" or loose "bales." None of these packets of tubers was found intact, so their exact shape and size could not be determined. They appear, however, to have been basically rectangular in form and longer than they were wide or thick. The rope-tied packets within which the potatoes and other root crops were entirely enclosed by straw were then placed in rectangular storehouses.

The storage technique differed substantially from that used for maize, reflecting the different requirements of root crops. It requires only a passing knowledge of these foods to know that they are exceedingly difficult to store in comparison with grain, and much of the success of highland Andean subsistence strategies depended on the development of storage techniques that allowed the root crops to be stored at least from one harvest to the next.

Basically two different storage strategies were used. One of these was a prestorage processing strategy; the other involved the manipulation of the storage environment. The prestorage processing converted the tubers into an essentially new substance with storage qualities far superior to those of the plants as they were harvested. These new substances are of *chuño, moray,* and related products so familiar to the Andes. The process of alternately freezing, drying, and sometimes soaking takes advantage of the daily temperature oscillations in the dry season of the altiplano climate, particularly in the southern Andes, and it has been described by Troll (1958) among others. The products of such prestorage processing can be kept for long periods of time; however, they differ drastically in taste and other qualities from the tubers from which they are made. There is no doubt that these highly storable products played a major role in Andean subsistence, particularly in tiding the population over years of poor harvests. Surprisingly, we did not find these products stored at Huánuco Pampa. This could well be a consequence of the generally small sample of material preserved, but the storage system seems to have emphasized fresh tubers.

The extreme modification that takes place in the making of *chuño* is indicative of the inherent difficulties in storing Andean tubers. Unlike maize and other grains, these tubers do not naturally lie dormant for long periods of time. They contain sufficient moisture for germination and tend to sprout if kept at an appropriate temperature for a long enough period of time. The high moisture content also makes them susceptible to a large number of bacterial and fungal infections, particularly if the skin of the tuber is broken. In addition, chemical and structural changes may take place during storage that affect the taste of the tubers; as will be seen, these changes tend to be amplified by the storage conditions necessary to control sprouting and bacterial problems. Insect and rodent invasion of stored tubers is seldom discussed in the literature. Although these consumers of stored foods probably have less effect on root crops than on grains, it is also possible that they have been underemphasized in the literature because of the far greater losses from other factors.

Any discussion of the pre-Columbian storage of Andean tubers must keep certain factors in mind. First of all, there are enormous varietal differences in the potatoes and their relatives, and many of these varietal differences effect storage requirements. To my knowledge these differences have not been adequately studied for modern species and varieties.[1] We may never be able to reconstruct special storage requirements and/or advantages of early varieties no longer cultivated. Second, some storage diseases may be of European origin—just as there may have been problems in antiquity that we no longer recognize. Third, it is necessary to consider the effects of storage procedures on taste, and this of course is largely a cultural matter for which we have no data from prehistoric periods. Finally, prestorage handling and processing plays a more important role for tubers, even when they are stored fresh, than it does for grain. They must be free of water film, but not allowed to dry out. Diseases acquired during growth are more important to the storability of tubers than of grains; tubers must therefore be carefully culled before warehousing. Methods of harvest are also directly related to difficulties encountered in storage. For example, modern machinery, means of transportation, and sharp metal tools probably produce more skin damage leading to deterioration in storage than did the procedures and implements employed in pre-European times.

In spite of these complications and the dearth of information, it is obvious that the Inka made a systematic and probably very successful effort to store potatoes and some other tubers in large quantities in their fresh state—in addition to making the famous *chuño*. Again the emphasis appears to have been mainly on temperature manipulation through storage in an appropriate climate. But the more difficult demands of the tubers resulted in more sophisticated use of ventilation and insulation and may have involved some control of moisture in the storage environment as well.

As was the case with maize, much of the pattern of tuber storage by the Inka emerges by looking at relationships between the storage procedures observed archaeologically and major problems known to be connected with the storage of root crops, including some of the side effects of storage itself.

1. *Sprouting.* The tendency of potatoes and many other tubers to sprout after a relatively brief period of dormancy following harvest poses one of the most serious limitations on their storage. Sprouting results in serious weight loss to the edible tuber, affects its nutritive value, and modifies its flavor (Phillips 1957). In modern commercial storage operations chemical suppressants are used to control sprout growth (Burton 1966:283–84; Christiansen 1967:191–92). In preindustrial technologies only one effective means of sprouting control was probably available—maintenance of a temperature at which the

tubers are "latent," that is, below the point at which sprout growth normally occurs.

At least in most modern varieties of potatoes, "sprout growth is, for all practical purposes, negligible at 4°C and below, and increases with increasing temperature" (Burton 1966:262). According to Phillips, a temperature of 38°F (3.33°C) is required to keep potatoes completely latent; at 40°F (4.44°C) slight swelling of the buds is followed by slow sprouting after several months, but temperatures above 40°F can be tolerated for only a few months (Phillips 1957:14–15).

The general climatic conditions of the *puna,* as well as our lack of data on temperatures inside the storehouses found there, have been discussed above. If the 3°-to-6°C average yearly temperature cited for regions similar to Huánuco Pampa could be maintained within the storage facilities, there probably would have been little problem with sprouting. However, the temperature demands and other storage requirements of potatoes were much more difficult to achieve than were those of maize, and the facilities built to accommodate those products at Huánuco Pampa are our best evidence of the problems involved. The rectangular storehouses that housed the tubers were as much as 300 meters higher on the hill than those that contained maize. Although this difference might seem insignificant, and we lack the statistics to show what the temperature implications actually are, they should not be discounted in an area famous for its altitudinal microclimates. The heavier frosts, more frequent accumulations of hail, and the occasional snows on the higher hillsides near the city (including the upper storage areas) suggest that the temperature differences are significant.

The narrow limits on storage conditions that must be maintained for the root crops is also suggested by a complicated set of floor features found in many of the rectangular storehouses. Most commonly, these take the form of a stone floor as much as 50 cm thick laid loosely over the prepared ground surface with little or no binder. The stones are laid in such a way that ample open space remains between them. These floors were usually associated with small trapezoidal openings in the wall of the storehouse at the level of the stones—that is, between the surface of the floor and the surface of the ground over which the floor was laid. In several cases, all in the second highest row (Row 10) where such floors dominated, stone-lined ducts or canals were incorporated into the floors. These ranged in number from a single duct to as many as four per room (Figures 8-2 and 8-3). Some ducts led to openings in the downhill side, some to openings in the higher uphill side, some to both, and some terminated at the foundations. Figure 8-2 illustrates an example with a single duct. One example had a less open floor than usual with both uphill and downhill openings at the floor level. Provision was made for closing both openings of this storehouse floor with stones, and they were, in fact, closed when excavated. When these ducts and "open" storage floors were first encountered, it was thought that they might have been associated with drainage or perhaps related to cleaning operations. However, the discovery that the ducts sometimes lead to an opening at their highest elevation indicated that the removal of a liquid from the building was not their only function.

Unfortunately no actual remains of stored goods were found in any of the qollqa with ducts. The presumption that they were used for rootcrops is based solely on the indirect evidence that only such products were found in that general sector of the depository zone, and those were the only goods associated with rectangular storehouses. It is necessary to stress once again the small size of the sample in which evidence of stored commodities was encountered. If tubers were stored over these "open" floors, it is almost certain that the major function of the floors was ventilation rather than drainage. In fact it is rather amazing how closely these floors match recommendations for potato warehouse construction given by modern experts: Phillips (1957), for example, recommends a slatted floor under storage bins, noting that the coolest air is available at ground level and that the recirculation of the cool air from underneath the stores is better than ventilation with outside air when exterior temperatures are undesirably high.

The ventilation systems in the floors were complemented by windows (doors) in both the uphill and downhill sides. Even chambers that lacked the complicated floor features appear to have had opposing windows (in contrast to the structures in which maize was stored). It seems clear that the principal function of these architectural features was temperature control.

It is not possible here to present a full discussion of the variables affecting the temperature of stored tubers. Not only would many pages be required, but such a discussion should necessarily involve particular characteristics of storage densities and procedures as well as more precise data than we have now on outside air temperatures, wind velocities, and the like. We can reconstruct, however, what were probably the principal outlines of temperature management. As was the case with maize storage, the roof served as insulation against warmer daytime temperatures. The large quantities of straw more loosely incorporated into the packetlike storage units described above provided additional insulation. The "open" floors in some structures enabled continuous air circulation within the building. This air flow could be increased by opening the windows. It is presumed that the windows could have been closed over with cloth or some other material; otherwise the sun would have produced seriously negative effects. No door or window covering material has been preserved anywhere in the storage complex. Finally, the duct system could be closed by placing stones at the open ends; however, the closing stones were seldom present at the time of excavation.

The opening and closing of the ventilation systems could have provided a flow of cool outside air at night while insulating against the warmer daytime temperatures. It should be noted that the velocity of the wind hitting the slope tends to be considerably greater than in the main part of the site below and that the warehousing zone was placed so as to avoid any interference to the prevailing winds from other nearby hills. In other words, the location of the rectangular qollqa and the positions of their windows and vents took good advantage of the winds blowing across the *pampa* and, of course, cooling effectiveness depends on the velocity of the air as well as its temperature.

The relatively rare openings at ground level on the uphill sides of the storehouses present further intriguing possibilities. One of these openings was in a storehouse that had to be reached via a narrow duct dug down beside the uphill storehouse wall. The diameter of that duct was only about 30 cm, and the constriction combined with an abrupt angle of entry would not have produced a particularly effective ventilator. Is it possible that water (or some other liquid?) was poured into the duct allowing the lower portion of the "open" floor to be flooded? Of course we can never be certain of this. But if true, it would have provided a simple but fairly effective means of cooling the interior of the storehouse as the water evaporated; in addition, it would have provided some control over humidity.

Returning specifically to the subject of sprouting, we are still faced with the critical question: Was the temperature control achieved by the combination of storehouse location, insulation, ventilation, and perhaps evaporation of water in some cases, adequate to prevent the sprouting of fresh tubers in relatively long-term storage? It should already be apparent that a definitive answer is yes, and the important question that remains is, How long could the tubers be held in a latent condition? It is here that experimental data would be so useful.

Discontinuous ventilation utilizing outside air can hold potatoes at 4°C from November through April in the Netherlands and, at that temperature, for a somewhat shorter period in England and Wales. Based on these data, Burton (1966:280) states that potatoes can be stored in most of Northern Europe without "serious sprout growth" from harvest time through the northern hemisphere winter until planting time in the spring. The limitations of temperature control with ambient air of course come with the normal planting and grow-ing season of the crops, at which time the climatic conditions to which they are adapted encourage sprouting. In the Andean *altiplano* the seasonal temperature variations are much less marked than in temperate zones, and the day-night contrasts of the Andean dry season are evened out somewhat by the cloud cover of the rainy season. The mean temperature is on the average only about 3° to 5°C greater. This would make temperature management much easier than in temperate latitudes. Nevertheless, in his brief mention of modern storehouses near Cajamarca and Cuzco, Christiansen (1967:192) says only that at 3,500 meters sprouting can be controlled during the months from May through September using ventilation with outside air. It is likely that at somewhat higher altitudes the Inka could have held potatoes longer and that fresh tubers could have been supplied from the storehouses from one harvest to the next with little deteriora-tion from sprouting. It seems unlikely, however, that any of the root crops could have been held for much more than a year, and for famine or poor harvest the Inka would have had to rely on chuño and the other processed tubers or on an organizational system that redistributed the harvests of areas not adversely affected.

One aspect of sprouting control that merits further investigation is the fact that the sprouting rates of different species and varieties of tubers are affected in different ways by temperature and temperature changes (Burton 1966:43, 244). For example, could potatoes adapted to lower altitudes, and therefore to sprouting at relatively higher temperatures, be stored longer at higher altitudes where the colder climate would presumably be more effective in maintaining a state of latency? It is only an hypothesis that the Inka might have been manipulating such altitude variation in tubers for purposes of storage. But given the well-documented Andean sensitivity to vertical ecological zones and the Inka's ability to move people and goods to take advantage of the varied ecology, it would not be surprising for them to have noted that the natural zone best suited to the production of a food crop was not necessarily the zone best suited to its storage. In fact, just such a principle may have been operative in maize storage, although corn could certainly have been stored effectively at altitudes lower than that of Huánuco Pampa.

Before leaving the discussion of sprouting, I would like to mention one further characteristic of the storage facility at Huánuco Pampa that calls attention to both the difficulties of tuber storage and the seriousness of the Inka attempt to surmount them. Row 10 of the Huánuco Pampa qollqa is noteworthy as the only group of storehouses with ducts built into its floors. It is also noteworthy for the variety of its floor constructions and even for its variation in floor plan—being the only place where more than two rooms occur in any one storage unit. The ducts appear to have been the major focus of attention, varying in the number of ducts per room and in the orientation of their openings. They are the most sophisticated attempts to control the storage atmosphere observed in the Inka storehouses. With the standardization so evident in many other things Inka, it is very interesting that no two of the floors with ducts were alike. The variation is quite clearly deliberate, and it almost appears as if these units were built to experiment with varying conditions that might improve their storage function.

2. *Fungi and other storage diseases.* A great variety of bacteria and fungi can contribute to devastating losses in stored tubers. In addition to great regional differences, these so-called storage diseases vary greatly in their effects on the many species and varieties of tubers and are conditioned by the weather of a particular year. Their histories

are thus very uneven, and it is difficult to suggest which of these diseases may have caused problems for the Inka and thus influenced their storage practices.

It is possible, however, to comment about storage diseases in general and to indicate how conditions at Huánuco Pampa were well suited to controlling many of them—provided that certain precautions were followed, such as removing obviously diseased or damaged tubers before storage and making periodic checks to see that the stores had not been infected. Storage diseases are usually contracted before harvest, but most of the causal organisms spread rapidly from infected to noninfected tubers in storage, given the appropriate conditions. As previously noted, damaged tubers are particularly susceptible to infection. Although hand-harvesting techniques with the traditional tools, such as those illustrated by Salaman (1949: Figures 40–49, pp. 48–49), may have produced little damage in comparison to modern tools and techniques, we must still remember that many of the tubers stored in Huánuco Pampa had to travel considerable distances from the fields of the Inka to the storage area. Both care in transport and careful prestorage inspection would thus have been important.

Aside from chemicals, the most effective means of reducing storage disease is, once again, the maintenance of low temperatures. Most modern texts on potatoes (e.g., Burton 1966:263; Christiansen 1967:261–62) recommend a two-stage procedure. First, wound healing should be encouraged by holding at 10° to 20°C under relatively humid conditions for about 2 weeks after harvest. This causes the formation of "wound cork" in lesions, protecting the vulnerable interior tissue from infection. By using a form of temperature management quite different from that suggested above for achieving low temperatures, it would probably be possible to obtain a relatively continuous temperature at the lower end of the 10°–20°C range. Of course such temperatures could be most easily provided at lower altitudes. We encountered no direct archaeological indication of anything interpreted as a "curing area" at Huánuco Pampa or elsewhere, and it would be idle to speculate further about such practices in the absence of evidence.

The second stage is to keep the long-term storage facility at a temperature of 2° to 5°C, being sure that no water film is allowed to condense on the surface of the tubers.[2] The one notable exception to the general advantage of low-temperature storage in preventing rots and other diseases is gangrene (*Phoma solanicola* Prill and Delacor). The optimum temperature for the growth of this fungus is 0°–5°C. However, "curing" at about 21° for a period of 10 days prior to long-term storage was found very effective in controlling the spread of the infection (Burton 1966:256).

Besides the generally low temperatures in the Huánuco Pampa storage facility, a second feature of Inka storage practices would almost certainly have been effective in the control of storage disease. That is the process, described above, of placing the tubers between layers of straw and tieing them into fairly loose "packages" with rope. There are several advantages to this procedure of isolating the stored tubers in small units (Burton 1966:282–83).

- Depending on how the "packages" are placed in the storehouses, air circulation can be increased, lowering the interior temperature and getting cool air more quickly and effectively to the stored commodity.
- Breaking up the storage bulk into smaller units tends to reduce the cumulative effects of temperature increase as a result of respiration of the tubers themselves.
- The straw would tend to prevent the condensation of water that frequently occurs, particularly at the top of large bulks.
- Finally, and most important, the relative isolation of the tubers in the straw would limit contamination of healthy specimens by diseased ones. This last feature may have been especially important in the storage of many small lots of tubers derived from fields over a large region. The isolation of the various lots would have made it much easier to contain the disease in any infected lot.

3. *Side effects of storage.* Low temperatures and the use of ventilation to help obtain them produce some deleterious side effects on the stored root crops. The most serious of these are changes in tissue structure of tubers when they are stored at low temperatures for substantial lengths of time. These changes lead, among other things, to the conversion of starch to sugar, thus causing a sweetening in taste (Christiansen 1967:193–94). Two somewhat different forms of sweetening are recognized. One of these, known as low-temperature sweetening, occurs in potatoes when they are held at temperatures below 10°C. The other, known as senescent sweetening, occurs at higher temperatures and starts after several months of storage. It shows varietal differences related to precocity of sprout growth. In

long-term storage a temperature as low as 7°C may be necessary to prevent senescent sweetening (Burton 1966:261).

In the temperature ranges probable at Huánuco Pampa it is unlikely that senescent sweetening would have been a problem. But at temperatures low enough to limit sprouting and the growth of most fungi and bacteria effectively, low-temperature sweetening is apparently inevitable. Fortunately low-temperature sweetening is partially reversible and holding potatoes for a few weeks at 20°C reconverts much of the sugar to starch. Of course if such a temperature is maintained for too long some of the damage that low-temperature storage had prevented in the first place would occur.

Another side effect of storage is dehydration. It is a common problem in modern warehouses where continuous forced air ventilation is used to maintain acceptable storage conditions. However, little water loss occurs with low-velocity, discontinuous ventilation of the sort possible at Huánuco Pampa, with its dependence on convection and wind currents. The possibility that water was being added to the "open" floors of some storehouses has been mentioned. If practiced, this would have helped control humidity and thus counteract dehydration. However, it seems likely that the benefits in terms of temperature control would have outweighed those resulting from the increased humidity.

SUMMARY

Burton (1966:265) points out that "all methods of potato storage are but compromises struck between a number of opposing requirements, and differences in practices may often have arisen because of a different emphasis placed upon these different requirements." It is the *emphasis* that we have difficulty reconstructing for a people whose warehouses were involuntarily abandoned almost 450 years ago. However, the major requirements of successful root-crop storage now seem clear for modern situations; it is equally clear that the Inka understood these requirements and combined an impressive ingenuity in warehouse engineering with a deep understanding of the natural environments available to them.

Both maize and tuber storage benefitted from the advantages of the *puna* climate, but aside from the mutual benefits of relatively low temperatures, their requirements were rather different. The facilities for storing potatoes and other tubers were placed and designed to take best advantage of cold temperatures and show evidence of experimentation toward increasingly sophisticated ventilation and temperature control. The maize qollqa had no windows on their downhill sides and no ventilators in their floors. Temperatures advantageous for maize storage were easily attained at Huánuco Pampa without such complications of storehouse construction. The use of large jars for corn storage, however, suggest there were other problems to be solved. In addition to being a convenient container for the shelled product, the jars may have been necessary to protect the valuable grain from rodents. The differences in floor construction between the storehouses used for maize and those used for the highland root crops likewise reflect an important difference in storage requirements. Although both maize and tubers conserve better under cold conditions, they differ substantially in their humidity requirements. The paved floors of the maize storehouses served to isolate their contents from the damp ground. The tuber storage arrangements, in contrast, protected the stored goods from water but either covered the ground loosely with stones or left the earth of the floor exposed. Both the extra cooling effects and the humidity were beneficial in this case. The planning and effort that went into providing specialized conditions for the various foods tell us almost as much about the importance of storage to the Inka as does the overall capacity of their storage system.

CONCLUSION AND IMPLICATIONS

It is evident that the food storage system in the highland areas of Tawantinsuyu was a remarkable achievement. In the construction of their storehouses, the Inka showed a sophisticated understanding of the use of insulation and ventilation to improve storage environments for their products. The evidence also suggests ongoing experimentation to improve their storehouses. The real genius of Inka storage, however, does not lie in the artificial manipulation of environments. It was based, instead, on a finely tuned understanding of natural environments for storage coupled with an elaborate organizational framework that was able to build massive storage facilities and to move people and goods to regions advantageous to storage. The complex sociopolitical organization was able to manage a wide variety of natural resources and environments on a vast multiregional scale. The perception of valuable resources and environments was not limited to raw materials and climates suitable for food production; it also recognized critical storage zones and incorporated them into its overall scheme of resource coordination.

Just as the terracing and irrigation of the *kechwa* regions of the Urubamba Valley near Cuzco extended the utilization of that area, the building of storage facilities in the higher zones helped take maximum advantage of their resources. Each zone was developed in the direction of its own potential, and impressive citylike centers could be built even in zones that at first glance might seem economically marginal. In fact, because concentrations of food could best be located in high areas, they may have been the best locations for the centers that served urban functions in such a system.

Although the evidence for pre-Inka storage is now substantial (Browman 1970; Anders 1975, 1977; Day 1973, 1982; Klymyshyn 1987; Mackey 1987; Pozorski 1987; Shimada 1978, 1987), it is still not sufficient to begin to plot developmental patterns. But the relation of storage to broader social and economic contexts is now much more conducive to analysis as a result of recent progress in the understanding of many facets of Andean organization. The relationship between the use of natural storage zones, stressed in this study, and the model of "control vertical de pisos ecologicos" elaborated by Murra (1972) should be apparent. Storage, or storage climate, was another critical resource that could be effectively managed through such a "vertical system." By Inka times, and at the level of the state, the vertical or "archipelago" model had been extended and fulfilled functions that were not strictly ecological (Murra 1972:465). Indeed the whole set of state-built administrative centers mentioned here and described elsewhere (Morris 1972a) as a strategy of "compulsory urbanism" can be seen as an elaboration of some of the principles of "vertical control." The centers were in many respects colonies set up by the state to serve urban functions.

ACKNOWLEDGMENTS

Most of the material in this chapter was written in 1976 and published in 1981 as part of "Tecnología y Organización Inca del Almacenamiento de Víveres en La Sierra," in *Runakunap Kawsayninkupaq Rurasqankunaqa: La Tecnología en el Mundo Andino*, edited by Heather Lechtman and Ana María Soldi. I am grateful to the National Science Foundation and to the Cornell University Library.

CHAPTER 9 **The Architecture and Contents of Inka State Storehouses in the Xauxa Region of Peru**

TERENCE N. D'ALTROY AND
CHRISTINE A. HASTORF

ARCHAIC expansionist states used a variety of economic mechanisms to finance their activities, including tribute levies, direct taxation, control of mercantilism, and mobilization of labor. In the Inka empire, the state was funded primarily through a corvée labor program, assessed to each household (see, for example, Murra 1982). The state also drew support from an increasing number of attached specialists from a vast pool of forcibly resettled subjects (*mitmaqkuna*) (Rowe 1946; Murra 1980), and, in some instances, from a levy on administered exchange (Salomon 1986). Together these sources produced the subsistence, utilitarian, and prestige supplies used by the state to support its personnel throughout the Andes.

As discussed in Chapter 2, a centrally planned storage system played a pivotal role in the management of Inka staple finance (Morris 1967, 1976; D'Altroy 1981; Earle and D'Altroy 1982). To review, the principle functions of centrally managed stockpiling in the Inka economy can be seen in (1) the regular maintenance of permanent administrative, military, religious, artesanal, and service personnel and the temporary support of corvée laborers; (2) provision of a buffer against fluctuations in state needs caused by both anticipated and unpredictable environmental, economic, and political changes; and (3) provision of a subsistence safeguard for local populations in the event of shortages (Morris 1967; Earle and D'Altroy 1979, 1982; Murra 1980). Analysis of this storage system affords a direct method for studying Inka staple finance. The state's concern for quantitative order, as reflected in its political structure and accounting system, makes storage facilities a singularly useful data source for research on the complex systems of production and consumption.

In this chapter we discuss results from our archaeological investigations into the Inka state storage system in the Xauxa region of the central Andean highlands (Figure 9-1). Two issues are of particular

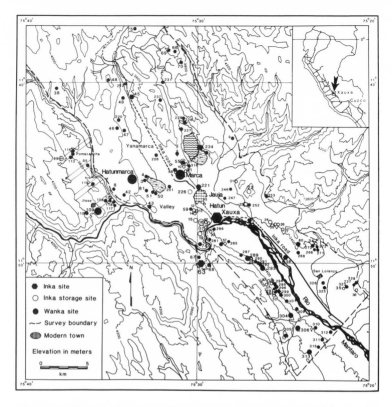

Figure 9-1. The distribution of sites in the Upper Mantaro Valley, during the Inka occupation.

interest: the spatial distribution of storage capacity (discussed in Chapter 6) and the contents of the storehouses (*qollqa*). These questions are significant because the distribution of stored goods may arguably reflect the state's intent and its ability to fund its activities at specific locations. By extension, the composition of the supplies should provide direct evidence of the types of activities to be supported. For instance, if we assume that the state stored its goods at the points of consumption rather than production, differential distributions of foods or craft goods among storage facilities may reflect different state-financed activities at these locations. We recognize that determining the sources of production and the points of final disposition of the supplies are also pertinent to this study; however, present data are insufficient to address these problems adequately, and we therefore concentrate on more accessible features of the system.

The early Spanish references to Inka storage overwhelmingly support a concept of storage organization in which the state concentrated supplies at state centers for consumption nearby (e.g., Cieza 1984: Ch. lx:190). An exception may be found in the case of a large storage facility in the Cochabamba area of Bolivia that may have housed agricultural goods produced in the immediate vicinity but that were intended for consumption elsewhere by the military (Wachtel 1982). This seems to be an unusual circumstance, however, and not a standard characteristic of Inka principles of economic organization (For a more extensive discussion of the spatial correlates of possible models of production, storage and consumption of the products kept in Inka storehouses, see Earle and D'Altroy 1982 and Chapter 6).

The data discussed here derive from study of the layout of the state facilities in the Xauxa region, from early documentary sources, and from test excavations in the core complexes above the provincial administrative center, Hatun Xauxa. These data show systematic patterning both in the regional distribution of storage capacity and in the organization of the contents among buildings. The results further show that many of the data needed to address these issues are readily recoverable through standard archaeological techniques, such as water flotation of soil samples.

THE STUDY REGION

The Xauxa region, conquered by the Inkas *ca.* 1460, was logistically and environmentally critical to the central part of the empire. Under Inka rule, the communities of the native Wanka population moved downslope from their defensive hilltop communities to inhabit more dispersed settlements along valley margins (LeBlanc 1981). At the same time, the Wanka politics were drawn into state government through a policy of centralizing local authority and inducting Wanka elites into the state administrative structure (D'Altroy 1981).

The main Inka highland road from Cuzco to Quito ran throughout the Mantaro Valley into the provincial center, Hatun Xauxa, and trunk roads ran west from the valley to the coast and east to the *montaña* and *selva*. Smaller state settlements along the road supported transient state personnel, controlled traffic, and provided message service (see Morris 1972a). This resulted in a dual settlement system in the region, with a planned series of Inka administrative and logistical sites superimposed over the resettled Wanka communities.

The complex highland topography made the products of a wide range of environmental zones available to the residents of the Xauxa region. Flat valley bottomlands (3,150 to 3,400 m) were most suited to maize agriculture, whereas the adjacent rolling uplands and hillslopes (3,400 to 3,800 m) were more conducive to tuber and quinoa cultivation. The *puna* grasslands (3,800 to 4,800 m) to the west, east, and north, were suited to camelid herding, whereas products such as coca, capsicum peppers, and fruit could be procured either directly or through exchange from the nearby *montaña* and *selva* on the eastern side of the Andean cordillera (Earle et al. 1980: 6–8). The conquest of the Upper Mantaro region and of the Wankas thus provided the Inka state with key human and environmental resources in a logistically important position.

STATE STORAGE ORGANIZATION

Fifty-three storage facilities have been recorded along the hillslopes lining the Mantaro Valley (Browman 1970; Parsons and Hastings 1977). These are consistently located on crests or high slopes, where they would have benefitted from water drainage and air circulation, enhancing the preservation of perishable goods. As discussed in Chapter 6, regularity characterized state storage facilities in the central Andes. Both the limestone and mud mortar (*pirka*) masonry and structure size were standardized, although not invariant. Morris (1967) has observed that the latter feature was probably partially an accounting device. The large sites also exhibit a few buildings (15 to 20; i.e., 3 to 4%) slightly offset from the principal rows. Functions suggested for these structures include administration, security, and residence of maintenance personnel (Morris 1967; D'Altroy 1981).

For the present study, we have investigated in detail only the 30 storehouse complexes in the northern half of the Mantaro Valley (Figure 9-1). These sites contain from four structures (J91; estimated volume 183 m^3) to an estimated 479 structures (J17; 27,075 m^3). The distribution of storage facilities strongly suggests that state-financed

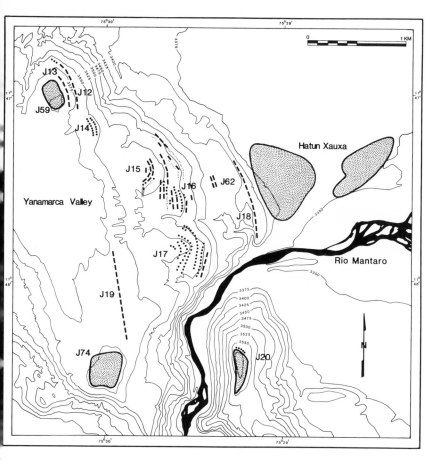

Figure 9-2. The distribution of storage complexes (J12-20, J62) and Wanka villages (J59, J74, and unnumbered site adjacent to J20) above the Inka administrative center of Hatun Xauxa. The dashes and dots are schematic representations of areas of the storage facilities dominated by rectangular and circular buildings, respectively. Elevations are in meters.

activity decreased rapidly as distance from the administrative center increased. Of the estimated total of 1,992 qollqa (123,716 m³), 1,069 (64,618 m³) lie in five major sites (J15–19) in the hills above Hatun Xauxa (Figure 9-2). The remaining storage capacity is distributed among 25 smaller sites, with an additional 23 small sites located south of the present study area (Browman (1970: map 14). The centralization of finance in this manner would have been cost-effective for supporting administrators, state-controlled craft specialists, and the military, housed at the administrative center. Conversely, the dispersed storage may have been useful in supporting corvée labor projects and craft production throughout the valley and for underwriting local elites acting on behalf of the state in their local communities.

Most of the small storage complexes away from the center were built adjacent to but separate from Wanka villages. In contrast, the main facilities above Hatun Xauxa were not associated with local habitation. This isolation of state storehouses from Wanka habitation underscores the actual and conceptual separation of state provisioning and local access to the goods provided.

STORAGE CONTENTS: DOCUMENTARY EVIDENCE

Early colonial documents, such as censuses, inspections, and litigation, provide insight into the role of centralized storage in the regional state economy. According to the Spanish chronicler Cieza, the organizational capacities of the state were reflected as much in the diversity of goods warehoused as in the extent of the storage facilities themselves.

> [I]n the more than 1200 leagues of coast they governed, they had their delegates and governors, and many lodgings and great storehouses full of necessary things, which were for provisioning the soldiers. Because in one of them, there were lances, and in others darts, and in others sandals, and in others the remaining arms they had.
>
> Moreover, some storehouses were filled with rich clothing, and others with more goods and others with food and all manner of supplies. In this manner, once the lord was lodged in his housing, and his soldiers nearby, not a thing, from the most trivial to the greatest, was lacking, because it could be provided (Cieza 1967: ch. xliiii:143–44).[1]

As the Wanka testified in a 1582 Spanish inspection (Vega 1965:169), the Inka required them to provide laborers to produce subsistence supplies on state lands and artisans to manufacture a variety of material goods that were then placed in the qollqa. The comprehensiveness of state stores was described in Wanka testimony to the inspector Andrés de Vega.

> [The Wanka were] ordered to tend fields of food, and [to make] clothing, and maids were named as their wives; and native clothing and everything

that they could produce was ordered put into storehouses, from which gifts were made to soldiers and to the lords and to the valiant Indians and to whomever seemed [appropriate to the Inka]; and similarly, it was ordered that those who worked in their fields and houses receive something from the storehouses [Vega 1965:169].[2]

This passage emphasizes the role of storage in the management of state finance and explicitly lists the major uses of goods: support of the military, the elites, corvée laborers, and retainers.

It may be further inferred from the documentary evidence that Wanka elites and accountants contributed directly to management of state storage. After the initial Inka defeat in the region (1533), the Wanka continued to stock the state storehouses until 1554, when nothing remained. The supplies were maintained in part to keep the Spaniards from raiding the local communities' own stores (Polo 1916:77; Zárate 1917:563; Cieza 1967: ch. xii:37). In 1558–1561 the Wanka filed depositions in the Audiencia Real in Lima, asking for restitution for goods and services provided the Spaniards up to 1554 (Espinoza 1971). In presenting the petitions, the Wanka lords relied on their personal accountants, who had itemized the information on the *khipu* (mnemonic knot records), the lords being unaware of the precise quantities themselves. Among the goods listed in the order presented from the *khipu* were gold, silver, *qompi* (fancy cloth), blankets, maize (*Zea mays*), quinoa (*Chenopodium quinoa*), potatoes (*Solanum* spp.), sandals, saddlebags, rope, ceramics, birds, coarse and fine firewood, charcoal, grass, straw, *chicha* (maize beer), "all fruit," salt, fish, and other unspecified goods. Also included on the lists, but not likely to have been kept in storehouses, were camelids, birds, and fresh fish. Murra (1975:241–254, 1982) has drawn attention to the consistent ordering of the materials on the *khipu* and has inferred a set of pre-hispanic Andean materials classifications based on the organization of the mnemonic system (see also LeVine 1979). Additional goods are listed that were Spanish in origin (introduced as early as 1537) or that could not reasonably have been kept in storehouses (e.g., chickens, eggs, camelids).

From 1533 to 1537 the Lurinwanka and Hatunxauxa provincial divisions (*saya*) repeatedly mobilized certain classes of goods in direct proportion to the relative populations of the two *saya*. In the last Inka census of the mid-1520s the Lurinwanka were recorded as having

Table 9-1. List of Goods Voluntarily Provided the Spaniards by the Wankas, 1533–1537 (cf. Espinoza 1971; Murra 1975:243–54; Levine 1979; Earle et al. 1980:36–37)

Event	Saya	Gold		Silver		Mature Camelids	
		Pesos	%[a]	Pesos	%	Frequency	%
Wankas meet	Lurinwanka	596	66.4	596	66.4	40	66.7
Pizarro in	Hatunxauxa	301	33.6	301	33.6	20	33.3
Cajamarca (1532)							
Pizarro arrives in	Lurinwanka					55,656	80.7
Hatun Xauxa	Hatunxauxa					13,320	19.3
(1533)							
Pizarro leaves for	Lurinwanka						
Cuzco	Hatunxauxa						
Treasurer	Lurinwanka					1,942	75.2
Requelme in	Hatunxauxa					642	24.8
Xauxa (1533–34)							
Soto battles	Lurinwanka					192	66.7
Quisquis	Hatunxauxa					96	33.3
Soto returns	Lurinwanka					439	68.7
	Hatunxauxa					200	31.3
Pizarro leaves for	Lurinwanka					245	67.1
Lima	Hatunxauxa					120	32.9
Spanish expedition	Lurinwanka					110	64.7
against Quizo	Hatunxauxa					60	35.3
Yupanki							
Alvarado received	Lurinwanka					876	60.9
(1537)	Hatunxauxa					563	39.1

12,000 "men of war," whereas Hatunxauxa had 6,000 (Vega 1965:167). Table 9-1 contains the list of goods reported to have been given to the Spaniards by each of the political divisions during these first years, in which the Spanish reorganization had yet to take effect. The 2:1 ratio can be seen principally in goods with prestige value, such as precious metals, mature camelids, *qompi* cloth, blankets, maize, quinoa, and potatoes. The first gift, to Francisco Pizarro in Cajamarca in 1532, where he held the emperor Atawalpa captive, effectively demonstrates the coordination between *saya*. These goods, almost certainly given by volition (i.e., not requested by the Spaniards), reflect the ratio in all classes of goods provided, with the exception of the 20 *hanegas* of potatoes given by Hatunxauxa. Later prestations, particularly those involving a large quantity of goods, such as maize, quinoa, and pota-

Table 9-1. (Continued)

Young Camelids		Qompi Cloth		Blankets		Maize	
Frequency	%	Frequency	%	Frequency	%	Hanegas[b]	%
		80	66.7	4	66.7	149	65.9
		40	33.3	2	33.3	77	34.1
20,386	100.0					20,542	62.3
		19	100.0	2	100.0	12,406	37.7
				4	66.7	11,931	61.1
				2	33.3	7,582	38.9
238	64.3	5	55.6			5,952	64.7
132	35.7	4	44.4			3,249	35.3
12	100.0					1,000	66.7
						500	33.3
12	16.4	24	66.7	12	66.7	4,260	65.9
61	83.6	12	33.3	6	33.3	2,202	34.1
12	66.7					1,193	66.5
6	33.3					602	33.5
18	64.3					665	66.7
10	35.7					332	33.3
65	60.7					21,319	61.2
42	39.3	23	100.0	4	100.0	13,488	38.8

toes, show the Hatunxauxa *saya* providing slightly more than 33.3%. It may be that the population of Hatunxauxa exceeded one half that of Lurinwanka by a small margin, which became important when large quantities were mobilized.

It cannot be assured that all goods listed were drawn from state stores even in the earliest Hispanic years, because as Murra (1975; cf. LeVine 1979:57) suggests, community stores could have been used to provide some of the goods. However, no archaeological evidence has been found to indicate that such stores existed apart from domestic stockpiles and elite household supplies in the Hatunxauxa region. On the contrary, the Wanka were drawing directly from Inka state stores to provision the Spaniards at least as late as Pizarro's 1537 expedition to the coast to establish the new capital of

Table 9-1. *(Continued)*

Event	Saya	Quinoa		Potatoes		Alpargatas	
		Hanegas	%	Hanegas	%	Frequency	%
Wankas meet	Lurinwanka						
Pizarro in	Hatunxauxa			20	100.0		
Cajamarca (1532)							
Pizarro arrives in	Lurinwanka	238	65.7	2,386	65.6		
Hatun Xauxa	Hatunxauxa	124	34.2	1,249	34.4		
(1533)							
Pizarro leaves for	Lurinwanka	224	56.7	600	61.8		
Cuzco	Hatunxauxa	171	43.3	371	38.2		
Treasurer	Lurinwanka	390	66.0	590	55.7		
Requelme in	Hatunxauxa	201	34.0	470	44.0		
Xauxa (1533–34)							
Soto battles	Lurinwanka						
Quisquis	Hatunxauxa			349	100.0		
Soto returns	Lurinwanka						
	Hatunxauxa	202	100.0				
Pizarro leaves for	Lurinwanka						
Lima	Hatunxauxa						
Spanish expedition	Lurinwanka	24	66.7	183	66.5		
against Quizo	Hatunxauxa	12	33.3	92	33.5		
Yupanki							
Alvarado received	Lurinwanka	279	59.7	398	60.9	123	100.0
(1537)	Hatunxauxa	188.5	40.3	255	39.1		

Ciudad de los Reyes (Lima). The Spaniard Alonso de Mesa, testifying on behalf of the Lurinwanka paramount don Jerónimo Guacrapáucar (Guacrapáucar 1971:244), stated that

> said Marquis Francisco Pizarro descended from said Xauxa Valley to the province of Los Llanos to look for a seat in which to settle the city of Los Reyes [Lima] and took from said Xauxa Valley all the Indians who he needed for cargo [bearers] and that the rest of the supplies that were in said valley from which the Marquis and those of his royal domain were provided were from the storehouses that they had in said valley that said Indians of said valley had given in tribute to the Inka and those were from said don Jerónimo Guacrapáucar and from the other Indians of said valley.[3]

In the mid-1540s, Spanish soldiers burned six structures the contents of which were duly recorded by Wanka accountants (Cusichaca

Table 9-1. (Continued)

Ojotas		Carrying Bags		Rope		Large Ceramics	
Frequency	%	Frequency	%	Frequency	%	Frequency	%
209	53.0					2,983	69.4
185	47.0					1,316	30.6
						1,430	100.0
50	40.0					1,430	65.7
75	60.0	4	100.0			745	34.3
120	56.6					6,003	85.7
92	43.4	6	100.0	12	100.0	1,002	14.3
						845	66.7
						422	33.3
						4,035	60.9
182	100.0	5	100.0			2,589	39.1

et al. 1971:308). The goods lost included 3,099 *hanegas* of maize, 18 *hanegas* of quinoa, and 370 *hanegas* of potatoes. The maize and quinoa were listed as a single item and the potatoes as another, but it is not clear if this occurred because of the storage organization itself or for some other reason. Although the measure *hanega* (or *fanega*) varied in Colonial Spanish America from one region to the next, a best estimate for Peru would be about 1.6 bushels per *hanega* (Haggard and McClean 1941:76). By this measure, an average of about 697.4 *hanegas* (39.4m^3) would have been stored in each structure. That is, the burned goods would have occupied about 75.8% of the potential storage volume of an average circular storehouse (52 m^3) or 55.5% of the potential volume of an average rectangular qollqa (71 m^3), as estimated from the archaeological field data. The estimated volume

Table 9-1. (Continued)

Event	Saya	Small Ceramics		Partridges		Rough Firewood	
		Frequency	%	Frequency	%	Cargas^c	%
Wankas meet Pizarro in Cajamarca (1532)	Lurinwanka Hatunxauxa						
Pizarro arrives in Hatun Xauxa (1533)	Lurinwanka Hatunxauxa	95	100.0	2,386 1,240	65.8 34.2	360,000 200,071	64.3 35.7
Pizarro leaves for Cuzco	Lurinwanka Hatunxauxa						
Treasurer Requelme in Xauxa (1533–34)	Lurinwanka Hatunxauxa	1,253	100.0	1,365	100.0	35,693 28,076	60.0 40.0
Soto battles Quisquis	Lurinwanka Hatunxauxa						
Soto returns	Lurinwanka Hatunxauxa	624	100.0	115	100.0	44,394 24,074	64.8 35.2
Pizarro leaves for Lima	Lurinwanka Hatunxauxa						
Spanish expedition against Quizo Yupanki	Lurinwanka Hatunxauxa					4,400 2,200	66.7 33.3
Alvarado received (1537)	Lurinwanka Hatunxauxa	1,635	100.0	153	100.0		

for the state storehouses in general thus appears to be reasonable, although perhaps a bit high.

Despite the warfare, Spanish and Inka theft, and gifts from the Wanka, the storage system was still fully viable after 15 years. When Presidente Gasca passed through the region in 1547, he stayed at Jauja for seven weeks with about 100 men, ultimately assembling about 1,500 (Zárate 1862:563). His force was fed without making a dent in the goods that were still stored in the state qollqa, even though the men consumed more than 15,000 *hanegas* of maize (about 24,000 bu, 850 m^3, or 14 average storehouses) (Polo 1916:77). At the time that Gasca took his supplies, goods for 2, 3, and even 4 years were said to still be stockpiled.

That the Wanka could partially maintain this system to their own

Table 9-1. (Continued)

Fine Firewood		Charcoal		Grass		Straw	
Cargas	%	Cargas	%	Cargas	%	Cargas	%
30,404	100.0	56,862	100.0	48,989	100.0	321,354	100.0
8,665	100.0			12,112	100.0	6,145	100.0
1,213	100.0			8,915	100.0	11,123	100.0
				10,134	100.0	10,133	100.0
				34,220	100.0	11,113	100.0

advantage for 20 years without Inka control implies that the Wanka were privy to the mechanics of the finance/storage system, most likely as managerial functionaries. It also implies that the Wanka socioeconomic organization, which had been centralized under the Inkas, did not collapse immediately with the Inka defeat but continued functioning for several decades thereafter (D'Altroy 1981). The documents thus clearly describe a complex system in which regional elites and laborers were essential to providing and maintaining the staple and sumptuary supplies employed in the empire's political economy.

TEST EXCAVATIONS

In 1979, six qollqa were test excavated at the two largest storage complexes above Hatun Xauxa, J16 (359 structures) and J17 (479

Table 9-1. *(Continued)*

Event	Saya	Chicha		"All Fruit"		Salt	
		Cántaros	%	Frequency?	%	Frequency?	%
Wankas meet Pizarro in Cajamarca (1532)	Lurinwanka Hatunxauxa						
Pizarro arrives in Hatun Xauxa (1533)	Lurinwanka Hatunxauxa	1,322	100.0				
Pizarro leaves for Cuzco	Lurinwanka Hatunxauxa						
Treasurer Requelme in Xauxa (1533–34)	Lurinwanka Hatunxauxa	2,118	100.0				
Soto battles Quisquis	Lurinwanka Hatunxauxa						
Soto returns	Lurinwanka Hatunxauxa	1,005	100.0				
Pizarro leaves for Lima	Lurinwanka Hatunxauxa						
Spanish expedition against Quizo Yupanki	Lurinwanka Hatunxauxa	10	100.0				
Alvarado received (1537)	Lurinwanka Hatunxauxa	2,424	100.0	354	100.0	120	100.0

structures; Figure 9-3). The principal goals of the excavations were as follows:

1. To determine the quality and quantity of botanical remains, in part for development of a research design for more extensive fieldwork. Botanical material is seldom reported in any quantity from Andean highland sites, but water flotation of soil samples from sites in the Xauxa region has consistently recovered identifiable remains (Hastorf 1981, 1983). Additionally, early documents report that the Inkas deliberately burned some portion of the storage facilities in Hatun Xauxa in 1533 to keep the Spaniards from using the contents (Sancho 1917:141), potentially preserving plant materials exceptionally well.
2. To determine whether the contents of the two shapes of structures— circular and rectangular—were systematically different. Morris (1971:139) has proposed that maize may have been kept in circular

Table 9-1. (*Continued*)

Fish Frequency?	%	Other
23,863	65.8	
12,404	34.2	
12,341	100.0	
1,500	100.0	
10	100.0	
322	100.0	5 chickens, 811 eggs

NOTE: This list includes only the prestige goods, camelids, and subsistence supplies given up to the introduction of European goods into the *khipu* lists, in the 1537 presentation to Alvarado. No stolen materials are included in this table, although the goods stolen by the Spaniards and Inka were recorded by the Wanka.
[a]Percentage is of the total given at one time from both Lurinwanka and Hatunxauxa.
[b]An *hanega*, a variant of a *fanega*, is about 1.60 bushels.
[c]The precise quantity of a *carga* is unclear, although it may be presumed to be either a human or llama load.

qollqa and tuber crops in rectangular qollqa, on the basis of evidence excavated from Huánuco Pampa. This hypothesis has become increasingly accepted in the literature, apparently without additional testing (e.g., Gasparini and Margolies 1980:303). A sample of six structures is clearly insufficient to test this proposition rigorously, but evidence for mixing or strict segregation of crops could contribute to understanding storage organization and to devising testable models of the staple finance system.

3. To study storage techniques. Early documents, confirmed in part by archaeological data collected elsewhere, report that a variety of goods, such as root crops, were stored in bales, whereas some products, such as shelled maize, were kept in ceramic containers (Morris 1967:96, 139).

4. To assess, in a preliminary fashion, the diversity and complexity of storehouse architecture.

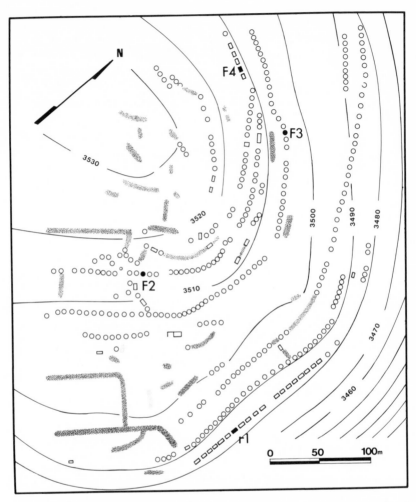

Figure 9-3. Inka state storage site J17, above Hatun Xauxa, consisting primarily of rows of circular and rectangular buildings; mottled areas designate zones of rubble from destroyed buildings. Contour intervals are approximate, in meters. Blacked-in structures F1, F2, F3, F4 were text excavated.

At J16, one circular and one rectangular structure were chosen randomly (i.e., using a random numbers table) from all structures clearly identifiable from surface remains. J17 was arbitrarily stratified into halves, and one structure of each shape was chosen randomly from each half. Only those structures in the main rows were considered for testing because of the higher probability that buildings displaced from the principal rows would have had functions other than storage. One quadrant was randomly chosen for excavation in each structure and a 1 m wide trench was excavated, with all dirt being sifted through a ¼ in. mesh screen. This procedure resulted in the sampling of about 15% of each structure (Figure 9-4 and 9-5).

Because of our primary interest in botanical remains, three cloth bags of soil (about 6 kg each) were taken for flotation analyses from each natural stratum yielding adequate soil for collection and from each concentration of burned material. A soil sample was also taken from a rectangular structure (J17=5) the wall of which had recently collapsed, revealing a layer of carbonized botanical remains. The soil samples were processed in a simple water flotation system (Minnis and LeBlanc 1976) in which carbonized remains floated to the water's surface where they could be collected with fine mesh chiffon.

STOREHOUSE ARCHITECTURE

All six excavated storehouses share a set of basic architectural characteristics, notably limestone *pirka* masonry, but display some variability in detail. The walls (55 to 60 cm thick) of the excavated buildings were intruded through sterile soil to rest on bedrock in every case but one (J16=F1). No entrances are preserved in the excavated structures, but at other sites rectangular openings (50 to 70 cm on a side) were systematically built either on the uphill or downhill sides of qollqa. On or just above sterile soil, each structure retains at least one layer (20 to 50 cm deep) of loose limestone rocks (5 to 10 cm maximum dimension) with little or no dirt intermixed. Two structures (J16=F1 and J17=F3) were built with two drainage levels, between which was a layer (10 cm deep) of loose soil. The regular size of the loose rock suggests a conscious effort to provide a porous but solid layer to support the floor. The apparent purpose was to lower the humidity of the floor, thus aiding the preservation of the contents.

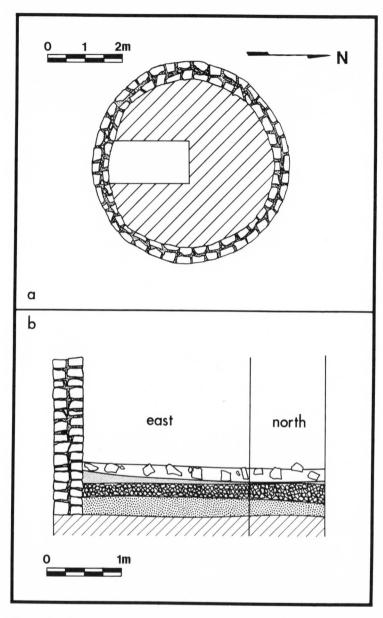

Figure 9-4. Storage structure J17=F2: *a,* plan view, showing stone and mud mortar foundation, unexcavated area shown by diagonal lines; *b,* cross-section of test trench and structure wall; from top to bottom, strata are loose wallfall, packed earth floor, loose limestone rock, packed earth leveling stratum, and unexcavated bedrock.

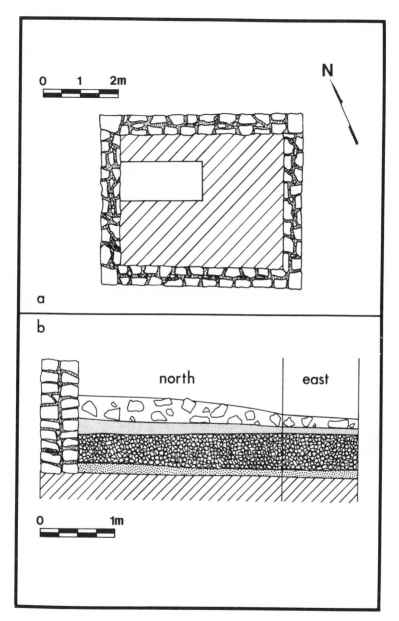

Figure 9-5. Storage structure J17=F4; a: plan view, showing stone and mud mortar foundation, unexcavated area shown in diagonal lines; b: cross-section of test trench and structure wall; from top to bottom, strata are loose wallfall, packed earth floor, loose limestone rock, packed earth leveling stratum, and unexcavated bedrock.

No evidence was found for drainage channels inside or outside the structures such as those Morris (1967:204) found at Huánuco Pampa. The contrast may be attributed in part to lower rainfall and higher evapotranspiration in the Xauxa region, or perhaps to a greater technological refinement at Huánuco. The floors of five structures were simply packed dirt, 10 to 15 cm thick. In structure J16=F1, however, a thin (4 cm thick), neatly laid, slate floor covered the entire area exposed by the trench and very likely the entire structure. This may be a local variant of the packed stone floors observed in the Huánuco area (Morris 1967:204) and may reflect the types of goods stored in the buildings (see below).

STOREHOUSE CONTENTS

Only ceramics and botanical remains were recovered intact from good archaeological contexts. No bone, metal, or lithic materials were recovered, and textile material (thread) was found only in a context. that could not be definitively assigned to prehistoric activities.

CERAMICS

Even allowing for the small number of structures tested, three features of the ceramic assemblage are notable (Table 9-2). First, the diagnostic assemblage on the storehouse floors is almost exclusively Inka; most Wanka ceramics recovered came from construction fill. Second, the assemblage was dominated by large flared-rim jars (aríbalos), although some fragments of platelike ceramic pieces, probably jar lids, were also recovered. The lack of hearths in the trenches and of carbonized organic deposits on any sherds argues against domestic use of the vessels, and it seems likely that the jars were used for storage, although this shape of vessel was also used for brewing maize beer (Rowe 1946:292).

Third, only two structures, both circular in floor plan, yielded an appreciable quantity of ceramics. Three structures contained no ceramics in the floor level, and one had only 16 sherds in the test trench (Table 9-2). As will be discussed shortly, the soil in the immediate vicinity of sherd concentrations yielded high quantities of carbonized maize and quinoa, suggesting that the seeds had been stored in the jars. A similar concentration of jars associated with

Table 9-2. Ceramics Excavated from Storehouses at Sites J16 and J17

Structure	Context	Total Diagnostic Ceramics	Total Inka Ceramics	Inka Jar Sherds	Inka Plate/Lid Sherds	Wanka Ceramics	Ceramics of Indeterminate Style
J16=F1[a]	Fill on floor	16	16	16			
J16=F2[b]		0					
J17=F1[b]		0					
J17=F2[a]	Fill on floor	198	188	188		7	3
J17=F3[a]	Fill on floor	151	151	150	1		
	Upper rocky layer	4	1	1			3
	Lower rocky layer	32	6	6		24	2
	Fill on sterile	1				1	
	Total	188	158	157	1	25	5
J17=F4[b]	Fill on floor	5	2	2			3
	Floor	8	3	3			5
	Rocky layer	39	7	6	1	31	1
	Fill on sterile	39				39	
	Total	91	12	11	1	70	9

[a]Circular floor plan.
[b]Rectangular floor plan.

maize in circular structures has been found at Huánuco Pampa (Morris 1967).

BOTANICAL REMAINS

The botanical materials recovered from the flotation procedure, once dried, were sorted and identified in the Ethnobotany Laboratory at the University of California, Los Angeles, by C. Hastorf, using a 10- to 15-power dissecting microscope. Several of the larger, incomplete plant fragments were identified from their tissue anatomy by use of a scanning electron microscope. In each procedure, the archaeological remains were compared to modern wild and cultivated species collected for the laboratory. Only charred material has been considered potentially prehistoric in this analysis because moisture and oxygen in the soil decompose uncharred remains; any uncharred material may be suspected of being recently intrusive. Not all charred remains can be assumed to have been deposited prehistorically, however, because Andean farmers frequently burn their fields today, leaving charred contaminants on the ground surface. An example of the consequences may be seen in the surface-level samples of J16=F2 (Table 9-3, row 2), which contain carbonized wheat (*Triticum* sp.), removing this provenience unit from consideration as an undisturbed, prehistoric context.

The results of the sorting are presented in Table 9-3. Each taxon is represented by a raw count and by *ubiquity,* which measures the proportion of samples containing a specific taxon (Hubbard 1980:51–52). This measure is useful because it partially controls for differential preservation (Monk and Fasham 1980). The interpretive value of the ubiquity measure is highest with large numbers of samples (Asch and Asch 1975), but it helps in assessing the relative importance of each crop within and among contexts, even with only a few samples. The ubiquity measure is used in Table 9-3 to present the major taxa recovered from each storehouse, in the floor proveniences and in the rocky subfloor strata. Not included are those taxa that occur very infrequently (e.g., one or two seeds per sample) or in less than 33% of the samples from each provenience.

Because all major highland crops are found in this set of 41 flotation samples, the crop distribution seen in the different structures can be attributed to depositional history rather than to differential preserva-

Table 9-3. Botanical Remains from Flotation Samples from Inka Storehouses at Sites J16 and J17

Provenience	Zea Mays No.[a]	Zea Mays Ub.[b]	Chenopodium spp. No.	Chenopodium spp. Ub.	Lupinus mutabilis No.	Lupinus mutabilis Ub.	Solanum spp. Tubers No.	Solanum spp. Tubers Ub.	Wood No.	Wood Ub.	Grasses No.	Grasses Ub.	Triticum hordeum No.	Triticum hordeum Ub.	Number of Samples
J16=F1, above floor			3	0.33					5	0.67	1	0.33			3
J16=F2, above floor	10	0.33	2	0.33							3	0.67	80	1.00	3
J16=F2, floor	100	1.00	4	0.16	6	0.33			5	0.84	7,100	1.00			6
J16=F2, pit	42	1.00	21	1.00					2	0.33	7,100	0.67			3
J17=F1, floor	2	0.67	70	1.00					18	1.00	1	0.33			3
J17=F1, rocky subfloor	14	0.67			4	0.33			11	1.00	1	0.33			3
J17=F2, above floor	3	0.33	13,485	1.00					12	1.00					3
J17=F2, rocky subfloor			40,472	1.00					16	1.00					3
J17=F3, floor					30	1.00	21	1.00	8	1.00	2	1.00			1
J17=F3, rocky subfloor (upper)	17	0.67	3	0.33	115	1.00			4	0.67					3
J17=F3, rocky subfloor (lower)			8	0.67	1	0.33					4	0.33			3
J17=F4, floor									3	0.67	6	0.33			3
J17=F4, floor			6	0.33					10	1.00	4	0.33			3
J17=F5, floor			72,000	1.00	6	1.00	1	1.00	25	1.00	1	1.00			1
													Total samples		41

[a]Total count of remains from all samples from each provenience.
[b]Ubiquity: Proportion of samples containing each type of botanical remains from each provenience.

tion. The presence of some plant remains (especially wood and grass) in samples from prehistoric contexts in all structures further indicates that the techniques used were consistent in recovering botanical specimens. (As noted above, however, we refer in this discussion only to charred material, because unburned plant remains are unfortunately not preserved in these contexts and we cannot evaluate remains that are not present.) For the purposes of this analysis, therefore, it is assumed that when a taxon is not present in a structure's plant assemblage, it was not present when the structure was abandoned.

The quantity of plant remains preserved differs markedly between the burned and unburned structures (see Table 9-3, column 4). The three structures (J16=F2, J17=F2, J17=F5) with clear evidence of rapid burning (in the form of heat-reddened clays) average about 11,000 specimens per sample, whereas the unburned structures average 48 specimens per sample. Two of the unburned structures have dense concentrations of quinoa, with little else in the plant assemblage. In the third burned structure, grass and wood were embedded in clay on the floor, accounting for much of the recorded counts of these plants. Despite the obvious higher quality of plant preservation in the burned structures, the buildings lacking evidence of fire had sufficient quantities of remains for this contextual comparison.

The variable composition of the plant remains in the qollqa is suggestive of the complexity of the storage organization. Among the six structures tested were (1) two buildings with essentially no crops, (2) two with a single crop, and (3) two with several crops. Wood and grass remains were recovered from all qollqa, perhaps reflecting either matting for storage or the thatched roofing characteristic of Inka structures (Morris 1967; Gasparini and Margolies 1980).

Of the two excavated structures with only one crop present, one (J17=F2; circular) had a dense quinoa concentration both on the floor and in the subterranean rocky level. The upper deposit of quinoa was directly associated with a concentration of Inka jar sherds, suggesting that the seeds may have been stored in pottery vessels. Alternatively, the abundant wood found in these samples may derive from storage of quinoa on wood twigs or racks or from storage of firewood. A sample from an unexcavated storehouse (J17=F5; rectangular) also yielded only quinoa, from a carbonized stratum 15 cm thick. Because this sample was obtained from a profile exposed by a collapsing sidewall, however, this sample may not reflect the overall composition of the structure's contents.

A second excavated structure (J16=F2; rectangular) yielded only maize from the floor and from an associated pit, along with wood and grass. Robert Bird (personal communication) suggests that one kernel found on the floor could be from the Cuzco maize race, thought to have been bred and distributed by the Inkas. Identification of Cuzco maize is based on low numbers of rows, inferred from the great kernel width (Grobman et al. 1961:252).

Two structures have a mixture of crops in their samples. J17=F1 (rectangular) contains both quinoa and maize, along with wood, lupine (*Lupinus mutabilis*), and grasses. J17=F3 (circular) has a more complex architecture and should be divided into two proveniences for analysis of crop remains. The floor yielded both lupine and seeds and fragments of potato, with a low frequency of wood. The rocky stratum directly below the floor also yielded lupine and, in contrast to the floor provenience, maize and quinoa. The second, lower rocky stratum had fewer remains—*Chenopodium,* wood, and grass. Because Inka pottery was found between the two rocky strata, we may infer that the structure was at least partially rebuilt during the Inka occupation. The differences in crops recovered from the various architecture strata thus suggest that the types of crops stored were changed during the use of the structure or that earlier refuse was incorporated into the construction of the drainage strata.

The potatoes and lupine in the upper floor of J17=F3 were associated with large Inka jars sherds. In traditional highland practice, tubers are stored either on ceiling beams or on a shrub matting on the floor (*pirwa* storage; see Morris 1967:92), the most frequently used matting being mint branches (*Mintostachys* sp.) (Werge 1977). The mint is a shrubby herb that grows on the hillslopes surrounding the valley and that is said to deter bugs from entering the storage area. Modern farmers in the Mantaro Valley leach and dry lupine seeds, storing them either in cloth or in ceramic jars (Hastorf, personal observation); by analogy, the Inka jars could have been used for this latter crop.

Chenopodium, wood, and grass occur with greater ubiquity than any other taxa (11 of 14 proveniences for *Chenopodium,* 12/14 for wood, and 11/14 for grass). As suggested above, the wood and grass may be attributed to either roofing or matting, but the consistent presence of quinoa requires an alternative explanation. Two lines of evidence suggest that a low frequency of *Chenopodium* in a high proportion of samples should be considered cultural background or processing contamination, not firm evidence of quinoa storage. First, these three taxa occur together in structures J16=F1 (circular) and J17=F4 (rectangular), where no other plant remains were found. However, only three quinoa seeds were recovered from J16=F1, and only six from J17=F4. Considering the quantities of remains recovered from the other qollqa, these buildings may be considered to be essentially without plant remains. Second, quinoa was consistently present in those rocky strata that contained sufficient dirt for flotation, including those in structures J17=F3 and J17=F4, from whose floors no quinoa was recovered. It therefore seems likely that low frequencies of quinoa may normally have been present in construction fill, perhaps because the crop was being cultivated in nearby fields when the storehouses were built.

While it is highly probable that architectural design was directly correlated with storage contents, present data are too sketchy to clarify this relationship. Both circular and rectangular structures contained dense concentrations of botanical remains, whereas other qollqa of each shape apparently held few or no plant remains. Relying on data from his extensive excavations at Huánuco Pampa, Morris (1967, 1971) has suggested that maize may have been consistently stored in circular qollqa and tubers in rectangular qollqa. He observes, however, that relatively few of the Huánuco storehouses yielded macrobotanical remains and that crop mixes occurred that deviated from this pattern.

The evidence from our excavations does not support Morris's hypothesis. The mixture of maize and highland crops (e.g., tubers, lupine, and quinoa) in the same structures argues against strict association of specific crops with each structure shape. Whether this may be attributed to differing patterns between Huánuco and Xauxa, to an inadequate sample, or to a more complex system than has been proposed is not yet clear. It seems reasonable, however, to expect that crops produced in particular environmental zones or by specific social groups would be stored separately, considering the Inka penchant for systematic organization and for itemized accounting of labor obligations.

DISCUSSION

From the information presented above, we may draw some conclusions about Inka storage in the Xauxa region. Looking first at the broad picture of state staple finance, we may infer that the accumulation of staple supplies for the state was centrally planned, although the facilities themselves were partially dispersed. The spatial organization of storage facilities (detailed in Chapter 6), the standardized site layout, structure size, and masonry all support the perception of state economic management described in the early documents. Similarly, the distribution of the facilities indicates strongly that the principal intent was to support activities closely associated with the state administrative center, even though the consumption of staple finance goods was extended to areas occupied by the subject Wanka communities.

Second, the documentary and archaeological evidence indicates that the organization of stored goods was complex and probably variable over time. The excavation data show that controlled recovery techniques are required to distinguish among the structures with and without plant remains and ceramics, to help reconstruct storage organization. The historical accounts cited above described stockpiles of textiles and other craft products, which may have required specialized preservation techniques. It can be argued, for example, that damage resulting from dampness would represent a much greater loss of a valued manufactured commodity and its labor investment than would a comparable loss of crops, from which a certain proportion of spoilage could be accepted. More elaborate architecture could therefore be expected for qollqa designed to hold craft products; among the special features might be stone floors, deep drainage levels, or subterranean channels. Conversely, we would not expect to find the narrow-necked jars appropriate for seed and liquid storage.

Structure J16=F1, with its neat stone floor and lack of plant remains or ceramics, appears to have been suitable for storage of craft goods. Structure J17=F1 also contained no ceramic or plant remains on the floor, suggesting that any goods stored here were not food supplies. Although positive evidence, such as burned textiles, would be necessary to confirm the storage of clothing or blankets, systematic excavation of a large number of storehouses may be sufficient to distinguish between the proportion of qollqa given to food stockpiling and that used for other supplies. By extension, this may permit a more precise estimate of the amount and distribution of the labor that the state was prepared to support through the storage system.

Third, with respect to storage techniques, the consistent association of ceramics with plant remains (especially quinoa, lupine, and tubers) suggests that certain foods may have been stored in pottery containers. Dried lupine seeds and quinoa are most easily stored in cloth bags or jars. Conversely, the abundant wood and grass remains found in all structures could be the remains of bale storage of potatoes or of deteriorated architecture. Maize, which is stored today in sacks or on the cob, appears to be less definitively associated with pottery within structures. Had maize been stored in sacks in Inka qollqa, it is likely that the material would have disintegrated and that the remaining kernels would appear to be dispersed on the floor, as they were found in our test trenches.

In sum, we have attempted to reconstruct partially the organization of centrally managed storage in the Inka provincial economy of the Xauxa area and to show that the data needed to address this problem are accessible through both archaeological and ethnohistorical research. It is equally clear, however, that a great deal of additional research will be needed to reconstruct the organization of the state economy in the region and its relationship to the imperial economy as a whole.

ACKNOWLEDGMENTS

We would like to thank Cathy Costin, Timothy Earle, James Hill, John Hyslop, Terry LeVine, William Macdonald, Craig Morris, Catherine Scott, and the editors and reviewers of *American Antiquity* for the comments on drafts of this paper. Although we have incorporated some of their ideas into the text, we, of course, remain responsible for any errors or omissions.

This chapter is reproduced by permission of the Society of American Archaeology from *American Antiquity* 49 (2):334–49 (1984).

CHAPTER 10

Stores and Homes

A Botanical Comparison
of Inka Storehouses
and Contemporary Ethnic Houses

**HEIDI A. LENNSTROM AND
CHRISTINE A. HASTORF**

INTRODUCTION

UNDER the hegemony of the Inka, an extensive state storage system, consisting of many thousands of storehouses, or qollqa, was constructed and maintained throughout the empire. The existence of these qollqa is well documented (see Snead, Chapter 3), and many, like those described in Chapters 5, 6, and 7, are still visible in the vicinity of Inka administration centers. However, relatively few qollqa have actually been excavated, and only recently have investigators begun to retrieve and make use of archaeobotanical materials in the analysis of Inka storage.

Two studies that have focused on the analysis of archaeobotanical materials from qollqa include Morris (1967, 1972a; Chapter 8, this volume) and D'Altroy and Hastorf (1984; Chapter 9, this volume). Morris described the contents recovered from qollqa at Huánuco Pampa. In that study, he suggests that specific crops were stored separately in differently shaped qollqa: maize (*Zea mays*) in circular structures and tubers (*Solanum tuberosum*, etc.) in rectangular structures. The study by D'Altroy and Hastorf in the Upper Mantaro Valley area demonstrated that the relationship between crop type and qollqa shape is not as straightforward as it appears to have been at Huánuco. In the Mantaro area, different crops often occurred within the same structure.

The purpose of the study described in this chapter is to take a more detailed look at Inka storehouses through a comparison of archaeobotanical material from the Upper Mantaro–area qollqa, with material recovered from contemporaneous habitation structures. Although we recognize the limitations of our small sample size, this comparison should be useful, first in assessing the resources utilized by the local inhabitants versus those that were appropriated by the

Inka in the same region for state-related use, and second, in providing a supplementary basis for identifying Inka state storage in the archaeological record. In addition we can begin to describe storage techniques, as well as to identify storage contexts in habitation sites.

AREA OF RESEARCH

The archaeobotanical data under consideration come from Sausa sites in the Jauja region of the central Peruvian Andes (Figure 10-1) excavated by the members of the Upper Mantaro Archaeological Research Project between 1979 and 1983 (D'Altroy 1981, and Chapter 6, this volume; Earle et al. 1980, 1987; Hastorf et al. 1989). The Sausa are a local ethnic subgroup that are part of the larger Wanka cultural group. The sites selected for this study are all firmly dated to the Inka period (known locally as Wanka III). During this time the Inka organized the construction of more than 2,000 qollqa in the Jauja area, and local inhabitants working on state owned land were required to stock the qollqa.

The two qollqa sites included in this study, J16 and J17, are large storage complexes of 359 and 479 structures, respectively (D'Altroy and Hastorf 1984, Chapter 9, this volume). These qollqa are situated just above the site of Hatun Xauxa, the Inka administration center of the Jauja district (D'Altroy Chapter 6). Each site consists of several parallel terraced lines of freestanding stone qollqa, with rows of both circular and rectangular structures. The storage structure excavations discussed here include seven randomly selected structures of both shapes from each site.

The habitation material comes from two local Wanka III sites, Hatunmarca (J2) and Marca (J54). Hatunmarca is located above the western portion of the Yanamarca Valley in the rolling uplands at 3,700 m, and Marca overlooks the Jauja and Paca valleys, at a lower elevation of 3,575 m. In order to have the same number of house structures as qollqa in the study, we chose seven habitations from these two sites. The selection criteria called for habitation structures that were securely dated, had unmixed contexts, were completely excavated, and had the most complete sampling for archaeobotanical remains.

Occupation at Hatunmarca began during the earlier Wanka II phase (A.D. 1300–1460) when the site was more widely occupied,

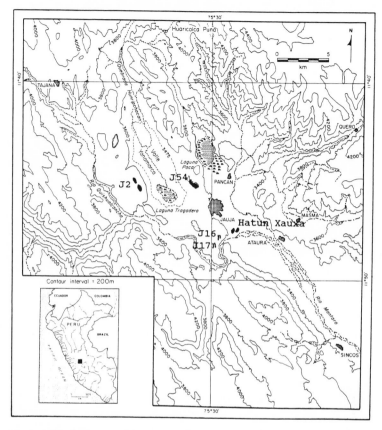

Figure 10-1. Study area: (From Hastorf 1983, Johannessen and Hastorf, 1990)

and continued, on a somewhat reduced scale, throughout the Wanka III phase. The site is made up mostly of circular stone structures, clustered in small groups of one to six around patio areas enclosed by walls. In 1983 excavations at Hatunmarca were conducted in six different patio groups, from which four structures were selected for comparison with the qollqa. These four met all the criteria listed above for inclusion in the study and contained at least five flotation samples each.

The site of Marca was first occupied in the Wanka III period and continued to be occupied into the early Colonial period. The site also

consists of stone structures in patio compounds. Most of the structures are circular, though there are some rectangular structures (such
as J54=4-20 included here [see Appendix]). From the 10 patio
groups excavated in 1982 and 1983 three complete Wanka III structures are used in this study: J54=2-1 and J54=7-1 had the highest
number of flotation samples, at 11 and 16 samples, respectively, and
were selected for this reason; J54=4-20 was chosen over two other
structures with similar numbers of samples as we decided that it
would be of special interest to include a rectangular habitation structure in the comparison. This made for a total sample of seven habitation structures, the same as the number of qollqa used in the study.

METHODOLOGY

The discussion presented here is based on archaeobotanical remains
retrieved from the habitation and qollqa structures. We focus on
material recovered from the water flotation of soil samples taken from
discrete locations that were recorded by the excavators on their site
plans. The samples were collected systematically from every 1.5 ×
1.5 m unit in each excavation level. Botanical material was also
recovered from the ¼ in. screens used during excavation, but this
material is not considered here, as it cannot be statistically analyzed
and does not contain a full array of small seeds and plant parts.

The bulk soil samples from the qollqa were processed by a simple
water flotation system (Minnis and LeBlanc 1976). The charred remains, which have a higher specific gravity than water, float on the
surface, and are scooped or syphoned off into a series of sieves. Any
plant material that becomes waterlogged and does not float is caught
in a sieve inside the machine. The qollqa samples were processed
with a 0.5 mm sieve to collect floating organic remains, called the
light fraction, and a 1.6 mm mesh to collect plant and artifact remains
that *do* sink to the bottom, called the heavy fraction (see Hastorf
1983:237–38).

Samples from the domestic structures were processed by a mecha-
nized water flotation system based on the SMAP (Shell Mound Archaeological Project) machine (see Watson 1976). In this system, soil
samples are gently poured into a 50 gallon drum of water that is
agitated by water from a shower head under the water's surface. The

mesh sizes for both the light and heavy fractions were the same as for the qollqa samples, at 0.5 mm and 1.6 mm, respectively.

Because of climatic and edaphic (soil) conditions that do not promote preservation of uncharred plant remains, only charred material will be considered to be of prehistoric origin. As seen in Table 10-1 some of the identified taxa could only be assigned to genus or family, whereas others are securely identified to species. Despite incomplete identifications, the groupings listed provide a series of intriguing results concerning storage practices and suggest what Inka storage looks like in the archaeological record.

We made quantifications based on counts of whole or fragmentary pieces of plant parts. Weights were not feasible as they are negligible for many of the smaller taxa. It must be kept in mind that the material represented in the archaeological record is biased against certain plant taxa and plant parts that never come into contact with fire.

A consideration of how plants become charred and preserved is of interest in any paleoethnobotanical study and is of particular importance here as the two types of sites we are considering represent different complexes of activities. Excellent studies of how plants get into habitation sites, and at what stage they may be exposed to fire, and hence charred, have been done by researchers such as Dennell (1976), Hillman (1981), and Pearsall (1988). Following their examples we needed to identify the possible sources of charred material in both our habitation structures and qollqa.

In domestic structures where food is processed and cooked, charred food remains are often a result of normal everyday life. Fuel remains are the result of purposeful burning, although food or fuel remains can also be charred as a result of home fires, whether intentional or not.

Qollqa sites serve a different function; they are the scene of different activities and have a different history. As a result, the plants in qollqa do not become charred in the same manner as those in domestic settings. We would expect to find less carbonized material in qollqa than in homes. Charred plants found in qollqa are most often a result of storehouses fires. In the Jauja area both the administrative center and the storehouse areas sustained fire damage during the Inkaic civil war (Espinosa Bravo 1964:95–96), and as a result of conflicts with

Table 10-1. Taxa Recovered from Habitation versus Qollqa Sites

Habitation Sites	Qollqa
Zea mays, kernels	*Zea mays*, kernels
Zea mays, embryos	*Zea mays*, embryos
Zea mays, cob fragments	*Zea mays*, cob fragments
Chenopodium quinoa	*Chenopodium quinoa*
Leguminosae, domesticated	Leguminosae, domesticated
	Lupinus mutabilis
Tubers, domesticated	Tubers, domesticated
	Solanum
Gramineae, small	Gramineae, small
Gramineae, medium (*Panicum* type)	Gramineae, medium (*Panicum* type)
Gramineae, large (*Stipa* type)	Gramineae, large (*Stipa* type)
Gramineae nodes	Gramineae nodes
Malvastrum	*Malvastrum*
Leguminosae, wild	Leguminosae, wild
Amaranthus	*Amaranthus*
Wood	Wood
	Triticum
	Triticum nodes
	Husk
Scirpus	
Verbena	
Plantago	
Cyperaceae	
Labiatae	
Nicotiana	
Compositae	
Polygonaceae	
Sisyrinchium	
Relbunium	
Ambrosia	
Solanaceae seed	
Eleocharis	
Salvia	

the Spanish (Espinoza Soriano 1971 [1561]:308). A minor source of charred material would have been occasional lightning strikes or wildfires.

Within the realm of charred remains, there is also a bias against the preservation and identification of different plant parts and plant taxa (Dennell 1976). For example, soft tissues such as large tubers can be quite fragile even when charred, and may break into fragments that are difficult to identify. Other pithy material, such as quinoa (*Chenopodium quinoa*) stalks, may simply be reduced to ash when they burn. In light of these biasing factors, quantitative results should be interpreted keeping in mind how different taxa would have entered the archaeological record and how sturdy these taxa are once charred. In the case of the major Andean food crops, this may mean that the tubers are underrepresented, whereas small, hard quinoa may be overly abundant in the archaeological record compared to their actual importance as a food.

Another bias that can affect the deposition of plant remains is their size and cultural value. For example, in an ethnobotanical study of traditional Andean households, Sikkink (1988a, 1988b) found that even in households where maize was stored and consumed there were no charred maize remains found in flotation samples taken from hearths or floors. Sikkink suggests that this is a result of the large and conspicuous size of the kernels and the care with which the highly valued maize crop is treated (Sikkink 1988a:66).

Because of both the biases inherent in our data and those biases associated with different quantification schemes, we have chosen to present the data in more than one way. Here we use ubiquity, sample diversity, ratios, and relative proportions to present a more complete picture of the plant distributions. The simplest quantification used is ubiquity (percentage presence). This is expressed as a percentage, based on the number of samples where a given taxon is present divided by the total number of samples (Popper 1988:60). In this way the occurrence and quantity of the different taxa do not affect the score of the others. This analysis tends to overemphasize rare taxa and ignores quantitative differences of a given taxon in different samples. Ubiquity may also be biased if the sample size is not uniform.

To view taxa with respect to others in the sample, the relative proportion of taxa has also been applied. This also is expressed as a percentage, but in this case the percentage is of all charred material within a single sample of each taxon. Using relative proportions, we can compare samples with differing amounts of charred material, as each adds up to 100% whether the sample contains 5 or 500 specimens.

Sample diversity, as used here, presents the number of different taxa recorded for each sample or within each site. Ratios are simply calculated between one taxon and another and are used to observe the differences or changes in the relationship between the two. These results can be especially revealing with respect to crops and their by-products, for example, maize and its kernel and cob fragments.

THE ARCHAEOBOTANICAL REMAINS

In the broadest sense, the taxa recovered from habitation and qollqa sites have some fundamental differences (see Table 10-1). Structures on habitation sites contain many more plant taxa, including domesticated foods, such as maize, quinoa, domesticated tubers, and domesticated legumes (*Leguminosae*), as well as weeds, fuel remains, industrial plants, medicinal plants, and the like. There are several taxa (especially wild seeds) that are found only in the habitation sites, reflecting their inclusion due to domestic activities. These would not have occurred in qollqa. The list of taxa from the qollqa is shorter, yet each list contains the four major food crops.

Interestingly, the only items that are regularly found in the qollqa and not in the houses are two that are identified to the species level: *Lupinus mutabilis* (tarwi), and *Solanum tuberosum* (potato). These species may indeed be present in habitation structures but in an unidentifiable condition. This suggests that plants in the qollqa were less damaged than those in homes, due to different types and intensities of activities that took place there. Other taxa found in qollqa, such as wood and grass, very likely represent storage packing or roofing material. Absence of many weed taxa in the qollqa indicate that the crops stored for the state had been carefully processed before storage and were in a relatively pure form upon entry into the structures.

An important contrast can be seen in the ubiquities of the major food crops in the two types of sites. In this analysis we have included all 124 of the samples from the 14 structures that were selected to represent qollqa and domestic sites, as outlined above. There are 86 flot samples from the seven domestic structures, and 38 samples from the seven qollqa. Table 10-2 shows that while the four food groups are found in both the habitation and qollqa structures, crops are often less regular within the qollqa. The only exception is the domesticated legumes that are more widely distributed in the qollqa. However,

Table 10-2. Ubiquity of Major Crops by Site Type

Site Type	N	Maize (N)	Quinoa (N)	Tubers (N)	Legumes (N)
Habitation	(86)	73.3% (63)	73.3% (63)	23.3% (20)	7.0% (6)
Qollqa	(38)	44.7% (17)	47.4% (18)	2.6% (1)	21.1% (8)

%=percentage of samples in which crop is present
N=number of samples

this may be a function of the process by which legumes enter into archaeological deposits.

Another way to look at the crop distributions is to examine which crops are encountered within the same *structure*. In habitation structures, we found that an average three of the four different domesticates were recovered (mean = 3.3). For example, structure J2=2-1 contains three crops, quinoa, maize, and tubers (see appendix). In the qollqa, the average is only two different domesticates in any single structure (mean = 2.0).

Similarly, individual *samples* from the two different structure uses show differences in the number of crop taxa per *sample*. In an examination of the number of crop taxa per sample, we see that 43% of samples from habitation structures have two crop taxa, and 21% have three or four taxa. On the other hand, 40% of the qollqa samples have only one crop, whereas only 3% have three or four. In sum, these figures indicate that even though all crops may occur in both structure types, they are more likely to be deposited together (through cooking, discard, etc) within habitation sites. A qollqa is much more likely to contain only one or two crops. This suggests that while separate crops were perhaps not specifically stored in certain shaped qollqa, they were kept separate within the structure, and all four major foods were not stored in the same structure.

Related to these differences in ubiquities and sample contents are differences in overall sample diversity. Following Sikkink's modern results (1988a, 1988b), we expect that storage contexts would show low taxa diversity, whereas high diversity would be linked to areas where many different activities took place. In our data we find that many of the domestic structures do show a higher diversity than the qollqa. Within the habitation sites, the number of identifiable taxa per sample ranges from 0 to 15, with an average of 5.5. In the qollqa each sample has significantly fewer taxa, with a range of 0 to 6, averaging 2.6. The plant data again suggest that the use of space and forms of deposition in the qollqa are different than those in habitations. Further, the range of plant products stored for the state was more limited than that utilized by the Sausa.

To compare this spatial distribution of plant remains, individual samples from each structure were plotted in plan view. Each map represents one use level within each individual structure, showing the walls and the location where float samples were collected. Pie diagrams (relative proportions) are used to show the composition of each sample, so that samples of differing densities of plant remains can be compared. (These results are also summarized in Appendix 10-1.) We originally plotted all of the samples in each level in every structure to examine similarities and differences. It became obvious that there were several trends and that it was unnecessary and cumbersome to present all of the maps in this chapter. Instead, we have chosen examples from three qollqa and three habitations that show the representative range of patterns we discovered. On each of the maps presented, each different taxon is labeled; maize is separated into categories of kernels, embryos, and cupules (cob fragments) to show the differences in distributions of each. The category "frags" represents charred fragments of plant tissue that could not be identified but were definitely not small seeds; most likely they represent eroded tubers or other fleshy remains. Small seeds that could not be identified to at least the family level are labeled "unidseed". The category "other" contains all taxa that represented less that 5% of the sample. The number above the "other" label indicates how many other taxa there were.

Qollqa Sites

The botanical material distributions from the seven tested qollqa falls roughly into two categories. One type of qollqa deposit contains high densities of charred plant material, usually with a high proportion of one crop. The other type contains few charred remains, with no one taxon dominating the assemblage. These general features can be used to characterize qollqa, though there is a great deal of variation as will be seen in the descriptions below.

One example of the first type of qollqa is J16=2. The uppermost level contains a large quantity of wheat (*Triticum* spp.), indicating that it continued to be used as a storehouse even after the Spanish invasion (Figure 10-2). The lower Wanka III levels show a dominance of maize, indicating that this qollqa was used mainly for the storage of this crop during the Inka period (see Figure 10-3). Presence of both kernels and cupules would suggest that some of the maize was stored on the cob. A pit in this qollqa suggests belowground, as well as the usual aboveground, storage in this structure. The high concentration of charred material and ash indicate that this structure and its contents were burned while it was still in use.

A circular qollqa, J17=3, is another example of this first type. An examination of this qollqa indicates that, at a point in time when the floor was rebuilt, there was a possible change in the crops stored. Although the upper floor is dominated by quinoa and potato, the lowest levels contain a few seeds of quinoa and tarwi (see Appendix 10-1). Samples from this qollqa are not as spatially discrete as are others of this type, as all four crops are present, with maize and quinoa occurring in small amounts in several different levels. This is likely a result of reworked deposits from the rebuilding of the floor.

In a variation of this type, J17=1, both the floor and rock subfloor are dominated by quinoa and maize, though a few legumes are included. Cupules are rare, suggesting that the maize was probably shelled prior to storage. The low density of sherds from this structure makes it ambiguous whether or not the crops were stored in jars.

A rectangular structure, J17=5, and one of the circular structures, J17=2, display the most dense deposits of charred crop material (Figure 10-4 shows J17=2). Each structure contains a very high concentration of quinoa (up to 45,545 seeds per 6-liter sample), with very little else, and each shows signs of burning. The deposits of J17=2 also contain many Inka vessel sherds, suggesting that storage of quinoa could have been in jars.

The two remaining qollqa display the second pattern of plant deposition we found for storage structures. In the circular structure, J16=1, and the rectangular structure J17 = 4, deposits contained very little charred material. This can be seen, for example, in level 3 of J17=4 shown in Figure 10-5. The relatively high proportions of wood and grass suggests that these may be remnants of the roof,

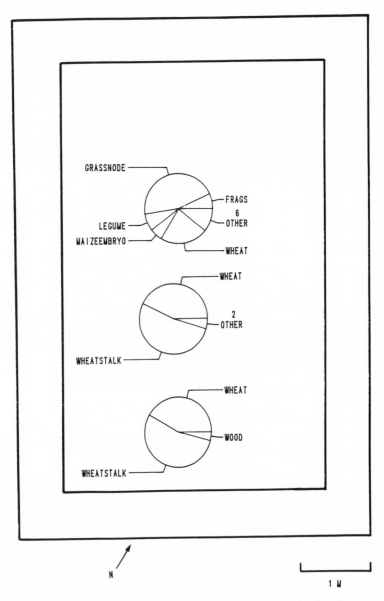

Figure 10-2. Type 1 qollqa pattern: Plan view of J16=2 level 2 showing relative proportions of plant taxa from flotation samples.

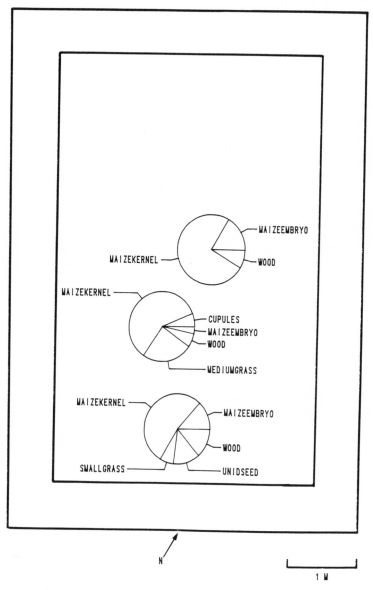

Figure 10-3. Type 1 qollqa pattern: Plan view of J16=2 level 4 showing relative proportions of plant taxa from flotation samples.

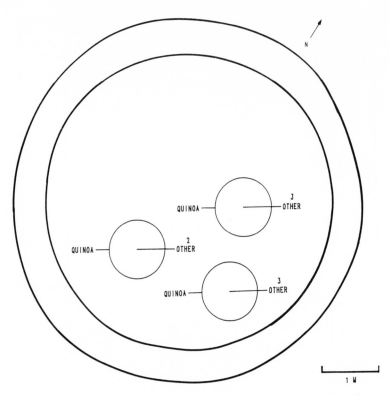

Figure 10-4. Type 1 qollqa pattern: Plan view of J17=2 level 1 showing relative proportions of plant taxa from flotation samples.

storage containers, or stored fuel. Artifacts in J16=1 were very sparse, and there do not appear to be any Inka storage vessels. J17=4 contained few sherds but did include camelid bone and stone tools. Several conclusions are possible: J16=1 may have been cleaned out; the main contents were not charred and therefore not preserved; or, the storehouse contained other perishable nonbotanical goods. This may also be true for J17 = 4, although another explanation of this pattern may be that this structure was used to store nonperishable goods, for example, tools.

In sum, the samples from the qollqa show the following: (1) a high proportion of identifiable material; (2) a low sample diversity; (3)

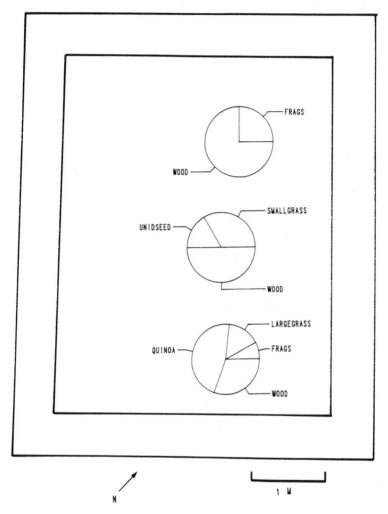

Figure 10-5. Type 2 qollqa pattern: Plan view of J17=4 level 3 showing relative proportions of plant taxa from flotation samples.

ubiquitous wood and grass, probably used as roofing and/or storage materials; (4) few taxa and low incidence of weed species left in with stored crops; (5) usually only one or two crops per structure; and, (6) when more than one crop was stored in a single qollqa it is most often maize with quinoa or tarwi with tubers (the tarwi/tuber combination is less common than quinoa/maize). The last point suggests to us that crops may have entered together from specific resource zones: for example, quinoa and maize are both from lower elevation agricultural zones, whereas tubers and tarwi are characteristic of higher elevation zones (Hastorf 1992).

Habitation Sites

The sites of Hatunmarca and Marca are contemporaneous with the Inka storehouses and were inhabited by the local Sausa people who were responsible for filling these qollqa with food and craft goods (see D'Altroy Chapter 6 and D'Altroy and Hastorf Chapter 9). In our samples we found three major patterns of botanical remains. The first type, Pattern 1, is characterized by dense charred remains, by a high proportion of unidentifiable plant material, and by a wide diversity of taxa. Pattern 2 shows dense remains with a high proportion (greater than 50%) of a single taxon. Pattern 3 is characterized by an overall low density of charred remains.

Pattern 1 is the most typical of the habitation sites. This pattern can be seen, for example, in level 4 of circular structure J2=1-1 (Figure 10-6), which contains a variety of contexts with associated plant remains such as general occupation debris, cultural fill, and a pit. The samples yielded abundant material that is unidentifiable ("frags," see above), and the material that was identified is highly diverse. For example, the average sample contains over seven taxa, usually in very small quantities. In the 27 samples from all of the levels of J2=1-1 there are only 2 samples that are dominated by a single taxon, one by small grass seeds, the other by wood (see samples 1056 and 1380 in the Appendix 10-1).

The four domesticates occur within the Pattern 1 structure and are very often found together within the same 6-liter sample. From these data we would suggest that the deposits were probably a result of accidental charring and discard and that there was a fair amount of activity within the household that led to the dispersion and eroded state of the plant remains. Pattern 1 is representative of the main occupation deposits of J2=3-1, J54=4-20, and J54=7-1 (not shown in the diagrams), though of course the pattern of botanical remains is not always identical.

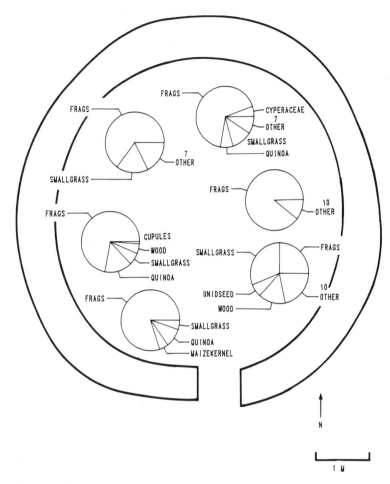

Figure 10-6. Type 1 habitation pattern: Plan view of J2=1-1 level 4 showing relative proportions of plant taxa from flotation samples.

Level 3 of structure J2=2-1 represents an example of Pattern 2 (Figure 10-7). The plant remains from the occupation zone display some characteristics of houses and some of storage areas. In this case some of the samples contain a very large proportion of quinoa, suggesting a cache of some sort. Even though the samples are 57% to 85% quinoa, they are not exactly like those of the qollqa in that

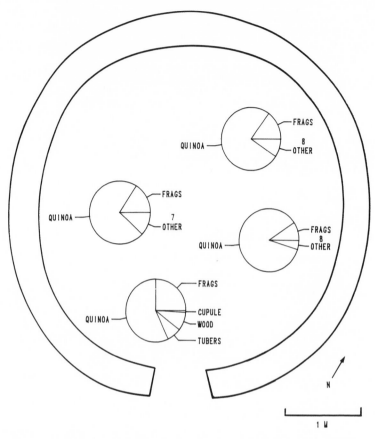

Figure 10-7. Type 2 habitation pattern: Plan view of J2=2-1 level 3 showing relative proportions of plant taxa from flotation samples.

there is still a high sample diversity with many other taxa present. Perhaps J2=2-1 was the storehouse of the patio group at one time during its use life. However, the inclusion of maize and tubers, as well as many taxa of wild seeds, also suggests the structure was probably lived in. Using both Sikkink's (1988a, 1988b) data and our findings from the qollqa to model the relationship between plant remains and activities, the relatively low percentage of unidentifiable material supports the hypothesis that this building was not visited as

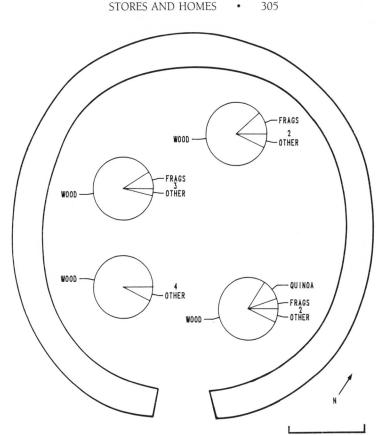

Figure 10-8. Type 2 habitation pattern: Plan view of J54=2-1 level 2 showing relative proportions of plant taxa from flotation samples.

frequently as other habitation structures, or there is the possibility that it was inhabited for a shorter period of time.

Pattern 2 was found in the uppermost levels of J54=2-1 (Figure 10-8), and also in the upper levels of structures J2=2-1, and J2=5-2 (not shown). All of these show higher concentrations of wood than those from the underlying occupation debris. The presence of high wood density in the uppermost levels of these structures is also suggested in one of the qollqa, and we believe it may be the remnants of roofing material. Although no structures had roofs at the time of

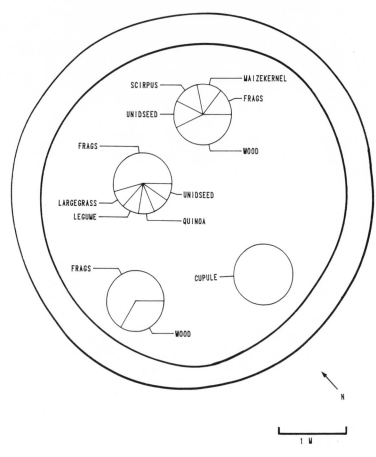

Figure 10-9. Type 3 habitation pattern: Plan view of J54=2-1 level 3 showing relative proportions of plant taxa from flotations samples.

excavation, it is likely that roofs would have been made of wood and grass, similar to those seen on field huts today.

Pattern 3 is characterized by a low overall density of charred plant remains, as seen in J54=2-1, level 3 (Figure 10-9). This pattern is not unlike a few of the qollqa and may be a consequence of a structure that had been cleaned out or one that had not been used for activities resulting in the deposition of charred plant remains.

There are a number of characteristics that habitation structures have in common. The charred plant remains are more damaged than those in the qollqa, making them difficult to identify using morphological characteristics. Samples tend to contain a wide range of plants, both wild and domesticated, as opposed to clusters of minimum taxa found in qollqa samples. Several different crops often occur together in the same structure, and even within the same sample. Deposits very rarely consist of a high proportion of a single crop. Compared with the discrete clustering of taxa in the qollqa, there is very little variation in the plant remains across space in the domestic sphere.

These patterns lead us to suggest that the daily activities taking place within habitation structures resulted in both greater diversity in taxa and increased destruction of plant remains. Even though roofs of wood and grass were not found in situ, the presence of these plants in the uppermost levels in many of the structures suggests that they probably represent roofing materials.

Maize Distribution

Maize morphology offers us the opportunity to investigate the storage of this particular crop more closely. From what is known of contemporary traditional maize storage, maize is usually kept either shelled in jars or sacks, or braided on the cob and suspended from the ceiling or walls (personal observation; Bird 1970:114–15; Sikkink 1988b:70). Therefore, kernels can be stored with or without the cob, but to be hung from roof beams they must be stored on the cob. We assume that the relationship between the amounts of cob and kernel fragments may help illuminate storage and use patterns within different contexts.

In the broadest terms, ubiquity analysis shows that the percentage of samples containing maize kernels is similar in both qollqa and habitation sites, 50% and 46%, respectively (see Table 10-3). On the other hand, cob fragments (cupules) are more common in habitation sites (63%) than in qollqa (16%). Similar evidence can be seen in an examination of the ratios between kernel and cob fragments (Table 10-4). The *overall* mean ratio of kernel to cob fragments is 5:1 for habitation sites, whereas it is 12:1 for qollqa, although within individual habitation structures and across sites it varies a great deal.

Table 10-3. Ubiquity of Maize Kernel and Cob Fragments by Site Type

Site Type	N	Kernel Fragments	Cob Fragments
Habitation	86	50% (43)	63% (54)
Qollqa	38	46% (17)	16% (6)

% = percentage of samples in which plant part is present
N = number of flotation samples

Table 10-4. Ratio of Maize Kernel to Cob Fragments by Site

Habitation Sites	Kernel:Cob
2=1	5:1
2=2	1.8:1
2=3	9.4:1
2=5	0:1
54=2	0.1:1
54=4	1.6:1
54=7	0.5:1
Average 5:1	

Qollqa	Kernel:Cob
16=1	—
16=2	13:1
17=1	8.5:1
17=2	3:1
17=3	7.5:1
17=4	—
17=5	—
Average 12:1	

Although in some of the habitation sites (e.g., 54=2 and 54=7) there are more cupules than kernel fragments, this situation is never found in the qollqa deposits. This suggests that some of the maize might have been stored on the cob in qollqa, although most was probably stored shelled in jars. The interpretation of the maize remains from the habitation sites is more complex, as storage is only one of many activities represented. An explanation for the higher cupule frequencies in the homes is that maize may have been stored or cooked on the cob. In addition, the high ubiquity of charred cupules in the houses could indicate that cobs were used as fuel.

From these data we suggest that maize from the qollqa represents more than one type of storage (but still only storage), whereas in the habitation structures maize distributions represent the presence of multiple activities. The state of preservation of the maize does not appear to be a factor in this result. That is, it is not simply that the cob fragments in the habitation sites are smaller and therefore represent the same number of cobs as fewer larger pieces. Both homes and qollqa show cobs in a poor state of preservation, whereas maize kernels seem to be somewhat better preserved in qollqa. In any case, if the counts in habitation sites are artificially high due to postdepositional breakage, it would only make the case stronger for the differences in kernel:cob ratios, with even fewer cob pieces per kernel than the figures given above. If this is the case, the maize difference between home and qollqa would then be even more acute.

SUMMARY AND CONCLUSIONS

The differences between plant material retrieved from Inka storehouses and contemporary Sausa habitation sites are summarized in Table 10-5. From this we suggest that these botanical distributions can identify and separate out these two contexts. The patterns of the plant remains show that the local Sausa peoples produced the same four major crops for themselves as they produced to fill the nearby Inka state storehouses. Given what we know about habitation and qollqa sites, we propose that the difference in sample diversity indicates that the more varied activities carried out in habitation sites *are* reflected in the botanical data. The lower sample diversity and higher sample "purity" in the qollqa samples lead us to suggest that stored state crops were processed before they entered the storehouses. And although there may be more than one crop per qollqa, they seem to have been stored discretely within each structure.

Although we recognize that our sample size is small, it indicates that maize and quinoa were stored together, whereas tarwi more often was stored with tuber crops. In habitation sites, of course, all the crops cooccurred in the deposits. Perhaps detailed carbon and nitrogen isotope studies would help discover whether or not these crops were actually cooked together, or whether they were mixed once discarded (Hastorf and DeNiro 1985).

Another major difference between the two contexts is that plant material from habitation sites is much more eroded, perhaps due to the impact of day-to-day life in the homes of the Sausa people. Qollqa,

Table 10-5. Summary of Botanical Analysis of Qollqa versus Habitation Sites

Qollqa	Habitation
Mainly crop plants	Crops and wild plants
All taxa here also occur in habitation sites	Contain all qollqa taxa plus many other wild taxa
Low sample diversity	High sample diversity
Samples relatively pure	Samples with low frequencies of many different taxa
Most material identifiable	Most material not identifiable

used only for state storage of food and other goods for the Inka administrative center, Hatun Xauxa, were under close control and were off limits to local peoples, leaving the deposits much less disturbed. This same pattern of single taxon dominance and lesser amounts of unidentifiable material can be used to suggest that some structures on habitation sites (e.g., J2=5-1) may have been used for household storage.

The presence, and the higher diversity, of weedy and wild taxa in habitation sites (as opposed to their low presence in the qollqa), can be taken as an indication that many nonfood or nondomesticated plants were brought in unintentionally, were used for industrial, ceremonial, or medicinal purposes, or were foods not demanded in tribute by the Inka.

The regular inclusion of wood and grass seed in the qollqa can be interpreted either as roof material or common material brought in as tribute (see Chapter 9). But because the same pattern appears in the habitation sites, it is likely that they represent roof remains.

In sum, the patterns recognized here should be of value not only for this study region but for the discussion of Inka state storage facilities anywhere within the empire and the homes of contemporary local groups that were responsible for the production of the food and goods that filled them. Despite the limitations of the number of structures used, this study demonstrates the potential of differential distributions of plant remains for informing archaeologists about the variety of cultural contexts present on Andean sites. Future work in qollqa should test whether our interpretations are sound, as well as provide more details on the contents of both qollqa and local homes.

Botanical Data (Percentage Present and Raw Counts)

HABITATION SITES
Hatunmarca

J2=1−1 LEVEL 2

Sample 1266

Frags	54.17%	(13)
Small grass	20.83	(5)
Amaranthus	12.50	(3)
Large grass	4.17	(1)
Wood	4.17	(1)
Unidentifiable seeds	4.17	(1)
	Total = 24	

Sample 1216

Frags	87.50%	(35)
Maize cupules	5.00	(2)
Small grass	5.00	(2)
Wild legumes	2.50	(1)
	Total = 40	

Sample 1196

Frags	100.00%	(2)
	Total = 2	

J2=1−1 LEVEL 3

Sample 1272

Frags	86.81%	(500)
Small grass	3.82	(22)
Unidentifiable seeds	3.47	(20)
Quinoa	1.56	(9)
Tubers	1.56	(9)
Cyperaceae	1.22	(7)
Scirpus	0.69	(4)
Maize cupules	0.35	(2)
Wood	0.35	(2)
Maize kernels	0.17	(1)
	Total = 576	

Sample 1066

Frags	88.05%	(700)
Tubers	4.91	(39)
Wood	3.02	(24)
Quinoa	1.51	(12)
Small grass	1.01	(8)
Maize kernels	0.75	(6)
Cyperaceae	0.50	(4)
Maize cupules	0.13	(1)
Unidentifiable seeds	0.13	(1)
	Total = 795	

Sample 1057

Frags	78.24%	(187)
Small grass	11.72	(28)
Tubers	5.43	(13)
Unidentifiable seeds	2.09	(5)
Quinoa	1.67	(4)
Amaranthus	0.42	(1)
Cyperaceae	0.42	(1)
	Total = 239	

Sample 1211

Frags	88.08%	(1,300)
Quinoa	5.83	(86)
Wood	2.64	(39)
Maize kernels	2.10	(31)
Tubers	1.15	(17)
Maize embryos	0.20	(03)
	Total = 1,476	

Sample 1056

Small grass	71.88%	(588)
Quinoa	5.26	(43)
Cyperaceae	4.89	(40)
Unidentifiable seeds	4.65	(38)

J2=1−1 LEVEL 3, cont'd.

Frags	4.03	(33)
Verbena	3.55	(29)
Large grass	2.32	(19)
Wild legumes	1.71	(14)
Relbunium	0.49	(4)
Malvastrum	0.24	(2)
Solanaceae	0.24	(2)
Sisyrichium	0.24	(2)
Polygonaceae	0.24	(2)
Maize cupules	0.12	(1)
Scirpus	0.12	(1)
	Total = 818	

Sample 1055

Frags	86.62%	(615)
Small grass	4.93	(35)
Quinoa	1.83	(13)
Cyperaceae	1.69	(12)
Wood	1.55	(11)
Tubers	1.27	(9)
Domesticated legumes	1.13	(8)
Unidentifiable seeds	0.70	(5)
Maize cupules	0.14	(1)
Wild legumes	0.14	(1)
	Total = 710	

Sample 1192

Frags	80.31%	(359)
Maize kernels	9.17	(41)
Wood	3.58	(16)
Quinoa	2.46	(11)
Tubers	1.34	(6)
Maize cupules	1.12	(5)
Small grass	1.12	(5)
Maize embryos	0.22	(1)
Verbena	0.22	(1)
Malvastrum	0.22	(1)
Relbunium	0.22	(1)
	Total = 447	

Sample 1250

Frags	71.80%	(191)
Quinoa	7.89	(21)
Tubers	7.52	(20)
Maize kernels	5.64	(15)
Unidentifiable seeds	3.76	(10)

Maize cupules	1.13	(3)
Small grass	1.13	(3)
Maize embryos	0.38	(1)
Cyperaceae	0.38	(1)
Sisyrinchium	0.38	(1)
	Total = 266	

Sample 1274

Frags	95.70%	(4,585)
Wood	2.25	(108)
Tubers	1.17	(56)
Cyperaceae	0.33	(16)
Maize kernels	0.19	(9)
Unidentifiable seeds	0.08	(4)
Quinoa	0.08	(4)
Small grass	0.08	(4)
Maize cupules	0.06	(3)
Maize embryos	0.04	(2)
	Total = 4,791	

Sample 1225

Frags	77.47%	(801)
Quinoa	7.25	(75)
Wood	7.06	(73)
Maize kernels	6.19	(64)
Tubers	0.97	(10)
Unidentified seeds	0.87	(9)
Maize cupules	0.19	(2)
	Total = 1,034	

J2=1−1 LEVEL 4

Sample 1123

Frags	64.91%	(37)
Small grass	17.54	(10)
Maize kernels	3.51	(2)
Quinoa	3.51	(2)
Polygonaceae	3.51	(2)
Verbena	1.75	(1)
Large grass	1.75	(1)
Unidentifiable seeds	1.75	(1)
Wood	1.75	(1)
	Total = 57	

Sample 1139

Frags	66.45%	(101)
Small grass	11.18	(17)
Quinoa	7.24	(11)

Cyperaceae 5.23 (8)
Wood 3.95 (6)
Maize cupules 1.97 (3)
Unidentifiable 1.32 (2)
seeds
Maize kernels 0.66 (1)
Tubers 0.66 (1)
Scirpus 0.66 (1)
Eleocharis 0.66 (1)
Total = 152

Sample 1082
Small grass 31.07% (32)
Frags 25.24 (26)
Wood 15.53 (16)
Unidentifiable 6.80 (7)
seeds
Wild legumes 4.85 (5)
Quinoa 4.85 (5)
Verbena 2.91 (3)
Amaranthus 2.91 (3)
Maize cupules 0.97 (1)
Scirpus 0.97 (1)
Large grass 0.97 (1)
Cyperaceae 0.97 (1)
Relbunium 0.97 (1)
Polygonaceae 0.97 (1)
Total = 103

Sample 1238
Frags 89.09% (800)
Maize kernels 3.23 (29)
Small grass 2.23 (20)
Quinoa 2.00 (18)
Tubers 1.00 (9)
Wood 0.78 (7)
Scirpus 0.78 (7)
Unidentifiable 0.45 (4)
seeds
Maize cupules 0.22 (2)
Verbena 0.11 (1)
Malvastrum 0.11 (1)
Total = 898

Sample 1215
Frags 80.00% (16)
Quinoa 10.00 (2)
Maize kernels 5.00 (1)
Small grass 5.00 (1)
Total = 20

Sample 1116
Frags 71.79% (56)
Quinoa 15.38 (12)
Small grass 6.41 (5)
Wood 5.13 (4)
Maize cupules 1.28 (1)
Total = 78

J2=1−1 LEVEL 5
Sample 1184
Small grass 23.94% (17)
Frags 15.49 (11)
Wood 15.49 (11)
Quinoa 8.45 (6)
Unidentifiable 5.63 (4)
seeds
Polygonaceae 5.63 (4)
Maize kernels 4.23 (3)
Scirpus 4.23 (3)
Wild legumes 4.23 (3)
Amaranthus 2.82 (2)
Large grass 2.82 (2)
Verbena 2.82 (2)
Medium grass 1.40 (1)
Salvia 1.40 (1)
Relbunium 1.40 (1)
Total = 71

Sample 1176
Frags 27.03% (20)
Quinoa 24.32 (18)
Small grass 24.32 (18)
Wood 13.51 (10)
Maize cupules 5.41 (4)
Unidentifiable 2.70 (2)
seeds
Verbena 1.35 (1)
Plantago 1.35 (1)
Total = 74

Sample 1080
Small grass 39.71% (54)
Wood 16.91 (23)
Quinoa 8.82 (12)
Frags 8.09 (11)
Wild legume 5.15 (7)
Verbena 5.15 (7)
Unidentifiable 5.15 (7)
seeds

J2=1−1 LEVEL 5, cont'd.

Scirpus	4.41	(6)
Maize cupules	2.94	(4)
Maize kernels	0.74	(1)
Domestic legumes	0.74	(1)
Malvastrum	0.74	(1)
Labiatae	0.74	(1)
Relbunium	0.74	(1)
	Total = 136	

Sample 1388

Wood	44.44%	(4)
Frags	33.33	(3)
Maize cupules	11.11	(1)
Wild legumes	11.11	(1)
	Total = 9	

Sample 1387

Wood	37.50%	(3)
Small grass	25.00	(2)
Quinoa	25.00	(2)
Domesticated legumes	12.50	(1)
	Total = 8	

Sample 1078

Wood	31.22%	(69)
Small grass	21.27	(47)
Frags	18.10	(40)
Maize kernels	7.24	(16)
Quinoa	5.43	(12)
Maize cupules	3.62	(8)
Wild legumes	3.62	(8)
Large grass	3.62	(8)
Unidentifiable seeds	2.26	(5)
Cyperaceae	0.90	(2)
Compositae	0.90	(2)
Verbena	0.45	(1)
Sisyrinchium	0.45	(1)
Relbunium	0.45	(1)
Polygonaceae	0.45	(1)
	Total = 221	

Sample 1380

Wood	50.00%	(8)
Frags	31.25	(5)
Large grass	6.25	(1)
Unidentifiable seeds	6.25	(1)
Polygonaceae	6.25	(1)
	Total = 16	

Sample 1776

Wood	28.26%	(13)
Maize kernels	23.91	(11)
Frags	19.57	(9)
Small grass	19.57	(9)
Large grass	4.35	(2)
Wild legumes	2.17	(1)
Grass stalks	2.17	(1)
	Total = 46	

Sample 1077

Frags	39.47%	(30)
Wood	21.05	(16)
Maize kernels	13.16	(10)
Small grass	13.16	(10)
Maize cupules	5.26	(4)
Quinoa	3.95	(3)
Nicotiana	1.32	(1)
Wild legumes	1.32	(1)
Verbena	1.32	(1)
	Total = 76	

J2=2−1 LEVEL 2

Sample 1059

Wood	87.57%	(148)
Frags	8.88	(15)
Quinoa	2.37	(4)
Labiatae	0.59	(1)
Relbunium	0.59	(1)
	Total = 169	

Sample 1047

Wood	81.40%	(35)
Frags	11.63	(5)
Quinoa	4.65	(2)
Wild legumes	2.33	(1)
	Total = 43	

Sample 1040

Wood	77.19%	(44)
Quinoa	10.53	(6)
Frags	5.26	(3)
Maize kernels	1.75	(1)
Maize cupules	1.75	(1)

Small grass	1.75	(1)
Malvastrum	1.75	(1)
	Total = 57	

Sample 1081

Wood	92.76%	(141)
Quinoa	3.95	(6)
Frags	1.97	(3)
Maize cupules	0.66	(1)
Verbena	0.66	(1)
	Total = 152	

J2=2−1 LEVEL 3

Sample 1180

Quinoa	71.96%	(77)
Frags	15.89	(17)
Wood	4.67	(5)
Small grass	1.87	(2)
Unidentifiable seeds	1.87	(2)
Maize cupules	0.93	(1)
Maize embryos	0.93	(1)
Scirpus	0.93	(1)
Relbunium	0.93	(1)
	Total = 107	

Sample 1120

Quinoa	75.77%	(172)
Frags	14.98	(34)
Wood	2.64	(6)
Small grass	2.20	(5)
Maize kernels	1.76	(4)
Scirpus	0.88	(2)
Maize cupules	0.44	(1)
Verbena	0.44	(1)
Large grass	0.44	(1)
Unidentified seeds	0.44	(1)
	Total = 227	

Sample 1182

Quinoa	85.92%	(653)
Frags	9.47	(72)
Maize kernels	1.32	(10)
Tubers	0.92	(7)
Wood	0.92	(7)
Maize cupules	0.53	(4)
Plantago	0.26	(2)
Small grass	0.26	(2)

Wild legumes	0.26	(2)
Maize embryos	0.13	(1)
	Total = 760	

Sample 1053

Quinoa	57.01%	(61)
Frags	25.23	(27)
Wood	9.35	(10)
Tubers	7.48	(8)
Maize cupules	0.93	(1)
	Total = 107	

J2=3−1 LEVEL 3

Sample 1500

Quinoa	36.28%	(119)
Frags	24.39	(80)
Maize kernels	17.38	(57)
Wood	17.38	(57)
Malvastrum	2.13	(7)
Maize cupules	0.91	(3)
Scirpus	0.91	(3)
Maize embryos	0.61	(2)
	Total = 328	

Sample 1384

Frags	50.00%	(3)
Quinoa	33.33	(2)
Maize kernels	16.67	(1)
	Total = 6	

Sample 1342

Frags	47.83%	(22)
Quinoa	32.61	(15)
Malvastrum	6.52	(3)
Small grass	4.35	(2)
Scirpus	2.17	(1)
Compositae	2.17	(1)
Wood	2.17	(1)
Sisyrinchium	2.17	(1)
	Total = 46	

Sample 1345

Quinoa	51.79%	(29)
Frags	25.00	(14)
Maize kernels	8.93	(5)
Maize cupules	5.36	(3)
Wood	5.36	(3)
Small grass	3.57	(2)
	Total = 56	

Sample 1546

Quinoa	36.96%	(34)

J2=3−1 LEVEL 3, cont'd.

Frags	23.91	(22)
Wood	19.57	(18)
Maize kernels	11.96	(11)
Tubers	4.35	(4)
Maize cupules	2.17	(2)
Small grass	1.09	(1)
	Total = 92	

Sample 1385

Maize kernels	56.41%	(44)
Frags	24.36	(19)
Wood	11.54	(9)
Quinoa	5.13	(4)
Maize embryos	1.28	(1)
Small grass	1.28	(1)
	Total = 78	

Sample 1696

Frags	58.43%	(766)
Maize kernels	17.16	(225)
Quinoa	15.64	(205)
Wood	5.26	(69)
Maize cupules	1.22	(16)
Tubers	1.07	(14)
Small grass	0.53	(7)
Maize embryos	0.46	(6)
Unidentifiable seeds	0.08	(1)
Sisyrinchium	0.08	(1)
Relbunium	0.08	(1)
	Total = 1,311	

Sample 1361

Frags	61.72%	(453)
Quinoa	20.44	(150)
Maize kernels	8.17	(60)
Wood	6.81	(50)
Maize cupules	0.54	(4)
Maize embryos	0.54	(4)
Large grass	0.41	(3)
Scirpus	0.27	(2)
Malvastrum	0.27	(2)
Relbunium	0.27	(2)
Wild legumes	0.14	(1)
Small grass	0.14	(1)
Unidentifiable seeds	0.14	(1)
Sisyrinchium	0.14	(1)
	Total = 734	

Sample 1377

Frags	72.84%	(2,631)
Maize kernels	17.94	(648)
Quinoa	2.93	(106)
Wood	2.46	(89)
Maize cupules	2.38	(86)
Maize embryos	0.91	(33)
Small grass	0.17	(6)
Wild legume	0.11	(4)
Scirpus	0.08	(3)
Large grass	0.08	(3)
Malvastrum	0.03	(1)
Unidentifiable seeds	0.03	(1)
Relbunium	0.03	(1)
	Total = 3,612	

J2=3−1 LEVEL 4

Sample 1687

Frags	43.53%	(37)
Quinoa	32.94	(28)
Small grass	9.41	(8)
Wood	5.88	(5)
Maize kernels	4.71	(4)
Maize cupules	2.35	(2)
Scirpus	1.18	(1)
	Total = 85	

J2=3−1 LEVEL 5

Sample 1350

Frags	60.00%	(9)
Quinoa	13.33	(2)
Wood	13.33	(2)
Maize cupules	6.67	(1)
Small grass	6.67	(1)
	Total = 15	

J2=5−2 LEVEL 1

Sample 1600

Wood	90.16%	(55)
Frags	4.92	(3)
Small grass	3.28	(2)
Relbunium	1.64	(1)
	Total = 61	

Sample 1444

Wood	83.33%	(10)
Quinoa	8.33	(1)
Relbunium	8.33	(1)
	Total = 12	

Sample 1441

Wood	42.86%	(3)
Small grass	28.57	(2)
Maize cupules	14.29	(1)
Frags	14.29	(1)
	Total =	7

Sample 1442

Small grass	50.00%	(3)
Quinoa	33.33	(2)
Wood	16.67	(1)
	Total =	6

J2=5−2 LEVEL 2
Sample 1401

Quinoa	100.00%	(1)
	Total =	1

Marca

J54=2−1 LEVEL 2
Sample 447

Maize cupules	60.00%	(3)
Quinoa	20.00	(1)
Tubers	20.00	(1)
	Total =	5

Sample 440

Wood	100.00%	(3)
	Total =	3

Sample 438

Wood	100.00%	(1)
	Total =	1

Sample 452

Frags	50.00%	(1)
Wood	50.00	(1)
	Total =	2

J54=2−1 LEVEL 3
Sample 463

Frags	54.55%	(6)
Quinoa	9.09	(1)
Domestic legumes	9.09	(1)
Tubers	9.09	(1)
Large grass	9.09	(1)
Unidentifiable seeds	9.09	(1)
	Total =	11

Sample 458

Wood	42.86%	(3)
Maize kernels	14.29	(1)
Frags	14.29	(1)
Scirpus	14.29	(1)
Unidentifiable seeds	14.29	(1)
	Total =	7

Sample 456

Maize cupules	100.00%	(12)
	Total =	12

Sample 485

Frags	66.67%	(2)
Wood	33.33	(1)
	Total =	3

J54=2−1 LEVEL 4
Sample 462

Wood	33.33%	(4)
Tubers	25.00	(3)
Frags	16.67	(2)
Quinoa	8.33	(1)
Scirpus	8.33	(1)
Verbena	8.33	(1)
	Total =	12

Sample 452

Quinoa	40.00%	(2)
Domestic legumes	20.00	(1)
Scirpus	20.00	(1)
Wood	20.00	(1)
	Total =	5

Sample 460

Maize cupules	62.50%	(5)
Frags	12.50	(1)
Scirpus	12.50	(1)
Small grass	12.50	(1)
	Total =	8

J54=4−20 LEVEL 2
Sample 1564

Frags	68.46%	(89)
Wood	11.54	(15)
Maize kernels	7.69	(10)
Quinoa	3.85	(5)
Maize cupules	2.31	(3)
Small grass	2.31	(3)

J54=4−20 LEVEL 2, cont'd.

Wild legumes	1.54	(2)
Scirpus	0.77	(1)
Large grass	0.77	(1)
Unidentified seeds	0.77	(1)
	Total = 130	

Sample 1559

Frags	70.00%	(105)
Wood	14.00	(21)
Quinoa	3.33	(5)
Small grass	3.33	(5)
Maize cupules	2.67	(4)
Unidentifiable seeds	2.00	(3)
Maize kernels	1.33	(2)
Tubers	1.33	(2)
Large grass	0.67	(1)
Compositae	0.67	(1)
Chenopodium/ Amaranthus	0.67	(1)
	Total = 150	

Sample 1568

Wood	42.86%	(9)
Frags	28.57	(6)
Maize cupules	9.52	(2)
Wild legume	9.52	(2)
Maize kernels	4.76	(1)
Quinoa	4.76	(1)
	Total = 21	

Sample 1503

Wild legumes	40.00%	(2)
Maize kernels	20.00	(1)
Maize cupules	20.00	(1)
Large grass	20.00	(1)
	Total = 5	

J54=4−20 LEVEL 3

Sample 1501

Frags	56.36%	(62)
Wood	19.09	(21)
Maize cupules	10.00	(11)
Maize kernels	3.64	(4)
Quinoa	3.64	(4)
Unidentifiable seeds	2.73	(3)
Small grass	1.82	(2)

Scirpus	0.91	(1)
Grass stalks	0.91	(1)
Sisyrinchium	0.91	(1)
	Total = 110	

Sample 1505

Frags	56.57%	(56)
Maize cupules	9.09	(9)
Maize kernels	9.09	(9)
Sisyrinchium	8.08	(8)
Wood	5.05	(5)
Grass stalks	4.04	(4)
Quinoa	3.03	(3)
Unidentifiable seeds	2.02	(2)
Scirpus	1.01	(1)
Small grass	1.01	(1)
Large grass	1.01	(1)
	Total = 99	

Sample 1507

Frags	40.63%	(13)
Quinoa	12.50	(4)
Scirpus	12.50	(4)
Wood	12.50	(4)
Maize kernels	6.25	(2)
Verbena	6.25	(2)
Small grass	6.25	(2)
Sisyrinchium	3.13	(1)
	Total = 32	

J54=7−1 LEVEL 2

Sample 1762

Frags	64.86%	(24)
Maize cupules	21.62	(8)
Maize kernels	13.51	(5)
	Total = 37	

Sample 1759

Frags	37.50%	(3)
Maize kernels	12.50	(1)
Maize cupules	12.50	(1)
Quinoa	12.50	(1)
Small grass	12.50	(1)
Wood	12.50	(1)
	Total = 8	

Sample 1764

Frags	50.00%	(2)
Maize cupules	50.00	(2)
	Total = 4	

Sample 1765

Frags	54.55%	(6)
Sisyrinchium	27.27	(3)
Large grass	9.09	(1)
Ambrosia	9.09	(1)
	Total = 11	

Sample 1768

Frags	66.67%	(8)
Maize cupules	16.67	(2)
Wood	16.67	(2)
	Total = 12	

Sample 1763

Ambrosia	66.67%	(2)
Sisyrinchium	33.33	(1)
	Total = 3	

J54=7−1 LEVEL 3
Sample 1595

Frags	36.36%	(4)
Maize kernels	27.27	(3)
Wood	18.18	(2)
Maize cupules	9.09	(1)
Quinoa	9.09	(1)
	Total = 11	

Sample 1721

Frags	55.56%	(5)
Wood	33.33	(3)
Quinoa	11.11	(1)
	Total = 9	

Sample 1570

Frags	23.19%	(16)
Maize cupules	20.29	(14)
Maize kernels	17.39	(12)
Tubers	17.39	(12)
Wood	11.59	(8)
Ambrosia	4.35	(3)
Sisyrinchium	2.90	(2)
Quinoa	1.45	(1)
Small grass	1.45	(1)
	Total = 69	

Sample 1588

Frags	72.28%	(73)
Maize cupules	13.86	(14)
Maize kernels	8.91	(9)
Wood	4.95	(5)
	Total = 101	

Sample 1587

Frags	50.00%	(3)
Maize cupules	16.67	(1)
Scirpus	16.67	(1)
Small grass	16.67	(1)
	Total = 6	

J54=7−1 LEVEL 4
Sample 1718

Frags	75.00%	(57)
Maize cupules	7.89	(6)
Scirpus	3.95	(3)
Wood	3.95	(3)
Maize kernels	2.63	(2)
Quinoa	2.63	(2)
Wild legumes	1.32	(1)
Malvastrum	1.32	(1)
Polygonaceae	1.32	(1)
	Total = 76	

Sample 1725

Frags	50.00%	(23)
Maize cupules	6.52	(3)
Quinoa	6.52	(3)
Scirpus	6.52	(3)
Small grass	6.52	(3)
Cyperaceae	6.52	(3)
Wood	6.52	(3)
Unidentifiable seeds	4.35	(2)
Wild legumes	2.17	(1)
Large grass	2.17	(1)
Malvastrum	2.17	(1)
	Total = 46	

Sample 1775

Frags	51.06%	(24)
Wood	31.91	(15)
Maize cupules	8.51	(4)
Domestic legumes	4.26	(2)
Quinoa	2.13	(1)
Scirpus	2.13	(1)
	Total = 47	

Sample 1771

Wood	100.00%	(1)
	Total = 1	

J54=7−1 LEVEL 4, cont'd.

Sample 1637

Frags	33.33%	(3)
Maize cupules	22.22	(2)
Quinoa	22.22	(2)
Scirpus	22.22	(2)
	Total =	9

QOLLQA SITES

J16=1 LEVEL 1

Sample 9055

Wood	100.00%	(4)
	Total =	4

Sample 9210

Quinoa	50.00%	(3)
Wild legumes	16.67	(1)
Unidentifiable seeds	16.67	(1)
Wood	16.67	(1)
	Total =	6

Sample 9054

Frags	33.33%	(1)
Small grass	33.33	(1)
Leaves	33.33	(1)
	Total =	3

J16=2 LEVEL 2

Sample 9201

Wheat stalks	52.44%	(43)
Wheat kernels	42.68	(35)
Small grass	3.66	(3)
Wood	1.22	(1)
	Total =	82

Sample 9209

Grass node (cf. wheat)	45.54%	(46)
Wheat kernels	22.77	(23)
Domestic legumes	7.92	(8)
Frags	6.93	(7)
Maize embryos	5.94	(6)
Maize kernels	3.96	(4)
Unidentifiable seeds	2.97	(3)
Maize cupules	1.98	(2)

Small grass	0.99	(1)
Compositae	0.99	(1)
	Total =	101

Sample 9211

Wheat stalks	48.15%	(26)
Wheat kernels	37.04	(20)
Small grass	11.11	(6)
Wood	3.70	(2)
	Total =	54

J16=2 LEVEL 3

Sample 9207

Wood	30.56%	(11)
Maize kernels	30.56	(11)
Maize cupules	25.00	(9)
Small grass	8.33	(3)
Maize embryos	2.78	(1)
Unidentifiable seeds	2.78	(1)
	Total =	36

Sample 9190

Maize kernels	54.17%	(39)
Maize embryos	26.39	(19)
Small grass	6.94	(5)
Wood	6.94	(5)
Quinoa	5.56	(4)
	Total =	72

Sample 9062

Maize kernels	68.75%	(22)
Maize embryos	31.25	(10)
	Total =	32

Sample 9061

Wood	77.59%	(90)
Small grass	9.48	(11)
Maize kernels	6.03	(7)
Maize embryos	3.45	(4)
Domestic legumes	1.72	(2)
Maize cupules	0.86	(1)
Malvastrum	0.86	(1)
	Total =	116

Sample 9049

Maize kernels	75.00%	(9)
Wood	16.67	(2)
Maize cupules	8.33	(1)
	Total =	12

Sample 9060
Maize kernels	48.15%	(13)
Domestic legumes	14.81	(4)
Wood	14.81	(4)
Maize embryos	11.11	(3)
Frags	7.41	(2)
Unidentifiable seeds	3.70	(1)
	Total = 27	

J16=2 LEVEL 4
Sample 9053
Maize kernels	59.38%	(19)
Medium grass	25.00	(8)
Maize cupules	6.25	(2)
Wood	6.25	(2)
Maize embryos	3.13	(1)
	Total = 32	

Sample 9050
Maize kernels	75.00%	(9)
Maize embryos	16.67	(2)
Wood	8.33	(1)
	Total = 12	

Sample 9024
Maize kernels	53.33%	(8)
Maize embryos	13.33	(2)
Unidentifiable seeds	13.33	(2)
Wood	13.33	(2)
Small grass	6.67	(1)
	Total = 15	

J17=1 LEVEL 3
Sample 9005
Frags	47.06%	(8)
Quinoa	23.53	(4)
Wood	17.65	(3)
Maize kernels	11.76	(2)
	Total = 17	

Sample 9004
Frags	45.00%	(9)
Domestic legumes	20.00	(4)
Wood	15.00	(3)
Unidentifiable seeds	10.00	(2)

Maize kernels	5.00	(1)
Large grass	5.00	(1)
	Total = 20	

J17=1 LEVEL 4
Sample 9003
Quinoa	40.54%	(15)
Frags	29.73	(11)
Maize kernels	21.62	(8)
Wood	5.41	(2)
Amaranthus	2.70	(1)
	Total = 37	

Sample 9001
Quinoa	50.00%	(1)
Frags	50.00	(1)
	Total = 2	

Sample 9006
Wood	60.61%	(20)
Maize kernels	15.15	(5)
Quinoa	12.12	(4)
Maize cupules	6.06	(2)
Malvastrum	3.03	(1)
Unidentifiable seeds	3.03	(1)
	Total = 33	

J17=2 LEVEL 1
Sample 9194
Quinoa	99.99%	(54,538)
Maize kernels	<0.01	(3)
Frags	<0.01	(2)
Wood	<0.01	(2)
	Total = 54,545	

Sample 9204
Quinoa	99.86%	(8,380)
Wood	0.11	(9)
Frags	0.02	(2)
Unidentifiable seeds	0.01	(1)
	Total = 8,392	

Sample 9020
Quinoa	99.94%	(5,000)
Wood	0.04	(2)
Frags	0.02	(1)
	Total = 5,003	

J17=2 LEVEL 2
Sample 9199

Quinoa	99.95%	(6,432)
Wood	0.05	(3)
	Total =	6,435

Sample 9195

Quinoa	99.84%	(5,000)
Frags	0.10	(5)
Wood	0.06	(3)
	Total =	5,008

Sample 9187

Quinoa	99.96%	(26,000)
Wood	0.04	(10)
	Total =	26,010

J17=3 LEVEL 1
Sample 9071

Tarwi	45.76%	(27)
Potatoes	35.59	(21)
Wood	6.78	(4)
Domestic legumes	5.08	(3)
Frags	3.39	(2)
Small grass	3.39	(2)
	Total =	59

J17=3 LEVEL 2
Sample 9083

Tarwi	96.08%	(49)
Frags	1.96	(1)
Wood	1.96	(1)
	Total =	51

Sample 9202

Frags	49.02%	(25)
Tarwi	35.29	(18)
Quinoa	5.88	(3)
Maize kernels	3.92	(2)
Maize cupules	3.92	(2)
Maize embryos	1.96	(1)
	Total =	51

Sample 9188

Tarwi	73.97%	(54)
Maize kernels	16.44	(12)
Frags	8.22	(6)
Amaranthus	1.37	(1)
	Total =	73

J17=3 LEVEL 4
Sample 9189

Husk	50.00%	(4)
Frags	25.00	(2)
Unidentifiable seeds	12.50	(1)
Wood	12.50	(1)
	Total =	8

Sample 9203

Quinoa	100.00%	(3)
	Total =	3

Sample 9206

Quinoa	45.45%	(5)
Wood	27.27	(3)
Tarwi	9.09	(1)
Malvastrum	9.09	(1)
Unidentifiable seeds	9.09	(1)
	Total =	11

J17=4 LEVEL 2
Sample 9208

Small grass	40.00%	(4)
Large grass	20.00	(2)
Unidentifiable seeds	20.00	(2)
Wood	20.00	(2)
	Total =	10

Sample 9052
No charred
  remains

9074

Wild legumes	50.00%	(1)
Wood	50.00	(1)
	Total =	2

J17=4 LEVEL 3
Sample 9020

Wood	50.00%	(3)
Small grass	33.33	(2)
Unidentifiable seeds	16.67	(1)
	Total =	6

Sample 9193

Wood	75.00%	(3)
Frags	25.00	(1)
	Total =	4

Sample 9191

Quinoa	46.15%	(6)
Wood	30.77	(4)
Large grass	15.38	(2)
Frags	7.69	(1)
	Total =	13

J17=5 LEVEL 4

Sample 9021

Quinoa	97.94%	(1,000)
Wood	1.96	(20)
Large grass	0.10	(1)
	Total =	1,021

PART V

**COMMENTS AND SUGGESTIONS FOR
FUTURE RESEARCH**

Storage and the Inka Imperial Economy
Archaeological Research

TIMOTHY K. EARLE

RECENT anthropological interest in Inka storage derives from the seminal research of Karl Polanyi (1957), who discussed the role of storage in centrally organized, redistributive economies. In redistribution, goods were thought to be given over to a central authority who then distributed them according to need. Central stores were seen as a common characteristic of redistribution needed to hold goods awaiting distribution. John Murra's (1980 [1956]) revolutionary study of the Inka economy introduced a Polanyian analysis to Andean studies. The role of storage in the Inka economy was argued to be important for redistributive functions ranging from the direct support of the imperial army to local disaster relief. The underlying assumption of this substantivist approach was that the specific historical character of Andean society was responsible for its unique structural characteristics, such as reciprocity and redistribution in the absence of a developed price-setting market.

Whether his work is being supported or questioned, Murra set the agenda for research on the relationship between economy and society in the Andean world that the present research on storage continues. Murra (e.g., 1975, 1980) has shown that the Inka underwrote their activities through control over production of staples and wealth, for example, in coca farms and semiindustrial textile shops. Although some scholars have suggested that market behavior was widespread in the Andes, especially in long-distance exchange relationships (e.g., Browman 1984, 1985), the more widely held view is that market behavior among Andean societies occurred primarily below the level of the state economy, in specific restricted areas, such as in highland Ecuador (Salomon 1986, 1987); on the north coast of Peru, where communities specialized in the production of certain commodities for exchange (see Netherly 1978; Rostworowski 1983); and among various ethnic groups where specialty crops and goods were produced for exchange among neighbors in different environmental zones (e.g., along the eastern side of the Andean *cordillera* [see Burchard 1974]).

The Inka political economy differed from those of other early empires, such as the Aztecs, Chinese, and Romans, in which markets and money were central to imperial finance. This does not imply, however, a total lack of comparability in economy, nor does the lack of widespread market systems within the Andes in itself preclude all principles underlying market behavior. A central point of our work (D'Altroy and Earle 1985; D'Altroy 1992) has been to examine aspects of the Inka empire using a conceptual vocabulary amenable to cross-cultural research. If it can be shown, for example, that institutional reorganization was moving in the direction of greater efficiency, then it becomes reasonable to draw comparisons with other early empires, in which similar changes occurred. Similarly, the nature of the demand population and the means of exchange, per se, do not imply that efficiency of production or transportation costs can be eliminated from consideration in evaluating economic behavior. Conversely, we should not assume that the Inka were markedly more or less efficient in their use of resources and labor than other Andean groups or early empires. These should be issues for research, rather than assumptions.

Serious archaeological research on Inka storage began with the doctoral project of Craig Morris (1967, Chapter 5), who described the extensive storage complex at Huánuco Pampa in conjunction with Murra's ethnohistorical research in the region. Morris set the standard for all subsequent work on Inka storage. The archaeological work on storage illustrates how our understanding of the close interrelationships between economy and society, the basic tenant of Polanyi's work, has been extended by the detailed substantial studies reported here. After a brief consideration of the methods applied to studying storage, I will devote the body of this commentary to a consideration of a number of the central theoretical issues that the work on storage addresses.

THE ARCHAEOLOGY OF STORAGE

The original research on Inka storage reported in Murra's dissertation was based on a detailed reading of the early chroniclers including Cobo, Cieza, and especially Polo. The goal was to use the fragmentary references to economic organization, including storage, found in the early commentaries to construct a consistent and uniform picture of the Inka economy.

For his Huánuco project, conducted during the 1960s, Murra initiated a major change in the ethnohistorical research on Inka economy by advocating a shift away from the general chroniclers' accounts to the detailed information on specific locales available in *visitas* and other administrative and judicial documents. Using such documents with specific information on storage, for example, Wachtel (1982) studied the Inka state agricultural development project in the Cochabamba Valley, and LeVine (1979) studied Inka finance in the Mantaro. This new generation of ethnohistorical research, emphasizing individual locales, has begun to investigate *variation* within the Inka empire, as opposed to the earlier work that sought to frame uniform cultural principles. Studying the variation has particular importance for understanding the strategies of Inka conquest and incorporation when faced with the tremendous variability in the types of societies, economies, and ecologies incorporated into its expanding territories (see, for example, Salomon 1983).

The shifting interest toward describing and explaining variability within the Inka empire has naturally spurred an interest in archaeological research. Although the vivid data available from the historical documents continue to provide essential understanding for the economic processes, the spotty availability of the documents makes systematic comparative studies of variability across the empire difficult. The more uniform availability of archaeological evidence from region to region makes such comparative work a natural goal of the ongoing research reported here. Different from the historical sources, by using archaeology it is possible to study where storage is *not* found and the meaning that this has for imperial strategies. In fact, more emphasis on the study of storage systems in pre-Inka polities, to the extent that negative as well as positive evidence for storage management can be determined, would aid in interpretations of earlier economic strategies. We need to document whether there was continuity, as well as change, in storage management practices over time.

Accepted procedures for conducting research are proving unusually fruitful for addressing a set of questions that I will discuss momentarily. Because of Morris's landmark investigations, archaeological studies of storage are being conducted at three levels.

At the broad interregional level, the goal has been to describe generally the patterned variability in the use of storage within the empire. This work, reported especially in Part II, relies heavily on existing descriptive work done in coordination with other archaeological research. Although the quality of existing research varies considerably, as Snead shows in Chapter 3, it is possible to pull together consistent information on the location, size, and association of storage complexes that can be used to construct a typology of storage and consider its role in the imperial economy.

At the regional level, comprehensive site survey can be used to describe the full extent of storage, its structural arrangements within and between storage complexes, and the association of the storage with specific state and local settlements. To date, such regional analyses are available only for Huánuco (Chapters 5, 8), the Upper Mantaro (Chapter 6, 9 and 10), Huamachuco (Chapter 7), and Pumpu (Chapter 4). Other areas, especially on the coast, have been intensively surveyed for archaeological sites, but few Inka storage complexes have been found (see Chapter 3). Such regional work is especially important for describing the nature of Inka mobilization and distribution of goods within a region; from region to region, differences in Inka economic strategies are becoming apparent with the work on storage.

At the site level, following mapping, excavation of individual structures can provide information on the technology of storage. Morris's original research (Chapter 8) outlined clearly how particular characteristics of the architecture could be understood as solutions to particular storage problems. More recently the application of new ethnobotanical techniques for recovery and analysis of plant remains (Chapters 7, 9, 10) have proven effective for studying staple storage. A future goal of such research must be to determine as specifically as possible the sources of goods amassed in the storage facilities. Needed are compositional analyses of ceramics and inventories of plant varieties that could pinpoint sources and the specific patterns for mobilization used by the state.

PRIMARY ISSUES FOR ARCHAEOLOGICAL INVESTIGATION OF STORAGE

Archaeological investigation of storage in the Inka empire has addressed five main issues: identification of storage facilities, the technology of storage, the function of storage in the Inka economy, the structure of storage facilities as related to accounting, and continuity and change in storage from pre-Inka periods. These issues range in theoretical importance but form an interdependent set of questions that are helping to unravel the economic organization of the Inka empire.

IDENTIFICATION OF STORAGE FACILITIES

Identification of storage facilities has been based on (1) characteristics of storage technology that include their location on the hills for lower temperature and dryness and particular architectural configurations such as small doors with raised sills, and thick walls for insulation (Morris, Chapters 5 and 8); and (2) the formalized arrangement and standardized size of the individual storage structures that suggests some accounting function (D'Altroy and Earle, Chapter 6).

The main problem with such identification is that the specific character of the storage facilities may vary from region to region either because of varying technological requirements for particular goods under specific environmental conditions (Morris, Chapter 8) or because of historical differences in how storage is handled (Snead, Chapter 3; Topic and Chiswell, Chapter 7). For this reason, definitive identification of storage can be accomplished by contrasting the material recovered from excavation of both normal houses and suspected storage structures. Useful indicators of storage include the lack of hearths noted consistently in all excavations, Inka aryballoid containers for maize and quinoa storage (Morris, Chapter 8; D'Altroy and Hastorf, Chapter 9), packing straw for storage of tubers (Topic and Chiswell, Chapter 7), and a distinctive low diversity in the macrobotanical remains (Lennstrom and Hastorf, Chapter 10).

THE TECHNOLOGY OF STORAGE

To maximize preservation of goods being held in storage several problems, including fungi, insects, rodents, and sprouting, must be dealt with. As general problems in the history of technology, the effectiveness of Andean storage technology and the role of the Inka state in developing that technology are significant. In Chapter 8, Morris argues for the effectiveness and ingenuity of traditional storage practices. The effectiveness of the Inka's massive storage system, he argues, may have depended less on specific technical details of the facilities than it did on the strategic *placement* of the facilities in locations naturally suited for storage. As seen in the cases reported here, Inka storage was found characteristically on the slopes of hills. Placement at high and exposed locations decreased temperature and humidity by exposing the storage units to the lower air temperature and the ever present winds.

Morris's further suggestion that fairly large-scale movement of goods *within* regions may have been carried out because of the desirability of a specific area for storage is intriguing. Essentially the most productive agricultural zone often lies at elevation less suited to storage than the upper zones with low temperatures and more wind. This argument emphasizes the economic complementarity between zones at different elevations within the Andes, a position made famous by Murra (1972). On the surface of it, this argument is appealing. A quick review of Snead's summary data shows that the "six large state centers with storage components" are found at high elevations (3,300–4,100 m). It has long been noted that the largest Inka administrative settlements are located high along the backbone of the Andes where storage conditions would be ideal but agricultural production marginal. For the Huánuco region, for example, the richest agricultural lands and the primary local population were located in the Huallaga River Valley, below 3,000 m; however, the administrative center of Huánuco Pampa was placed not in this locale but in the barren *puna* at 3,800 m, from 50 to 90 km distance from the agricultural zone that filled its vast storehouses.

What appears evident, however, is that this vertical movement of goods for storage is not an ancient Andean tradition but a specific strategy developed by the Inka state as part of its newly developed staple finance system (see D'Altroy and Earle, Chapter 2). Definitive evidence for organized staple storage prior to the Inka is lacking (see LeVine, Chapter 1). Rather it would appear that the Inka instituted a novel, large-scale staple finance system in which central storage at nodes through the empire was critically important. To maximize the efficiency of this financial system, they apparently positioned their administrative centers in locations best suited to the storage on which the staple finance depended.

The three chapters discussing the excavation of storage features at

Huánuco Pampa (Morris, Chapter 5), in the Mantaro (D'Altroy and Earle, Chapter 6), and in Huamachuco (Topic and Chiswell, Chapter 7) speak of specific architectural and artifactual details that facilitate storage of grains and root crops. Although these functionalist arguments seem reasonable and are most probably true, I am struck by the variability from region to region. If the storage of shelled maize in jars is so beneficial in Huánuco and the Mantaro, why is it not found in Huamachuco; if floor drainage/aeration is so important in Huánuco and Huamachuco, why are they absent in the Mantaro? Such variability raises questions about the degree of standardized technology that the Inka state may have imposed from above versus the local adoption of traditional storage techniques closely adjusted to local conditions.

The two sources of information on storage technology—the consistent placement of storage at high elevation and the local variability in specific storage technologies—seem to point in quite different directions. The first suggests the importance of central planning with technological change imposed from above. The second suggests the Inka adoption of storage technologies from local traditions (see Topic and Chiswell, Chapter 7). Both may of course be true, emphasizing the scope and adaptability of the Inka imperial economy.

THE FUNCTION OF STORAGE IN THE INKA EMPIRE

Various potential functions for Inka storage have been presented and discussed in the chapters of this volume. Roughly, the functions break into three nonexclusive spheres—subsistence maintenance, commodity distribution, and institutional finance. Subsistence maintenance involves the storage of goods to compensate for seasonal and unpredictable variation in availability (see D'Altroy and Earle, Chapter 2). Such storage is common in virtually all societies and is essential in agricultural economies with demarcated harvest cycles. As I have argued elsewhere (Johnson and Earle 1987), such storage is characteristically handled at the household level; households are in fact reluctant to give up the autonomy and security of personal supplies for some promise of support from a larger group or leader. Although there is some evidence that the Inka coopted household storage at least in part (Earle et al. 1987), the primary goal of the imperial storage was certainly not subsistence maintenance of its population.

Murra (1980 [1956]) shows this clearly in his review of the historical sources; although he believes that the state stores provided a safety net to protect populations in times of disaster, regular provisioning out of the storehouses was unlikely.

Commodity distribution was a primary function proposed by Polanyi (1957) for redistribution and its associated storage. A point made by Polanyi was that the economy was imbedded in broader institutional contexts such that an economic function such as commodity distribution can be accomplished in alternative ways depending on the institutional context. Redistribution in centrally organized societies, such as the Inka empire, could thus be viewed as a functional alternative to reciprocity and market exchange. In a redistributive economy it was thought that commodities generally flowed through the hands of the central leadership, who collected and distributed according to ability and need. Murra (1980 [1956]) seems to follow this position at least in part. In the first archaeological evaluation of storage, however, Morris (1967) showed definitively that the redistributive system of the Inka did not serve a commodity distribution function. Rather the goods found in storage were exclusively regionally available food products (Morris, Chapter 5). Morris argues against direct state intervention into interregional exchange so as to provide a marketlike function for the distribution of specialized goods. The amount of exchange that existed both before and after Inka expansion was quite limited (Earle 1985) and was most probably handled by reciprocal exchange both within and between communities.

The primary function of storage in the Inka empire seems quite clearly to be for institutional finance, especially involving staple goods (D'Altroy and Earle, Chapter 2). The Inka empire was unusual in history as a large-scale and institutionally complex state without a developed market system throughout much of its territory. Staple finance minimizes or eliminates the need for market involvement by mobilizing staples from the local subsistence economy to support those working for the state. Such a financial system is a simple and direct means for compensation; its main problem is logistical, involving large-scale storage facilities and dispersed economic control (D'Altroy and Earle, Chapter 2).

The extensive evidence for the staple finance function of Inka storage can be summarized at the three levels of available archaeology data:

At the interregional level, the empirewide pattern of storage emphasizes its association with state facilities where it would serve for support of state personnel, and with locales of agricultural production. Snead (Chapter 3) shows the clear association of state storage with Inka administrative and special purpose facilities where the distribution of foods could have provided direct support for state activities (see also D'Altroy and Earle, Chapter 2). Several storage complexes, quite obviously designed to hold massive staple stores, are also found in direct association with major agricultural development projects in Cochabamba, Campo de Pucara (Snead, Chapter 3), and perhaps Colcabamba (Topic and Chiswell, Chapter 7). In her interregional comparison of three administrative districts, LeVine shows an apparent association between population size (and available agricultural labor) of a region and the size of its storage volume.

At the regional level, the fact that the storage held primarily staples is shown by its volume and distribution. The large-scale of the storage is apparent. In the Mantaro, over 3,000 individual storage units have been recorded (D'Altroy and Earle, Chapter 6). At Huánuco Pampa, 12% of the total number of structures at the site were for storage (Morris, Chapter 5). This scale alone would argue for the bulk of stored product. The additional fact that the storage complexes are by and large out in the open (i.e., not within the boundaries of the administrative sites) would seem to emphasize that their contents where not sufficiently valuable to require high security or very limited access. It was sufficient simply to separate the storage spatially to make access more visible. Although there is an association between storage and population size between regions, *within a region* storage is not associated with local population (LeVine, Chapter 4). In the Mantaro (D'Altroy and Earle, Chapter 6), local population avoided an area of prime agricultural land associated with extensive storage; the authors argue that this area was a state agricultural development similar to the famous Cochabamba case.

At the site level, it is clear from excavations that virtually all of the storage was devoted to food products and that the foods were all regionally available staples such as maize, tubers, and quinoa. Morris

(Chapter 5) was the first to argue that the goods stored in the administrative complexes were local foods and not special products moved by the state over long distances. Subsequent excavations in both the Mantaro Valley (D'Altroy and Hastorf, Chapter 9) and Huamachuco (Topic and Chiswell, Chapter 7) emphasize the staple contents of the storehouses, goods in both cases that would have been produced within the administered region.

Evidence for staple storage prior to the Inka conquest is problematical. The storage rooms at Chan Chan may have stored foods, but their association with major compounds seems uncharacteristic (cf. Klymyshyn 1987). Repetitive room blocks at Wari sites such as Pikillaqta, Jargampata, and Azángaro have frequently been taken to be storage rooms perhaps for staples, although there is not yet a consensus on the function of the architecture (Isbell 1977; Anders 1986; Schreiber 1987a, 1991).

An alternative function for the Inka storage would have been part of the wealth finance system that may have provided more central control to the Inka political economy (D'Altroy and Earle, Chapter 2). Wealth finance and associated wealth storage were characteristic of pre-Inka Andean states, especially the Chimú (Netherly 1978; Topic 1982; Moseley 1985). The centralized manufacture and storage of wealth were extremely important at the capital Chan Chan, and the Inka coopted this preexisting system by moving the northcoast smiths to Cuzco. Topic (1982), for instance, shows a pattern of craft specialization in the lower class architectural areas of Chan Chan and argues that these were probably the residences and workshops of specialists attached to the elite residences at the center.

Now the identification of storage of wealth, as opposed to staples, relies on three criteria: (1) smaller volumes for the less bulky goods, (2) restricted access to provide security for the valuable and more easily transported goods, and (3) the lack of evidence for stored goods, if one assumes that wealth objects would have been more carefully curated.

In the Andes the evidence for wealth storage prior to the Inka conquest seems relatively good. At the major Chimú center of Chan Chan, for example, storage units were fairly small scale, were located within the private palace compounds and in elite compounds where access would have been highly restricted, and when excavated, were clean of artifactual or botanical remains. This pre-Inka pattern contrasts with the pattern just described for the Inka storage of staples. We cannot depend on the assumption that pre-Inka storage was analogous to Inka period storage. In order to assess the extent to which wealth goods versus staple materials was being emphasized, the same kind of systematic study of the function of pre-Inka storage management is needed as has been attempted for the Inka. In addition to issues of access, we need more data on volume, in order to estimate the number of people storage could have served, and more ethnobotanical analysis to identify actual storehouse contents.

The evidence for the importance of storage in a wealth finance system in the Inka empire as well is problematical but suggestive. Morris (Chapter 5) describes how the storage facilities around the capital city of Cuzco were comparatively small-scale in comparison to the large complexes around Huánuco Pampa or Hatun Xauxa. The chroniclers frequently mention storehouses around Cuzco, but Morris proposes that these more likely held wealth rather than staple goods. D'Altroy and Earle (Chapter 2) suggest that the staples would have been held locally in contrast to the wealth that would have been moved into Cuzco so as to control centrally its distribution. Out in the provinces, LeVine (Chapter 4) proposes that the location of storage off of the hillside at Pumpu may have been for nonstaples that did not require careful temperature control; the absence of botanicals in one of the Mantaro storage structures with a unique slate floor indicated to D'Altroy and Hastorf (Chapter 9) that the structure might have held nonstaples. In both cases, however, the lack of restricted access for the units seems not to fit my expectation for wealth storage. Ethnohistorical evidence for the production of wealth in the hinterlands indicates that storage for these goods did exist, but logically it seems likely to have been restricted to within the administrative sites where controlled access could be maintained (see Morris, Chapter 5).

Preliminary results of ongoing research conducted by Terence D'Altroy, Christine Hastorf, and me in the Valle Calchaquí, Salta Province, in northwest Argentina (see Figure 3–4), offers a case of production and distribution of wealth outside of the empire's core (D'Altroy et al. 1990). This region, known for its mineral wealth, was primary for Inka exploitation of copper resources (González 1983).

Prior research undertaken by other archaeologists indicated that this was an area of intensive Inka occupation (e.g., Ambrosetti 1907–8; Tarragó 1975; Tarragó and Díaz 1977; Deambrosis and de Lorenzi 1977; Pollard 1981; Díaz 1983; Raffino 1983; Hyslop 1984). The Inka settlements in the northern part of the valley, where our work was conducted, include the Inka center of Potrero de Payogasta (Difrieri 1948), the fortress and associated settlement of Cortaderas, and a string of smaller sites along the Inka road north toward Tastil and south toward the major sites of Shincal and Chilecito (Hyslop and Díaz 1983; Hyslop 1984).

In 1990 our investigations at Potrero de Payogasta and the contemporaneous Santamariana subject community of Valdéz revealed distinctive patterns of production and access to state-related wealth objects. Large hearths, raw materials, and by-products of manufacture such as slag indicate that objects of gold, copper, mica, and obsidian were manufactured at Potrero. The only finished objects of metal recovered in our fieldwork also came from this settlement. In contrast, 24 surface collections and 5 excavations at Valdéz yielded extensive evidence for manufacture of copper objects (e.g., 11 crucible fragments from one particular 1 × 1 m test pit in a midden), but no evidence for access to the final products. Although more data and further analysis will be necessary for us to argue that this is representative of a regional pattern, this distribution does fit the model of intense production of wealth goods under state auspices with control over the output being administered through the state settlements.

Little evidence exists for Inka storage facilities in the Valle Calchaquí. One small facility lies in a defended position above Potrero de Payogasta, and a rectangular enclosure at the fortress of Cortaderas contained a set of rectangular qollqa. The relatively small scale of the storage facilities here and their direct association with Inka settlements suggest that their uses were tied closely to Inka institutions and that the goods stored therein were not widely distributed to regional populations. The documentary and archaeological evidence for military activity and late fortification of northwest Argentina suggests that a major function of storage in this peripheral region was to guarantee supply for the Inka garrisons (see Raffino 1981; Lorandi and Boixadós 1987–88; Hyslop 1990). We surmise that support of ceremonial hospitality at provincial centers may also have been a significant use of stored goods in the Valle Calchaquí, because of the relative lack of domestic remains in the areas excavated at Potrero de Payogasta, a planned settlement with extensive ceremonial areas. Importantly, Inka storage here was apparently quite different from that found in the Central Highlands (Chapters 4, 5, 6, and 7).

THE STRUCTURE OF STORAGE FACILITIES AS RELATED TO ACCOUNTING

One point made repeatedly in the chapters of this volume is that Inka storage sites have a rigid internal organization. An individual storage complex consists of long rows of circular or rectangular structures of standard sizes. In the absence of a writing system, other nonliterate accounting devices, such as the famous *khipu*, must have been essential. It seems probable that the storage structures themselves were also constructed so as to provide units of accounting.

Perhaps the strongest evidence for the accounting function of the storage units is their consistent size. Units were also arranged into sites or lines within sites that held a singular structural form. As seen especially in the regions of Huánuco, the Mantaro, and Pumpu, the distribution of structural shape is highly patterned both within and between storage complexes. In the Mantaro, for example, the two largest complexes above Xauxa are distinct one from the other—one largely with rectangular structures and the other largely with circular structures. This division is then mirrored in the heavy concentration of sites with rectangular structures on the eastern side of the Mantaro Valley and with circular structures on the western side (D'Altroy and Earle, Chapter 6; LeVine, Chapter 4).

What is to be made of the structured separation into storage units with circular or rectangular forms? Morris (Chapter 8) suggests, based on the distribution of macrobotanical remains from the Huánuco Pampa excavations, that the circular structures may have been designed for maize and the rectangulars for tubers. Although based on small samples of buildings, the botanical remains recovered systematically from the storage structures of the Mantaro (D'Altroy and Hastorf, Chapter 9) and Huamachuco (Topic and Chiswell, Chapter 7) do not correspond to this proposed division. Alternatively, LeVine (Chapter 4), noting the dominance of circular structures on the plain adjacent to the administrative center of Pumpu, proposes that the circulars, on the plain, in contrast to the mixed circular and rectangular structures on the hillside, may have held craft goods or raw materials. Excavations at Huánuco Pampa and in the Mantaro, however, show evidence for staple storage in both rectangular and circular structures. D'Altroy and Earle (Chapter 6) note that the rectangular structures were associated with the western side of the valley where excellent agricultural land without local population may have been connected with a state farm development in the Mantaro. The rectangular and circular structures may designate different mechanisms of mobilization: rectangulars for state development projects versus. circulars for community mit'a labor. Regrettably this pattern does not fit the use of circular structures at Cotapatchi, where they are associated with the state farm project in Cochabamba (Snead, Chapter 3).

An answer to the meaning of formal structural arrangement of building forms is ellusive. The strong pattern would seem to indicate a clear plan the explication of which may hold an important key for understanding the nature of Inka imperial finance. The contributions to this volume seem clearly to show the direction for future research more than an answer to this intriguing question. The potential of archaeological research as a detailed data source for investigating issues of structure and meaning of imperial finance should be evident.

CONTINUITY AND CHANGE IN THE INKA POLITICAL ECONOMY

A major issue regarding the character of the Inka political economy is the degree to which the economy was built on existing traditional Andean precedent versus the degree to which it was designed as a revolutionary solution to the novel problems of a highland state. The storage facilities provide some intriguing evidence that the extent of change instituted by the Inka empire was in fact profound.

Prior to the Inka imperial expansion evidence for storage was limited either to residential contexts or to highly controlled access areas. The evidence would appear to indicate that most staple storage was found within individual households and that central storage facilities were designated rather for items of wealth. In the highland Wari state, an obvious potential prototype for the Inka state (LeVine, Chapter 1), evidence for staple storage is limited. The best potential example of staple storage is at Pikillaqta. Roughly 500 standardized rectangular units found at the site would, on the basis of form and volume, suggest staple storage; however, the position of the storage within the site's architectural core indicates a degree of control perhaps more related to direct military provisioning than to a staple finance system prototypical of the later Inka empire. The best evidence for continuity for storage is rather in specific technologies of storage, not its overall function and organization (see Topic and Chiswell, Chapter 7).

The changes in how storage was handled by the Inka were profound. Storage volume designated for staples increased dramatically and became separated from household contexts. Most of the storage was concentrated in direct association with Inka facilities, either areas of state agricultural projects or Inka administrative facilities. A regional pattern was instituted whereby storage was often moved away from areas of production and to locations ideal for preservation of the staples. The locations of the administrative settlements were then mapped onto this high-elevation distribution of the storage. The massive staple storehouses of the Inka appear to have been constructed almost without precedent in earlier Andean societies; this emphasizes the revolutionary redesign of economic relations that made the Inka state viable.

CONCLUSIONS

The creation of a massive staple finance system in highland Andean areas was apparently a novel solution to a problem of large-scale institutional support required by a far-flung empire in the absence of an established market system. Investigation of this staple finance system deriving initially from historical sources is shifting increasingly to archaeology as it provides evidence for variation in imperial financial strategies.

Archaeology has unusual potential for studying the character of the Inka political economy. Already the archaeological evidence is beginning to solve critical questions concerning the mobilization of staples from local populations, the regional movement of the staples to high elevations best suited for preservation, and the support of state administrative, military, and economic activities. The next generation of research promises to be able to track in more detail the specific flows of goods and the system of accounting developed to monitor these flows.

It has been a continuing problem to explain the rapid expansion and success of the Inka, but the storage data may point to the scope of economic change that made this political expansion possible. The design of the staple finance system based on large-scale mobilization and warehousing of staples apparently solved the problem of financing institutions of governance in the absence of a market economy. Other dramatic solutions included extensive internal population displacement, the development of state farms, elaboration of community self-sufficiency, and the creation of attached specialists working outside of their traditional community contexts (Murra 1980 [1956]). It is probably wrong to overemphasize the continuity with the past. Certainly much of what the Inka used was borrowed from the existing repertoire of Andean economic patterns, but the success of the Inka seems based on the effectiveness of their redesign of these traditional solutions to novel problems of statehood in the high Andes.

ACKNOWLEDGMENTS

Some of the material presented here is derived from D'Altroy 1992. The archaeological research in the Valle Calchaquí was funded in part by a grant from the National Science Foundation (BNS–88–05471).

Notes

1. THE STUDY OF STORAGE SYSTEMS

1. "[D]e las tierras que estavan lexos se traya poco . . . sino era oro y ropa, porque era poco el peso . . . y de las demás comarcas se traya la comida quanto más çerca trayan más, y quanto mas lexos menos" (Polo 1940:170).

2. STAPLE FINANCE, WEALTH FINANCE, AND STORAGE IN THE INKA POLITICAL ECONOMY

1. Exceptions to this may be found in early inspections (e.g., Ortiz de Zuñiga 1967 [1562]:47; Martinez de Rengift [1571] in Espinoza 1963:63; see Salomon 1983, 1986), primarily in the form of direct prestations of finished craft goods and gathered materials. Murra (1975:242–54; see also 1982) has argued that, because the raw materials from which these were made or collected were owned by the state, the local populations were only giving their labor. We do not find this explanation satisfactory for all cases but prefer not to explore the issue in detail here because of its complexity.

2. An exception to the localized consumption of stored agricultural products has recently been documented for the Cochabamba area of Bolivia. According to early sources cited by Wachtel (1982), the maize produced here was intended for consumption by the military in other areas of the em-pire, with transport being provided by llama caravan.

3. The convertibility of these kinds of goods into subsistence or utilitarian products is an issue that has not yet been addressed, largely because of a lack of data on the topic. Wealth goods, such as *qumpi,* were directly and indirectly (e.g., through Spanish coinage) convertible into other types of goods in the early colonial economy. Although it is possible that such conversions took place prior to Spanish contact, this point cannot be demonstrated with current information, and we do not wish to assert it here.

4. Acosta (1894 [1590]:142) reports that the Andean peoples used coca and, in the Santa Cruz area of eastern Bolivia, cotton cloth as currency. Murra (1980 [1956]:143) has expressed reservations about the accuracy of this passage for pre-Columbian economies, and we share them in part, because of the general content of the passage.

4. INKA STATE STORAGE IN THREE HIGHLAND REGIONS: A COMPARATIVE STUDY

1. Many investigators consider Tarmatambo a separate administrative entity for the small ethnic groups located north and northeast of the site. However, because of its limited size, limited storage volume, and its proximity to Hatun Xauxa, it is included here as part of the Xauxa general region. My

reading of the documents suggests to me that Tarmatambo, as a separate administrative entity, may have been a Colonial-period construct.

2. Due to differences in the number of kilometers travelers walked on a daily basis, many more wayside *tampu,* of limited size and with very limited storage space, probably existed (see Hyslop 1984:77–82, 294–303). The more important *tampu* and those with known storage facilities are shown on the map in Figure 4-1.

3. In order to estimate Inka-period population, Colonial census figures were increased according to formulae worked out by Cook (1981) for all of Peru; by Hadden (1967), using analyses of Huánuco documents; and by D'Altroy (1981; D'Altroy and Earle 1985), based on his research in the Xauxa area (see also LeVine 1985).

4. In Chapter 6, D'Altroy and Earle use a different method for grouping rectangular versus circular storehouses, differentiating only between storehouses within a 1-kilometer range of Hatun Xauxa, and those from 1- to 3-kilometers of the Inka center. Also, although site #J20 lies within the 1–3 km range of Hatun Xauxa, its position is across the Mantaro River. Because of the location of the Inka-period bridge, 3 kilometers up river, the problems involved in the transfer of materials to the center made it reasonable to include J20 with sites from within the 3–17 km range, on the west side of the river (see D'Altroy 1992) for a description of the location of this bridge).

5. HUÁNUCO PAMPA AND TUNSUKANCHA: MAJOR AND MINOR NODES IN THE INKA STORAGE NETWORK

1. "Toda esta forteleze Sacasahuaman era un deposito de armas, porras, lanzas, arcos, flechas, hachas, rodelas, jubones fuertes acojinados de algodon, y otras armas de diversas maneras, y vestidos para los soldados, recogidos aqui de todos los rumbos de la tierra sujeta a los Senores del Cuzco. . . . Desde esta forteleza se ven en torno de la ciudad muchas casas . . . y muchas de ellas son de placer y recreo de los senores pasados y otras de los caciques de toda la tierra que residen de continuo en la ciudad: las otras son casas o almacenes llenos de mantas, lana, armas, metales y ropas, y de todas las cosas que se crian y fabrican en esta tierra. Hay casas donde se conservan los tributos que traen los vasallos a los caciques y casa hay en que se guardan mas de cien mil pajaros secos, porque de sus plumas que son de muchos colores se hacen vestiduras, y hay muchas casas para esto. Hay rodelas, adargas, vigas para cubrir las casas, cuchillos y otras herraminentas: alpargatas y petos para provision de la gente de guerra, en tanta cantidad que no cabe en el juicio como han podido dar tan gran tributo de tantas y tan diversas cosas."

7. INKA STORAGE IN HUAMACHUCO

1. Between 1981 and 1983 we surveyed and test excavated Inka storerooms in Huamachuco. Because this work was done as part of a wider program of research in which the focus was on earlier periods, the results reported here must be considered preliminary.

2. For example, the will of Juan Felipe (1621) mentioned an *estancia* that had been vacant and uncultivated since the time of Topa Inka Yupanqui. The will is located in the Archivo Departmental de Cajamarca, sección Corregimiento, Causas Ordenarias, Legajo 11. We thank Eric Deeds for bringing this document to our attention.

3. We thank John H. Rowe and

María Rostworowski de Diez Canseco for providing us with copies of this unpublished document. The manuscript is #3035 in the collection of the Biblioteca Nacional, Madrid.

4. Site maps for Cerro Santa Barbara and Cerro Mamorco are not available.

5. Of course, because of the persistence of Late Intermediate Period ceramic forms throughout the provinces, after the Inka conquest, these might actually date to the Inka period.

6. This information is from a report prepared by Eric Deeds for the Project. He cites a manuscript in the Archivo Departmental de La Libertad, sección Judicias, Corregimiento, Causas Ordenarias, Legajo 168, expediente 336.

8. THE TECHNOLOGY OF HIGHLAND INKA FOOD STORAGE

1. I have not had access to literature that may exist on this subject in languages other than English or Spanish, and my familiarity with the large agricultural literature in those languages is incomplete.

2. Burton (1966:252–60) offers a convenient discussion of storage diseases common in Europe. Because most storage diseases are the result of infection before harvest, it is useful to compare Burton's discussion with that of Christiansen for Peru (1967:196–220), although the latter does not elaborate on the effects of the field diseases in storage.

9. THE ARCHITECTURE AND CONTENTS OF INKA STATE STOREHOUSES IN THE XAUXA REGION OF PERU

1. "[Y] cómo en más de mill y dozientas leguas que mandaron de costa, tenía sus delgados y gouernadores, y muchos aposentos y grandes depósitos llenos de todas las cosas necessarias, lo qual era para prouisión de la gente de guerra. Porque en vno destos depósitos auía lancas, y en otros dardos, y en otros oxotas, y en otros las demás armas que ellos tienen.

"Assímismo vnos depósitos estauan proueydos de ropas ricas, y otras de más bastas: y otros de comida, y todo género de mantenimiento. De manera que oposentado el señor en su aposento, y alojada la gente de guerra, ninguna cosa desde la más pequeña hasta la mayor y más principal dexaua de auer, para que pudiessen ser proueydos" (Cieza 1967:lxiiii:143–44).

2. "[L]es mandó que le hiciesen chácaras de comidas, y ropa, y le nombrasen doncellas para sus mujeres; y ropa de la tierra y de todo cuanto podían trabajar, mandaba que lo tuviesen en depósitos, de lo cual hacían mercedes a la gente de guerra y a los caciques y a los indios valientes y a quien le parecía; y asimismo, a los que trabajaban en las chácaras y casas suyas, les mandaba repartir destos depósitos algo" (Vega 1965:169).

3. "[E]l dicho marqués don Francisco Pizarro bajó del dicho Valle de Xauxa a la provincia de Los Llanos a buscar asiento a donde poblar la ciudad de Los Reyes e sacó del dicho Valle de Xauxa todos los indios que tuvo necesidad para cargas a que los mas de los bastimentos que en el dicho Valle se proveyó el dicho marqués e los de su Real era de los depósitos que tenían en el dicho Valle que los dichos indios del dicho Valle los habían tributado al inga y estos eran del dicho don Jeronimo Gaucrapaucar e de los demás indios del dicho valle" (Guacrapáucar 1971:244).

Glossary of Spanish and Quechua Terms

Aji. *Capsicum* peppers

Aqlla (aqllakuna, akllakuna). Woman (women) chosen to devote their lives to service to the state.

Altiplano. High plateau of the South-Central Andes.

Audiencia. Judicial and advisory body in Colonial Spanish America

Ayllu. A corporate, endogamous, descent group with collective ownership of communal territory and resources.

Ceja de montaña. Wet, warm, lower part of the eastern Andean slopes.

Chacra. Agricultural field.

Chaquira. Metal, shell, or stone beads.

Ch'arki (charqui). Dried (jerked) llama meat.

Chicha. A fermented drink usually made from maize.

Chuño. Freeze-dried potatoes.

Cordillera. Chain of mountains.

Fanega. Grain measure equal to about 1.6 bushels.

Huaca. A physical awe-inspiring place or thing having the qualities of holiness and/or magic.

Hunu. Unit of 10,000 heads of households in the idealized Inka decimal administrative system.

Khipu (quipu). Recording device based on information encoded in the patterned distribution of knots on strings.

Kichwa (quechua). Zone of temperate climate (2,300–3,500 m).

Kuraka. An ethnic lord or leader in the Inka political hierarchy; controller of a political unit called a curacazgo.

Macca. Highland root crop.

Mercaderes. Traders.

Mindaláes. In prehispanic Ecuador, long-distance traders under the protection of a political leader.

Mit'a. Rotational, periodic labor service quota that the Inka state exacted from administered populations.

Mitayo. Person performing mit'a.

Mitmaq. State directed population transfer; also, a relocated person.

Mitmaqkuna. State-relocated populations, the plural form of mitmaq.

Montaña. Term used to designate the eastern slopes of the Andes.

Pachaka. Unit of 100 household heads in the Inka decimal system.

Pampa. Extensive plain.

Parcialidad. A part of an ethnic sociopolitical unit.

Pirka. Unshaped fieldstone used in the construction of walls.

Puna. High altitude grassland (4,000–4,800 m) where frosts are frequent.

Qollqa. Storehouse.

Quinoa. Lentil-like cereal native to the Andean highlands.

Qumpi (qompi). Fine, woven cloth.

Saya. A provincial political subunit.

Selva. Tropical forest zone.

Sierra. Highlands.

Tampu (tambo). State installation (inn) along Inka roads, serving traveling personnel.

Tawantinsuyu. Inka name for its empire ("Land of the Four Quarters").

Visita. A survey, inspection, or inquiry conducted by a colonial official.

Visitador. A colonial official conducting a visita.

Waranqa. A political unit composed of 1,000 tax-paying household heads in the idealized Inka decimal administrative system.

Yana. A retainer in service to the Inka elite.

Yunga. Warm lowlands (500–2,300 m).

Bibliography

Acosta, José de
1894 [1590] *Historia natural y moral de las Indias.* Madrid: R. Anglés.

Adams, Richard
1978 Man, energy, and anthropology. *American Anthropologist* 80:297–309.

Adams, Robert Mc C.
1974 Anthropological perspectives on ancient trade. *Current Anthropology* 15 (3): 239–58.

Agurto Calvo, Santiago
1986 *Lima prehispánica.* Lima: Empresa Financeria.

Alcock, Susan
1989 Archaeology and imperialism: Roman expansion and the Greek city. *Journal of Mediterranean Archaeology* 2:87–135.

Ambrosetti, Juan B.
1907–8 Exploraciones arquelógicas en la ciudad prehistórica de "La Paya" Valle Calchaquí, Provincia de Salta. *Revista de la Universidad de Buenos Aires* 8 (Sección Antropología, Facultad de Filosofía y Letras, 3), 2 vols. Buenos Aires: M. Biedma é hijo.

Anders, Martha B.
1975 Formal storage facilities in Pampa Grande, Peru: A preliminary report of excavation. Manuscript, Cornell University, Ithaca, N.Y.
1977 Sistema de depósitos en Pampa Grande, Lambayeque. *Revista del Museo Nacional* (Lima) 43:243–79.
1981 Investigations of state storage facilities in Pampa Grande, Peru. *Journal of Field Archaeology* 8:391–404.
1982 Diseño para la Investigación de los funciones de un sítio Wari. *Investigaciones* (Universidad Nacional San Cristobal de Huamanga, Ayacucho), 2:27–44.
1986 Wari experiments in statecraft: A view from Azángaro. In *Andean archaeology: Papers in memory of Clifford Evans,* edited by Ramiro Matos M., Solveig A. Turpin, Herbert H. Eling, Jr., 201–24, Monograph 27, Institute of Archaeology, University of California, Los Angeles.

Anderson, John A., and A. W. Alcock, editors
1954 *Storage of cereal grains and their products.* Monograph Series, no. 2. St. Paul, Minn.: American Association of Cereal Chemists.

Asch, David L., and Nancy Asch
1975 Plant remains from the Zimmerman site—grid A: A quantitative perspec-

tive. In *The Zimmerman site: Further investigations at the grand village of Kaskaskia,* edited by Michael R. Brown, 2: 116–19. Illinois State Museum, Springfield, Reports of Investigations.

Atienza, Lope de
1931 [1575?] Compendio historial del estado de los indios del Perú. In *La religión del imperio de los Incas,* edited by Jacinto Jijón y Caamaño, apéndices, vol. 1. Quito: Escuela Tipográfica Salesiana.

Baldini, Lidia
1981–1982 *Observaciones al trabajo de Gordon C. Pollard titulado "Nuevos aportes a la prehistoria del Valle Calchaquí, Noroeste Argentino."* Anales de Arqueología y Etnología 36-37:161–76. Mendoza: Universidad Nacional de Cuyo, Facultad de Filosofía y Letras.

Baudin, Louis
1928 *L'empire socialiste des Inka.* Paris: Institut d'Ethnologie.

Bawden, Garth
1982 Galindo: A study in cultural transition during the Middle Horizon. In *Chan Chan: Andean desert city,* edited by Michael E. Moseley and Kent C. Day, pp. 285–320. Albuquerque: University of New Mexico Press.

Beavers, A. H., and I. Stephens
1958 Some features of the distribution of plant opal in Illinois soils. *Soil Science* 86:1–5.

Bennett, Wendell C.
1948 Northwest Argentine archaeology. *Yale University Publications in Archaeology* (New Haven) 38.

Berdan, Frances
1975 Trade, tribute, and market in the Aztec empire. Ph.D. dissertation, University of Texas, Austin. Ann Arbor: University Microfilms.

Betanzos, Juan de
1880 Suma y narración de los Incas. In *Biblioteca Hispana Ultramarina,* edited by Jiminez de la Espada. Madrid: Atlas.
1987 [1551] *Suma y narración de los Incas.* Madrid: Atlas.

Bingham, Hiram
1922 *Inca land: Explorations in the highlands of Peru.* Boston: Houghton Mifflin.
1930 *Machu Picchu: A citadel of the Incas.* New Haven: Yale University Press.

Bird, Robert
1970 Maize and its cultural and natural environment in the Sierra of Huánuco, Peru, Ph.D. dissertation, University of California, Berkeley. Ann Arbor: University Microfilms.

Bohannan, Paul
1955 Some principles of exchange and investment among the Tiv. *American Anthropologist* 57:60–70.

Boman, Eric
1908 *Antiquités de la région Andine de la république Argentine et du désert d'Atacama.* 2 vols. Paris: Imprimerie Nationale.

Bradfield, Maitland
1971 *The changing pattern of Hopi agriculture.* London: Royal Anthropological Institute.

Bram, Joseph
1941 An analysis of Inca militarism. Ph.D. dissertation, Department of Anthropology, Columbia University, New York.

Browman, David L.
1970 Early Peruvian peasants: The culture history of a central highlands valley. Ph.D. dissertation, Department of Anthropology, Harvard University, Cambridge, Mass.
1984 Development of interzonal trade and economic expansion in the altiplano. In *Social and economic organization in the prehispanic Andes,* edited by D. L. Browman, R. L. Burger, and M. A. Rivera, pp. 117–42. British Archaeological Reports, International Series, no. 194. Oxford, England.
1985 Comment on, Staple finance, wealth finance, and storage in the Inka political economy, by T. D'Altroy and E. Earle. *Current Anthropology* 26: 197–99.

Bruch, Carlos
1904 Descripción de algunos sepulcros Calchaquis. *Revista del Museo de La Plata* (Buenos Aires) 11: 13–37.

Brumfiel, Elizabeth
1976 Specialization and exchange at the Late Postclassic community of Huexotla, Mexico. Ph.D. dissertation, University of Michigan: Ann Arbor.
1980 Specialization, market exchange, and the Aztec state. *Current Anthropology* 21:459–78.
1983 Elite and utilitarian crafts in the Aztec empire. Paper delivered at the eleventh International Congress of Anthropological and Ethnological Sciences, Vancouver, August.
1987 Elite and utilitarian crafts in the Aztec state. In *Specialization, exchange, and complex societies,* edited by E. Brumfiel and T. Earle, pp. 102–18. Cambridge: Cambridge University Press.

Brush, S. B.
1976 Man's use of an Andean ecosystem. *Human Ecology* 4:147–66.

Burchard, Roderick
1974 Coca y trueque de alimentos. In *Reciprocidad e intercambio en los Andes Peruanos,* compiled by Giorgio Alberti and Enrique Mayer, pp. 209–51. Lima: Instituto de Estudios Peruanos.

Burton, R.
1975 Why do the Trobriands have chiefs? *Man* 10:544–58.

Burton, W. G.
1966 *The potato: A survey of factors influencing its yield, nutritive value, quality and storage.* N. V. Wageningen, Netherlands: H. Veenman and Zonen.

Byrne de Caballero, Geraldine
1974 Los circulos misterios de Cotopachi. *Los Tiempos* (Cochabamba), March 11.

1975 La arquitectura de almacenamiento en la logística Incaica. Manuscript on file, Universidad Mayor de San Simon, Cochabamba, Bolivia.
1978 Incarracay: Un centro administrativo Incaico. *Arte y Arqueologia: Revista del Instituto de Estudios Bolivianos* (Academia Nacional de Ciencias de Bolivia, La Paz), 5–6: 309–316.
1981 El Cerro de "Las rueditas." *Santa Cruz de la Sierra* (Bolivia), November 22.

Castro, Cristóbal de, and Diego de Ortega Morejón
1936 [1558] Relación y declaración del modo que este valle de Chincha. . . . In *Quellen zür Kulturgeschichte des präkolumbischen Amerika*, edited by Hermann Trimborn, pp. 236–46. Stuttgart, Germany.

Cespedes Paz, Ricardo
1982 La arqueologia en el area de Pocona. *Cuadernos de Investigación, Serie Arqueológica* (Instituto de Investigaciones Antropologicas [Museo Arqueologico], Universidad Mayor de San Simon, Cochabamba), 1:89–99.

Chapman, Anne
1957 Port of trade enclaves in Aztec and Maya civilizations. In *Trade and market in the early empires*, edited by Karl Polanyi, Conrad M. Arensberg, and Harry W. Pearson, pp. 114–53. Chicago: Free Press.

Chavez Ballon, Manuel
1963 El sitio de Raqchi en San Pedro de Cacha. *Revista Peruana de Cultura* 1:105–11.

Cherry, John F.
1986 Politics and palaces: Some problems in Minoan state formation. In *Peer polity interaction and sociopolitical change*, edited by C. Renfrew and J. Cherry. London: Cambridge University Press.

Childe, V. Gordon
1951 *Man makes himself*. London: Watts.

Chiswell, Coreen E.
1984 A study of prehistoric Andean storage by means of phytolith analysis. M. A. thesis, Trent University, Ontario. Ottawa: National Library of Canada Microfilms.
1986 Analysis of organic remains from Huamachuco *qollqas*. In *Perspectives on Andean prehistory and protohistory*, edited by D. H. Sandweiss and D. P. Kvietok, pp. 123–30. Ithaca, N.Y.: Latin American Studies Program, Cornell University.

Christensen, C. M., and H. H. Kaufman
1969 *Grain storage: The role of funghi in quality loss*. Minneapolis: University of Minnesota Press.

Christiansen, G. Jorge
1967 *El cultivo de la papa en el Peru*. Lima: Centro Internacional de la Papa.

Cieza de León, Pedro de
1862 [1551] La crónica del Peru. In *Biblioteca de autores Españoles*, no. 26: 349–458. Madrid: Ediciones Atlas.
1967 [1553] *El señorío de los Incas*. Segunda parte de La *Crónica del Peru*. Lima: Instituto de Estudios Peruanos.

1984 [1551] *La Crónica del Peru. Primera Parte.* Lima: Pontífica Universidad Católica del Peru, Fondo Editorial.
1986 [1553] *Crónica del Peru, Segunda Parte.* Lima: Fondo Editorial de la Pontifica Universidad Católica del Peru.

Cobo, Bernabé
1956 [1653]. Historia del nuevo mundo. Vols. 2 and 3. *Biblioteca de autores Españoles,* no. 92. Madrid: Ediciones Atlas.

Conrad, Geoffrey
1977 Chiquitoy Viejo, an Inca administrative center in the Chicama Valley, Peru. *Journal of Field Archaeology* 4:1–18.

Cook, Noble David
1975 Introducción. In *Tasa de la visita general de Francisco de Toledo,* edited by N. D. Cook. Lima: Universidad Nacional Mayor de San Marcos.
1981 *Demographic collapse: Indian Peru, 1520–1620.* Cambridge: Cambridge University Press.
1982 Population data for Indian Peru: Sixteenth and seventeenth centuries. *Hispanic American Historical Review* 62 (1): 73–120.

Costin, Cathy L., and Timothy Earle
1989 Status distinction and legitimation of power as reflected in changing patterns of consumption in late prehispanic Peru. *American Antiquity* 54(4): 691–714.

Costin, Cathy, Timothy K. Earle, Bruce Owen, and Glen Russell
1989 The impact of the Inca conquest on local technology in the Upper Mantaro Valley, Peru. In *What's new? A closer look at the process of innovation,* edited by S. E. van der Leeuw and R. Torrence. London: Unwin Hyman.

Cusichaca, Don Francisco, Don Diego Eneupari [Ñaupari], and don Cristóbal Canchaya
1971 [1561] Probanza . . . In Los Huancas, Aliados de la Conquista, by Waldemar Espinoza Soriano. *Anales Científicos de la Universidad del Centro del Peru* (Huancayo), 1:260–387.

Dalton, George
1961 Economic theory and primitive society. *American Anthropologist* 63:1–25.
1967 *Tribal and peasant economies.* Garden City, N.Y.: Natural History Press.
1977 Aboriginal economies in stateless societies. In *Exchange systems in prehistory,* edited by Timothy Earle and Jonathan Ericson, pp. 191–212. New York: Academic Press.

D'Altroy, Terence N.
1981 Empire growth and consolidation: The Xauxa region of Peru under the Incas. Ph.D. dissertation, Department of Anthropology, University of California, Los Angeles. Ann Arbor: University Microfilms.
1987 Transitions in Power: Centralization of Wanka political organization under Inka rule. *Ethnohistory* 34 (1): 78–102.
1988 Personal communication, James Snead, Los Angeles.
1989 Field notes.
1992 *Provincial power in the Inka empire.* Washington, D.C.: Smithsonian Institution Press.

D'Altroy, Terence N., and Timothy K. Earle
1985 Staple finance, wealth finance, and storage in the Inka political economy (with comment). *Current Anthropology* 26 (2): 187–206.

D'Altroy, Terence N., and Christine A. Hastorf
1984 The distribution and contents of Inca state storehouses in the Xauxa region of Peru. *American Antiquity* 49 (2): 334–49.

D'Altroy, Terence N., Ana María Lorandi, and Verónica Williams
1990 Informe preliminar: Proyecto Arqueológico Calchaquí. Submitted to Ministerio de Educación y Cultura, Provincia de Salta, Argentina. Manuscript.

Dauelsberg, Percy
1983 Investigaciones arqueológicas en la Sierra de Arica, Sector Belen. *Chungara* (Universidad de Tarapaca, Arica, Chile), 11 (Nov.): 63–83.

Day, Kent C.
1973 Architecture of Ciudadela Rivero, Chan Chan, Peru. Ph.D. dissertation, Department of Anthropology, Harvard University, Cambridge, Mass.
1982 Ciudadelas: Their form and function, and, Storage and labor service: A production and management design for the Andean area. In *Chan Chan: Andean desert city,* edited by M. Moseley and K. Day, pp. 55–66, 333–49. Albuquerque: University of New Mexico Press.

Deambrosis, María Susana y Mónica de Lorenzi
1977 La influencia incaica en el noroeste Argentino (Sector Norte). *Estudios de Arqueología,* 2:43–60. Cachi: Museo Arqueológico de Cachi.

Dennell, R.
1976 The economic importance of plant resources represented on archaeological sites. *Journal of Archaeological Science* 3:229–47.

Díaz, Pío Pablo
1983 Sitios arqueológicos del Valle Calchaquí. *Estudios de Arqueología,* 2:93–104. Cachi: Museo Arqueológico de Cachi.

Diez de San Miquel, Garci
1964 [1567] *Visita hecha a la provincia de Chucuito por Garci Diez de San Miquel en el año 1567: Versión paleográfica de Waldemar Espinoza Soriano.* Lima: Casa de la Cultura del Peru.

Difrieri, H.
1948 Las ruinas del Potrero de Payogasta (Provincia de Salta, Argentina). In *Actes du XVIII Congrès Internacional des Americanistes,* pp. 599–604. Paris: Musée de l'Homme.

Dillehay, Tom D.
1976 Competition and cooperation in a prehispanic multi-ethnic system in the central Andes. Ph.D. dissertation, University of Texas, Austin.
1977 Tawantinsuyu integration of the Chillon Valley, Peru; A case of Inca geopolitical mastery. *Journal of Field Archaeology* 4:397–405.

Dixon, W. J., and M. B. Brown (editors)
1979 *BMDP-79. Biomedical computor programs P-series.* Berkeley: University of California Press.

Dougherty, Bernard
1972 Un nuevo yacimiento con cunstrucciones tumuliformes de piedra; Agua Hedionda. *Etnia* (Olavarria) 16 (July–Dec.): 20–29.

Drewes, W. U., and A. T. Drewes
1957 *Climate and related phenomena of the eastern Andean slopes of Central Peru.* Syracuse: Syracuse University Research Institute.

Duviols, Pierre
1974–76 [1614] Un petite chronique retrouvée: Errores, ritos, supersticiones y ceremonias de los yndios de la provincia de Chinchaycocha y otras del Piru. *Journal de la Societé des Américanistes,* 2d ser., 63: 275–86.

Earle, Timothy K.
1974 Evolution of Peruvian trade. Paper delivered at annual meeting of the Society for American Archaeology, Washington, D.C.
1977 A reappraisal of redistribution: Complex Hawaiian chiefdoms. In *Exchange systems in prehistory,* edited by Timothy K. Earle and Jonathan E. Ericson, pp. 213–29. New York: Academic Press.
1978 *Economic and social organization of a complex chiefdom: The Halelea district, Kaua'i, Hawaii.* Anthropological Papers of the Museum of Anthropology, University of Michigan Museum, no. 63. Ann Arbor.
1982 The ecology and politics of primitive valuables. In *Cultural ecology: Eclectic perspectives,* edited by John Kennedy and Robert Edgerton. Washington, D.C.: American Anthropological Association.
1985 Commodity exchange and markets in the Inca state: Recent archaeological evidence. In *Markets and Exchange,* edited by Stuart Plattner, pp. 369–97. Latham, Md.: University Press of America.
1987 Specialization and the production of wealth: Hawaiian chiefdoms and the Inka empire. In *Specialization, exchange, and complex societies,* edited by E. Brumfield and T. K. Earle, pp. 65–75. Cambridge: Cambridge University Press.

Earle, Timothy K., and Terence N. D'Altroy
1979 The function of storage in traditional economies. Paper presented at the forty-fourth annual meeting of the Society for American Archaeology, Vancouver.
1982 Storage facilities and state finance in the Upper Mantaro Valley, Peru. In *Contexts for prehistoric exchange,* edited by Jonathan E. Ericson and Timothy K. Earle, pp. 265–90. New York: Academic Press.
1989 The political economy of the Inka empire: The archaeology of power and finance. In *Archaeological thought in America,* edited by C. Lamberg-Karlovsky. Cambridge: Cambridge University Press.

Earle, Timothy K., Terence N. D'Altroy, Catherine J. LeBlanc, Christine A. Hastorf, and Terry Y. LeVine
1980 Changing settlement patterns in the Upper Mantaro Valley, Peru. *Journal of New World Archaeology* 4 (1): 1–49. Institute of Archaeology, University of California, Los Angeles.

Earle, Timothy, Terence D'Altroy, Christine Hastorf, Catherine Scott, Cathy Costin, Glen Russell, and Elsie Sandefur

1987 *Archaeological field research in the Upper Mantaro, Peru, 1982–83: Investigations of Inka expansion and exchange,* Monograph 28. Los Angeles: University of California, Institute of Archaeology Press.

Ellefsen, B.
1978 La dominación incaica en Cochabamba. *Bulletin de l'Institut Français d'Etudes Andines* (La Paz) 7 (1–2).

Engels, Donald W.
1978 *Alexander the Great and the logistics of the Macedonian army.* Berkeley: University of California Press.

Espinosa Bravo, C.
1964 *Juaja antiqua.* Lima: Talleres Graficos P. L. Villanueva.

Espinoza Campos, Diego de
1965 [1592] Los indios del repartimiento de Ichoc-huánuco contra los indios Pachas, sobre el servicio y mitas del puente del Rio Huánuco. BNP A 474, partially published by R. Mellafe in *Historia y Cultura* 1 (1): 65–113.

Espinoza Soriano, Waldemar.
1963 La guaranga y la reducción de Huancayo. *Revista del Museo Nacional* (Lima) 32:8–80.
1971 [1558–61] Los Huancas, aliados de la conquista. *Anales Científicos de la Universidad del Centro del Peru* (Huancayo), 1:3–407.
1973 Las colonias de mitmas multiples en Abancay, siglos XV y XVI. *Revista del Museo Nacional* (Lima) 39:225–99.
1974a Los señórios étnicos del valle de Condebamba y Providencia de Cajabamba: história de las huarancas de Llucho y Mitmas, siglos XV–XVI. *Anales Científicos de la Universidad del Centro del Peru* (Huancayo, Peru) 3: pp 5–371.
1974b Ichoc-Huánuco y el señorio del curaca Huanca en el reino de Huánuco siglos XV y XVI. In *Anales Científicos de la Universidad del Centro del Peru* (Huancayo, Peru) 4:7–70; fragment of La Visita de 1549, 4:49–61.
1975 Los mitmas huayacuntu en Quito o guarniciones para la represión armada, siglos XV y XVI. *Revista del Museo Nacional* (Lima) 41:351–94.
1978 Editor. *Los modos de producción en el imperio Inca.* Lima: El Mantaro.

Estete, Miguel de
1917 [1532–33] La relación que hizo el señor capitan Hernando Pizarro. . . . In *Verdadera relación de la conquista del Peru . . . ,* by Francisco de Xerez; edited by Horacio Urteaga, pp. 77–102. Lima: Sanmartí.

Fejos, Paul
1944 Archaeological explorations in the Cordillera Vilcabamba. *Viking Fund Publications in Anthropology* (New York) 3.

Fock, Nils
1961 Inka imperialism in northwest Argentina, and Chaco burial forms. *Folk* (Copenhagen) 3: 67–90.

Forde, C. Darryl
1931 Hopi agriculture and land ownership. *Journal of the Royal Anthropological Institute of Great Britain and Ireland* 61:357–405.

Franch, Jose Alcina
1978 Ingapirca: Arquitectura y areas de asentamiento. *Revista Espanola de Antropología Americana* (Facultad de Geografía e Historia, Universidad Complutense de Madrid), 127–46.

Franco, Efrain, Douglas Horton, and Francois Tardieu
1979 *Producción y utilización de la papa en el valle del Mantaro, Peru.* Unidad de Ciencias Sociales, Documentos de Trabajo, no. 1979-1. Lima: Centro Internacional de la papa.

Fried, Morton
1967 *The evolution of political society.* New York: Random House.

Friedman, J., and M. J. Rowlands
1977 Notes toward an epigenetic model of the evolution of "civilization." In *The evolution of social systems,* edited by M. J. Rowlands and J. Friedman, pp. 201–76. London: Duckworth.

Garcilaso de la Vega (el Inca)
1943 [1609] *Comentarios reales de los Incas.* Edited by Angel Rosenblatt. Buenos Aires: Emece Editores.
1960 [1604] *Primera parte de los comentarios reales.* Lima: Universidad Nacional Mayor de San Marcos.
1963 [1604] Primera parte de los comentarios reales de los Incas. *Biblioteca de autores Españoles,* 133. Madrid: Real Academia Española.

Gasparini, Graziaño, and Luise Margolies
1980 *Inca architecture.* Translated by Patricia J. Lyon. Bloomington: Indiana University Press.

Genel, M. R.
1966 *Almacenamiento y conservación de granos y semillas.* México.

Godelier, Maurice
1977 The concept of "social and economic formation": The Inca example. Translated by Robert Brain. In *Perspectives in Marxist anthropology,* pp. 63–69. Cambridge: Cambridge University Press.

Goldman, Irving
1970 *Ancient Polynesian society.* Chicago: University of Chicago Press.

Gonzalez, Alberto Rex
1963 Cultural development in northwestern Argentina. In *Aboriginal cultural development in Latin America: An interpretative view,* edited by Betty Meggers and Clifford Evans. *Smithsonian Miscellaneous Collections* (Washington, D.C.), 46 (1): 102–17.
1982 Las "provincias" Inca del antiguo Tucuman. *Revista del Museo Nacional* (Lima), 46:317–80.
1983 Inca settlement patterns in a marginal province of the empire: Sociocultural implications. In *Prehistoric settlement patterns: Essays in honor of Gordon R. Willey,* edited by Evon Z. Vogt and Richard M. Leventhal, pp. 337–60. Albuquerque: University of New Mexico Press.

González, A. Rex, and Cravotto, A.
1977 *Estudio arqueológico e inventario de las ruinas de Inkallajta* [Bolivia]. Paris: UNESCO.

González Hoguin, Diego
1952 [1608] *Vocabulario de la lengua general de todo el Peru llamda lengua quichua o del inca.* Lima: Edición del Instituto de Historia.

Grobman, Alexander, W. Salhuana, and R. Sevilla
1961 *Races of maize in Peru.* National Academy of Sciences, National Research Council Publication no. 915. Washington, D.C.

Guacrapáucar, Don Jerónimo
1971 [1560] Información hecha en la audiencia [de Lima] a pedimento de Don Jerónimo [Guacrapáucar sobre los servicios de su parcialidad de Lurinhuanca y propios desde que llegó Francisco Pizarro]. In *Los Huancas, aliados de la conquista,* by Waldemar Espinoza Soriano. *Anales Científicos de la Universidad del Centro del Peru* (Huancayo), 1:216–59.

Guaman Poma de Ayale, Felipe
1936 [1613] *Nueva corónica y buen gobierno.* Paris: Institut d'Ethnologie.
1980 [1613] *El primer nueva corónica y buen gobierno.* 3 vols. Edición crítica de John V. Murra y Rolena Adorno. Mexico: Siglo Veintiuno.

Hadden, Gorden J.
1967 Un ensayo de demografia histórica y etnológica en Huánuco. In *Visita de la provincia de León de Huánuco en 1562,* edited by John V. Murra, 1:371–80. Huánuco, Peru: Universidad Nacional Hermilio Valdizán.

Haggard, J. Villasana, and Malcolm D. McLean
1941 *Handbook for translators of Spanish historical documents.* Austin: Archives Collection, University of Texas Press.

Hainz, Walter
1966 Beiträge zür Archäologie Boliviens. *Bässler-Archiv Beiträge zür Völkerkunde,* supplement ser. Z, 4.

Handy, E. S. Craighill
1923 *The native cultures in the Marquesas.* Bishop Museum Bulletin 9.

Harris, Marvin
1979 *Cultural materialism: The struggle for a science of culture.* New York: Random House.

Hartmann, Roswith
1971 Mercados y ferias prehispánicos en el área andina. *Boletín de la Academia Nacional de Historia* 54 (118): 214–35. Quito.

Hassiq, Ross
1981 The famine of One Rabbit: Ecological causes and social consequences of a pre-Columbian calamity. *Journal of Archaeological Research* 37:172–82.
1985 *Trade, tribute, and transportation: The sixteenth-century political economy of the Valley of Mexico.* Norman: University of Oklahoma Press.

Hastorf, Christine A.
1981 Preliminary report on land and plant use from flotation recovered remains in the Jauja-Mantaro region, Peru. Manuscript on file, Department of Anthropology, University of California, Los Angeles.
1983 Prehistoric agricultural intensification and political development in the Jauja region of Central Peru. Ph.D. dissertation, Department of Anthropol-

ogy, University of California, Los Angeles. Ann Arbor: University Microfilms.

1990 The effect of the Inka State on Sausa agricultural production and crop consumption. *American Antiquity* 55(2): 262–90.

1992 *Resources to power: Agricultural and political change before the Inka.* Cambridge: University of Cambridge Press.

Hastorf, Christine A., and Michael DeNiro
1985 Reconstruction of prehistoric plant production and cooking practices by a new isotopic method. *Nature* 315:489–91.

Hastorf, C. A., T. Earle, H. Wright, L. LeCount, G. Russell, and E. Sandefur
1989 Settlement archaeology in the Jauja region of Peru: Evidence from the Early Intermediate Period through the Late Intermediate Period: A report on the 1986 field season. *Andean Past* 2:81–129.

Helmer, Marie
1955–56 [1549] La visitación de los yndios Chupachos: Inca et encomendero, 1549. *Travaux de l'Institut Français d'Etudes Andines* (Lima and Paris), 5:3–50.

Hemming, J.
1970 *The conquest of the Inca.* New York: Harcourt, Brace, and Jovanovich.

Hillman, G.
1981 Reconstructing crop husbandry practices from charred remains of crops. In *Farming practice in British prehistory,* edited by R. Mercer, pp. 123–62. Edinburgh: University of Edinburgh Press.

Hough, Walter
1915 *The Hopi Indians.* Cedar Rapids, Iowa: Torch Press.

Hubbard, R. N. L. B.
1980 Development of agriculture in Europe and the Near East: Evidence from quantitative studies. *Economic Botany* 34(1):51–67.

Hunt, Robert
1988 The role of bureaucracy in the provisioning of cities: A framework for analysis of the ancient Middle East. In *Organization of power: Aspects of bureaucracy in the ancient Near East,* edited by M. Gibson and R. Biggs, pp. 161–92. Chicago: Oriental Institute, University of Chicago.

Hyslop, John
1979 El area Lupaqa bajo del dominio Incaico; Un reconocimiento arqueológico. *Historica* 3(1): 53–95.

1984 *The Inka road system.* Studies in Archaeology. New York and San Francisco: Academic Press.

1985 *Inkawasi: The new Cuzco.* British Archaeological Reports, International Series, no. 234. Oxford, England.

1990 *Inka settlement planning.* Austin: University of Texas Press.

Hyslop, John, and Pío Pablo Díaz
1983 El camino Incaico: Calchaquí-Tastil (N.O. Argentina), *Gazeta Arqueológica Andina,* 1(6): 6–8. Lima: Instituto de Estudios Andinos.

Isbell, William H.
1977 *The rural foundations for urbanism.* Illinois Studies in Anthropology, no. 10. Urbana: University of Illinois Press.
1987 State origins in the Ayacucho Valley, central highlands, Peru. In *The origins and development of the Andean state,* edited by J. Haas, S. Pozorski, and T. Pozorski, pp. 83–90. Cambridge: Cambridge University Press.
1988 City and state in Middle Horizon Huari. In *Peruvian Archaeology,* edited by R. W. Keatinge. Cambridge: Cambridge University Press.

Isbell, William H., and Katharina J. Schreiber
1978 Was Huari a state? *American Antiquity* 43 (4): 372–89.

Johnson, Allen W., and Timothy K. Earle
1987 *The evolution of human societies: From foraging group to agrarian state.* Stanford: Stanford University Press.

Johannessen, S., and C. Hastorf
1990 A history of Andean fuel management (A.D. 500 to the present) in the Mantaro Valley, Peru. *Journal of Ethnobiology* 10, no. 1: 61–90.

Julien, Catherine J.
1978 Inca administration in the Titicaca Basin as reflected at the provincial capital of Hatunqolla. Ph.D. dissertation, University of California, Berkeley, California.
1982 Inca decimal administration in the Lake Titicaca region. In *The Inca and Aztec states 1400–1800,* edited by G. A. Collier, R. I. Rosaldo, and J. D. Wirth, pp. 119–51. New York: Academic Press.
1983 *Hatunqolla: A view of Inca rule From the Lake Titicaca region.* University of California Publications in Anthropology, no. 15. University of California Press, Berkeley.
1988 How Inca decimal administration worked. *Ethnohistory* 35: 257–79.

Kendall, Ann
1976a *Kin groups and social structure.* New York: Holt, Rinehart, and Winston.
1976b Descripción y inventario de las formas arquitectónicas Inca. Patrones de distribución e inferencias cronológicas. *Revista del Museo Nacional* (Lima), 42:13–96.
1985 *Aspects of Inca architecture: Description, form, and chronology.* BAR International Series, no. 242. Oxford, England: British Archaeological Reports.

Klymyshyn, Alexandra M. Ulana
1987 The development of Chimu administration in Chan Chan. In *The origins and development of the Andean State.* Edited by J. Haas, S. Pozorski, and T. Pozorski, pp. 97–110. Cambridge: Cambridge University Press.

Kolata, Alan L.
1986 The agricultural foundations of the Tiwanaku state. *American Antiquity* 51: 748–62.
1989 *Arqueología de Lukurmata 2.* La Paz, Bolivia: Instituto Nacional de Arqueología y Ediciones Puma Punku.

Krapovikas, Pedro
1968 Una construcción novedosa en la quebrada de Humahuaca (Jujuy). *Etnia* 7 (Jan.–July): 20–26.

La Lone, Darrell
1978 Historical contexts of trade and markets in the Peruvian Andes. Ann Arbor: University Microfilms.
1982 The Inca as a nonmarket economy: Supply on command versus supply and demand. In *Contexts for prehistoric exchange,* edited by Jonathan E. Ericson and Timothy K. Earle, pp. 291–316. New York: Academic Press.
1985 Comment on T. D'Altroy and T. Earle, Staple finance, wealth finance, and storage in the Inka political economy. *Current Anthropology* 26(2): 199.

La Lone, Mary B., and Darrell E. La Lone
1987 The Inka state in the Southern Highlands: State administrative and production enclaves. *Ethnohistory* 34(1): 47–62.

Latcham, Ricardo E.
1927 Tumulos del Copiapo que no son sepulturas. *Publicaciones del Museo de Etnología y Antropología de Chile* (Santiago de Chile), 4 (3–4).

Lavallée, Danielle, and Michele Julien
1973 Les établissements asto à l'époque préhispanique. *Travaux de l'Institut Français d'Etudes Andines,* book 15, vol. 1.

LeBlanc, Catherine J.
1981 Late prehispanic Huanca settlement patterns in the Yanamarca Valley, Peru. Ph.D. dissertation, Department of Anthropology, University of California, Los Angeles.

Lee, Vincent R.
1985 *Sixpac Manco: Travels among the Incas.* Wilson, Wyo.: by the author.

LeVine, Terry Yarov
1979 Prehistoric political and economic change in highland Peru: An ethnohistorical study of the Mantaro Valley. Master's thesis, Archaeology Program, University of California, Los Angeles.
1985 Inka administration in the Central Highlands: A comparative study. Ph.D. dissertation, University of California, Los Angeles. Ann Arbor: University Microfilms.
1987 Inka labor service at the regional level: The functional reality. *Ethnohistory* 34 (1): 14–36.

Lorandi, Ana María, y Roxana Boixadós
1987–88 Etnohistoria de los valles Calchaquíes en los siglos XVI y XVII. *Runa* 17–18: 263–420.

Lumbreras, Luis G.
1974 *The peoples and cultures of ancient Peru.* Translated by Betty Meggers. Washington, D.C.: Smithsonian Institution Press.
1978 Acerca de la aparición del estado Inka. In *III Congreso Peruano. El hombre y la cultura andina,* edited by Ramiro Matos M., 1: 101–9. Lima: Universidad Nacional Mayor de San Marcos.

Mackenzie, Janet
1980 Coast to highland trade in precolumbian Peru: Dendritic economic organization in the North Sierra. Master's thesis, Department of Anthropology, Trent University, Peterborough, Ontario.

Mackey, Carol J.
1987 Chimu administration in the provinces. In *The origins and development of the Andean state,* edited by J. Haas, S. Pozorski, and T. Pozorski, pp. 121–29. Cambridge: Cambridge University Press.

MacNeish, Richard S., Thomas C. Patterson, and David L. Browman
1975 The Central Peruvian prehistoric interaction sphere. In *Papers of the Robert S. Peabody Foundation for Archaeology,* 7. Andover, Mass.

Madrazo, Guillermo B., and Marta Ottonelo de Garcia Reinoso
1966 Tipos de instilación prehispanico en la región de la puna y su borde. Monografia 1. Olavarria, Buenos Aires: Museo Etnológico Municipal "Damaso Arce."

Malinowski, Bronislaw
1965 *Coral gardens and their magic.* Bloomington: Indiana University Press.

Malo, David
1971 [1898] 2d ed. *Hawaiian antiquities.* Bernice P. Bishop Museum Special Publications, no. 2. Honolulu: Bishop Museum Press.

Malpass, Michael A.
1983 Late prehispanic terracing at Chijra in the Colca Valley, Peru: Preliminary report I. In *Perspectives on Andean prehistory and protohistory,* edited by Daniel H. Sandweiss and D. Peter Kvietok, pp. 19–34. Papers from the Third Annual Northeast Conference on Andean Archaeology and Ethnohistory. Ithaca: Cornell University Press.

Marcos, Jorge G.
1978 Cruising to Acapulco and back with the thorny oyster set: A model for a linear exchange system. *Journal of the Steward Anthropological Society* 9 (1 and 2): 99–132.

Marcus, Joyce, Ramiro Matos M., and Maria Rostworowski de Diez Canseco
1983–85 Arquitectura Inca de Cerro Azul, Valle de Canete. *Revista del Museo Nacional* (Lima), 47:127–38.

Mathews, James E.
1987 Dual systems of agricultural production under the Inka imperial state in the Osmore Drainage, southern Peru. Master's thesis, University of Chicago.

Matos Mendieta, Ramiro
1975 Prehistória y ecología humana en la punas de Junín. *Revista del Museo Nacional* 41:37–80.

Matos Mendieta, Ramiro, and Jeffrey R. Parsons
1979 Poblamiento prehispanico en la cuenca del Mantaro. In *Arqueología Peruana,* edited by R. Matos M., pp. 157–71. Lima: Universidad Nacional Mayor de San Marcos.

Mayer, Enrique
1979 *Land use in the Andes: Ecology and agriculture in the Mantaro Valley of Peru with special reference to potatoes.* Lima: Centro Internacional de la Papa.
1985 Production zones. In *Andean ecology and civilization,* edited by S. Masuda, I. Shimada, and C. Morris, pp. 45–84. Tokyo: University of Tokyo Press.

McCown, Theodore D.
1945 Pre-Incaic Huamachuco: Survey and excavations in the region of Huama-

chuco and Cajabamba. *University of California Publications in American Archaeology and Ethnology* (Berkeley), 39: 223–399.

Menzel, Dorothy
1959 The Inca occupation of the south coast of Peru. *Southwest Journal of Anthropology* 15(2): 125–42.

Menzel, Dorothy, and Francis A. Riddell
1986 *Archaeological investigations at Tambo Viejo, Acari Valley, Peru 1954.* Sacramento: California Institute for Peruvian Studies.

Metraux, Alfred
1969 *The history of the Incas.* Translated by George Ordish. New York: Schocken.

Minnis, P., and S. LeBlanc
1976 An efficient, inexpensive arid lands flotation system. *American Antiquity* 41 (4): 491–93.

Mitchell, William
1980 Local ecology and the state: Implications of contemporary Quechua land use for the Inca sequence of agricultural work. In *Beyond the myths of culture,* edited by Eric B. Ross, pp. 139–54. New York: Academic Press.

Monk, M. A., and J. Fasham
1980 Carbonized plant remains from two Iron Age sites in central Hampshire. *Proceedings of the Prehistoric Society* 46:321–44.

Moore, Sally Falk
1958 *Power and property in Inca Peru.* Westport, Conn.: Greenwood Press.

Morris, Craig
1966 El tampu real de Tunsancancha. *Cuadernos de Investigación, Antropología* (Universidad Hermilio Valdizán, Huánuco), 1:95–107.
1967 Storage in Tawantinsuyu. Ph.D. dissertation, Department of Anthropology, University of Chicago.
1971 The identification of function in Inca architecture and ceramics. *Actas y Memorias of the XXXIX International Congress of Americanists, 1970* 3:135–44. Lima.
1972a State settlements in Tawantinsuyu: A strategy of compulsory urbanism. In *Contemporary archaeology,* edited by Mark P. Leone, pp. 393–401. Carbondale: Southern Illinois University Press.
1972b El almacenaje en dos aldeas de los Chupaychu. In *Visita de la provincia de León de Huánuco en 1562,* 2, edited by John V. Murra, pp. 383–404. Huánuco, Peru: Universidad Nacional Hermilio Valdizán.
1974 Reconstructing patterns of nonagricultural production in the Inca economy: Archaeology and documents in instituted analysis. In *Reconstructing complex societies,* edited by Charlotte Moore, pp. 49–68. Supplement to the Bulletin of the American Schools of Oriental Research, (Cambridge, Mass.), no. 20.
1976 The archaeological study of Andean exchange systems. In *Social archaeology: Beyond subsistence and dating,* edited by C. Redman, M. Berman, E. Curtin, W. Langhorne, Jr., N. Versaggi, and J. Wanser, pp. 315–27. New York: Academic Press.
1981 Tecnología y organización inca del almacenamiento de víveres en la sierra. In *Runakunap Kawsayninkupaq Rurasqankunaqa: La tecnología en el mundo*

andino, edited by Heather Lechtman and Anna Maria Soldi, pp. 327–75. Mexico City: UNAM.

1982 The infrastructure of Inka control in the Peruvian central highlands. In *The Inka and Aztec states, 1400–1800,* edited by George A. Collier, Renato I. Rosaldo, and John D. Wirth, pp. 153–71. New York: Academic Press.

1985 From principles of ecological complementarity to the organization and administration of Tawantinsuyu. In *Andean ecology and civilization,* edited by S. Masuda, I. Shimada, and C. Morris, pp. 477–90. Tokyo: University of Tokyo Press.

1986 Storage, supply, and redistribution in the economy of the Inka state. In *Anthropological history of Andean polities,* edited by J. Murra, N. Wachtel, and J. Revel, pp. 59–68. Cambridge: Cambridge University Press.

Morris, Craig, and Idilio Santillana
N.d. The Inca occupation of La Centinela. Unpublished manuscript.

Morris, Craig, and Donald E. Thompson
1970 Huánuco Viejo: An Inca administrative center. *American Antiquity* 35 (3): 344–62.

1985 *Huánuco Pampa, an Inca City and its hinterland.* New York: Thames and Hudson.

Moseley, Michael E.
1975 Chan Chan: Andean alternative of the preindustrial city. *Science* 187:219–25.

1985 Comment on T. D'Altroy and T. Earle, Staple finance, wealth finance, and storage in the Inka political economy, *Current Anthropology* 26(2):199–200.

Moseley, Michael E., and Kent C. Day
1982 *Chan Chan: Andean desert city.* Albuquerque: University of New Mexico Press.

Mostny, Grete
1948 Ciudades Atacamenas. *Boletín del Museo Nacional de História Natural* (Santiago de Chile), 24: 125–212.

Mujica, Elias
1985 Altiplano-coast relationships in the south-central Andes: From indirect to direct complementarity. In *Andean ecology and civilization,* edited by S. Masuda, I. Shimada and C. Morris. Tokyo: University of Tokyo Press.

Murra, John V.
1958 On Inca political structure. In *Proceedings of the 1958 annual spring meeting of the American Ethnological Society.* Seattle: University of Washington Press.

1962 The function of cloth in the Inca state. *American Anthropologist* 64:710–28.

1972 El 'control vertical' de un máximo de pisos ecológicos en la economía de las sociedades andinas. In *Visita de la Provincia de León de Huánuco en 1562,* 2, edited by John V. Murra, pp. 429–76. Huánuco, Peru: Universidad Nacional Hermilio Valdizán.

1975 *Formaciones económicas y políticas del mundo andino.* Lima: Instituto de Estudios Andinos.

1980 [1956] *The economic organization of the Inka state.* Greenwich, Conn.: JAI Press.

1982 The *mit'a* obligations of ethnic groups to the Inka state. In *The Inca and Aztec states, 1400–1800,* edited by George A. Collier, Renato I. Rosaldo, and John D. Wirth, pp. 237–62. New York: Academic Press.

Myers, Thomas P.
1985 Comment on T. D'Altroy and T. Earle, "Staple finance, wealth finance, and storage in the Inka political economy." *Current Anthropology* 26(2): 200–201.

Nash, Manning
1966 *Primitive and peasant economic systems.* San Francisco: Chandler Publishing Co.

Netherly, Patricia
1978 Local-level lords on the north coast of Peru. Ph.D. dissertation, Department of Anthropology, Cornell University, Ithaca, N.Y.

Niles, Susan A.
1980 Civil and social engineers: Inca planning in the Cuzco region. Ph.D. dissertation, University of California, Berkeley. Ann Arbor: University Microfilms.

Nordenskiold, Erland
1915 Inkallacta, Eine Befestigte und von Inca Tupac Ypanqui Agelegte Stadt. *Ymer* 35(2): .169–85.

1924 *Forschungen und Abenteuer in Südamerika.* Stockholm, Sweden.

Núñez del Prado, Oscar
1950 Exploración arqueológica en Raqc'i (Urubamba). *Tradición del Cuzco* 1 (1).

Nyanteng, V. K.
1972 *Storage of foodstuffs in Ghana.* Institute of Statistical, Social, and Economic Research Technical Publications Series, no. 18. Legon, Ghana.

Oberem, Udo
1968 La fortaleza de Montana de Quitoloma. *Boletín de la Academia Nacional de História* (Quito), 114: 196–204.

Ortiz de Zúñiga, Iñigo
1967 [1562] *Visita de la provincia de León de Huánuco en 1562.* Vol. 1, edited by John V. Murra. Huánuco, Peru: Universidad Nacional Hermilio Valdizán.

1972 [1562] *Visita de la provincia de Leon de Huánuco en 1562.* Vol. 2, edited by John V. Murra. Huánuco, Peru: Universidad Nacional Hermilio Valdizán.

O'Connor, David
1990 Abydos: Investigation of an Egyptian settlement in the Old Kingdom and First Intermediate period. National Science Foundation grant proposal.

Owen, Bruce
1986 Settlement in the Cochas Valley: A preliminary archaeological survey in the Central Andes. Paper presented to the Friends of Archaeology, UCLA.

1991 Metal and wealth good. In *Empire and domestic economy,* edited by Terence N. D'Altroy and Christine A. Hastorf. Washington, D.C.: Smithsonian Institution Press.

Papavizas, George C., and C. M. Christensen
1958 Grain Storage Studies 26: Fungus invasion and deterioration of wheats stored at lower temperatures and moisture contents of 15–18%. *Cereal Chemistry* (St. Paul, Minn.) 35:27–34.

Pardo, Luis A.
1937 Exposición de las ruinas del Santuario del Huiraccocha. *Revista del Instituto Arqueológico del Cuzco* 2: 3–32.

Parsons, Jeffrey R., and Charles M. Hastings
1975–1976   Field notes.
1976 Prehispanic settlement patterns in the Upper Mantaro, Peru: Preliminary report of the 1975 field season. Progress report submitted to the National Science Foundation.
1977 Prehispanic settlement patterns in the Upper Mantaro, Peru: A progress report for the 1976 field season. Submitted to the Instituto Nacional de Cultura, Lima, Peru, and the National Science Foundation, Washington, D.C.
1988 The Late Intermediate period. In *Peruvian archaeology,* edited by R. W. Keatinge, pp. 190–229. Cambridge: Cambridge University Press.

Parsons, Jeffrey R., and Ramiro Matos M.
1978 Asentamientos pre-hispánicos en el Mantaro, Peru: Informe preliminar. In *El hombre y la cultura andina: III Congreso Peruano,* edited by R. Matos M., pp. 539–55. Lima: Universidad Nacional Mayor de San Marcos.

Patterson, Thomas C.
1983 Pachacamac: An Andean oracle under Inca rule. In *Perspectives on andean prehistory and protohistory. Papers from the Second Annual Northeast Conference on Andean Archaeology and Ethnohistory,* edited by Daniel H. Sandweiss and D. Peter Kvietok, pp. 159–76. Ithaca: Cornell University Press.

Paulotti, Osvaldo
1967 Las ruinas de los Nevados de Aconquija. *Runa* (Buenos Aires), 10: 354–70.

Paulsen, Alison
1974 The thorny oyster and the voice of God. *American Antiquity* 74:597–607.

Pearsall, Deborah M.
1979 The application of ethnobotanical techniques to the problem of subsistence in the Ecuadorian formative. Ann Arbor: University Microfilms.
1982 Phytolith analysis: Application of a new paleoethnobotanical technique in archaeology. *American Anthropologist* 84:862–71.
1988 Interpreting the meaning of macroremain abundance: The impact of source and context. In *Current Paleoethnobotany,* edited by C. Hastorf and V. Popper, pp. 97–118. Chicago: University of Chicago Press.

Pease G. Y., Franklin
1982 The formation of Tawantinsuyu: Mechanisms of colonization and relationship with ethnic groups. In *The Inka and Aztec states, 1400–1800,* edited by George A. Collier, Renato I. Rosaldo, and John D. Wirth, pp. 173–98. New York: Academic Press.

Pereira H., David
1982a La Red Vial Incaica en Cochabamba. *Cuadernos de Investigacion,* Serie Arqueológia (Instituto de Investigaciones Antropologicas [Museo Arqueologico]), 1: 55–88. Cochabamba: Universidad Mayor de San Simon.
1982b Kharalaus Pampa: Tambo incaico en Quillacollo. *Cuadernos de Investigacion,* Serie Arqueológia (Instituto de Investigaciones Antropologicas [Museo Arqueologico], 1: 55–88. Cochabamba: Universidad Mayor de San Simon.

Peterson, Ulrich
1965 Regional geology and major ore deposits of Central Peru. *Economic Geology* 60 (3): 407–76.

Phillips, W. R.
1957 *Potato storage.* Ottawa: Canada Department of Agriculture.

Piperno, Delores R.
1987 *Phytolith analysis.* New York: Academic Press.

Pizarro, Hernando
1959 [1533] Carta a los oidores de Santo Domingo. *Biblioteca de autores Españoles,* 121, 5: 84–90. Madrid: Real Academia Española.

Pizarro, Pedro
1965 [1571] Relación del descubrimiento y conquista de los reinos del Peru. . . . *Blblioteca de autorres Españoles* 168: pp. 167–242. Madrid: Real Academia Española.
1986 [1571] *Relación del descubrimiento y conquista de los reinos del Perú,* 2d ed. Lima: Pontificia Universidad Católica del Perú, Fondo Editorial.

Plaza Schuller, Fernando
1976 *La incursión Inca en el septrion Andino ecuatoriano. Antecedentes arqueologicos de la convulsiva situacion de contacto cultural.* Primer Informe Preliminar. Instituto Otavaleno de Antropología, Serie Arqueologiá, no. 2. Otovalo.

Polanyi, Karl
1957 The economy as instituted process. In *Trade and market in the early empires,* edited by Karl Polanyi, Conrad Arensberg, and Harry Pearson, pp. 243–70. New York: Free Press.
1968 *Primitive, archaic, and modern economies: Essays of Karl Polanyi.* Edited by George Dalton. Garden City, N.Y.: Doubleday.

Pollard, Gordon C.
1981 The bronze artisans of Calchaquí. *Early Man* 3(4): 27–33.

Polo de Ondegardo, Juan
1916 [1567] Instrucción contra las ceremonias y ritos. . . . In *Colección de Libros y Documentos Referentes a la História del Peru,* 1st Ser., 3, no. 4. Edited by H. H. Urteaga. Lima.
1916–1917 [1571] *Relación de los fundamentos acerca del notable daño que resulta de no guardar a los Indios sus fueros.* Edited by Horacio Urteaga. Lima: Sanmartí.
1917 [1567] La Relación del linaje de los Incas y como extendieron ellos sus conquistas. Edited by H. H. Urteaga. *Colección de Libros y Documentos Referentes a la História del Peru.* 4:45–94. Lima: Sanmartí.

1940 [1561] Informe . . . al licenciado Breviesca de Munatones sobre la perpetuidad de las encomiendas del Peru. *Revista Histórica* (Lima), 13:125–96.

Popper, Virginia
1988 Selecting quantitative measurements in paleoethnobotany. In *Current Paleoethnobotany,* edited by C. Hastorf and V. Popper, pp. 53–71. Chicago: University of Chicago Press.

Pozorski, Shelia, and Thomas Pozorski
1986 Recent excavations at Pampa de las Llamas-Moxeke, a complex Initial Period site in Peru. *Journal of Field Archaeology* 13:381–401.
1989 Personal communication.

Pozorski, Thomas
1987 Changing priorities within the Chimu state: The role of irrigation agriculture. In *The origins and development of the Andean state,* edited by J. Haas, S. Pozorski, and T. Pozorski, pp. 111–20. Cambridge: Cambridge University Press.

Prescott, William
1961 [1847] *History of the conquest of Peru.* Edited by V. W. Von Hagen. New York: Times-Mirror.

Price, Barbara J.
1978 Secondary state formation: An explanatory model. In *Origins of the state: The anthropology of political evolution,* edited by Ronald Cohen and Elman R. Service, pp. 161–86. Philadelphia: Institute for the Study of Human Issues.
1982 Cultural materialism: A theoretical overview. *American Antiquity* 47:709–41.

Primeros Agustinos
1918 [*ca.* 1560] Relación de la religión y ritos del Peru hecha por los primeros religiosos agustinos que allí pasaron para la conversión del los naturales. *Colección de Libros y Documentos Referentes a la História del Peru,* 11:1–56. Lima: Imprenta y Librería Sanmartí y Cia.

Qasem, Subhi A., and C. M. Christensen
1960 Influence of various factors on the deterioration of stored corn by funghi. In *Phytopathology* (St. Paul, Minn.), 50:703–9.

Raffino, Rodolfo
1981 *Los Inkas del Kollasuyu.* La Plata: Ramos Americana Editora.
1983 Arqueología y etnohistoria de la región calchaquí. *Presencia hispánica en la arqueología argentina,* 2:817–61. Edited E. S. Morresi and R. Gutierrez. Museo Regional de Antropología e Instituto de Historia, Facultad de Humanidades UNNE.

Ramírez-Horton, Susan E.
1981 La organización economica de la costa norte: Un análisis preliminar del período prehispánico tardío. In *Etnohistória y antropología andina,* edited by A. Castelli, M. Koth de Paredes, and M. Mould de Pease, pp. 281–97. Lima: Museo Naccional de História.
1982 Retainers of the lords or merchants: A Case of mistaken identity? In *El hombre y su ambiente en los andes centrales,* edited by L. Millones and H.

Tomeda, pp. 123–36. Senri Ethnological Studies, no. 10. Osaka: National Museum of Ethnology.

Reed, Nelson
1964 *The caste war of Yucatan*. Stanford: Stanford University Press.

Regal, Alberto
1936 *Los caminos del Inca—En el antiguo Peru*. Lima: Sanmartí.

Renfrew, Colin
1972 *The emergence of civilization: The Cyclades and the Aegean in the third millennium B.C.* London: Methuen.

Rivera, Mario A.
1987 Inka strategies of occupation in northern Chile. Paper presented at the 52nd annual meeting of the Society for American Archaeology, Toronto.

Roman y Zamora, Jerónimo
1897 [1575] *Repúblicas de Indias*. Colección de Libros Raros Y Curiosas que Tratan de América, vols. 13 and 14. Madrid.

Rostworowski de Diez Canseco, María
1970 Mercaderes del valle de Chincha en la época prehispánica: Un documento y unos comentarios. *Revista Española de Antropología Americana* (Madrid), 5.
1977 *Etnía y sociedad: Costa peruana prehispánica*. Lima: Instituto de Estudios Peruanos.
1978 *Señoríos indígenas de Lima y Canta*. Lima: Instituto de Estudios Peruanos. (Also, Appendice 2 [1549], pp. 216–31.)
1981 *Recursos naturales, renovables, y pesca, siglos XVI y XVII*. Lima: Instituto de Estudios Peruanos.
1983 *Estructuras Andinas del poder*. Lima: Instituto de Estudios Peruanos.
1988 *Historia del Tawantinsuyu*. Lima: Instituto de Estudios Peruanos.

Rovner, Irwin
1983 Plant opal phytolith analysis: Major advances in archaeological research. In *Advances in archaeological method and theory*, edited M. B. Schiffer, 6: 225–66. New York: Academic Press.

Rowe, John H.
1944 An introduction to the archaeology of Cuzco. *Papers of the Peabody Museum of American Archaeology and Ethnology, Harvard University* (Cambridge, 27(2).
1946 Inca culture at the time of the Spanish conquest. In *Handbook of South American Indians*, edited by Julian R. Steward, 2: 183–330. Bureau of American Ethnology Bulletin 143.
1948 The kingdom of Chimor. *Acta Americana* 6 (July–Dec.) 26–59.
1967 What kind of settlement was Inca Cuzco? In *Ñawpa Pacha* 5:55–77.
1982 Inca politics and institutions relating to the cultural unification of the empire. In *The Inca and Aztec states 1400–1800*, edited by G. Collier, R. Rosaldo, and J. D. Wirth, pp. 93–118. New York: Academic Press.

Sahlins, Marshall
1958 *Social stratification in Polynesia*. Monograph of the American Ethnological Society. Seattle: University of Washington Press.

Salaman, Redcliffe
1949 *The history and social influence of the potato.* Cambridge: Cambridge University Press.

Salomon, Frank L.
1978 Pochteca and mindalá: A comparison of long-distance traders in Ecuador and Mesoamerica. *Journal of the Steward Anthropological Society* 9 (1 and 2): 231–46.
1983 The north-Andean *mindalá* complex under Inca rule. Paper presented at the 48th annual meeting of the Society for American Archaeology.
1985 Comment on T. D'Altroy and T. Earle, Staple finance, wealth finance, and storage in the Inka political economy. *Current Anthropology* 26 (2):201.
1986 *Native lords of Quito in the age of the Incas.* Cambridge: Cambridge University Press.
1987 A north Andean status trader complex under Inka rule. *Ethnohistory* 34(1):63–77.

Sancho, Pedro
1917 [1532–33] Relación para SM de lo sucedido en la conquista y pacificación de estas provincias. . . . In *Colección de Libros y Documentos Referents a la Históría del Peru* 1st ser. 5: 122–202. Lima: Sanmartí.

Sanders, William T.
1973 The significance of Pikillakta in Andean culture history. *Occasional Papers in Anthropology* (Department of Anthropology, Pennsylvania State University, University Park), 8:379–428.

Santa Gertrudis, Fray Juan de
1970 [1775] *Maravillas de la naturaleza,* Tomo I. Bogota: Biblioteca Banco Popular no. 10.

Santillán, Hernando de
1968 [1563–64] Relación del origen, descendencia política y gobierno de los incas. . . . In *Biblioteca de autores Españoles,* 209:97–149. Madrid: Ediciones Atlas.

Sarmiento de Gamboa, Pedro
1965 [1572] Historia de los Incas. *Biblioteca de autores Españoles,* 135:195–279. Madrid: Real Academia Española.

Schaedel, Richard P.
1978 Early state of the Incas. In *The early state,* edited by Henri J. M. Claessen and Peter Skalnik, pp. 289–320. The Hague: Mouton.

Schjellerup, Inge
1979–80 Documents on paper and in stone. A preliminary report on the Inca ruins in Cochabamba, Province of Chachapoyas, Peru. *Folk* 21–22: 299–311. Copenhagen.
1984 Cochabamba: An Incaic administrative centre in the rebellious province of Chachapoyas. In *Current archaeological projects in the Central Andes: Some approaches and results,* edited by Ann Kendall, pp. 161–88. BAR International Series (Oxford), no. 210.

Schneider, Harold
1976 *Economic man.* New York: Free Press.

Schneider, Jane
1977 Was there a pre-capitalist world system? *Peasant studies* 6(1):20–29.

Schreiber, Katharina J.
1978 Planned architecture of Middle Horizon Peru: Implications for social and political organization. Ph.D. dissertation, State University of New York, Binghamton. Ann Arbor: University Microfilms.

1985 Comment on T. D'Altroy and T. Earle, Staple finance, wealth finance, and storage in the Inka political economy. *Current Anthropology* 26(2):201.

1987a Conquest and consolidation: A comparison of the Wari and Inka occupations of a highland Peruvian valley. *American Antiquity* 52: 266–84.

1987b From state to empire: The expansion of Wari outside the Ayacucho basin. In *The origins and development of the Andean state,* edited by J. Haas, S. Pozorski, and T. Pozorski, pp. 91–96. Cambridge: Cambridge University Press.

1989 Personal communication

1991 *The archaeology of imperialism: Ecology, settlement patterns, and political expansion in Middle Horizon Peru.* Ann Arbor: Museum of Anthropology, University of Michigan.

Scudder, Thayer
1962 *The ecology of the Gwembe Tonga.* Manchester, England: Manchester University Press.

Service, Elman R.
1975 *Origins of the state and civilization: The process of cultural evolution.* New York: Norton.

Shea, Daniel E.
1976 A defense of small population estimates for the Central Andes. In *The native population of the americas in 1492,* edited by William M. Denevan, pp. 157–80. Madison: University of Wisconsin Press.

Shimada, Izumi
1978 Economy of a prehistoric urban context: Commodity and labor flow at Moche V Pampa Grande, Peru. *American Antiquity* 43: 569–92.

1982 Horizontal archipelago and coast-highland interaction in North Peru. In *El hombre y su ambiente en los andes centrales,* edited by L. Millones and H. Tomoeda, pp. 137–210. Senri Ethnological Studies, no. 10. Osaka: National Museum of Ethnology.

1987 Horizontal and vertical dimensions of prehistoric states in North Peru. In *The origins and development of the Andean state,* edited by J. Haas, S. Pozorski, and T. Pozorski, pp. 130–44. Cambridge: Cambridge University Press.

Sikkink, L.
1988a Ethnoarchaeology of harvest and crop-processing in traditional households in the Mantaro Valley, Central Andes of Peru. Master's thesis, University of Minnesota, Minneapolis.

1988b Traditional crop-processing in Central Andean households: An ethnoarchaeological approach. *Multi-disciplinary Studies in Andean Archaeology* (Ann Arbor), 8.

Smelser, Neil
1959 A comparative view of exchange systems. *Economic Development and Cultural Change* 7:173–82.

Smith, Carol A.
1976 Exchange systems and the spatial distribution of elites. In *Regional analysis*, edited by C. A. Smith, 2:309–74. New York: Academic Press.

Smith, C. T.
19790 The depopulation of the central Andes in the 16th century. *Current Anthropology* 11:453–64.

Squier, G. E.
1973 [1877] *Peru: Incidents of travel and exploration in the land of the Incas.* New York: Macmillan.

Steponaitis, Vincas P.
1978 Location theory and complex chiefdoms: A Mississippian example. In *Mississippian settlement patterns,* edited by B. D. Smith, pp. 417–53. New York: Academic Press.
1981 Settlement hierarchies and political complexity in nonmarket societies: The Formative period in the Valley of Mexico. *American Antiquity* 83 (2): 320–63.

Stevenson, Matilda
1905 The Zuñi Indians: Their mythology, esoteric fraternities, and ceremonies. In *Twenty-third Annual Report of the Bureau of American Ethnology,* 1901–1902, pp. 1–608. Washington, D.C.

Steward, Julian
1960 *Theory of culture change.* Urbana: University of Illinois Press.

Strong, William Duncan, and Clifford Evans, Jr.
1952 *Cultural stratigraphy in the Virú Valley, Peru.* Columbia studies in Archaeology and Ethnology, no. 4. New York: Columbia University Press.

Strube Erdmann, Leon
1963 *Vialidad imperial de los Incas.* Serie Histórica, no. 33. Instituto de Estudios Americanistas, Facultad de Filosofía y Humanidades, Universidad Nacional de Córdoba, Argentina.

Tarragó, Myriam
1975 Panorama arqueológico del sector septentrional del valle Calchaquí, Salta. In *Actas y Trabajos del I Congreso Nacional de Arqueología Argentina,* Rosario.

Tarragó, Myriam, and Pío Pablo Díaz
1977 Sitios arqueológicos del valle Calchaquí (II). *Estudios de Arqueología* (Museo Arqueológico de Cachi), 2:61–71.

Thompson, Donald E., and John V. Murra
1966 The Inca bridges in the Huánuco region. *American Antiquity* 31(5):632–39.

Thurnwald, Richard
1932 *Economics in primitive communities.* Oxford: Oxford University Press.

Toledo, Francisco de
1940 [1570] Información hecha por orden de don Francisco de Toledo en su

visita de las províncias del Peru. . . . In *Don Francisco de Toledo, supremo organizador del Peru, su vida, su obra [1515–1582]*, edited by Roberto Levillier, 2:14–37, 122–77. Buenos Aires: Espasa-Calpe.

1940 [1571] Información comenzada en el Valle de Yucay el 2 de junio. . . . In *Don Francisco de Toledo, supremo organizador del Peru, su vida, su obra [1515–1582]*, edited by Roberto Levillier, 2:122–77. Buenos Aires: Espasa-Calpe.

Topic, John R.

1982 Lower-class social and economic organization at Chan Chan. In *Chan Chan: Andean desert city*, edited by Michael E. Moseley and Kent C. Day, pp. 145–75. Albuquerque: University of New Mexico Press.

1985 Comment on T. D'Altroy and T. Earle, Staple finance, wealth finance, and storage in the Inka political economy. *Current Anthropology* 26(2):201–2.

1991 Huari and Huamachuco. In *Huari Administrative Structure: Prehistoric Monumental Architecture and State Government*, edited by William H. Isbell and Gordon McEwan. Washington: Dumbarton Oaks.

Topic, John R., and Theresa Lange Topic

N.d. A summary of the Inca occupation of Huamachuco. Paper presented to the 52nd annual meeting of the Society for American Archaeology, May 1987, Toronto.

1982 Huamachuco Archaeological Project: Preliminary report on the first season, July–August 1981. Manuscript on file, Department of Anthropology, Trent University.

Topic, Theresa Lange, and John R. Topic

1984 *Huamachuco Archaeological Project: Preliminary report on the third season, June–August 1983*. Trent University Occasional Papers in Anthropology (Peterborough, Ontario), no. 1.

Tosi, Joseph A.

1960 Zonas de vida natural en el Peru. *Boletín Técnico*, 5. Lima: Instituto Interamericano de Ciencias Agrícolas de la OAS, Zona Andina. Proyecto 39.

Trimborn, Hermann

1967 Archäologische Studien in den Kordillern Boliviens. *Bässler-Archiv. Beitrage zür Völkerkunde* (Berlin), Neu Folge, Beiheft, 5.

1985 *Quebrada de la Vaca, Eine vorspanische Siedlung im Mittleren Süden Perus*. Munich: Verlag C.H. Beck.

Troll, Carl

1958 Las culturas superiores andinas y el medio geográfico. *Revista del Instituto de Geografía* (Lima), 5:3–55.

Uhle, Max

1903 *Pachacamac; Report of the William L. Pepper, M.D., LL.D., Peruvian expedition of 1896*. Philadelphia: Department of Anthropology, University of Pennsylvania.

1969 *Estudios sobre história Incaica*. Edited by Toribio Mejia Xesspe. Lima: Universidad Mayor de San Marcos.

Urteaga, Horacio H.
1939 Tambo Colorado. *Boletín de la Sociedad Geográfica de Lima* 51(1): 85–94.

Vaca de Castro Cavallero, Cristóbal
1908 [1543] Ordenazas de Tambos. *Revista Histórica* (Instituto Histórica del Peru, Lima), 3:427–92.

van Creveld, Martin
1977 *Supplying war: Logistics from Wallenstein to Patton.* Cambridge: Cambridge University Press.

Vásquez de Espinoza, P. Antonio
1969 [1617] Compendio y descripción de las Indias Occidentales. *Biblioteca de autores Españoles,* no. 231. Madrid: Ediciones Atlas.

Vega, Andres de
1965 [1582] La descripción que se hizo en la provincia de Xauxa por la instrucción de su Majestad que a la dicha provincia se invio de molde. In *Biblioteca de autores Españoles,* no. 183, pp. 166–75. Madrid: Ediciones Atlas.

Vermeule, Emily
1964 *Greece in the Bronze Age.* Chicago: University of Chicago Press.

Wachtel, Nathan
1977 *The vision of the vanquished.* Translated by Ben and Sian Reynolds. Hassocks, Sussex: Harvester Press.
1982 The *mitimas* of the Cochabamba Valley: The colonization policy of Huayna Capac. In *The Inca and Aztec states, 1400–1800,* edited by George A. Collier, Renato I. Rosaldo, and John D. Wirth, pp. 199–235. New York and London: Academic Press.

Wallace, Dwight T.
1971 Sítios arqueologicos del Peru (segunda entrega)—Valles de Chincha y Pisco. Translated by Luis Watanabe M. *Arqueológicas* 13, (Museo Nacional de Anthropología y Arqueología, Lima).

Watanabe, Luis, Michael E. Moseley, and Fernando Cabieses, compilers.
1990 *Trabajos arqueológicos en Moquegua, Perú.* 3 vols. Ilo, Peru: Programa Contisuyo del Museo Peruano de Ciencias de la Salud. Southern Peru Copper Corporation.

Watson, P.
1976 In pursuit of prehistoric subsistence: A comparative account of some contemporary flotation techniques. *Mid-Continental Journal of Archaeology* 1 (1): 77–100.

Werge, Robert W.
1977 *Potato storage systems in the Mantaro Valley region of Peru.* Lima: International Potato Center, Socioeconomic Unit.

White, Leslie
1959 *The evolution of culture.* New York: McGraw-Hill.

Wilcox, G.
1974 A history of deforestation as indicated by charcoal analysis of four sites in Eastern Anatolia. *Anatolian Studies* 24:117–133.

Willey, Gordon
1953 *Prehistoric settlement pattern in the Virú Valley, Peru.* Bureau of American Ethnography Bulletin 155. Washington, D.C.

Wright, Henry T.
1977 Toward an explanation of the origin of the state. In *Explanation of prehistoric exchange,* edited by James N. Hill, pp. 215–30. Albuquerque: University of New Mexico Press.

Wright, Henry T., and Gregory Johnson
1975 Population, exchange, and early state formation in southwestern Iran. *American Anthropologist* 77:267–89.

Xérez, Francisco de
1862 [1533–34] Conquista del Peru. *Biblioteca de autores Españoles,* 26:319–46. Madrid: Ediciones Atlas.

Zárate, Augustin de
1862 [1555] Historia del descubrimiento y conquista de la provincia del Peru. *Biblioteca de autores Españoles,* 26:459–574. Madrid: Ediciones Atlas.
1917 [1532–1533] *Verdadera relación de la conquista del Peru.* . . . Edited by Horacio Urteaga. Lima: Sanmartí.

Zuidema, R. Tom
1964 *The ceque system of Cuzco.* Leiden: Brill.

Contributors

Coreen E. Chiswell, Department of Anthropology, University of California, Los Angeles

Terence N. D'Altroy, Department of Anthropology, Columbia University, New York

Timothy K. Earle, Department of Anthropology, University of California, Los Angeles

Christine A. Hastorf, Department of Anthropology, University of Minnesota, Minneapolis

Heidi A. Lennstrom, Center for Ancient Studies, University of Minnesota, Minneapolis

Terry Y. LeVine, Institute of Archaeology, University of California, Los Angeles

Craig Morris, Department of Anthropology, American Museum of Natural History, New York

James E. Snead, Department of Anthropology, University of California, Los Angeles

John R. Topic, Department of Anthropology, Trent University, Ontario, Canada

Index

Accounting devices, 23, 32–33, 139, 190, 194–95, 339–41

Administrative (provincial) centers, 19, 21, 48, 49, 168, 170, 177, 182, 195, 338; under Chimú, 15; under Wari 15. *See also* Hatun Xauxa; Huamachuco; Huánuco Pampa; Pumpu

Aegean cultures: Bronze Age storage in, 44; Dorian-Malthi, storage in, 9; Mycenaean, 5; palace economies in, 5; Pylos, storage in, 9; staple finance in, 44; storage control in, 44

Agriculture: cycles, 4, 41; intensification, 12, 39,, 33, 137; irrigation, 6, 39, 170

Agua Hedionda (Argentina), 77, 94–95

Amazon basin. *See* Tropical forest

Anocariri (Bolivia), 105

Aqllaquna (aqllakuna), 39, 49, 206

Ayllu, 113, 118, 130, 176–77; defined, 34–35; and labor tax, 38

Azángaro, 11, 12, 227, 229, 336

Aztec empire: cacao and cloth as currency in, 51–53, 57–58; conquests, 52; economy in, 328; finance system of, 33–34; and market economy, 52, 53; storage in, 45; wealth control and, 51–52, 59

Babylon, staple finance in, 44

Belen. *See* Cuzco-vicinity sites

Botanical analysis, 27, 143–44, 222–24, 330, 331, 337, 339; and continuity and change, 16; and flota-

tion, 144, 224, 261, 272, 275, 280, 284, 289–93; of habitation sites, 302–7, 311–20; maize in, 307–9; methodology in, 223–24, 280, 290–94, phytoliths in, 222–24, 233; pollen in, 9; ratios in, 293, 307, 309; relative proportion in, 280, 293, 296, 298–301, 303–6; sample diversity in, 293–95, 300, 304, 309; of storehouses (qollqa), 296–302, 307, 320–33; ubiquity in, 280, 286, 293, 295, 301, 307, 308

Cacao, 52, 53

Cajabamba, 225

Cajamarca, 11, 17, 57, 85, 206, 266, 344n.2

Calchaquí Valley (Argentina): copper, 337; metalworking, 337–38; wealth goods, 338

Callejón de Huaylas, 155

Camata (Moquequa Valley), 84, 97

Campo del Pucara (Lerma Valley, Argentina), 21, 75–77, 92–93, 335

Canta Valley, 85

Capinota (Argentina), 76

Case studies, 25, 27; Hatun Xauxa (Mantaro Valley), 176–205; Huamachuco, 206–33; Huánuco Pampa, 151–75

Casma Valley, 6

Ceramics, 39, 77, 127, 136, 143, 144, 240, 246–47; Huamachuco, 218, 229–30; Huánuco Pampa, 154, 162; Mantaro Valley, 177,

192–94, 265, 278–80, 285–86;
Tunsukancha, 166; Wanka, 14
Cerro Azul (Cañete Valley), 79
Cerro Cacañan, 211
Cerro Mamorca, 210–11
Cerro de las Rueditas (Bolivia), 78,
95
Cerro Santa Barbara, 208–10
Chacamarca, 78, 94, 111, 123, 127–
28, 133, 134–36, 140, 142. *See
also* Pumpu
Chachapoyas, 81, 99, 134
Charred remains, 9, 10, 160, 213–
15, 219, 220, 224, 239, 246,
280–82, 290, 296–97, 300, 302,
306–8; and preservation, 291–93
Chicama Valley, 83
Chicha (maize beer), 23, 39, 178,
179, 265
Chichipampa (Arequipa), 104
Chile, sites in, 12, 66, 82, 86; Capis-
Cerrillos, 76, 93–94; Catarpe, 86;
Copiapo, 76; Santiago, 16; Turi,
82, 103
Chilicito (Argentina), 338
Chillón Valley, 40, 84–85, 143; Hu-
ancayo Alto in, 85
Chimú: administrative centers, 15;
Chan Chan, 13–14, 336; and con-
trol of storage, 11, 13–14, 16;
Farfan, 13–14; and household
stores, 43; under Inka 57; Man-
chan, 14; metalsmiths, 57; wealth
finance and, 336;
Chincha Valley: food production in,
172; Inka presence at La Centinela
in, 83, 172; traders in, 56
Chinchaycocha (Lago Junín), 118,
133, 135. *See also* Pumpu
Chincheros. *See* Cuzco-vicinity sites
Chinese empire, economy in, 328
Chucuito (Lake Titicaca area), 40,
56–57
Chuño, 24, 43, 247, 248
Chuquibamba (Condebamba Valley),
225
Civic/ceremonial rituals, 39, 71, 110,

126, 130, 135; hospitality, 19–20,
44, 177, 338–39; gift exchange at,
20
Cloth, 39; as currency, 51, 57–58,
343n.4; as tribute, 53; as wealth
goods, 56–58, 171
Coca, 37, 177; as currency, 343n.4;
as hospitality, 58–59
Cochabamba (Bolivia): production
for military, 343n.2; state farms
near, 261, 329, 335, 340; storage
near, 65, 76–77, 79
Cochabamba (Chachapoyas), 81, 99
Colcabamba, 225, 335
Comestibles: at Huánuco Pampa,
161; in Moche period, 10
Communication in Inka empire, 72,
86, 87, 110, 134, 147, 170, 174
Comparative models: increasing energy, 136–45; nonmarket, 129–
36, 180–81
Complex society: central control and,
31; communication and, 31, 110,
134, 147, 237; increasing energy
and, 31, infrastructure and, 151;
logistics and, 151–52; production
and, 151; and revenue organization, 31–32; and storage, 43–47,
170
Continuity or change: administrative
center, 15; botanical analysis and,
16; Chimú as source for, 15–16;
decimal hierarchy and, 15; discussed, 15–16, 28, 329, 340–42;
road systems and, 15; storage in,
6
Corral Blanco (Argentina), 16, 82,
101
Cortaderas (Argentina), 75, 338
Corvée labor, 259, 264, 265
Cotapachi (Cochabamba, Bolivia),
21, 22, 75–77, 92, 172–73, 340
Craft goods, 17, 260; allocation of,
36; transport of, 18; use of, 39;
utilitarian vs. prestige, 49
Craft production: 119, 135, 138–40,
141, 264; Chimú control of, 12;

metalsmiths and, 49, 57; Moche control of, 10; specialization in, 17, 34, 35, 39, 130, 177, 179, 181, 259, 264, 336; storage of, 140, 161; of textiles, 24; workshops for, 19

Culluma Baja (Carhuarzo Valley), 78, 96

Cuzco, 34, 45, 152, 175, 177, 182, 258, 283, 336; allegiance to, 47; ceramic style in, 164, 166, 168; as control center, 19, 26, 34, 110, 130, 131, 151; description of, 167–71; and Inka road, 5, 48–49, 127, 132, 184, 261; storage at, 20, 22, 23, 26, 63–64, 85, 87, 167–71, 337; storage near, 154, 159, 168–71; traders at, 56; transport to, 17, 18, 123, 139, 145, 172; and tribute, 39; wealth goods at, 18, 139, 144, 171

Cuzco-vicinity sites, 167–70

Dahomey, 45

Decimal system, 15; and Wanka, 48

Dendritic system, 180–81

Documents, 3–4, 20–24, 328; administrative records 20–21, 24; anthropological perspective, 21; census records, 24, 265; Cochabamba archives, 22, 76–77; court cases, 21–24, 265–73; storehouses, 20–24, 142–45; *visitas,* 24, 154, 264–65

Economic surplus, 4, 24

Economy, Marxian, 31, 178–80

Economy, nonmarket, 129–36

Economy, political, 3, 5, 56, 108, 129–30, 328, 336, 340–41; and barter, 52; characterized, 34–36; and control of values, 58; defined, 51, 38–41; and fluctuating demand, 45–46; and Inka, 26, 34–37; integration of, 60; in nonindustrial states, 24; storage in, 41–

47, 176–83; and war, 45; wealth finance in, 51–59

Economy, subsistence: 37–38

Ecuador, 56, 66, 77, 79, 81, 82, 177, 181, 184; coca as currency in, 58; under Inka, 55–56, 59; markets in, 327; pre-Inka, 54; subsistence economy in, 38; wealth goods in, 54

Ecuador (Quito), 40, 55, 177, 261; under Inka, 16; Inka road and, 48–49; prestige goods in, 52–56

Ecuador, Inka installations: Ingapirca (Canar), 82, 103–4; Millpu, 101; Otavalo, 55; Paradones (Azuay), 97–98; Quitaloma, 79, 102; Tambo Blanco, 66, 102

Egypt, staple finance in, 44

Elites: Chimú period, 13–15; in Inka bureaucracy 35, 60, 110, 130, 144, 176–81, 190; religious, 19; Wanka, 27; and wealth goods, 17

Energy capture and social complexity, 31–32, 36, 60, 136–45

Ethnic groups: Chinchaycocha, 178; Chupaychu, 155, 163, 164, 175, 177; diversity of, 112–13; in Huánuco region, 113, 135, 142–43, 145, 155, 163, 177; and labor service, 178–79; pre-Inka growth, 183; in Pumpu region 118, 143; state and, 107; state centers and, 110, 112, 131–32, 145–46; and storage volume, 108, 118, 138–39; and transport, 110; in Xauxa (Jauja) region, 125–26, 144; Yacha, 155, 163. *See also* Wanka ethnic groups

Ethnic populations, distribution of: Cuzco, 170; in Huánuco, 113–14; in Pumpu, 114–23; and storage, 134–36, 174, 191–95, 198–201, 204; in Xauxa (Mantaro Valley), 183–84, 123–29

Excavation, 64, 65, 83, 84, 261, 330–32, 335–36, 338, 339–40; and botanical analysis, 287–323;

at Huamachuco, 211–19; at Huánuco Pampa, 154–55, 159–60, 238, 251; in Mantaro Valley, 271–75; of metals, 53–54, 337–38; in storehouses, 140, 142–44, 154; at Tunsukancha, 166

Exchange: and barter (in a political economy), 52; Inka control of, 17; and markets, 38; pre-Inka, 12; and trade, 108, 129, 142–43, 175, 259, 262, 327–28, 334

Feathers, 24, 52, 114, 142–44, 168, 171, 177
Finance systems: Aztec, 33–34; Hawaii, 34; storage in, 41–47, 334; staple, 32–34; wealth, 32–34

Ghana, storage in, 43
Gift exchange: ceremonial elite, 20, 22, 36, 39, 40, 52, 53, 56, 58, 171; obligatory, 53; goods transfer in, 52
Graneros (Argentina), 103

Hatunmarca, 53, 288–89, 302
Hatunqolla, 71, 92
Hatun Xauxa, 21–26, 71, 85, 89–90, 154, 173–74, 226, 229, 232, 261, 263–64, 271–72, 288, 309, 337, 339; Spanish view of, 49; storage distribution at, 49–50; storage facilities in, 49–50, 184–204. See also Mantaro Valley; Xauxa region
Hawaii: craft specialization, finance system in, 34; staples finance in, 44; storage in, 47
Herding, 111–13, 114, 118, 123, 127, 142–43
Hopi storage, 43
Household storage, 9, 14, 43–45, 47, 302–7, 310, 333
Huacas, 9, 207
Hualfin (Argentina), 99
Huallaga River Valley, 14, 113–14, 118, 135, 143, 145, 155, 332. See also Huánuco as a region

Huamachuco, 71, 72, 85, 91, 133–34, 330, 333, 336, 339; botanical analysis at, 222–24; ceramics at, 218, 229, 230; excavations at, 211–19; historical context of, 208, 225–30; Inka center at, 22, 26, 27; Inka conquest of, 207–8; storage in, 206–33
Huamachuco-region sites: 208–11, 225–26, 335
Huancari. See Cuzco
Huánuco as a region, 26, 107–14, 330
Huánuco Pampa, 85, 177, 232, 284, 287, 328; center described, 22, 66, 71, 90, 145, 154–64; documents for, 142–43; excavation at, 64, 155, 160, 273, 339, 340; in geographical model, 130–35; housing capacity of, 163; storage distribution from, 166, 173, 229; storage of maize at, 239, 240–46, 278–80; storage of tubers at, 239, 246–56; storage volume, 138–39, 147, 335, 337; storehouse architecture, 139–40, 155–59, 168, 226; storehouse organization, 160–64

Incahuasi (Argentina), 76, 77
Incarracay (Bolivia), 74
Inka empire: administered divisions in, 34; administrative flexibility, 108, 145; arrogation of rights by, 38, 107–8, 177; authorized prerogatives in, 130; bureaucratic hierarchy in, 47; continuity/change and, 15–16, 329; cross-cultural research, 328; and elites, 176–81, 190; and expansion, 3, 16; food storage in, 174–75; and hospitality, 172; lack of markets in, 327–28; and messengers, 49, 261; military, 172, 207; mobilization/redistribution in, 40–41; people's rights in, 34–37, 178; political economy in, 34–37; production

in, 176, 178–81, 183, 195, 199, 204; production enclaves in, 17; road network in, 152, 170, 261; staple finance and, 37–41, 259, 273, 285; storage function in, 327–28; storage network in, 47–50, 152, 171; Tawantinsuyu, 15, 62, 63, 72, 82–84, 86, 87, 173, 179; traffic control in, 49, 262; variability of, 329; wealth finance and, 33–34

Inkallajta (Bolivia), 79, 81, 101
Inka Tampu (Carhuarazo Valley), 98
Inkawasi (Cañete Valley), 78–79, 81, 83–84, 93, 154, 172
Irrigation agriculture: in Casma Valley, 6; in Inka expansion, 17, 39

Jargampata, 227, 229, 336
Jauja and Jauja Valley. See Hatun Xauxa; Mantaro Valley

Kharalaus Pampa (Bolivia), 77, 95
Khipu, 242, 265; as accounting device, 23, 339, in court case, 182
Kullku Tampu (Bolivia), 81, 102

Labor service, 3, 25, 71, 76, 85, 87, 108, 110, 114, 118, 126, 130–31, 135, 137, 138–39, 143, 145, 170, 177–82, 198, 204; census as tax base for, 3, 35–36, 38–40, 47, 59; corvée labor, 259, 264, 265; crafts and, 33; decimal system and, 3; management of, 17–18, 59; or prestation, 343n.1; and usufruct, 38
La Centinela (Chincha Valley), 83, 85, 172
La Cima, 81, 101, 123, 133, 140. See also Pumpu
Lerma Valley (Argentina), 64, 77
Llagaday Saddle, 225–26
Llama, 23; as meat, 139, 142; in transport, 17, 123, 131, 139; 343n.2; and Tiwanaku, 12

Long-distance exchange and prestige goods, 52

Mantaro Valley, 78, 145–47, 261, 262, 287, 329–30, 333–39, 340; Inka conquest of, 48; Late Intermediate in, 14; metals excavated in, 53–54; pre-Inka, 14; resources in, 144, 177; roads through, 135–36; settlement system in, 123, 126–28, 183–84; and Spanish, 59; storage in, 47–50, 64, 79, 82, 86, 96–97, 141–42, 176, 184–204; Wanka population in, 48. See also Hatun Xauxa; Xauxa region
Marañón River (valley), 113, 134, 155
Marca, 53, 288–90, 302
Markets, 108, 129–31, 327, 334, 341–42; under Inka control, 17
Market systems: absence of, 341; Aztec, 51–52; economy, 51–53; exchange in, 34, 37–38, 54–56, 178–82, 205
Marquesan storage, 43
Military, 39, 43–44, 49, 52, 63, 78, 79, 81, 87, 110, 134, 147, 153, 161, 170, 177, 180, 182, 207, 259–60, 264–65, 338, 341, 343n.2
Mining and metals, 53–54, 123, 138, 141, 142, 143, 177, 337–39
Mit'a, 17, 118, 138, 143, 204, 304; defined, 39
Mitmaq (mitmaqkuna) (colonists), 17, 77, 207, 225, 232, 259; services by, 39
Mobilization, 72, 85, 86, 130, 330; economies, 26; from elites, 40; in Hawaii, 44; Inka empire and, 179–82, 204; versus redistribution, 40–41; and staples, 33, 341–42; and storehouse design, 340
Moche: Early Intermediate, 6–10; Galindo site, 10; household stores and, 43; at Pampa Grande (Lam-

bayeque Valley) site, 9–10, 64;
specialization in, 10
Murra, John V., 21, 35, 56, 151,
177–80, 182, 258, 265, 267,
327–29, 332, 334, 343n. 1

Nevados de Aconquija (Argentina),
82, 103

Ollantaytampu (Urubamba Valley).
See Cuzco-vicinity sites

Paca Valley: 288
Pachacamac (Lurín Valley), 83–85,
132, 152
Pampa Grande. *See* Moche
Phytoliths. *See* Botanical analysis
Pikillaqta, 11, 336, 340
Pisaq. *See* Cuzco-vicinity sites
Pocona (Bolivia), 81, 100
Pollen analysis. *See* Botantical
analysis
Population estimates, 112, 344n.3;
Huánuco, 113; Pumpu, 118;
Xauxa, 123, 126–29
Potrero de Payogasta (Argentina), 82,
103, 338–39
Pottery. *See* Ceramics
Pre-Inka polities, 113, 118, 123–26,
155; Chimú, 12–14; in Initial period, 6; and land-use rights, 130;
in Mantaro Valley 14–15; Moche,
6–10; and storage management, 3,
329, 331, 336–37; Tiwanaku, 12;
and warfare, 177, 183; Wari, 10–
12; and wealth storage, 340
Production enclaves, 17, 24, 35, 72–
79, 130, 146, 195–204
Pumpu, 20, 22, 71, 78, 85, 90–91,
154, 166, 173, 330, 337, 339;
documents for, 143–44; storage
distribution, 133–35; storehouses
in, 139–42, 145, 147
Pumpu, as a region, 107–12, 114–
23

Puna, 37; Huaricolca, 127, 133; as
refrigerator, 27
Punta de Balasta (Argentina), 106

Qhata-q'asa. *See* Cuzco-vicinity sites
Qollqa. *See* Storehouse architecture;
Storehouse contents; Storehouse-
contents preservation
Quebrada de la Vaca, 83, 98
Quito. *See* Ecuador (Quito)

Raqchi, 71–72, 91. *See also* Cuzco-
vicinity sites
Reciprocity: asymmetrical, 36, 178–
79; and economics, 26; in Moche
period, 10
Redistribution, 26, 130, 178–79,
327, 334; to hinterlands, 163–64;
minimized, 20; in Moche period,
10; and staples, 33, 40; Tiwanaku
and, 12; wealth goods and, 171
Religion, state, 17, 132, 179, 181,
194; and storage, 152, 162. *See
also* Civic/ceremonial rituals
Road system (Inka), 5, 137, 146–
47; in Central Highlands, 131–36;
in Chimú period, 15; in Huamachuco, 27, 207; in Huánuco, 113–
14; Inka centers and, 5, 66–68,
71, 72, 81, 86, 87; in Pumpu,
118–19; in Wari period, 15; in
Xauxa, 127
Roman empire, 6; economy in, 328

Sacsayhuaman, storage at, 23. *See
also* Cuzco-vicinity sites
Salt, 38, 49, 54, 55, 58, 118, 143,
177, 178, 265
San Sebastian. *See* Cuzco-vicinity
sites
Sausa subethnic group: 288, 296,
302, 309
Saya (political subunit), 34, 48,
265–67
Shincal (Argentina), 105, 338
Spondylus, 52, 53, 56
Staple finance, 19; in Inka finance,

16–17, 37–41; in Mantaro Valley, 48; in political economies, 32–33, 145, 176, 204, 341–42; risks of, 60; and seasonality, 44; and storage, 41–47, 181, 259, 273, 285; in Sumeria, 44

Staples: in accounting, 32–33; allocation of, 36; conversion of, 53; indirect evidence for, 15–16; function of, 18, 39, 174–75; management of, 50, 59; storage and, 15–16; transport of, 6, 18, 25, 33, 47; as wealth, 174–75

State farms: and population displacement, 342; as production enclaves, 24, 26, 77, 141, 195–204; and staples, 24; storage at, 50, 147

Storage: and accounting, 190, 194–95, 339–40; continuity, change, and, 340–42; distribution of, 3, 25, 49–50, 145–46, 172; function of, 3, 4, 16–20, 41–43, 161, 333–39; household identification of, 331; long-term, 123, 139, 143, 145, 147, 166–67, 241; organization of, 176–83; pre-Inka, 258, 336–37; for religion (state), 72, 160, 162; short-term, 111, 145, 160, 162, 166, 172. *See also* Storage, controlled access; Storage facilities; Storage management; Storage volume

Storage, controlled access: in Aegean, 44; by Chimú, 13, 14, 16; discussed, 336–40; in Initial period, 6; by Moche, 9–10; at Pylos, 9; by Wari, 11

Storage facilities: archaeology and, 151; at Calchaquí, 338; characteristics of, 65–82; and Chimú, 13–14; continuity, change, and, 15–16; in Cuzco area, 167–71; described, 89–106; distribution of, 26, 28, 48, 151, 195–97, 237, 232; at Hatun Xauxa, 184–204; highland and coast compared, 82–86; in Huamachuco, 206–33; at

Huánuco Pampa, 155–67; identification of, 63–65; in Initial period, 6; Inka attributes of, 15, 18–20, 63–82, 137; in Late Intermediate period, 4; military and, 153; mobilization and, 181, Moche and, 9–10; as a network, 151–52, 171–72; organization of, 162, 190, 262–64; and populations, 50, 86, 151, 195–201; processing at, 162; and production sites, 72–79, 92–96; psychological value of, 19–20; at Pumpu, 118–23; and research, 28; Spaniards' view of, 3, 21–24, 170–71, 182; at state farms, 198–201; and state centers, 68–72, 89–92, 151, 152; state religion and, 152, 162; and state roads, 19; and Tiwanaku, 12; and Wari, 10–12

Storage management: in archaic states, 4–5; centralized control and, 4, 6, 47; and Chimú, 12–14; coast and highlands compared, 25; continuity/change in, 6; in Inka period, 16; late Moche, 9; in a political economy, 4, 41–47; pre-Inka polities and, 1–16; and shortfalls, 4–5; Wanka role in, 27; Wari and, 2

Storage volume, 108, 111, 114, 117–19, 123, 127–31, 133–42, 146–47, 184, 186–87, 189, 192, 194–95, 263–64, 335–37; need for data on, 28, volume distribution, 195–204, 260, 261, 263–64

Storehouse architecture, 27–28, 144–45; in accounting, 339–40; circular versus rectangular, 1, 9, 11, 19, 72, 82–83, 114, 117, 119–23, 127, 129–44, 147, 155–61, 184–95, 199, 202–4, 226, 237–39, 246, 249, 269, 272–77, 278, 282–84, 287, 288, 297, 339–40, 344n.4; construction, 185–93; and dimensions, 159, 185–90, 210–11, 237–38; drainage, 8, 9, 10, 217, 218, 238, 250, 252, 262, 275, 278, 283, 285, 333; and floors, 159, 215, 219, 220, 224, 231, 232, 238, 249–51; and roofs, 218; windows and doors in, 238

Storehouse (qollqa) contents, 153, 154, 220, 260, 278–85; and ceramics, 162, 163, 164; *chuño,* 247; diseases, 41, 219, 345n.2; in documents, 21–24, 142–45, 264–73; indirect evidence for, 13; maize in, 161, 177–79, 183, 190, 224, 231–32, 239, 240–46, 262, 265–66, 269–70, 272–73, 278, 280, 283, 284, 286, 287, 293–97, 302, 331, 333, 335, 339; metals and textiles in, 3, 123, 139, 144; *quinoa,* 49, 183, 262, 265, 266, 269, 278, 282–84, 286, 293–97, 302, 303, 309, 331, 335; records of, 23; staples, 3, 48; tubers in, 161, 177, 190, 224, 231, 232, 239, 246–56, 283–86, 287, 292–96, 302, 331, 333, 335, 339; wealth goods as, 336. *See also* Botanical analysis

Storehouse-contents preservation, 3, 22–23, 27, 152, 220, 232, 262, 331–33; climate in, 237; fungi and, 241, 242–47, 253–55; humidity in, 242, 243–44, 245, 275; insects in, 241, 244–47; insulation for, 248; rodents in, 241, 245–47; and sprouting, 241, 245–53; temperature and, 242–44, 245, 248, 249–56; ventilation and, 248, 249–53

Sumerian staple finance, 44

Sumptuary goods. *See* Wealth goods

Tambo Colorado (Pisco Valley), 81–84, 102, 154, 172

Tambo Viejo (Acari Valley), 81–84, 97

Tampu, 48, 140, 145, 152; function of, 66; spacing, 111, 344n.2; stor-

age at, 66, 77–78, 81–83, 86, 111, 128, 172–73, 226; supply for, 173

Taparaku, 100, 114

Tarmatambo, 78, 81, 98, 121, 127–29, 132–33, 136, 142, 154, 173–73; as province, 343n.1

Tarma Valley, 126–27, 136

Tawantinsuyu. *See* Inka empire

Taxation, 32, 35, 259; institutionalized, 32. *See also* Labor service

Telarnioj, 101, 122, 133, 140. *See also* Pumpu

Titicaca (lake), 12, 56

Tiwanaku period, 12

Transport, 110, 111, 131, 143, 147; cost of, 17, 50–51, 58, 59, 180, 328, 336; of crafts, 18; logistics of 85; for military, 17–18, 343n.2; porters and, 17–19, 20; problems of, 12, 18, 182; of staples, 25, 33, 47; and state roads, 132–35; of wealth goods, 33, 51. *See also* Llama

Trobriands, storage in, 43

Tropical forest (Amazon basin): and agriculture, 127, 132; described, 44, 111–14; as Inka empire border, 111; resources of, 52, 177

Tumuyo (Bolivia), 78–80, 95–96

Tunsukancha, 99, 114, 154, 155, 164–67

Urubamba Valley, 169–70, 258

Usufruct and the *ayllu,* 38, 176

Virú Valley, 83

Wanka ethnic groups: Hatunxauxa, 265–73; Lurinwanka, 265–73; Sausa, 288, 296, 302, 309

Wankas: ceramics, 193, 278–80; elites and Inka, 48, 261–62; exchange for sale, 178; habitations of, 189–90, 192; and Inka center, 86, 146; Inka resettlement of, 48, 261; litigation (with Spanish),

144, 182, 265–73; and mining, 53–54, 143; population distribution, 50; in pre-Inka period, 14, 126–27; *saya* divisions, 34; and staple finance, 27, 285; and storage locations, 198–204, 264; as storage managers, 27, 265

Wanka sites: Hatunmarca, 53, 288–89, 302; Jauja Valley, 288; Marca, 53, 288–90, 302; Paca Valley, 288; Tunanmarca, 53; Umpamalca, 53; Yanamarca Valley, 86

Wari period: Azángaro site of, 11–12, 227, 229, 336; Jargampata site in, 227, 229, 336; long-distance trade in, 12; Pikillaqta site in, 11, 336, 340; road system of, 15; storage in, 10–12, 336, 340; wealth goods in, 12

Warfare, 41, 59, 183, 170; in Dahomey, 45; in Late Intermediate period, 14, 123, 143; Spanish conquest, 270

Wealth finance: discussed, 33; pre-Inka period, 336

Wealth goods, 24, 36, 39; and Chimú elite, 12–14; cloth and, 56–58, 123, 139, 146; control of, 60; convertibility of, 343n.3; and Cuzco, 18, 123, 139, 171; in Early Intermediate period, 52; in Ecuador, 38; elite gifts and, 36, 40; and finance, 33; in Hawaii, 34; in long-distance exchange, 18; management of, 36, 53, 59; and metals, 53–54, 111, 123, 139, 146; in Moche period, 10; storage of, 146, 340; and Tiwanaku, 12

Xauxa region, 53, 107–12, 123–29, 130, 132–36, 138, 141–42, 259, 262, 268, 270, 272, 278, 284, region described, 176, 183–84, 285, 286; documents for, 144–47; storage in, 184–204. *See also* Hatun Xauxa; Mantaro Valley

Yacorite (Argentina), 103
Yana (*yanakuna*) (servants), 39
Yanamarca Valley, 50, 86, 123–28, 135, 145, 195, 288
Yucay. *See* Cuzco-vicinity sites

Zimbabwe, storage in, 43
Zuni, storage among, 43